Nomadic New Women

Renée M. Silverman
Esther Sánchez-Pardo
Editors

Nomadic New Women

Exile and Border-Crossing between Spain
and the Americas, Early to Mid-Twentieth Century

Editors
Renée M. Silverman
Department of Modern Languages
Florida International University
Miami, FL, USA

Esther Sánchez-Pardo
Department of English Studies
Complutense University
Madrid, Spain

ISBN 978-3-031-62481-0 ISBN 978-3-031-62482-7 (eBook)
https://doi.org/10.1007/978-3-031-62482-7

© The Editor(s) (if applicable) and The Author(s), under exclusive license to Springer Nature Switzerland AG 2024

This work is subject to copyright. All rights are solely and exclusively licensed by the Publisher, whether the whole or part of the material is concerned, specifically the rights of translation, reprinting, reuse of illustrations, recitation, broadcasting, reproduction on microfilms or in any other physical way, and transmission or information storage and retrieval, electronic adaptation, computer software, or by similar or dissimilar methodology now known or hereafter developed.
The use of general descriptive names, registered names, trademarks, service marks, etc. in this publication does not imply, even in the absence of a specific statement, that such names are exempt from the relevant protective laws and regulations and therefore free for general use. The publisher, the authors and the editors are safe to assume that the advice and information in this book are believed to be true and accurate at the date of publication. Neither the publisher nor the authors or the editors give a warranty, expressed or implied, with respect to the material contained herein or for any errors or omissions that may have been made. The publisher remains neutral with regard to jurisdictional claims in published maps and institutional affiliations.

This Palgrave Macmillan imprint is published by the registered company Springer Nature Switzerland AG.
The registered company address is: Gewerbestrasse 11, 6330 Cham, Switzerland

If disposing of this product, please recycle the paper.

Acknowledgments

Nomadic New Women—Exile and Border-Crossing Between Spain and the Americas, Early to Mid-Twentieth Century began life as a conversation between Esther Sánchez-Pardo and Renée Silverman during 2014–2015, a year which Renée spent researching in Madrid. During that year, Esther and Renée, who had previously collaborated on the study of modernism and the avant-garde, began a long conversation about modernism and women. Our exploration of the influence of gender on modern artistic and cultural production began to include themes of border-crossing, exile, and migration, perhaps as a reflection on our own intercultural lives and collaborative scholarship. We decided to continue this conversation, now about modernism in relation to women crossing borders, expanding it into a double seminar at the 2017 conference of the American Comparative Literature Association (ACLA) in Utrecht, the Netherlands. In the course of the seminar, we found that several of the presentations in our seminar coalesced not only around the particular time-period of modernism, but also around specific geographical areas and cultural geographies. Most of the women featured in our seminar turned out to have moved in and around Anglo- and Hispanic spaces.

The ACLA conference gave our conversation a new and pointed focus, from which our initial book project was born. Gathering momentum, the book project had its course inevitably changed by the crisis of 2020, which altered the roster of participants, as well as the warp and woof of its content. New contributors made our project even more specific to the time period of the first half of the twentieth century and the way in which the exigencies of this period led to the cross-border movement and

vi ACKNOWLEDGMENTS

intercultural collaboration of women artists, writers, and intellectuals, between Spain and the Americas. We moved forward with a sharper sense of the factors that affect the movement of women and, especially, the border crossings of creative women.

Our most important acknowledgment is to our contributors, past and present: Their brave intellectual flexibility and creativity have shaped *Nomadic New Women*. We are grateful to the participants in the ACLA seminar, whose ideas sowed the seeds that made the project blossom initially. We are also deeply indebted to the authors of each chapter for their outstanding contributions, which have engendered this book's ultimate flowering.

Esther Sánchez-Pardo would like to acknowledge the teachings and intellectual exchanges that over the years have nurtured and sustained her work. From early on the work of women scholars who were models in her formative years and postgraduate work, from her much admired Professors Susan Stanford Friedman and Nellie McKay (U. Wisconsin–Madison), outstanding scholars of modernism, to the continued conversations she had the honor to maintain with Professors Barbara Godard (York University, Canada) and Robert Silhol (U. Paris VII). Attending the seminar on Maria Zambrano offered by Professor Elena Laurenzi and organized by the Autonomous Feminist Platform in Madrid many years ago is at the origin of her work on Zambranian philosophy and writing. Esther wishes to acknowledge the support and intellectual friendship of poet Noni Benegas (and her impressive background on Gertrude Stein and avant-garde women), Pilar Sánchez Calle, and Fátima Arranz, dear colleagues and professors of English and Sociology, respectively. Her graduate and undergraduate students at the Universidad Complutense have been the best and most devoted community of readers and researchers she might have imagined, a permanent source of inspiration and laboratory of ideas.

Renée Silverman would like to express her sincere gratitude to the individuals and centers at Florida International University (FIU) who have supported her research: the Department of Modern Languages and Chair Pascale Bécel, and the Steven J. Green School of International and Public Affairs and Dean Shlomi Dinar. Renée and Esther also wish to recognize our late friend and colleague in the field of Women's and Gender Studies, Aurora Morcillo (FIU), whose work we had intended to include in the pages of this book. Similarly essential for Renée have been the conversations that she has maintained with her doctoral students over the years, in graduate seminars and while working together on their dissertations; several of them have since become valued colleagues. In relation to her research on Maruja Mallo, Renée wants to profusely thank the late Juan Pérez de Ayala for generously sharing his insights into the Spanish artist, as well as to Guillermo de Osma and everyone at the Guillermo de Osma Gallery for providing her with access to art by Mallo as well as other key materials. Finally, crucial to Renée's scholarship have been the ideas and incisive commentary of her fellow specialists in Spanish literature at the South Atlantic Modern Languages Association.

It is likewise essential for us to gratefully acknowledge all those at Palgrave Macmillan for their crucial support: Editors Carly Silver and Victoria Peters for their deft direction of the whole process; Susan Westendorf; and Steven Fassioms and Linda Berlin for their adept management of the technical aspects of publication. Last, but certainly not least, we wish to sincerely thank our anonymous peer reviewers for their judicious consideration, comments, and suggestions, for which every part of our book is much the better.

Finally, we wish to thank our families for the loving support and understanding that they have shown for this project and ourselves.

RMS and ESP

Miami and Madrid, May 2024

CONTENTS

1 Introduction: Nomadic New Women: Border-Crossing
and Intercultural Encounter   1
Renée M. Silverman and Esther Sánchez-Pardo

Part I   Women Writing (in) Exile: Art, Life, Politics   23

2 The Intimacy of Distance: Homelessness and
Homecoming in the Poetry of Marina Romero   25
Ana Eire

3 A Voice in the Margins: Ana María Martínez Sagi's
Poetry in Exile   51
Javier Sánchez

4 Words in Space: The Exile Diary of Zenobia Camprubí   75
Leonor María Martínez Serrano

5 "A Gem of Many Colors": Articulating Migration in
Isabel de Palencia's *I Must Have Liberty* (1940)   101
Lisa Nalbone

x CONTENTS

6 María Zambrano's Caribbean Imaginings: Philosophy
from Island to Continent and Back   121
Esther Sánchez-Pardo

7 The Scene of the Firing Squad: Zambrano's
Delirium and Destiny and Goya's *The Third of May*   147
Juli Highfill

Part II   Border-Crossing: Displacement and Creativity   179

8 Gertrude Stein Off Center in Spain (1901–1916)   181
Anett K. Jessop

9 *La Americanita*: Janet Riesenfeld's Nomadic Crossings
of the Spanish Civil War and Exile   211
Maria Labbato

10 From British Sorcery to *El Mundo Mágico De Los Mayas*:
Leonora Carrington's Cultural Hybridity   237
Javier Martín Párraga

Part III   New Women, New Art Forms   263

11 How to Narrate a War: Kati Horna's Photography
During the Spanish Civil War (1936–1939)—Moving
Across the Real and the Symbolic   265
Aránzazu Díaz-Regañón Labajo

12 "It's where she belongs, isn't it?" Lupe Vélez and
Dolores del Río in Hollywood   295
R. Hernández-Rodríguez

13 A Double Exile: Crossing the Female Figure in Maruja
Mallo's Art—From Spain to America   323
Renée M. Silverman

Index   351

NOTES ON CONTRIBUTORS

Ana Eire is a Professor of Hispanic Studies at Stetson University in DeLand, Florida. She received her Ph.D. from Vanderbilt University. Her articles on contemporary Spanish poetry have appeared in many journals and collections. She is the author of *Conversaciones con poetas españoles contemporáneos* (Renacimiento, 2005), and has edited the anthologies *Sin fronteras* (Renacimiento, 2018) and *El misterio de la felicidad. La poesía de Miguel d'Ors* (Renacimiento, 2009).

R. Hernández-Rodríguez is a Professor of Spanish at Southern Connecticut State University, where he teaches literature, culture, language, and film. He has taught at universities in Mexico, the United States, and Canada. He has contributed essays to multi-authored volumes and published articles in academic journals on film, literature, and culture. He is the author of *Una poética de la despreocupación* (2003), *Splendors of Latin Cinema* (2009), and *Food Cultures of Mexico* (2021).

Juli Highfill is a Professor Emerita in the Department of Romance Languages and Literatures at the University of Michigan. Her research concerns the literary and visual production of the Spanish historic avant-garde, as well as popular film in the 1920s and 30s. She is the author of *Portraits of Excess: Reading Character in the Modern Spanish Novel* (1999) and *Modernism and Its Merchandise: The Spanish Avant-garde and Material Culture* (2014). Her current book project—*Images in Flight: Popular and Political Affect in Spanish Film*—addresses early cinema and

xi

xii NOTES ON CONTRIBUTORS

spectatorship leading up to the Civil War, tracing the turn from the avant-garde to political engagement.

Anett K. Jessop is an Associate Professor of English at The University of Texas at Tyler (USA). Her recent publications include essays in *The Robert Graves Review* (2023), *The Classics in Modernist Translation* (2019), *Women Poets and Myth in the 20th and 21st Centuries: On Sappho's Website* (2018), *Brill's Companion to Classical Receptions: International Modernism and the Avant-Garde* (2017), and *Mediterranean Modernism: Intercultural Exchange and Aesthetic Development, 1880–1945* (2016). Her monograph, *Remediating Antiquity in Modernism: Laura Riding and Robert Graves' Restaging of the Trojan War*, is under contract with Edinburgh University Press's Critical Studies in Modernism, Drama and Performance series.

Aránzazu Díaz-Regañón Labajo Aránzazu Díaz-R. Labajo has been a teacher in Public Secondary Education in Castile and Leon, Spain, since 2012. She received her Ph.D. in History from the University of Salamanca (2010), and was awarded a *Premio Extraordinario de Doctorado* (2009–2010). Her work focuses on the exile of physicians, psychologists, psychoanalysts, and other scientists as a consequence of the Spanish Civil War (1936–1939), and the impact of this diaspora on Argentina's science and education. She has recently widened her research to include the work of foreign female photographers during the Spanish Civil War.

Maria Labbato is an adjunct lecturer at UNC Charlotte and teaches history at an independent school. She earned her Ph.D. in History from Florida International University, researching gender, the Spanish Civil War, and exile. Her dissertation employs feminist theory and life stories to examine the transnational impact of the Spanish conflict and its displacement during the early Cold War years within an Atlantic framework. Her broader research and teaching interests include women's transnational activism and anti-fascism, gender and sexuality history, queer theory, and Latinx studies.

Lisa Nalbone is a Professor of Spanish at the University of Central Florida. She has published over 20 articles/book chapters, a co-edited volume on Spanish literature and culture at the turn of the nineteenth to twentieth century, and a book on the novels of Spanish author Carmen Conde, with her latest book, *Negotiating Discursive Spaces: Censorship and Women's Novels in Spain (1950s–1960s)*, appearing in 2023. Her research engages with sociocultural representations of social constructs in the context of modernity and gender.

Javier Martín Párraga is an Associate Professor at the Department of English and German Studies at the University of Córdoba, where he obtained his Ph.D. degree. His main fields of research focus on American literature, film, cultural studies, and women studies. He has worked as a Visiting Scholar at Wheaton College, United States; Louisiana School for Math, Science, and the Arts, United States; the University of Toronto, Canada; Wellesley College; and several Polish universities. His academic publications include seven books and numerous book chapters and articles in peer-reviewed academic journals.

Javier Sánchez is a Professor of Spanish at Stockton University in New Jersey. He received his Ph.D. in comparative literature from the University of North Carolina at Chapel Hill. In addition to his book *Constructing Meaning in the Spanish and French New Novel: Juan Benet and Alain Robbe-Grillet*, Dr. Sánchez's articles have appeared in peer-reviewed journals such as *Dissidences: Hispanic Journal of Theory and Criticism, L'Érudit Franco-Espagnol, Ojáncano, Letras Hispanas: Revista de Literatura y Cultura, MIFLC Review, Hispanic Studies Review*, and *South Atlantic Review*.

Esther Sánchez-Pardo is a Professor of English at Complutense University, Madrid, Spain. She is the author of *Cultures of the Death Drive. Melanie Klein and Modernist Melancholia* (Duke UP, 2003) and *Antología Poética. Mina Loy* (2009). She has published four critical editions and edited (and co-edited) seven books. Among the latest, *L'Écriture Désirante. Marguerite Duras* (2016), *On Sappho's Website* (2018), *Poéticas Comparadas de Mujeres* (Brill 2022), and *Myth and Environmentalism* (Routledge 2023). Prof. Sánchez-Pardo is the translator of the *Complete Correspondence Sigmund Freud–Ernest Jones* (2001) and serves on the editorial board of several international journals.

Leonor María Martínez Serrano is an Associate Professor in the Department of English and German Philology at the University of Córdoba (Spain). Her research interests include Canadian Literature, American Literature, Ecocriticism, High Modernism, and Comparative Literature. She has been a visiting scholar at the University of Toronto and the University of British Columbia (Canada), the University of the West of

Scotland (United Kingdom), the University of Bialystok (Poland), and Oldenburg University (Germany). She has authored the monograph *Breathing Earth: The Polyphonic Lyric of Robert Bringhurst* (Peter Lang, 2021) and coedited *Modern Ecopoetry: Reading the Palimpsest of a More-Than-Human World* (Brill, 2021).

Renée M. Silverman is an Associate Professor of Spanish at Florida International University. She is the author of *Mapping the Landscape, Remapping the Text: Spanish Poetry from Antonio Machado's* Campos de Castilla *to the First Avant-Garde (1909–1925)* (2014) and the editor/co-editor of *The Popular Avant-Garde* (2010), the 2017 *International Yearbook of Futurism Studies*, and *Mediterranean Modernism: Intercultural Exchange and Aesthetic Development* (2016). Dr. Silverman has also published several articles and book chapters on the European, Latin-American, and Spanish avant-gardes and modernisms. She is a past recipient of the National Endowment for the Humanities (NEH) Award for Faculty.

LIST OF FIGURES

Fig. 7.1	Francisco de Goya y Lucientes. *The Third of May in Madrid.* 1814. Prado Museum, Madrid	168
Fig. 11.1	CNT-FAI Foreign Propaganda Office of CNT. *España?* 1938. CDMH, Salamanca, CDMH BIB FA00431 001	274
Fig. 11.2	Kati Horna. "The Spanish Woman Before the Revolution." March 1938. CDMH, Salamanca, photo No. 184	286
Fig. 12.1	Promotional photo of Novarro and Vélez in *Laughing Boy.* 1934	297
Fig. 12.2	Lupe Velez and Gibson Gowland in a still photo from *Hell Harbor.* 1930	304
Fig. 12.3	Lupe Velez, publicity portrait for *Mexican Spitfire*	307
Fig. 12.4	Still from the movie *Bird of Paradise.* 1932	311
Fig. 13.1	Maruja Mallo. *Cabeza de mujer (Cabeza de negra).* 1946. Museo de Pontevedra. © 2024 Artists Rights Society (ARS), New York / VEGAP, Madrid	342
Fig. 13.2	Maruja Mallo. *La cierva humana.* 1948. Patrimonio Museo de Bellas Artes de La Boca de Artistas Argentinos "Benito Quinquela Martín." © 2024 Artists Rights Society (ARS), New York / VEGAP, Madrid	343

CHAPTER 1

Introduction: Nomadic New Women: Border-Crossing and Intercultural Encounter

Renée M. Silverman and Esther Sánchez-Pardo

The early to mid-twentieth century witnessed an era of unprecedented upheaval and transformation, marked by political turmoil, social unrest, and radical artistic movements. This turbulent period gave rise to a remarkable generation of women writers and artists who challenged societal norms and boldly explored new frontiers of creative expression. These women dared to confront the social norms that were imposed on their gender and carved out their own paths in a hostile world that excluded or relegated them to domesticity and subordination. Their experiences of exile and cultural exchange profoundly shaped their artistic production and intellectual development, rendering their work a testament to the power of resilience and the transformative potential of cross-cultural encounters.

R. M. Silverman
Department of Modern Languages, Florida International University,
Miami, FL, USA
e-mail: silvermr@fiu.edu

E. Sánchez-Pardo (✉)
Department of English Studies, Complutense University, Madrid, Spain
e-mail: estsanch@ucm.es

© The Author(s), under exclusive license to Springer Nature
Switzerland AG 2024
R. M. Silverman, E. Sánchez-Pardo (eds.), *Nomadic New Women*,
https://doi.org/10.1007/978-3-031-62482-7_1

1

The movements of all twelve women in our study bridge Anglo- and Hispanic spaces and cultures, connecting Europe and the Americas. This book examines how their nomadic journeys mark their contributions to the arts and literature of Spain and both the Anglo- and Hispanic Americas, including the Caribbean. The practice of border-crossing, and the art made under circumstances of displacement and uncertainty, is defined by juxtaposition, contrast, and transformation. For the art of women crossing borders, of nomadic women, is essentially the art of mobility, versatility, creative fulfillment, and intellectual restlessness.

The chapters comprising this volume pay tribute to the women writers and artists from the early to mid-twentieth century who made the momentous decision to cross the Atlantic, establishing new lives in Spain, North and South America, and the Caribbean. These women, driven by a variety of personal and professional aspirations, migrated and traveled, seeking opportunities for self-expression, creative growth, and a liberated social and cultural environment. Many sought new collaborations and thriving artistic milieux in cultural hubs. Some fled political unrest, discrimination, or persecution in their home countries to find safety and freedom elsewhere. Still others moved to pursue educational opportunities or establish themselves professionally in their artistic fields. These migrations profoundly influenced their lives and work, shaping their perspectives and allowing them to contribute to the cultural landscapes of their adopted homes. Their creative endeavors, molded by their experiences of border-crossing and cultural exchange, enriched the artistic and literary scenes on both sides of the Atlantic and across the Americas.

The women writers, philosophers, dancers, actresses, and artists on whom we focus decided, or saw themselves forced, to go beyond the borders of their countries of origin, forming a true diaspora. Many of them remained permanently in transit across national and other sorts of boundaries, experiencing the trauma of exile or a disturbing sense of displacement. The present volume centers on the life experiences and careers of twelve of these outstanding women who moved between Anglo- and Hispanic spaces, Europe and the Americas. The women here under study fit within two contiguous generations, although we recognize, at the same time, that their lives and work form a continuum due to their many similarities and shared experiences. If we were to follow the established 'generational' pattern in literary, art, and world history, we would place Gertrude Stein (1874–1946), Zenobia Camprubí (1878–1956), and Isabel de Palencia (1878–1974) within the first. The second generation would then include Maruja Mallo (1902–1995), María Zambrano (1904–1991), Dolores del Río (1904–1983), Ana María Martínez Sagi (1907–2000), Marina Romero (1908–2001), Lupe Vélez (1908–1944), Kati Horna (1912–2000), Leonora Carrington (1917–2011), and Janet Riesenfeld (1918–1998).

We contend that all twelve embody the qualities of what we call 'nomadic New Women.' They were independent, professional women, forging a career and making a living on their own. Not only were they focused on their creative and artistic work, but also, they vindicated the role of women in society as freethinking political subjects and became active participants in their communities and social life. This volume examines their important work as authors (in literature, diaries, poetry, philosophy, and the political essay), visual artists, dancers, and practitioners of the modernist arts par excellence of photography and film, and explains how they deftly navigated the gendered discourses surrounding their professional and personal lives and civic engagement. Through cross-border exchange, mobility, collaboration, reciprocity, and solidarity, they were able to connect Anglo- and Hispanic spaces and both sides of the Atlantic, breaking fresh ground and establishing new traditions in their fields. In this way, María Zambrano (the subject of Chaps. 6 and 7, by Esther Sánchez-Pardo and Juli Highfill) became one of the most important philosophers of her generation. The same applies to Maruja Mallo and Leonora Carrington in art, as masterful innovative painters, Zenobia Camprubí, as an outstanding diarist and translator, and Marina Romero, as a splendid yet still, to date, virtually unknown poet.

For many of our nomadic New Women, history and politics remained closely entwined, and well before second wave feminism raised as a slogan the reality that the 'personal is political,' they had already internalized this tenet, manifesting it in their lives and deeds. The idea that the personal is political formed part of the struggle of women for equality ever since the modern feminist ideas of pioneers Virginia Woolf, Margaret Sanger, and Clara Campoamor first circulated in the public sphere. We map the spaces in which these nomadic women engaged in their pursuits, describing the territory in which they lived and made art on the vanguard of change. The cartography of our volume draws a spatiotemporal geography of the migrations of our women writers and artists in and through the Anglo-Hispanic world, from the turn of the twentieth through mid-century. Our critical intervention charts the connections among these women's movements, as they engaged in their quest for liberty, opportunity, and freedom from confining socio-economic and political boundaries. This quest led to their crossing of borders of many kinds (the gendered nature of which effect and enforce women's marginalization), and at times led to an exile made double by their gender and sexuality. Our cartography brings into relief the relations created for and by women among the United Kingdom, United States, and Spain in response to World War I and its aftermath; Mexico and the United States, as a result of the socio-political, economic, and technological upheaval that occurred during the first half of the twentieth century (with special reference to the Mexican Revolution of 1910–1920); and Spain, Mexico, the United States, Caribbean, and South America, as a consequence of the Spanish Civil War (1936–1939) and World War II. Our map is not, therefore, an objective spatial diagram but, rather, a subjective rendering that shows how such border-crossings become inflected by gender and sexuality, as well as the particularities of Anglo-Hispanic linguistic communities and cultural spaces.

Part of this volume focuses on the nomadic New Women who found that Spain could be a privileged space on the margins of Europe for their lives and work. Spain was, at the time, a place where the confluence of faded national glory, picturesque attraction, and preservation of old traditions acted as a magnet, drawing intellectuals and travelers curious about the Spanish *Weltanschauung* and way of life. Gertrude Stein, Ernest Hemingway, Gerald Brenan, Laura Riding Jackson, Robert Graves, and Muriel Rukeyser, to name but a few, experienced Spain and distilled their experiences of the land in their writings and testimonial narratives. Neutral during World War I, Spain (especially Madrid and Barcelona) also stood, before the Civil War, as a beacon to the international creative community, including modernists and members of the avant-garde like Jorge Luis Borges and Norah Borges (who were siblings), the artists Robert Delaunay and Sonia Delaunay-Terk, and the impresario and founder of the *Ballets Russes* Sergei Diaghilev. Gertrude Stein, who traveled and lived in Europe from the time she was young, felt strongly attracted to Mallorca and intermittently resided in Spain; Chap. 8, authored by Anett Jessop, addresses Stein's important literary production inspired by the Spanish character, ethos, and terrain.

In terms of the geography of our nomadic New Women's lives, many of them took the path of exile when the government of the Second Spanish Republic was overthrown in a coup d'état (1936). Out of this volume's selection of Spanish women—Zenobia Camprubí, Isabel de Palencia, Maruja Mallo, María Zambrano, Ana María Martínez Sagi, and Marina Romero—left Spain for Latin American or Caribbean locations, Mexico, or the United States; the American Janet Riesenfeld and the Hungarian Kati Horna also left active lives led in Spain, eventually emigrating to Mexico. The Spanish-speaking countries to which fled the largest number of "literary intellectuals" among the Civil War exiles were Mexico, considered by some to be the most hospitable of destinations, Argentina, Chile, Venezuela, and the Dominican Republic (Gray 54, 69, 74). Smaller groups of well-known literary-intellectual exiles secured their refuge in Cuba, Puerto Rico, Uruguay, Bolivia, Ecuador, Colombia, Costa Rica, Guatemala, and Panama (Gray 74). The United States and United Kingdom became the favored English-speaking landing places for such exiles; notably, one of the women studied in this volume, Zenobia Camprubí (with her lifelong spouse, the modernist poet Juan Ramón Jiménez), found shelter and inspiration in the beauty of Coral Gables (Miami), after living in Cuba and Puerto Rico (Gray 76–78). In Mexico, President Lázaro Cárdenas opened the country's borders to Spanish exiles. Mexico was the preferred destination for many exiles from Spain—a country where they could feel at home and preserve their 'national' identity while acquiring a new and hybrid sense of self. Photographer Kati Horna, for instance, fled Spain in 1937 for France and, in 1939, escaped Nazi-occupied Paris to take refuge in Mexico, where she remained for the rest of her life. British-born painter Leonora Carrington is also a case in point: She fled World War II France for what turned out to be a traumatic stay in Spain (1939–1940), then left for New York, and later, Mexico (1942). Her escape from a European continent threatened by violence, Fascism, and dictatorship testifies to the importance of Mexico as a refuge, and fertile ground for artistic creation and a renewed sense of life. Mexican actresses Lupe Vélez and Dolores del Río crossed the linguistic, geographical, and socio-cultural boundaries between Mexico and the United States, becoming well known during the Golden Age of Hollywood cinema. Closing the circle, Janet Riesenfeld traversed various Hispanic spaces, and after her sojourn in Spain (starting in July, 1936), she became known in the New York press as "the first North American actress to make a film career in Latin America" (Adelson 7). She arrived in Mexico on an undetermined date, between 1937 and 1938, and settled there for life.

New Women Navigating the Atlantic

The figure of the New Woman represented in this volume is an epochal sign that emerged in the late nineteenth and early twentieth centuries to describe a cultural shift in the status and the social perception of the role of women, which had been traditionally tied to family values, domesticity, social class, and responsibility to the nation. This figure came to be characterized by the gradual public appearance of women who challenged traditional gender roles and sought greater freedom and independence in their personal and professional lives. In Einav Rabinovitch-Fox's view, "The New Woman image was often positioned in opposition to the Victorian 'True Woman,' which was associated with an understanding of femininity as an essential, timeless concept that emphasized domesticity and submissiveness" (n. pag.). The new designation was used to portray women who rejected the strict gender norms of their time and embraced new ideas about femininity, education, work, and sexuality; the proponents of the New Woman figure were mainly writers, activists, and artists who sought to challenge the prevailing social norms and stereotypes about women. Certainly, the emergence of the New Woman in different locations in the first decades of the twentieth century was influenced by broader social and cultural changes in the West and the world at large, such as the struggle for women's suffrage, incorporation into the work force, and vindication of equal status to men under the law. In order to achieve a fair social occupation of public spaces by women, and women's political representation, gaining the right to vote was essential. According to Margaret Walters, "In the course of the 19th century, the vote gradually became central to feminist demands. It was seen as important both symbolically (as a recognition of women's rights to full citizenship) and practically (as a necessary way of furthering reforms and making practical changes in women's lives). But winning the vote proved a complicated struggle, and one that lasted for decades" (68). Some of the most notable proponents of the struggle for women's rights and the idea of the New Woman were organizations such as the Women's suffrage movement— under the leadership of Emmeline and Christabel Pankhurst in the United Kingdom, M. Carey Thomas and Alice Paul in the United States, the International Alliance of Women (Berlin, 1904), the League of Women Voters (1920–present), and the Spanish Federation of Women's Societies (1918)—as well as intellectuals for the advancement of the cause like Annie Besant, Virginia Woolf, Marie Stopes, Charlotte Perkins Gilman, Margaret Sanger, Rebecca West, Maria Deraismes, Käthe Schirmacher, and Clara Campoamor.

In *A Room of One's Own* (1927), Virginia Woolf examines the challenges faced by women who want to break free from traditional gender roles and become professional writers. Upon entering the British Museum, the narrator wonders, "Why did men drink wine and women water? Why was one sex so prosperous and the other so poor? What effect has poverty on fiction? What conditions are necessary for the creation of art?" (19). As if in answer to the narrator's rhetorical questions, Woolf argues that women need to overcome the societal expectations that have held them back and find their own voice. One of the most significant figures in the emergence of the New Woman in Spain was Carmen de Burgos (1867–1932), a writer and journalist who wrote under the pseudonym Colombine. Burgos was a leading voice in the feminist movement in Spain, writing extensively about women's issues, including education, work, and sexuality. In her book *La mujer moderna y sus derechos* (*The Modern Woman and her Rights*), published in 1927, Burgos argued that women should have the same rights and opportunities as men, and that they should be free to pursue their own interests and careers.

The marginalized condition of women at the beginning of the twentieth century was aggravated by the stagnancy of domesticity. Women were prohibited from moving freely outside the home, and acquiring higher education and culturally rich experiences that could only be had through exchanges in the public social sphere. The women who inherited Burgos's mantle of women's-rights advocacy—María Teresa León, Maruja Mallo, Concha Méndez, Josefina de la Torre, Margarita Manso, Ernestina de Champourcín, María Zambrano, Rosa Chacel, Ángeles Santos, and Marga Gil Roësset—insisted on their corporeal freedom (Balló 19). One fine day during the 1920s, Mallo and Manso staged a rebellion against the social convention that 'respectable' Spanish women would wear hats in public, strolling bareheaded through the Puerta del Sol in the center of Madrid, accompanied by Federico García Lorca and Salvador Dalí (Balló 33). In challenging the then-prevailing sartorial rules, Mallo and Manso asserted control over their own bodies, as well as where and how these bodies could move. Thus, mobility and exteriority were achievements that progressively put an end to the confinement of women and contributed to beginning a new stage that went hand-in-hand with the first wave of feminism.

Mobility played a key role in the emergence of the New Woman in modernist literature. With the advent of transportation technologies such as trains and automobiles, women were able to travel more freely and explore new opportunities beyond their traditional social roles. The figure of the New Woman in literature was often portrayed as an independent, free-spirited woman who embraced mobility as a means of breaking free from traditional gender roles and social conventions. According to Ann Ardis, even "the woman who metaphorically kills the angel in the house ... [leaves] the Victorian social order intact" (66). For this reason, an increased mobility was a must, a form of escape from the rigid constraints imposed upon women. Such opportunities for travel also had significant cultural implications, as movement beyond national borders and intercultural exchange became possible, allowing people to connect with one another in new and unprecedented ways.

NOMADISM AND THE MODERN WOMAN

Travel and mobility—nomadism—are crucial aspects of the modern and Modernism. During the first half of the twentieth century, industrialization, urban development, and transnational movement, traditionally related to the male, provided new avenues for the lived experience and artistic expression of women. As Virginia Woolf declares, "As a woman I have no country. As a woman I want no country. As a woman, my country is the whole world" (*Three Guineas* 99), and as Theodor Adorno argues, "For a man [or a woman, as we hold] who no longer has a homeland, writing becomes a place to live" (87). These polemical declarations express fundamental truths about modernity—and modernity in relation to gender. The ability to cross national borders is a key condition of women's liberation; creative and artistic expression replace home when these boundaries are traversed.

Our view that the resistance and rebellion against patriarchal and heteronormative hegemonies play essential roles in the subject-formation and creative production of the woman nomad follows from Woolf's argument, in her anti-war essay *Three Guineas* (1938), that such hegemonies are part and parcel of women's socio-economic, political, and cultural marginalization, as well as a root cause of the violence and war that send them into exile and force them to migrate. Woolf's *Three Guineas* and Rosi Braidotti's *Nomadic Subjects* (1994) are foundational to our consideration of women's experiences of border-crossing. In concordance with Woolf, we question the patriarchal and heteronormative premises of national identity, as well as the entwining of patriarchy and nation with the cord of violence. Yet in questioning these patriarchal and heteronormative premises, we widen the scope of vision, looking beyond the nation and national identity to examine the subjectivities of border-crossing creative women and the spaces that they must create for themselves.

In *Nomadic Subjects*, Braidotti argues that traditional concepts of identity are no longer sufficient to describe the complex and rapidly changing world in which we live in the late twentieth century. Instead, she proposes the concept of a nomadic subjectivity, which is defined by a willingness to embrace difference and move beyond traditional notions of identity. As Braidotti observes, "The nomadic subject as a performative image allows me to weave together different levels of my experience; it reflects some autobiographical aspects, while also expressing my own conceptual preference for a postmetaphysical vision of subjectivity" (7). Her influential account of the subject under very advanced global capitalism draws from a Deleuzian framework. It portrays and critically responds to the proliferation of centers of power, scattered around the globe, flows of capital, and a virtual reality obfuscating the realities of dispossession and oppression. Braidotti argues for the necessity of lines of flight, creative alternative spaces of becoming, and complicating ingrained binaries (e.g., mobile/immobile, resident/foreigner), asserting the need for "new alliances and assemblages" ("Nomadic Subjects" 136).

In light of historical and other contextual specificities, our understanding of 'nomadic' cannot fully align with Braidotti's important feminist theorization around nomadic subjectivities within feminist philosophy. One of the central tasks of this volume is to (re)imagine the nomadic woman for the modern period under study. For reasons related to the precise characteristics of the time-period, the path that we take in our exploration of nomadism diverges significantly from the line of Braidotti's work on the topic, shaped as it is by the postmodern conception of subjectivity formulated by Gilles Deleuze and Félix Guattari. Notably, we do not conceptualize subjectivity according to the rhizomic model of Deleuze and Guattari, nor do we couple nomadism with their notion of 'deterritorialization,' since such ideas respond to the particularities of the postmodern condition and context.

At the same time, we have been inspired by the "cartographic method" that has proven integral to Braidotti's feminist nomadic theory—a method that she describes as "a theoretically based and politically informed reading of the process of power relations" (*Portable* 4). For, in this volume, we focus on socio-cultural and political power relations in connection with hierarchies of gender and sexuality, the material body, language, and creative expression. We envisage modern women's nomadic subjectivity in terms of multiplicity and hybridity, recalling the feminist-psychoanalytic notion of the 'sex which is not one,' which regards female corporeality and sexuality as inherently double (Irigaray, *This Sex*). The perspective that we adopt is likewise informed by modern-period creative and theoretical work that posits hybridity as constitutive of culture, yet eschews an ahistorical decentering of subjectivity and identity.

In the context of our volume, (New) women's displacement and exile are foregrounded. Both displacement and nomadism represent a rejection of fixed, stable identities in favor of more fluid and flexible conceptions of self. In modernist literature, the emerging figure of the *flâneuse*, as is the case with the protagonist in Virginia Woolf's "Street Haunting" (1930), is frequently depicted as a character who is in a state of perpetual motion, moving through the city and engaging with a variety of experiences and perspectives. The *flâneur* was originally a male figure who traversed the urban environment with a sense of detachment and curiosity, observing and experiencing the city in new and unconventional ways.[1] Similarly, Braidotti's nomadic subjectivities are defined by a constant state of transformation and evolution, as individuals move beyond traditional social and cultural boundaries to embrace novel forms of identity and experience.

The perspective that we adopt is shaped by modern-period creative and theoretical work that posits hybridity as constitutive of culture. How, we ask, can we conceptualize the modern woman nomad through the lens of multiplicity and hybridity, while simultaneously differentiating this (non-monolithic) woman nomad from the postmodern one? Braidotti, for example, conceives of a "transmobile materialist theory of feminist subjectivity ... within the parameters of the postmodern predicament" (*Nomadic Subjects* 2); to our mind, the postmodern is defined by a marked performativity, and the relative absence of historical anchoring, fixity, and permanence with respect to subjectivity and identity. Contrastingly, we locate the modern woman nomad squarely in the period spanning the early through mid-twentieth century, keeping the historical, socio-political, and cultural conflicts of the time in full view. Although the modern women nomads featured in our volume certainly retain agency over their lives and movements, they nevertheless remain circumscribed by contemporary socio-cultural norms governing gender and sexuality, their material bodies, politics, and the events of history. These nomadic New Women are

---

[1] One of the earliest and most significant instances of male *flânerie* is Charles Baudelaire's protagonist in "The Painter of Modern Life" (1863), in which the French poet characterizes modernity and speaks of how the *flâneur* experiences urban life, and in a detached and arrogant way relates to others.

encircled by gendered borders, but they are not without recourse for crossing these borders—via routes that they daringly chart for themselves. In other words, the modern women artists and writers of our volume are at once embedded in circumstance, and nomadic, characterized by their (interconnected) mobility, creativity, and hybrid identity.

Our viewpoint is that the hybridity of the modern woman nomad's flexible subjectivity and identity translates into particular kinds of creative activity. Visual artist Maruja Mallo and writer-philosopher María Zambrano, the subjects of three of the chapters in this volume, exemplify the transgressive creative work of the modern woman nomad. As Renée Silverman holds, Mallo turns her subjectivity and identity, as a Spanish Civil War exile experiencing the natural and ethnic diversity of South America, into art that challenges the patriarchal and phallocentric order. According to Silverman, Mallo's art deviates from the predominant esthetic of abstraction by foregrounding the female figure and material body, and disrupts the desiring male gaze and masculine-centered classificatory ontology. An exile from the Spanish Civil War just as Mallo, Zambrano draws upon her multifaceted experience living in the Caribbean to cultivate generically and stylistically syncretic forms of writing. As Esther Sánchez-Pardo demonstrates in her essay, Zambrano's syncretic forms of writing reflect the inherent hybridity of her exilic and nomadic cultural production, and are designed to counter the psychic trauma that such a situation causes. Analogously, Juli Highfill's study centers on generic hybridity and intermediality in Zambrano's novel *Delirio y destino: los veinte años de una española* (*Delirium and Destiny: A Spaniard in Her Twenties*, 1952); Highfill analyzes how Zambrano uses the art of Francisco de Goya for her novelistic meditation on death and the collapse of democracy. The interdisciplinary and inter-artistic crossing in Zambrano's novel parallels the hybrid subjectivity and identity of the modern women nomad.

For the authors and editors of this volume, women's nomadism in the modern period translates into acts of creation and transgression that challenge the patriarchal and phallocentric order. Yet these creative and transgressive ventures do not happen in the free spaces of postmodernity in which everything is, at least apparently, open to rhizomic growth, becoming, and performance. We stress that the modern woman nomad repeatedly runs up against, and must therefore find a way to traverse, the very real and material borders of her time. Along these lines, the relationship between displacement during the time-period of our focus and Braidotti's nomadic subjectivities lies in their shared commitment to mobility and fluidity in the face of rapidly changing social, cultural, and economic land-scapes. Both concepts represent a rejection of stable identities in favor of more dynamic and flexible forms of subjectivity, and each has had a signifi-cant impact on the development of modernist and post-modernist litera-ture and critical theory.

We find in Braidotti's reflections on (Deleuzian) deterritorialization the potential implicit in the lines of flight of our New Women, although we always maintain a historically grounded feminist perspective. In *A Room of One's Own*, Woolf advised women to "Travel and idle, contemplate the future or the past of the world, dream over books and loiter at street cor-ners, and let the line of thought dip deep into the stream" (79). She argued that this mobility had a significant impact on the way writers approached their craft, as it allowed them to engage with a broader range of experiences and perspectives. Woolf herself traveled widely, and both her rich fictional world and her work as an editor for Hogarth Press with Leonard Woolf, disseminating, editing, and translating many foreign authors, greatly benefited from her direct knowledge of life abroad.

Correspondingly, the relationship between mobility, the New Woman, and exile is a central concern in modern—and modernist—literature and culture. According to Wendy Parkins, "women's mobility is an important means through which the reconfigurations of the modern female subject are textually represented" (90), which leads her to "consider the mobility of the female subject as a trope of modernity" (77). As Parkins implies, the emergence of the New Woman in literature remained closely linked to the development of new transport technologies such as automobiles, steam-ships, and trains, which enabled women to travel more freely and explore new opportunities beyond their traditional social roles. In her book *Modernism and Mobility: The Passport and Cosmopolitan Experience*, Bridget Chalk argues that mobility was a central concern for modernist writers, who were often themselves exiles or otherwise displaced individu-als. Chalk foregrounds "the central role nationality plays in the modernist cosmopolitan context" (91) and the difficulties and conflicted negotiation over that context many were pushed to confront. For modernist writers, mobility was often a source of anxiety and uncertainty, as they found themselves constantly on the move and struggling to find a sense of belonging in a rapidly changing world. As Chalk notes, many modernist writers were themselves exiles who had been forced to leave their homes and move to new and unfamiliar places. Transience feels different depend-ing on one's origin and location; Chalk devotes attention to cases such as those of Claude McKay and Jean Rhys, en route to the United States and United Kingdom from Jamaica and the Caribbean island of Dominica, respectively. Certainly, displacement and exile were a common experience for many modern and modernist writers, who were often politically or culturally marginalized, or found themselves in a state of perpetual motion as they moved from one country to another.

Overall, the relationship between mobility, the New Woman, and exile in modern and modernist literature reflects the larger cultural and political changes of the early to mid-twentieth century. The emergence of new technologies and the changing role of women in society created a sense of excitement and possibility, but also a sense of dislocation and uncertainty as individuals and communities adapted to new ways of being in the world and relating to one another.

Spain at the Crossroads of Modernity

The loss of Cuba, Puerto Rico, and the Philippines as colonies, as a consequence of defeat in the 1898 Spanish-American War, compelled Spain to confront the destruction of its former empire and find meaning in the remnants of its past. The group of artists, writers, and philosophers commonly known as the Generation of 1898 made substantial progress in questioning the Spanish mindset within a turbulent political panorama. The writer and philosopher Miguel de Unamuno (1864–1936), in particular, returned to the idea of Spain as a crossroads for different cultures and traditions, situating the essence of Spanish identity, paradoxically, in this fundamental hybridity. Others, such as Antonio Machado (1875–1939), like his precursor, the Galician poet Rosalía de Castro (1837–1885), located Spain's identity in the character of the land. Ironically, the Spanish Civil War uprooted Machado, a supporter of the Second Spanish Republic, forcing him to flee his homeland (breathing his last in Collioure, over the French border), just as many of the women and men of the generations that succeeded him escaped into exile. Indeed, the so-named Generations of 1927 and 1936, to which Mallo and Zambrano belonged, embraced both their roots and hybridity, as did Unamuno.

Positioned on the outermost western edge of Europe, Spain, in our view, was at once peripheral and central to Modernism. One strand of Modernism, specific to Spain, created a space for New Women at the forefront of the Second Spanish Republic (1931–1939) across a wide spectrum of political positions and public life; we refer to Spanish New Women like Clara Campoamor, Victoria Kent, Margarita Nelken, Irene Falcón, Dolores Ibárruri (known as 'Pasionaria'), and Federica Montseny. These women worked in favor of a politics of equality and the promotion of women in the public sphere.

During the Republican period in Spain, women politicians and representatives in Parliament advocated for the emancipation of women, women's education, and women's rights. These women played a crucial role in advancing the cause of gender equality in the country and their efforts paved the way for future generations to achieve greater political and social power. One of the most notable women politicians of the Republican era was Victoria Kent (1892–1987). Along with Campoamor and Nelken, Kent was one of the first three women to be elected to the Spanish Parliament in 1931, where she worked to advance women's rights and promote gender equality. She was a strong advocate for women's education and believed that greater access to education was key to improving women's status in society. Kent also played a key role in the passage of the 1931 Ley de Divorcio (Divorce Law), which made it easier for women to obtain a divorce and provided greater legal protection for women in marriage.

Another prominent women's rights advocate during the Republican era was Campoamor (1888–1972). Like Kent and Nelken, she was a member of Parliament. Campoamor fought for women's suffrage and played a key role in the passage of the 1931 Ley de Voto (Voting Law), which granted women the right to vote in Spain for the first time. She believed that political representation was essential to advancing women's rights and she worked tirelessly to ensure that women had a voice in Spanish politics (see *El voto femenino*). Other women politicians and representatives who advocated for women's rights during the Republican era included Nelken (1894–1968), Ibárruri (1895–1989), and Montseny (1905–1994). Nelken was a member of Parliament who fought for greater legal protections for working women, while Ibárruri was a communist and a Republican leader during the Spanish Civil War who championed the cause of women's rights and fought against Fascism. Montseny was the first woman to serve as a minister in a European government, and she played a key role in promoting gender equality and reproductive rights during her tenure in office.

The events that led to the Spanish Civil War became a laboratory for testing the limits, virtues, and imperfections of the democratic Second Republic. The Spanish Civil War marked the bounds of an era, which we observe critically from the privileged vantage point of our New Women's art and lives. It was at this time, in preparation for the fight over Fascism in Europe and the testing of the old machinery of war, when Spain became the somber scenario for operations of foreign powers, an insurgent military, and the Catholic Church (and, in parallel, anticlericalism), which resulted in the devastation of the Civil War and the dismantling of civil society.

The majority of the nomadic New Women—and all of those from Spain—represented in this volume went through the painful experience of exile. Whereas on the one side of the coin, exilic writing, life, and art originate from a space of 'otherness,' on the other side, there is always a reflection on the idiosyncrasies of the national community of origin. In consequence, the imprint left by Spain on the Anglo- and Hispanic cultures of the Americas and Caribbean, and by the Anglo- and Hispanic Americas and Caribbean on Spain, constitutes the common denominator of our critical assessment of the nomadic New Woman.

THE WOMAN EXILE

Exile has often been compared with other experiences of physical displacement: Emigration, migration, refuge, and diaspora are some typical examples. Yet we place emphasis on exile as a special form of movement and displacement across borders—one that is at least partially, if not wholly, involuntary (Wimbush 6). In so defining the term, we must ask, who should be considered an exile? In Edward Said's foundational work on the subject, exile usually occurs for political reasons, and the archetypal exiled individual tends to be a highly educated and socio-economically élite man, even when this élite man is non-European or participates in the critique of Eurocentrism (Said, "Reflections"). One of our main purposes in this volume is to imagine the woman exile, giving her form and shape, and thus visibility, and thereby expanding upon 'exile' as a concept.

The creative women exiles portrayed in this volume cross borders for reasons not only of politics, but also of ideology, broadly speaking, including cultural norms and expectations. For our conceptualization of the ideologies from which these creative women sought freedom in exile, we take as a premise Virginia Woolf's declaration, in *Three Guineas*, that woman has no country. The World War I context of Woolf's essay is the motivating factor behind her rejection of the nation as the basis of belonging, and related embrace of cosmopolitanism. From her standpoint, the same component parts that make up national borders serve to construct the boundaries that close off social and economic spaces to women. For this reason, in *Three Guineas*, the internal marginalization of women within the nation becomes comparable to exile. As Woolf points out, women are effectively banished by means of the segregation of public and commercial places on the basis of gender. She further demystifies the *patria* as having been consolidated and defended by male aggression; woman has 'no country' because she always already lives on the margins of the *patria*, the borders of which are policed by war and other forms of violence. Woolf stresses that such violence is organized and perpetrated primarily by men of the upper echelons of society, who have a proprietary interest in excluding women from competition for land and wealth, as well as access to the educational and professional institutions from which the ability to generate economic resources is derived.

In *Literature and Inner Exile*, his critical study of "authoritarian Spain" during Francisco Franco's dictatorship (1939–1975), Paul Ilie explains that exile can be internal as well as external, or "territorial" (6). Ilie defines "inner exile," essentially, as a dissident whose refusal to conform to authoritarianism and the cultural norms of an authoritarian regime brings about an uprooting from that individual's natural place in society, with repercussions ranging from marginalized disillusionment and clandestinity to ostracism and imprisonment (6, 3). From our standpoint, women's exile is 'double,' since even before women may be compelled to leave their countries as territorial exiles, they are already inner exiles, pushed toward the margins and driven underground by ideologies of gender and cultural norms, whose enforcement by authoritarian regimes tends to be stricter and more violent.

In this volume, our definition of the woman exile is she whose internal marginalization, combined with actual geographical displacement, occurs as the consequence of ideologies of gender that banish her from full participation in the culture, society, education, politics, or economic activity of her home territory. We also consider a form of exile the alienation of women from their own bodies, sexuality, and consciousness, from which linguistic, creative, and artistic capabilities originate. Luce Irigaray has argued that women experience such estrangement because patriarchal societies make corporeality and sexuality so dependent on masculinity and the phallus. This phallocentrism, from Irigaray's perspective, exiles women from their "auto-eroticism" and, as a result, from fully expressing their sexuality ("Women's Exile" 65). According to Irigaray, the expression of sexuality remains intimately tied to language and linguistic expression; the "masculine imaginary" dominates the "feminine imaginary," since validity is assigned exclusively to the male body and sexuality ("Women's Exile" 66–67). For us, and for several of the contributors in this volume, in taking back their bodies and sexuality, women emerge from their inner exile, transforming their linguistic and creative capacities.

As previously indicated, crucial to our volume are the Spanish Civil War and its fallout. The war worked as a magnet, attracting many in solidarity with the Republic and repelling others who could not, or would not, live under Franco's regime. In *Las palabras del regreso* (2009), Zambrano wrote about her lengthy and painful exilic condition: "I think that exile is an essential dimension to human life, but upon saying that my lips burn, because I wish that I had never been exiled, that we were all human and cosmic beings, that exile was something unknown. It's a contradiction, what can I do, I love my exile, is it because I didn't look for it, because I didn't go chasing it" (66). For the nomadic women in this volume, exile was a formative experience that shaped their literary, artistic, and intellectual identities. We learn of the pre-civil war and wartime period through Isabel de Palencia's *I Must Have Liberty* (1940); Palencia was able to flee from Stockholm to Mexico City in 1939, where she lived for the rest of her life. Janet Riesenfeld provides a direct, eyewitness account of the revolutionary atmosphere in Madrid right after the coup d'état, through her work as a press translator and performer throughout her stay in Spain (1936–1937), her autobiographical account of which makes her *Dancer in Madrid* (1938) a unique testimony from the standpoint of a nomadic woman artist. Photographer Kati Horna has similarly given us a fundamental 'documentary' account of the everyday life of communities— women, children, and the elderly—including the most vulnerable of civilians who suffered the effects of the war. Many of Horna's war images, commissioned by the Spanish Republican government between 1937 and 1939, constitute an idiosyncratic approach to photographic reportage that remains as an essential epochal testimony.

In this vein, Ana Eire explores the notion of 'homelessness' in relation to poet Marina Romero, a modern woman exile who could not return to her native Spain from the United States after the Spanish Civil War started. As Eire argues in her essay for the volume, Romero's non-conformity with the rules and boundaries surrounding the female body and sexuality leads her, as an exile, to try to find an ever-elusive home by inventing poetic dialogues with an absent interlocutor or object, which may be a lover or

18   R. M. SILVERMAN AND E. SÁNCHEZ-PARDO

place. Similar to Eire's study, Javier Sánchez's essay looks at how poet Ana María Martínez Sagi's lesbian sexuality and modern interest in sport—unconventional attitudes toward her own and other female bodies—left her displaced—an inner exile even prior to her move to the United States to escape the Spanish Civil War and conservative ideologies in Spain. Her uprooting from her country, where she had been a feminist journalist, tinges her poetic work with a sense of isolation and longing for a lost home.

In our volume as a whole, we survey the subjectivities, identities, and cultural production of women exiles, mapping the borders that they traverse and treating these borders as navigated and negotiated spaces.[2] Our collective cartography foregrounds hybridity and the in-between, concepts that we use to describe both the space surrounding the border and border-identities. In traversing borders, the woman exile transforms, and is transformed by, the in-between spaces of the borderland as the territory of exile, thereby at once increasing the hybrid nature of these spaces and the syncretic character of her exilic identity. These women's crossings are mirrored in the syncretic form and structure of their creative work, of which their subjectivities and identities are paradigmatic.

Implicit in our theorization of this essential hybridity is the concept of *transculturación* ('transculturation'), as conceived by the Cuban anthropologist and essayist Fernando Ortiz, and as developed in the work of his compatriot, the writer, folklorist, and ethnographer Lydia Cabrera.[3] Ortiz and Cabrera (for instance, in such foundational ethnographic studies of hers as *El monte*, or *The Wilderness*) recognized syncretism and cultural layering as paradigmatic of Cuban and Afro-Cuban identity (see Rodríguez-Mangual). Just as the notion of cultural hybridity in Ortiz and Cabrera gives focus to our vision of border and exilic identities, so does the concentration on hybrid identities and spaces in the field of Border Theory. Gloria Anzaldúa, one of Border Theory's major exponents, conceptualizes her experience of life as a *mestiza* (ethnically mixed woman) in the borderland as a simultaneity of diverse positionings, and reclaims for herself as a

---

[2] Mary Vásquez conceives of borders as "navigated, negotiated spaces" (14).

[3] Fernando Ortiz first explained his concept of *'transculturación'* in his *Contrapunteo cubano del tabaco y el azúcar* (*Cuban Counterpoint: Tobacco and Sugar*, 1940). Lydia Cabrera's *El monte* deals with Afro-Cuban religion. Ortiz happened to be Cabrera's brother-in-law.

Chicana this borderland and its transformative, because syncretic, power. In like fashion, we regard the characteristic hybridity of the border, and multiplicity of possible subject positions in the space of the borderland, as a distinct advantage for the creative woman exile. Exile means, for the creative women who are the subjects of our study, the need and opportunity to create a syncretic consciousness and, progressively, new forms of subjectivity, identity, and cultural production. Comparable to Irigaray, Anzaldúa regards language as the primary expressive vehicle of consciousness, understanding the hybrid "border tongue" of Chicano/a Spanish as intrinsic to the syncretic consciousness of the *mestiza*, or the Chicana who inhabits the in-between space of the border (55, 77). If, as Anzaldúa holds, the linguistic, cultural, and ethnic hybridity (*mestizaje*) of the borderland are defined and circumscribed by gender and sexuality, conversely, gender and sexuality can re-map and change the border, in this way giving rise to "a new *mestiza* consciousness, *una consciencia de mujer ...* a consciousness of the Borderlands" with the creative potential that stems from hybridity (77). We envision the cultural production of the woman exile as similarly syncretic because of her gender, and her consequent culturally, bodily, psycho-sexually, and linguistically hyphenated existence.

Relatedly, in his essay on Mexican actresses Lupe Vélez and Dolores del Río, Rafael Hernández-Rodríguez analyzes how these mobile women turn ethnic and linguistic difference to their creative and economic advantage. For Vélez and Del Río, their hybridity becomes a valuable resource and an entryway into the burgeoning film industry of Hollywood, while at the same time re-situating them in the space of the border, which remains in the shadow of persistent ethnic and gender inequality. Comparably, as Javier Martín-Párraga shows, the idiosyncratic British-born artist and writer Leonora Carrington, having escaped to Mexico following her mental breakdown and related captivity, transforms her psychological and corporeal deracination into a Surrealist body of work that explores the nature of women's subjectivity. Carrington defends the mutability of this gendered subjectivity in order to protect her inner self and creative force.

Hybridity becomes a source of creative power for the woman exile as she traverses borders. The warp and woof of her cultural production, and the in-between quality of the spaces that she inhabits, give shape and significance to each other. Dissociation and deracination as consequences of inner and territorial exile turn into fruitful crossing and syncretism, albeit not without great cost. Such generative transformations lay the foundations for a home-away-from-home, or something close to what Theodor Adorno meant by his observation that those bereft of a homeland find a place to live in writing (87), and what Woolf intended when she declared that woman's country is the whole world (*Three Guineas* 99).

In conclusion, this volume addresses the ways in which the border as margin serves as a particular space of influence and creativity, and how, as a consequence, our nomadic New Women shape artistic and cultural production from the margin to the center. Theirs is a journey from the 'no-man's land' of tradition and patriarchy. Crossing borders on the vanguard of history, the women here under study transform this no-man's land into open terrain, fertile for creativity, beyond national and gendered boundaries. In the hybrid space of the border, and through their border-crossings, our twelve women find a psychological and physical place to confront the harshest of social and political realities and conflicts, create, and pursue life- and art-enhancing opportunities that engender innovative ideas for the future. The fabric of their work, created on and across borders, becomes interwoven with the contradictions and contrasts characteristic of the borderland, displaying the power and transcendence of their adaptability.

In the course of their migrations and exile, our nomadic New Women map hitherto uncharted routes, traversing the gendered, as well as national and cultural, boundaries surrounding them. Through the intercultural exchanges and collaborations made possible by their newfound mobility, they challenge patriarchal and phallogocentric norms in the social, artistic, and cultural spheres. The syncretic consciousness made possible by crossing borders gives these women a vantage perspective and position on the avant-garde of creativity. Our subjective cartography demonstrates how such flexibility generates their cutting-edge cultural production within the historical context of the early to mid-twentieth century. These nomadic New Women's jettisoning of their former position on the margins of society to cross all sorts of boundaries would lead them to acquire a versatility and capacity for innovation that would transform their creative and artistic fields. Each and every one of the women studied in this volume provides not only unique personal perspectives, but also, useful critical lenses for understanding questions about the local, global, and national, exile, belonging and non-belonging, and the key role of feminist thought and action in the twentieth century.

Works Cited

Adelson, Dorothy. "Yankee-Born Actress Mexican Screen Star: Manhattan Miss in Film Triumphs South of Border." *Morning Herald*, New York, 29 June 1943, p. 7.

Adorno, Theodor. *Minima Moralia: Reflections from Damaged Life*. Translated by E. F. N. Jephcott, Verso, 2020.

Anzaldúa, Gloria. *Borderlands/La Frontera: The New Mestiza*. Aunt Lute Books, 1987.

Ardis, Ann. *New Women, New Novels: Feminism and Early Modernism*. Rutgers UP, 1990.

Baudelaire, Charles. *The Painter of Modern Life*. 1863. Translated by P. E. Charvet, Penguin, 1972.

Braidotti, Rosi. *Nomadic Subjects: Embodiment and Sexual Difference in Contemporary Feminist Theory*. Columbia UP, 1994.

———. "Nomadic Subjects." *Fragile Identities*, edited by Susanne Witzgall and Kerstin Stakemeier, Diaphanes, 2017, pp. 135–43, https://www.diaphanes.com/titel/nomadic-subjects-4356. Accessed December 2023.

———. *Nomadic Theory: The Portable Rosi Braidotti*. Columbia UP, 2011.

Burgos, Carmen de. *La mujer moderna y sus derechos*. Valencia, Sempere, 1927.

Cabrera, Lydia. *El monte*. 1954. E-book ed., Linkgua, 2017.

Campoamor, Clara. *El voto femenino y yo: mi pecado mortal*. 1935. Renacimiento, 2018.

Chalk, Bridget. *Modernism and Mobility: The Passport and Cosmopolitan Experience*. Palgrave Macmillan, 2013.

Deleuze, Gilles, and Félix Guattari. *Anti-Oedipus: Capitalism and Schizophrenia*. Translated by Robert Hurley, Mark Seem, and Helen R. Lane, preface by Michel Foucault, U of Minnesota P, 1983.

———. *A Thousand Plateaus: Capitalism and Schizophrenia*. Translated and forward by Brian Massumi, U of Minnesota P, 1987.

Gray, Rockwell. "Spanish Diaspora: A Culture in Exile." *Salmagundi*, no. 76–77, fall 1987–winter 1988, pp. 53–83.

Ilie, Paul. *Literature and Inner Exile: Authoritarian Spain, 1939–1975*. Johns Hopkins UP, 1980.

Irigaray, Luce. *This Sex Which is Not One* [*Ce sexe qui n'en est pas un*]. 1977a. Translated by Catherine Porter with Carolyn Burke, Cornell UP, 1985.

———. "Women's Exile: Interview with Luce Irigaray." Translated by Couze Venn. *Ideology & Consciousness*, vol. 1, no. 1, 1977b, pp. 62–76.

Ortiz, Fernando. *Contrapunteo cubano del tabaco y el azúcar*. 1940. Introduction by Bronislaw Malinowski, e-book ed., Linkgua, 2017.

Palencia, Isabel de. *I Must Have Liberty*. Longmans, 1940.

Parkins, Wendy. "Moving Dangerously: Mobility and the Modern Woman." *Tulsa Studies in Women's Literature*, vol. 20, no. 1, 2001, pp. 77–92.

Rabinovitch-Fox, Einav. "New Women in Early 20th-Century America." *Oxford Research Encyclopedia of American History*, edited by Jon Butler, Oxford UP, 2017, https://doi.org/10.1093/acrefore/9780199329175.013.427. Accessed March 2023.

Rodríguez-Mangual, Edna. *Lydia Cabrera and the Construction of an Afro-Cuban Identity*. U of North Carolina P, 2004.

Said, Edward W. "Reflections on Exile." *Reflections on Exile and Other Essays*, Harvard UP, 2000, pp. 173–86.

Vásquez, Mary. "The Grammar of Contested Memory: The Representation of Exile in Selected Female-Authored Texts of Diaspora." *Female Exiles in Twentieth and Twenty-First Century Europe*, Palgrave Macmillan, 2007, pp. 13–29.

Walters, Margaret. *Feminism. A Very Short Introduction*. Oxford UP, 2005.

Wimbush, Antonia. *Autofiction: A Female Francophone Aesthetic of Exile*. Liverpool UP, 2021.

Woolf, Virginia. *A Room of One's Own*. 1929. Edited by David Bradshaw and Stuart N. Clarke, Wiley, 2015.

———. *Three Guineas*. 1938. E-book ed., Blackwell, https://www.blackwellpublishing.com/content/BPL_Images/Content_store/Sample_chapter/9780631177241/woolf.pdf. Accessed December 2023.

———. "Street Haunting: A London Adventure." 1930. *The Death of the Moth and Other Essays*, Harvest, 1942, pp. 20–36.

Zambrano, María. *Las palabras del regreso*. Edited by Mercedes Gómez Blesa, Cátedra, 2009.

PART I

Women Writing (in) Exile: Art, Life, Politics

CHAPTER 2

The Intimacy of Distance: Homelessness and Homecoming in the Poetry of Marina Romero

Ana Eire

The homelessness of the Spanish poet Marina Romero stems from multiple sources: she was exiled in the United States as a result of the Spanish Civil War, and she was an orphan who never met her parents.[1] Her poetry has also been homeless. As is the case with most women poets associated with the Generation of 27 or with the Republican diaspora, scholars and critics have ignored her literary production. She is unknown in Spain, although her poetry—from the three books that she published between 1935 and 1945, to the rest of her poetic production in latter years— deserves recognition for her artistic insight and philosophical depth.

Marina Romero (Madrid, 1908–2001) left Spain in 1935 with a scholarship to study at Smith College. Once the Civil War started, Romero

[1] Her tutor, the renowned psychiatrist Luis Simarro, gave her an exquisite education, but died when she was a young girl. See Cotarelo for a detailed biography.

A. Eire (✉)
Stetson University, DeLand, FL, USA
e-mail: aeire@stetson.edu

© The Author(s), under exclusive license to Springer Nature Switzerland AG 2024
R. M. Silverman, E. Sánchez-Pardo (eds.), *Nomadic New Women*,
https://doi.org/10.1007/978-3-031-62482-7_2

26   A. EIRE

stayed in the United States and built her academic career at Douglass
College (Rutgers University). The question of whether Romero was a true
political exile or simply an émigré did not help her cause among scholars,
as studies of the Republican exile in the United States wanted clear demar-
cation lines. Cotarelo recently put that question to rest as she demonstrated Romero's credentials as an exiled (234–42). The references to
Romero's poetry tend to be glowing, if superficial, one liners—"Romero
attains a greater luminosity and depth through a simplicity of style in this
most personal and intimate of poetry" (Galerstein 227)—with Noël Valis'
study as the exception. Recently, both Valender and Merlo include Romero
in their anthologies of poetry of the Republican exile and women poets,
respectively. Valender states that Romero "is without a doubt one of the
most egregious cases of someone unjustly forgotten" (341).[2] Romero's
poetry deserves a homecoming. This chapter is an initial attempt to rescue
her poetry from the homelessness of the unknown. I will trace homelessness as a motif that underpins her poetry. The analysis will illuminate the
poetry's philosophical makeup and demonstrate that it cannot be reduced
to the sentimental lyricism that, as Merlo argues, serves as the all-purpose
label attached to most Spanish women poets in the first half of the twentieth century (44). The chapter will show how Romero's poetry unmasks
the intimate contradictions of exile. It directs attention away from the
outskirts of exile—its collective, social impact—to concentrate on its center: the within of exilic existence and thought.

Crossing Borders Before and After Exile

The concept of homelessness implies a dispossession that recalls the protection of home. It conjures up the positive connotations of asserting a self
within a space where one is at ease and in control. The poetry of Romero
begins by turning this concept upside down. Her first book exalts the
eagerness of crossing borders and presents the impulse to leave behind the
comfort of home and a self-contained self as the only way to find fulfill-
ment. A few years later, already in exile, those initial ideas are put to the
test when the poet unexpectedly loses her home and the border crossing
materializes as a permanent reality and not only a youthful dream.

Romero's first two books *Poemas A* and *Nostalgia de mañana* are separated by the experience of exile. *Poemas A*, published in Spain in 1935,

---

[2] My translation: "Es sin duda una de las figuras del exilio más injustamente olvidadas." All
further quotes from Valender are also my translation.

2 THE INTIMACY OF DISTANCE: HOMELESSNESS AND HOMECOMING... 27

right before Romero left for the United States, is followed by *Nostalgia de mañana*, published in México in 1943 by Editorial Rueca, a publisher that had welcomed Spanish exiles.

On the surface both collections seem to be closely connected: lyrical poetry where the speaker explores the dilemmas of an absent lover. The rupture, however, is clear. Romero underlines it simply by including most of *Poemas A* as the first part of *Nostalgia de mañana*.[3] The continuities and discontinuities between part I, before exile, and part II, the poems written in exile, reveal a fracture that is not only defined by the spatial crossing of borders. It is, above all, an epistemological and ontological upheaval.

In *Poemas A* Romero's poetry begins to construct a philosophical conviction that if one relies exclusively on personal subjectivity, if one sees the world and the other as separate and alien to the self, we place limits on existence and impoverish life. Hence, the need to cross the limits imposed on the self underpins the poems. The image of the young girl who explores the world around and beyond her like her male counterparts do surfaces repeatedly throughout the collection. The girl who either runs against all warnings not to—as in "Girl Running" (12)[4]—or is in synch with a wind that encourages her to run—as in "The Girl Sings Foolishness" (25)[5]—recall Lorca's "Preciosa and the Wind" (172–74). In this last poem, however, Romero's girl doesn't escape a wind that incarnates a threatening male desire. Instead, the girl yearns to run and her crazy singing embodies the force of the wind. Nature clamors to hear her voice, in a clear representation that a female desire to reach out into the world is in accord with nature: "Run, girl [...] / I want to listen to your song!" (25).[6]

Romero departs from the convention of reducing the girl's world to a protective home or other private space. The poet also tries to break the confines of the self-contained subject, which is a more arduous task. *Poemas A* portrays an image of the subject as encompassing the other. It does not seek a dissolution of the self but a total and radical openness to the loved one, in an action that should be reciprocated. "You" is the only home the speaker in *Poemas A* cares to inhabit. This "you" could be interpreted, in light of Romero's biography, as a safe expression of her lesbianism—which she always kept private—as the pronoun you and the adjectives

---

[3] For my discussion of *Poemas A*, I will use the edition of *Nostalgia de mañana*, as all the poems I will mention are included in that collection and *Poemas A* has no pagination.

[4] "Corría la niña." All translations are mine.

[5] "La niña canta locuras".

[6] "¡Corre, niña [...] / quiero escuchar tus cantares!".

28 A. EIRE

your, his, and her have no gender in the highly gendered Spanish language. But the abstract and all-encompassing you is, above all, a feeling of inhabiting someone or something other than oneself, and the expectation that the other would inhabit you. This conceptualization of self coincides with the new philosophy of her time, which posits that a being is always situated by inhabiting the world and the other. In the twenties, Heidegger had dismantled the rationalist and Cartesian tradition of seeing the world as separate and alien to the self. The individual doesn't exist within a mind, but immersed in the world. Existence is not simply to be or to think, but *Dasein*, to be there. As Wheeler explains, Heidegger is the father of the tradition of investigating dwelling for existence as a philosophical concept, an idea that was central to existentialism. Dwelling is a human activity that defines our relationship to the world, but it is not a given. In order to really embody who we are, we must learn to be at home in the world, which is the journey to build an existential dwelling.[7] Romero questions the true extent of being and wants to expand it and liberate it. Her "you" is a yearning for an engaged existence that coincides with the philosophical definition of dwelling: a self only achieves its authenticity—the house

[7] Heidegger may seem an odd choice to frame the poetic journey of Romero. A clarification is in order. Heidegger is "widely hailed as one of the greatest thinkers of our age; he is also one of the most controversial" (Dallmayr 1). His support of the National Socialist movement starting around 1933 "played a not insignificant role in giving the Nazis cultural prestige" (Polt 153). Heidegger relinquished the responsibility of the intellectual when faced with ethical choices of such magnitude. His philosophy, however, influenced almost every major philosopher of the twentieth century, even if some preferred to avoid mentioning the genealogy of their ideas for a long time. The two main attitudes regarding Heidegger are either to treat his politics as irrelevant to his philosophy, or to reject him and abandon his tradition of inquiry. Luc Ferry and Alain Renaut indict him as an anti-humanist. Hubert Dreyfus, arguably the main American philosopher who interpreted the Heideggerian tradition, follows the first option. Richard Polt summarizes the various ways in which scholars have dealt with the conflict between life and philosophy, and asserts that "Heidegger's postwar self-interpretation is cowardly and self-deceptive. To speak the language of *Being and Time*: it is glaringly *inauthentic*" (159). I generalize that statement to describe my own attitude: Heidegger betrayed his philosophy and in particular the authenticity needed for his *Dasein*, his concept of being in the world. By doing so he exposed the limitations of his concept and the dangers lurking within it. If existence is defined by connections and interactions, and if historicity, culture, and language determine most of those, one is doomed to immerse oneself in its cultural time, with all its advantages and its evils. Heidegger's life emphasizes the need to "wrestle with and against what the philosopher says" (Polt 164). My chapter will rely on a few of Heidegger's ideas, especially his "open quest for being" (Dallmayr 151) and his rejection of the self-contained subject that had dominated modern philosophy until that point. But the chapter will also illustrate the dangers and limitations of Heidegger's situational ontology, as it condemns dissent to homelessness when he limits being to its cultural roots.

of being—when it reaches outside of itself toward an encounter (Polt 42). *Poemas A* could be summed up as a subject's eagerness for such an encounter.

Rhetorically Romero expresses her intention with spatial metaphors— to run, to leave, to travel, to go out into the garden—that focus on the movement outward. More uniquely she combines first- and second-person pronouns and possessive adjectives so that the reader loses track of who is experiencing what:

> And your chest hurts me
> and your eyes cry me.
> I look in my coat
> which doesn't seem mine
> for a handkerchief that seems unknown,
> and I wipe you my tears
> [...]
> All my air
> enters my chest
> in your breathing. (43)[8]

The symbiotic union of the lovers is a topical concept of poetry that carries reverberations of Romantic and *modernista* ideals that are traditionally expressed by a male voice. The fact that the idea now comes from a female poet shouldn't force us to change the interpretation to a desire for dependency from a male lover. In *Poemas A* the notion of space as something to be explored regardless of its risks contradicts the temptation to interpret these images as acceptance of the traditional female role who needs a loved one to feel whole. Both beings are equal in *Poemas A*. The open conceptualization of the self seems an extension of breaking the physical boundaries that restrain us in our exploration of the natural world. The other for Romero is an epistemological entity akin to other spaces: the other to be known, the other that will open up possibilities of growth both outward and inward because Romero never accepts the duality imposed by those directions. In her poetry, moving outward is the only way to reach inward. The reciprocal rhythm—to love and be loved, to approach as something affects us—is the path to a meaningful existence. The desire to overcome

---

[8] "Y me duele tu pecho / y me lloran tus ojos. / Busco en mi abrigo / que parece tan no mío / un pañuelo que desconozco, / y te enjugo mis lágrimas / [...] / Todo mi aire / me va entrando en el pecho / por tu respirar".

30   A. EIRE

distances represents the speaker's burden, and in the poem "Horizontal My Angst," they intersect to form a cross:

Horizontal my angst,
vertical my distances.
In a cross you cover the space
of my wandering wide. (35)[9]

The common spatial representation of angst and distance is reversed: spatial distance becomes vertical as if moving within someone, while the angst of desire appears as horizontal, a terrain to cover toward the other who must be approached. The intersection merges inner and outer worlds and the image of the cross depicts the challenge of crossing both realms. The unification of the dichotomy would bring the ability to dwell in a true self that is free to wander in any and all directions.

Intuitively Romero yearns for the most difficult expression of Heidegger's *Dasein*: a being that reaches beyond itself (Polt 42) and whose subjectivity alone doesn't make her whole. This vision also implies a desire for freedom. Her occasional tentativeness—in "Mill Rotating" (24) or "My sailing heart" (18)[10]—comes from the sorrow of failing to achieve her herculean goal, but ultimately the problem is how to bridge distances, not whether one should try it. One of the most heartfelt poems insists that we do not go far enough in that attempt, even if we know our ambitious ideal may never be reached: "Lengths I dream off, / so short / in your ambition to grow!" (34).[11] The poetic voice prefers to be lost in fog than to be guided by the moon in "The Fog Challenges the Moon."[12] The moon, with its showy presence, may win when treacherously "stabs a silver lance" (26)[13] into the fog. The poetic voice, however, regrets that action and reinforces the sense that Romero's poetry prefers the freedom of the unknown and its daring attractiveness, in spite of the danger of being lost.

The reality of exile will transform Romero's existential aspirations. Romero writes the second part of *Nostalgia de mañana* in 1938–1943,

---

[9] "Horizontales mis ansias, / verticales mis distancias. / En cruz ganáis el espacio / de mi ancho correr".

[10] "Rueda molino" and "Corazón marinero".

[11] "Longitudes soñadas, / ¡qué cortas / en vuestro afán de crecer!".

[12] "La niebla reta a la luna"

[13] "le clava un rejón de plata".

2 THE INTIMACY OF DISTANCE: HOMELESSNESS AND HOMECOMING... 31

when she has realized that her stay in the United States in no longer temporary. The opening verse, "I was two" (49),[14] signals a radical separation within the self and marks the beginning of her exilic thinking. The dispossession of exile provokes a dual rupture: the loss of the outward projection and the tearing apart of the speaker's conception of inner self. Weariness and existential anxiety become the predominant tones of the second part of *Nostalgia de mañana*.

The central motif of dispossession is expressed as temporal and emotional uprootedness. From a poet who had relied on spatial metaphors to express the distances she wished to overcome, one would expect a continuation of the rhetorical device to represent the scope of exile. Instead, time becomes the major trope of distance. In what may seem counterintuitive for those who have not experienced any form of migration, distance in time is a deeper rupture than spatial distance since roots are not only a connection to a place, but the maintaining of temporal links to people, cultural history, and to hopes for the future in a community. For Romero, exile is not a space from here to there, but a separation from a past that can no longer provide continuity of connections and references. Time is the "most abstract of all humanity's homes" (Sebald 154) and temporal discontinuity leads to an intimate form of homelessness. The speaker in the second part of *Nostalgias de mañana* has "two new distances" (61)[15] that were not problematic earlier on: from past to present, and from present to future. The contrast between yesterday and today recurs in many poems. She pities herself "because yesterday was silent / my anxiety at my waist, / and today it overflows my soul (60).[16] Temporal discontinuity implies an epistemological rupture as time—historicity—is key to understand both the world and who we are. What she was told earlier "is up for sale without a price" (63)[17] in a reassessment of what one believes. The epistemological upheaval forces the speaker to relinquish the empirical—"I was feeling without my hands, / seeing without my eyes" (49)[18]—and to rely primarily on the emotional as a cognitive source. This groundlessness envelopes the subject in Romero's poetry. Her existence lacks continuity and points of reference. The distances brought about by exile cannot be measured or

---

[14] "Fui dos".

[15] "dos distancias nuevas".

[16] "porque ayer se me callaba / una angustia en la cintura, / y hoy se me sale del alma".

[17] "lo vendo a cualquier precio".

[18] "sentía sin mis manos, / veía sin mis ojos".

32   A. EIRE

grasped. Therefore, presence has to be defined in terms of absence and withdrawal while one actually is. As Schuback emphasizes, "the real struggle in exile is not so much the struggle to not lose the past or to forge a future, but to be above all present for the present, to be where one is" (120). The feeling of drowning and stagnation paralyzes life:

> submerged in shadows
> anchored in realities.
> Water in between
> and a life without hours. (78)[19]

Instead of the constant action of *Poemas A*, the speaker now only wants to sleep and wishes to abandon the tools of her life—a pine desk, a fountain pen—and return them to their origin (72), in a displacement that points to her desire to return to her own origin. The poet acknowledges elements of life in her: "air, light, kiss, / [...] / and it enters / and leaves you" (83);[20] however, the poem ends, "such great indifference inside you" (83).[21]

The problem of presence in exile leads to a reflection on Heidegger's view of detachment as a deficient state (*Being and Time* 158), with its problematic implication that life in exile is damaged existence and something to be avoided. However, it highlights the painful experience of detachment: "if our connections to other beings were cut, we would not end up inside our mind—we would end up without a mind at all" (Polt 57). Romero's speaker doesn't lose her mind, but wants to throw away her soul: "If I had here the paper / basket, / I would strip away my soul" (72).[22] The existential apathy is so pervasive that it seems that "a thousand year old tiredness / rises up in my bones" (70)[23] in the poem "Tiredness."[24] Her sense of loss takes the life out of her because, as Weil asserts, "Loss of the past, whether it be collectively or individually, is the supreme human tragedy" (119). In this situation, she cannot propel herself forward. The only occasion in which she admits hope is with uncharacteristic passivity:

---

[19] "sumergida en la sombra / anclada en realidades. / Agua por medio / y una vida sin horas".
[20] "La luz, el aire, el beso, / [...] / y entra / y sale en ti".
[21] "¡qué gran indiferencia en tu interior!".
[22] "Si tuviera aquí el cesto / de los papeles, / me despojaría del alma".
[23] "un cansancio de mil años / se me sube por los huesos".
[24] "Cansancio".

2 THE INTIMACY OF DISTANCE: HOMELESSNESS AND HOMECOMING...

And I will wait for the shape
of my freedom
with a round yawn
of tiredness. (73)[25]

Instead of the earlier impulse to seek encounters, the poetic voice is left
with an "empty loneliness" (49),[26] a loneliness that has no hope of regain-
ing the connection with the other. In "Blood Poem,"[27] dedicated to Spain,
the rhetorical devices Romero had deployed in *Poemas A* to express openness to the other are now transferred to her distant homeland:

I felt it fall,
and it wasn't mine,
drop by drop,
with the slow pain
of an open wound,
[...]
I patted my veins
drenched in eviction
[...]
They were full.
And still
I felt it fall,
and it was my blood;
it flowed towards my inside
nourishing the gurgling
of stagnant plumbing. (58–59)[28]

The speaker identifies with the pain and bloodshed caused by the war in
Spain, but she knows that she was safe away and didn't have to shed her
blood. Nevertheless, she bleeds emotionally. For someone whose definition of self was comprised of an involvement outward, the trauma implied
in the image of "stagnant plumbing" couldn't be more evocative. She is

[25] "y esperaré la forma / de mi libertad, / en un bostezo redondo / de cansancio".
[26] "la soledad vacía".
[27] "Poema de sangre".
[28] "Yo la sentía caer, / y no era mía, / gota a gota, / con el dolor lento / de la herida
abierta, / [...] / Palpé mis venas / saturadas en desahucio / [...] / Estaban llenas. / Y sin
embargo / yo la sentía caer, / y era mi sangre; / se vertía hacia dentro / nutriendo el bor-
boteo / de caños estancados."

34   A. EIRE

reduced to her inner world where vitality is congealed. Furthermore, the only flow is a form of internal bleeding. Cultural and personal ties cut off, her inner world stagnant, her vitality drained, Romero has lost all the elements that allow growth and flourishing. Exile immerses her in an ontological crisis.

Out of this homelessness of spirit, emerges the question of grammar, which appears for the first time in *Nostalgia de mañana* and will become a leitmotif in Romero's poetry. Language provides meaningful access to the world, and grammar, by holding language together, shapes a network that creates meaning beyond the impoverished referentiality of isolated words. Romero chooses it as the ideal metaphor to address the pervasive disconnectedness of exile. The poetic voice struggles between two grammars and the distinctive worldviews they signify for her. Spanish helps the speaker recall the nostalgia of community in "the faraway grammar / of your nouns and your verbs" (53),[29] while English in "Sentimental Grammar"[30] carries within a reduction of her self-expression:

> This impersonal one
> and that
> which they call neuter,
> detach me from a time
> that was imperfect tense
> in a longing
> for the subjunctive.
> [...]
> And such poor value
> in a pronoun! (75–76)[31]

English denotes a beggarly way of feeling when many of the elements that characterize Spanish—gender, subjunctive (so connected with potentiality), imperfect past tense (in which one reminisces)—fade away and the impersonal and neuter "one" takes center stage. It should be remembered that "during this assimilationist era, the English language and Anglo-American culture enjoyed virtually unquestioned hegemony" (Hondagneu-Sotelo

---

[29] "las gramáticas lejanas / de tus nombres y tus verbos".

[30] "Gramática sentimental".

[31] "Este uno impersonal / y eso / que llaman neutro, / se desligan de un mío / que fue tiempo imperfecto / en un ansia / de subjuntivo. / [...] / ¡Y qué valor tan pobre / en el pronombre!".

108) in the United States. In exile a grammar must be relinquished and its possibilities of expression are lost. The conflict for Romero, however, works both ways. Her life takes place in English, which complicates communication with the community of people she left behind in Spain. In "If You Knew English..." with the subtitle "(From the United States)" (79–80),[32] the speaker addresses a you who doesn't speak English. Spanish is depicted as one of the "tired languages" (79)[33] while English is:

> this universal air
> [...]
> And it searches in the stars
> for an expression of light
> and new sounds. (79)[34]

Romero captures in these poems the impossibility to translate a life experience into another language, not because there are no words, but because experience is anchored in new ideas, feelings, perceptions, that when expressed to a cultural outsider lose nuance and become meaningless. She encourages the recipient of the verses to cross the waters "as a good pilgrim / in search of truths" (80).[35] That arrival will give her hope. The longing for community and contact is heartbreaking. The image of the United States as a land of possibility who welcomes those who search for truth—the poem was written during World War II—doesn't negate the reality of discontinuity with personal relations, with a way of knowing and a way of living. It is not her adopted country that is the problem; it is the experience of exile which creates an experience that demands a new word from the poet, and Romero calls it "withoutworld" (67).[36] As the poem "I no longer have time" (66–67)[37] suggests, her two worlds and her two languages are at a turbulent standstill that make presence impossible:

> When subjunctive disappears,
> and time tires

---

[32] "Si supieras inglés... (Desde los Estados Unidos)".
[33] "idiomas cansados".
[34] "Este aire universal / [...] / y busca en las estrellas / una expresión de luz / y de nuevos sonidos."
[35] "como buen peregrino / buscador de verdades".
[36] "sinmundo".
[37] "Ya no hay tiempo".

> of never ending,
> then,
> for an equinox grammar,
> I will write a present
> that doesn't exist. (67)[38]

Said remarks that exile includes collective sentiments and private emotions and there is hardly a language adequate for both (177). Romero finds herself at that juncture and out of a situation that seems apocalyptic—time has stopped at the half-point, her present seems unreal—comes the determination to invent a grammar that can address it: when her new English reality imposes itself, she will be able to write a grammar of homelessness that will connect both halves of her being and create the presence she doesn't have. The poem expresses the desperation of living at a symbolic equinox, suspended in the in-between of exilic existence that Schuback argues is the truth of exile (7). This in-between life of dispossession and weariness, with its dissolution of certainties and identities, constitutes an intimate homelessness that Romero will inhabit in the rest of her oeuvre.

Homelessness and the Grammar of Homecoming

Romero's poetry of the 1950s and 1960s—mainly in *Presencia del recuerdo* (1952) and *Sin agua, el mar* (1961)—can be read as a long struggle with homelessness that goes beyond the groundlessness of *Nostalgia de mañana*. Romero continues to explore the "constant spiritual wear and tear that exile entails" (Valender 341),[39] but never relinquishes the idea of her potentiality. The ontological questions about the distortions brought forth by exile flood her poems. They represent a way to confront the symptoms of the exilic sickness, but are also a first step to recuperate a true dwelling.

In her determination to establish an order in her thinking, the poet catalogs what she brought to her loneliness as if testing different possibilities that will help her out of her suspended existence:

---

[38] "Cuando todo sea sin subjuntivo, / y el tiempo se canse / de no acabarse nunca, / entonces, / para una gramática de equinoccio, / escribiré un presente / que no existe".

[39] "sobre el constante desgaste espiritual que supone vivir en el exilio".

2 THE INTIMACY OF DISTANCE: HOMELESSNESS AND HOMECOMING... 37

I organize things:
[...]
from this self to that self,
order,
to feel myself in their existence. (*Presencia* 66)[40]

The only conclusion she can reach is that in her loneliness to be and to have been are separate entities (67), an idea that underlines once again the temporal fracture of exile, with the dissolution of ties that it implies. The actual exilic event may be transitory, but the exilic thinking is fixed in a sort of eternal return that persistently recurs. It is the albatross weighing the poet down. To free herself from it, the focus must shift to how to live in that situation. Can she root herself in homelessness to build a meaningful existence within it? The poet asks, "is that enough?" (*Presencia* 67).[41] The questions inundate her poems even if Romero rarely finds answers. In "How?" (*Presencia* 61–62),[42] the parallelistic repetition of "how" reaffirms the epistemic challenges that seep into the ontological: how to know, how to find, how to see, how to feel, how to grow. "Questions" (78–79)[43] lists unanswerable questions about how to dream and love, but also about physical sensations such as being thirsty or cold, and all the issues listed emphasize a lack. In "Where to?" (*Presencia* 80–81),[44] the issue is where to escape to find the plenitude that she is determined to achieve. Nowhere, it seems:

This prolonged death,
or this shortened life,
are not my beating heart.
[...]
I fulfill my duty.
I work,
I speak and listen...
I respond once in a while
to a laugh;
I read

---

[40] "voy poniendo las cosas: / [...] /de ese estante a este estante, / orden, / para sentirme en su existencia".

[41] "¿basta?".

[42] "¿Cómo?".

[43] "Preguntas".

[44] "¿Adónde?".

38 A. EIRE

what others like me
maybe
have left without saying
and I go to bed.
[...]
I change my suit
I don't know why,
[...]
I don't know what time it is.
But, who cares. (*Sin agua* 12–13)[45]

The tension between an inauthentic life limited to facticity and the search for a way to recuperate her beating heart lies at the center of *Presencia del recuerdo* and *Sin agua, el mar*. The poet's epistemological efforts to get rid of the dissatisfaction that exilic feeling provokes run into a sense of inevitability. The empirical doesn't seem to help as a guide to establish a solid foundation to her thinking. Even math, the epitome of an empirical activity outside of the subjective realm, is bent by feeling and pain in Romero's poetry. One plus one may be two for someone else, but for the poet zero is the "only number" (*Sin agua* 47).[46] She herself adds up yesterdays, but she doesn't know what the resulting amount is:

I am adding up
well,
I think,
all the yesterdays.

Digits
crowd me,
numbers
lose me,
truths
get confusing.

---

[45] "Esta prolongada muerte, / o esta acortada vida, / no son de mi latir. / [...] / Cumplo con mi deber. / Trabajo, / hablo y escucho... / Acompaño de vez en cuando / una risa; / leo / lo que otros como yo / tal vez / han dejado sin decir / y me acuesto. / [...] / Cambio de traje / no sé por qué, / [...] / No sé qué hora será. / Pero, qué importa".
[46] "cifra única".

So many zeroes!
On which side? (*Sin agua* 50)[47]

How do experience, feelings, and memories add up to a whole number? The challenge in this instance is not exclusively a matter of temporal dislocation, but an inability to assess existence lucidly in a failure to construct a narrative that adds up for the poet. The placement of a zero to the right or to the left of an amount can change accomplishment into failure and the dilemma underlines the ironic juxtaposition of plenty and nothing: "The more you add, the less you get. Thus, the notion of plenty is converted into the bitter poetry of subtraction" (Valis 260). Romero deromanticizes exile by not focusing on the movement from one place to another. She explores instead an exilic within in all its intimate contradictions. It constructs a self that "has become an after-itself: a constant movement, the movement within a suspension of movement.... [Exile] is, namely, a nonway out, ... a present's unmoving movement, inmoving or in-being, inescapably aporetic" (Schuback 180). The internal tension of accumulating life and being unable to orient oneself within it is the central trauma.

Romero acknowledges that one is bound to construct a life even if one cannot restore a sense of belonging. Her poetry resorts to conceptist word play to express the paradoxical feeling of an inauthentic life: "my want not wanting" (*Presencia del recuerdo* 11)[48] or "and you're not here, being here" (18).[49] These expressions allow the poet to reflect on how the present feels weightless since she is emotionally detached from it, even though she perceives its gravitational pull. Romero takes the idea a step further with paradoxical images in which she takes an object and empties its essence. They become a trademark of her poetry at this time:

> Without water,
> the sea.

> Without time
> the clock.

---

[47] "Yo voy sumando / bien, / creo, / todos los ayeres. / Se me agolpan / las cifras, / se me extrañan / los números, / se me confunden / las verdades. / ¡Tantos ceros! / ¿De qué lado?".

[48] "mi querer no queriendo".

[49] "y tú no estás, estando".

Without air
the sigh. (*Sin agua* 51)[50]

The disarticulated life of exile prevents the construction of a new dwelling for her-self because nothing lives authentically when the connection between a being and its world is shattered.

The question is reiterated in a unique way in a sort of *Ubi sunt* in the poem "Childhood Memories" (*Presencia* 59–60).[51] The poetic voice wonders what happened to childhood friends, to innocence, and to travel without tickets or passports. They all lead to the essential question of being: Is she herself without that yesterday? And are they themselves without her today?

And am I
without that yesterday so mine?
Where, without my today,
All of you? (60)[52]

The last question posits a forgotten facet of exile: what part of its identity has the homeland lost by forcing its people into exile?

Romero is aware of what others think: "They tell me I am lucky / and I don't complain" (*Sin agua* 45).[53] She has shoes, bread, friends (45). She is not dispossessed like refugees are. Her dispossession is invisible. Said suggests that exiles refuse to let go, exaggerate differences, and insist on the "right to refuse to belong" (182) and that "no matter how well they may do, exiles are always eccentrics who *feel* their difference (even as they frequently exploit it) as a kind of orphanhood" (182). Romero, as I mentioned, was actually an orphan and her original orphanhood underpins the importance that an existential dwelling has for her. There is no need to exaggerate. For Romero to construct an embodied and engaged self, she must connect emotionally and epistemologically to her life. She expresses her inability to do so when she describes life as shrouded in doubt, impermanent, and on loan (*Presencia* 30–31). How to belong when everything seems an emptiness of being, a vessel without purpose?

---

[50] Sin agua, / el mar. / Sin tiempo / el reloj. / Sin aire / el suspiro.
[51] "Memorias de niñez".
[52] ¿Y soy yo / sin ese ayer tan mío? / ¿En dónde, sin mi hoy, / vosotros?
[53] "Me dicen que tengo suerte, / y no me quejo".

2 THE INTIMACY OF DISTANCE: HOMELESSNESS AND HOMECOMING... 41

Ant without its grain.
Asphalt,
all asphalt.

Fish without its route.
Hooks,
all hooks.

[...]
Child without a story
and swan without a lake.

All impossible puddle,
all puddle. (*Sin agua* 19)[54]

Romero continues to hollow out mercilessly the direction and purpose of every being she writes about. Distance cannot be bridged and space lacks the quality that would help each being exist meaningfully. The speaker in *Sin agua, el mar* feels like a "sailor without sea on a broken shore" (52).[55] Crossing, at any level, is unachievable for the exiled. Even more tragic, the closeness of purpose is elusive. Romero is not alone in this dilemma, which is one of the central issues of modern ontology and the most common criticism of Heidegger's concept of being, so anchored in historicity and culture that there seems to be no way out for the self once it is uprooted and cast away. The idea that the only possible existential dwelling is within one's culture is one that is deeply ingrained, but it presents a limitation that needs to be confronted. Levinas takes issue with Heidegger's concept of being precisely because "it is absolutely not a philosophy of the émigré!" (*Entre Nous* 117). Levinas, a student and early admirer of Heidegger, was himself an émigré who fought against Germany in WWII and was taken prisoner of war, while most of his family was murdered by the Nazis. Philosophically and by experience he knew that Heidegger's idea ties one to a culture, avoids an ethics, and condemns displacement and dissent to suffering. Romero has not yet realized the limitations of a concept that seems intuitive: one belongs to their homeland and its culture. Her poetry,

---

[54] La hormiga sin su grano. / Asfalto, / todo asfalto. / El pez sin su camino. / Anzuelos, / todo anzuelos. / [...] / El niño sin su cuento / y el cisne sin su lago. / Todo charco imposible, / todo charco.

[55] "marinero sin mar en rota orilla".

42   A. EIRE

with its speaker cast away from her roots but searching for a true dwelling, is immersed in this existential dilemma of where to turn to in exile. The only path left in her search for belonging is to return. Homecoming could be a way to recuperate a house of being.[56]

Romero, unlike other exiles, has the opportunity to test that path and writes with poetic honesty about its unraveling. Her last book, *Poemas de ida y vuelta (1999)—Round Trip Poems*, problematizes the concept of return for the exiled. She leaves behind the elliptically constructed poems and the mostly metaphorical allusions to exile to face the denouement of homelessness: whether homecoming is possible. Her answer is not as happy or straight forward as one may expect. After years of yearning and longing, instead of a resolution, the poems of return represent the undoing of a possible grammar of homecoming. Exile is not a round-trip journey, but a voyage that never lands in a home(land).

Romero returned to Spain once she retired in 1970 and lived there until her death in 2001. In her poetry, however, her return is not a restoration of the homeland, but the uprooting of her American existence. Poem after poem describes the return to Spain as an abandonment of the United States, and her adopted country is portrayed as a truer dwelling than Spain:

> I left friends who spoke
> another language,
> and who sheltered me better
> than those who spoke
> mine. (13)[57]

The question of a different language is minimized in this instance to emphasize the warmth of the people who speak it. Nostalgic images of her American life surface repeatedly: from "those dense forests / with yellow

---

[56] As Cotarelo documents, in the late 1940s, once Romero became a US citizen and was protected by her American passport, she began to travel back to Spain during the summers (234–42). Out of those travels she publishes in 1957 *Landscape and Literature of Spain: Anthology of the Generation of 1898 (Paisaje y literatura de España: antología de la generación del 98)*, a book that will be her main claim to fame during her lifetime. Romero chooses the Spanish landscape as the theme of this anthology, and accompanies the text with her own photographs. The book is a bridge to her homeland and an examination of its space. Taken together with the poetry, it reaffirms the idea that Romero sees return as a path available to her.

[57] "Dejé amigos que hablaban / otro idioma, / y que me cobijaban mejor / que los que hablaban / el mío."

autumns" (13)[58] to scenes from her suburban life: rows of houses that look the same, nervous squirrels, picket fences, and white Christmases (16). The conundrum of belonging becomes a more complex issue: "I don't know how to solve / this riddle" (16).[59] She is aware of the harmony her life achieved in the United States, and the question emerges of how she will feel once in Spain, as her experiences will be mediated by the foreign life she has led:

> In a Madrid morning
> the Guadarrama light
> will lie down on the streets.
> What will happen
> when I return to them
> dimmed distances
> and memories,
> no more forced longing
> what, when I truly live them? (21–22)[60]

The answer is the reality of a double exile. The round trip of the title is not the crossing back to her origin, but the return to the original experience of exile. As in a merry-go-round, the exilic experience recurs without end:

> I have left my two lands
> and in each one
> half of what feeds
> my soul,
> and now I don't know
> in this double banishment,
> where can I bend my head
> from sadness. (13)[61]

Romero's poetry confronts this unexpected reality but is unable to settle within its ambiguity. The banishment from the possibility of a homeland

---

[58] "aquellos bosques densos / de otoños amarillos".

[59] "no me sé resolver / este problema".

[60] En Madrid mañanero / la luz del Guadarrama / se acostará en sus calles. / ¿Qué pasará / cuando al volver a ellas / apagadas distancias / y recuerdos, / sin forzada añoranza / los viva de verdad?

[61] "He dejado mis dos tierras / y en cada una / la mitad de lo que me alimenta / el alma, / y ahora no sé / si desterrada doble, / tengo donde agachar la frente / de tristeza."

44   A. EIRE

leaves her unmoored. For most of *Poemas de ida y vuelta*, however, Romero prefers the United States and would like to jump the ocean's "unassailable barrier" (15)[62] in order to relive American memories that are described as appealing tussle and healthy struggle, but also civil word (15). In Spain one must be Lázaro de Tormes, an orphan—like Romero—who had to survive on his wits. Romero complains of the picaresque culture, and of a country that has received the exiled without "invitation" (15).[63] The controversial Heideggerian idea that an authentic being embraces its historicity and immerses itself in its culture fails her as she discovers that returning doesn't imply belonging. Homecoming must be found elsewhere.

Romero could embrace other concepts of home. Levinas proposes an extraterritorial home where the self transcends its relation to place (Gauthier 192–193). Home is then not a goal or "the end of human activity" but "its condition, and in this sense its commencement" (Levinas, *Totality and Infinity* 152). It is a refuge where the self is simultaneously host and guest, a concept that disregards origin, return, homeland, and where exiles are on equal footing with others. Hannah Arendt adopts a similar attitude. After she experienced exile, danger, and deprivation, she welcomed "the possibilities inherent in limited existence without fear or illusions, sustained only by one's joyful awareness of the possibilities of Being" (Maier-Katkin 36). Arendt rejected the cultural baggage attached to Heidegger's concept of dwelling, and by embracing dissent, she expanded the concept of freedom. Adorno, for his part, states in a famous quote that "in his text, the writer sets up house.... For a man who no longer has a homeland, writing becomes a place to live" (87). But he ends his paragraph contradicting his own assertion because "in the end, the writer is not even allowed to live in his writing" (87), among other reasons because the rigors of intellectual tension have no room for self-pity. Said praises Adorno's intention and argues that the duty of the exiled is to stand away from home (185) as "homecoming is out of the question" (179).

In *Poemas de ida y vuelta* Romero takes neither of those paths. She appears ready to embrace an extraterritorial concept of home akin to Levinas': a refuge on both sides of her roundtrip, where she is host and guest, and has the comforts and discomforts of both roles and both lands.

---

[62] "barrera infranqueable".
[63] "tarjeta".

This is where Romero began her poetic journey in an intuitive manner, with the subject as a host for the other. The opening poem points in that direction. It transcends the uncertainties that have been tearing the poet apart and rises up beyond the personal to a more collective tone:

> Let's walk these streets,
> let's open those doors,
> let's say good morning
> in all the world
> languages. (11)[64]

The poem instills a hopeful attitude in the speaker and her readers. It suggests an openness to the ambiguity of multiplicity. That positive attitude is all one needs to face life, the poem concludes. However, the spirit of the poem doesn't carry through the rest of the book. Romero never rejects the concept of a home and, even though she questions homecoming constantly, she never abandons it as a goal. She comes to the edge of the idea and peers into the intrinsic ambiguity of a true dwelling, but never crosses into a new definition of homecoming that rejects the traditional one. Her poetry is too lucid and too aware of her double exile to reify Spain as a conventional homecoming. She cannot choose to retreat into an ontology of place, but Romero is anchored in an exilic thinking which depends on "a sense of origin and with it a desire to regain that origin, and a sense of being beyond all such origin" (Malpas). The ultimate homelessness of that situation pushes Romero's poetry to dwell momentarily into the bitter defeat of exile. The bitterness is understandable even if it indulges in self-pity. In "Part of the wrong"[65] the poet blames her suffering on the fact that she was born in Spain and the country's history doomed her to exile: "because / I never left it, / and will never find it again" (20).[66] Her life unraveled in the nostalgia for Spain and now she feels "as if they had defrauded / my soul" (20).[67] The image portrays the speaker as a victim whose homelessness is a crime perpetrated by her land. The sensation of a lack of freedom and personal agency reverberates through her poetry as the speaker assesses her life:

---

[64] "Andemos estas calles, / abramos esas puertas, / demos los buenos días / en todos los idiomas / de la tierra."
[65] "Parte del mal".
[66] "Porque / ni la dejé nunca, / ni nunca la volveré a encontrar".
[67] "como si me hubieran estafado / el alma".

46   A. EIRE

This life journey
with so many paths to choose
they gave it to me
with a suitcase already packed
shoes on
and a fixed destiny.
And even if I ask nonstop
at what time the train leaves,
the plane,
the boat,
the answer is the same.
In twelve hours,
in four days,
in a century and a half.
[...]
With insatiable hunger
of a quiet station
in any town
with love. (53)[68]

Romero feels cheated out of a life freely chosen. The irony of her comings
and goings is that her authentic life journey never begins. She looks for a
refuge where her emotions—love and affection—can be housed. Romero
realizes in this her last book that the language of poetry has comprised
that refuge for her all along and she returns to the metaphor of grammar
to express the emotional ties to her native language, which moreover
binds her to a place and a tradition.

Why—a poem asks—doesn't her heart feel in English given the amount
of time she lived in the United States and the feelings she has toward the
country? She has two lands and lives in two languages, "but my heart has
not yet learned / to write with those two spellings" (37).[69] She relished
not feeling like a foreigner in that American human babel (30), but she
cannot suppress a sentimental lack: "my heart doesn't know / how to

---

[68] "Este viaje de la vida / con tantos caminos a elegir / me lo dieron ya / con la maleta
hecha / con los zapatos puestos / y el destino fijo. / Y por más que pregunto / a qué hora
sale el tren, / el avión, / el barco, / la respuesta es la misma. / Dentro de doce horas, / de
cuatro días, / de siglo y medio. / [...] / con un hambre insaciable / de estación tranquila /
en cualquier pueblo / de amor."

[69] "pero mi corazón aún no ha aprendido / a escribir con las dos ortografías".

adapt its beat / how to translate its tears" (39).[70] It even becomes increasingly difficult "to learn to cry / in foreigner" (38).[71] For Romero, as for Adorno when he returned to Germany, the homecomer is not just "someone who has forever lost a naive relationship to what is his own, but also… someone who is driven by the attempt to rescue something valuable from the past that is at the very core of his subjectivity" (Bielsa 383). In the conflicting ambiguity between exile and return, poetic language endures as Romero's only way to express her true self. Romero holds onto language as the intimate space that is her own and that crystallizes the bond to her homeland.

Her poetry houses homecoming as a symbol, a desire, a mystery that ties her to her homeland, while it allows for autonomy of self. Now it even gives homecoming some degree of ambiguity. She can dismantle the concept of return back as she does throughout *Poemas de ida y vuelta*. Romero's poetry had always been anchored in the Spanish literary tradition, from the influence of Lorca to the Baroque conceptist word play I mentioned earlier. Her poetry in this way was imbued in homecoming formally. Thematically, the ceaseless confrontation between homelessness and homecoming—in another conceptist paradox—manifests that "exile is above all *present tension*" (Schuback, "Memory" 178), a transit camp "between worlds, languages, images, sensibilities, indeed, the movement of between-existence" (186) that never abates and where presence is always a lingering delay. The pain of that lingering delay can only be resolved symbolically with the creation of a poetic dwelling. Romero decides to end her poetic voyage doubling down on the concept of homecoming and determined to take control poetically of an ontology of place that she cannot abandon and that has eluded her.

In her last poem, Romero merges her identity, her homeland, and poetic language into a powerful symbolic form of homecoming: the lingering delay of presence can only end with death. "Let the ocean embrace me" (59)[72] depicts a dissolution of her identity into the Spanish land. The poet plays with her name, Marina Romero Serrano—the linguistic equivalent of identity and self—and develops each of its words as a metaphor of place that connects her to Spain. The name Marina derives from the word *mar*, sea. Romero means rosemary, a common bush in the Spanish land-

---

[70] "mi corazón no sabe / adaptar su latido / ni traducir su llanto".
[71] "aprender a llorar / en extranjero".
[72] "Que me abrace el mar".

48   A. EIRE

scape. Serrano is the inhabitant of a sierra. The poet's desire is to integrate herself lovingly into the landscape and become one with each of the components her name represents:

Let the ocean embrace me,
[...]
Surrounded by its blue,
its grey,
sea everywhere,
Marina I am, its lover.

[...]
Drowning in its green,
its red,
mountain everywhere.
Romero I am, its lover.

Let your snow encircle me, sierra,
Let your cold embrace me, sierra,
[...]
White in blue
an infinite ending.
Serrano I am, its lover. (59)[73]

The symbolic nature of poetic language conjures back home and self for Romero. In her last poem, her self becomes poetry and both—self and poem—refer to her land. Romero's poetic voyage reveals all the unease of exilic existence and the constant sense that something has gone awry. Poem after poem expressed her pain at not being able to define the situation on her own terms even when she is tirelessly trying to take control over uncertainty and lack. However, at the end, the poet offers us the joy of arriving home linguistically and poetically because "for those whose business is language, there is only in language that the unhappiness of exile can be overcome" (Sebald 166). In Romero's final poem, the journey home is the journey to death, as a return to the soil of home. Romero embraces in the closest intimacy the places she yearned for in an

---

[73] "Que me abrace el mar, / [...] / Rodeada de su azul, / de su gris, / por todas partes el mar. / Marina yo, su amante. / [...] / Anegada de su verde / de su rojo, / por todas partes el monte. / Romero yo, su amante. / Que me abarque tu nieve, sierra, / que me abrace tu frío, sierra, / [...] / Blanco en azul / infinito acabarse. / Serrano yo, tu amante."

irrevocable return. In a pyrrhic victory, she triumphs over exile and becomes one with the other, the loved one that she saw as part of her being from the beginning of her poetic journey. The poet embeds herself lovingly in her poetry as the only way to dwell in her land. The joyful and playful tone of the poem celebrates the achievement of her lifelong goal. But it is also a defeat. Romero entombs herself into the landscape of her homeland. It is the interment of a voice that wanted a joyful union while alive and found only distance.

WORKS CITED

Adorno, Theodor W. *Minima Moralia*, translated by E. F. N. Jephcott, NLB, 1978.

Bielsa, Esperança. "Theodor W. Adorno's Homecoming." *European Journal of Social Theory*, vol. 19, no. 3, 2016, pp. 374–90.

Cotarelo, Lucía. *Poetas de la otra Edad de Plata en exilio estadounidense (costa este): redes de socialización, biblioteca digital y geolocalización.* 2019. U Complutense Madrid, PhD dissertation.

Dallmayr, Fred. *The Other Heidegger.* Cornell UP, 1993.

Ferry, Luc, and Alain Reanut. *Heidegger and Modernity.* Translated by Franklin Philip, U Chicago P, 1990.

Galerstein, Carolyn L., and Kathleen McNerney, editors. *Women Writers of Spain: An Annotated Bio-bibliographical Guide.* Greenwood, 1986.

García Lorca, Federico. *Selected Poems.* Edited by Christopher Maurer, Penguin, 1997.

Gauthier, David. *Martin Heidegger, Emmanuel Levinas, and the Politics of Dwelling.* 2004. Louisiana State U, PhD dissertation.

Heidegger, Martin. *Being and Time.* Translated by John Macquarrie and Edward Robinson, Harper & Row, 1962.

———. *Poetry, Language, Thought.* Translated by Albert Hofstadter, Harper & Row, 1971.

Hondagneu-Sotelo, Pierrette. "Feminism and Migration." *The Annals of the American Academy of Political and Social Science*, vol. 571, no. 1, 2000, pp. 107–20.

Levinas, Emmanuel. *Entre Nous: On Thinking-of-the-Other.* Translated by M. Smith and B. Harshav, Columbia UP, 1998.

———. *Totality and Infinity: An Essay on Exteriority.* Translated by Alphonso Lingis, Duquesne UP, 1961.

Maier-Katkin, Daniel, and Birgit Maier-Katkin. "Love and Reconciliation: The Case of Hannah Arendt and Martin Heidegger." *Harvard Review*, vol. 32, 2007, pp. 34–48.

50   A. EIRE

Malpas, Jeff. "*Heidegger and the Issue of Space. Thinking on Exilic Grounds*, by Alejandro A. Vallega." *Notre Dame Philosophical Reviews*, 11 June 2004, https://ndpr.nd.edu/reviews/heidegger-and-the-issue-of-space-thinking-on-exilic-grounds/.

Merlo, Pepa, editor. *Peces en la tierra: antología de mujeres poetas en torno a la Generación del 27.* Fundación José Manuel Lara, Vandalia, 2010.

Polt, Richard. *Heidegger. An Introduction.* Cornell UP, 1999.

Romero, Marina. *Poemas A.* Asociación de Alumnas de la Residencia, 1935.

———. *Nostalgia de mañana.* Rueca, 1943.

———. *Presencia del recuerdo.* Ínsula, 1952.

———. *Paisaje y literatura de España: antología de la generación del 98.* Introduction by Julián Marías, Tecnos, 1957.

———. *Sin agua, el mar.* Ágora, 1961.

———. *Poemas de ida y vuelta.* Torremozas, Libros de Jacarandá, 1999.

Said, Edward. *Reflections on Exile and Other Essays.* Harvard UP, 2000.

Schuback, Marcia Sá Cavalcante. *Time in Exile. In Conversation with Heidegger, Blanchot, and Lispector.* SUNY Press, 2020.

———. "Memory in Exile." *Research in Phenomenology*, vol. 47, no. 2, 2017, pp. 175–89.

Sebald, W. G. *On the Natural History of Destruction.* Translated by Anthea Bell, Hamish Hamilton, 2003.

Valender, James, and Gabriel Rojo Leyva, editors. *Poetas del exilio español: una antología.* El Colegio de México, 2006.

Valis, Noël. "The Language of Treasure: Carolina Coronado, Casta Esteban, and Marina Romero." *In the Feminine Mode: Essays on Hispanic Women Writers*, edited by Noël Valis and Carol Maier, Associated U Presses, 1990, pp. 246–72.

Weil, Simone. *The Need for Roots.* Translated by Arthur Wills, Putnam, 1952.

Wheeler, Michael. "Martin Heidegger." *The Stanford Encyclopedia of Philosophy*, fall 2020 edition, edited by Edward N. Zalta, https://plato.stanford.edu/archives/fall2020/entries/heidegger/.

CHAPTER 3

A Voice in the Margins: Ana María Martínez Sagi's Poetry in Exile

Javier Sánchez

INTRODUCTION

This chapter contextualizes and provides an analysis of the poetry written by Ana María Martínez Sagi (1907–2000) in France and in the United States during her forced exile from Spain. Certainly, the early 1930s brought the promise of change from old regime, feudal hierarchies, and the dismantling of patriarchal traditions. However, when General Francisco Franco led a coup d'état against the democratically elected government of Spain and eventually won the Spanish Civil War (1936–1939), the fall of the second Republic (established in 1931) became a harsh reality. The ensuing dictatorship (1939–1975) proved to be a social and political danger for those who remained loyal to the democratic institutions of the country and exile became an alternative, albeit traumatic, for many citizens of all social classes and backgrounds. During the years of the Republic, Ana María Martínez Sagi had become a poet, an intellectual participating in conferences, a journalist, a winning athlete in national competitions,

J. Sánchez (✉)
Stockton University, Galloway, NJ, USA
e-mail: javier.sanchez@stockton.edu

© The Author(s), under exclusive license to Springer Nature Switzerland AG 2024
R. M. Silverman, E. Sánchez-Pardo (eds.), *Nomadic New Women*,
https://doi.org/10.1007/978-3-031-62482-7_3

51

52   J. SÁNCHEZ

and the director for the Barcelona Soccer Club. Moreover, she was willing to express her romantic love for her contemporary author Elisabeth Mulder. But the expansion of this new era of opportunity and self-realization for Sagi (and women in general) in Spain ended with Franco's social and political practices: isolationism, autarky, the closing of borders, persecution, repression, censorship, and the implementation of an ultra-Catholic and ultra-conservative regime. Crossing the border into France at the end of the war, escaping the military autocracy, meant survival for Sagi (as it did for many others). Yet, Sagi becomes a forgotten, silenced, and, at best, a peripheral literary figure during her life. Recently, however, she has been the focus of study for Spanish writer Juan Manuel de Prada who published *Las esquinas del aire. En busca de Ana María Martínez Sagi* in 2000.

Sagi's work reflects her sentiments for being uprooted from her native land through profound nostalgia. Small vignettes of various Spanish geographical places with high emotional overtones, what I call *estampas*, predominate in her poetic, artistic production in exile. Her writing is intended to soothe the pain of her exile and becomes a medium for coping with the physical separation from her culture and people.[1] Sagi's poems also show the difficulties of her exilic life, the nomadic experience of a permanent wanderer without a home. Over time, hope and the possibility of returning to her land progressively diminish. In fact, even when she finally returns to Spain after the end of Franco's regime, her sense of isolation prevails. Facing such continued alienation, her poetry explicitly conveys intentions to silence a conscious mind full of memories to avoid further pain. A self-imposed silence is meant to act as a coping mechanism to deflect her sorrow of expatriation and consistent marginalization. Rather than mourning the loss of land any longer, rather than persevering and keeping such a traumatic experience alive, Sagi desires to embrace oblivion. In the end, crossing the border out of Spain signifies residing in limbo, in a place in-between, neither in France nor the United States nor Spain. Her poetic writing during her exile expresses this existential ambivalence.

---

[1] Her middle-class bourgeois family also exiled Sagi due to her sexual orientation.

3 A VOICE IN THE MARGINS: ANA MARÍA MARTÍNEZ SAGI'S POETRY IN EXILE 53

BIOGRAPHICAL NOTES: MARGINALITY

Trying to emphasize her life and her literary work, Juan Manuel de Prada writes *Las esquinas del aire. En busca de Ana María Martínez Sagi* in 2000 and edits *La voz sola*, an anthology of Sagi's poetry and journalistic essays, in 2019.[2] These two volumes offer a detailed account of Sagi's life. Following Prada's works, we learn that Sagi was born in Barcelona (1907) into a wealthy family with a business in the textile industry. In contrast to certain liberal tendencies of her father, her conservative mother believed in educating her children under socially accepted gender roles at the time.[3] Her mother wanted her to be a "prudish and traditional girl" (*Las esquinas* 430).[4] But Sagi constantly rebelled against such an approach to her education.[5] Soon, young adult Sagi breaks expectations and shows genuine and particular interest in poetry and in sports. Indeed, Sagi's poetic work and literary style also reflect her marginal condition. Her approach to poetry did not conform to the avant-garde trends of the time. When Sagi publishes her first book of poems *Caminos* (1929), critic César González-Ruano interviews Sagi.[6] She declares to him that "I am not an avant-garde writer" (107–8).[7] González-Ruano in fact identifies influences from Latin American writers such as Delmira Agustini, Juana de Ibarbourou, and

---

[2] *Las esquinas* is a fictionalized narrative of Prada's research on Sagi which he denominates a "biografía detectivesca" or a biographical quest (11). See essays by Hans-Jörg Neuschäfer, Christian von Tschilschke and Javier Sánchez for analysis on *Las esquinas*.

[3] What literary writer Emilia Pardo Bazán defines as "marital fishing" [la pesca conyugal] (101).

[4] "muchachita pudibunda y tradicional." All translations from Spanish to English in this chapter are mine.

[5] In her testimonial interview with Prada, Sagi explains that "My mother ... hated me for upsetting her desire of having another son, and later, for rebelling against the female model she wanted me to accept. My mother thought that women's mission in the world was to attract suitors with money" [Mi madre...me odió primero por haber contrariado sus designios de procrear otro hijo varón, y luego, por sublevarme contra el modelo femenino que pretendía inculcarme. Pensaba mi madre que la misión de la mujer en el mundo era la de reclamar a pretendientes adinerados] (*Las esquinas* 405).

[6] González-Ruano's impressions appear in a brief essay titled "Ana María Martínez Sagi, poeta, sindicalista y virgen del stadium" included in *Caras, caretas y carotas* (100). "Ana María Martínez Sagi, Poet, Syndicalist and Virgin of the Stadium."

[7] The full quote reads: "yo no soy ni vanguardista, ni ultraísta, ni clasicista...me fastidian mucho los 'istas' y los ismos.'"

54   J. SÁNCHEZ

Gabriela Mistral in her early poetry (101).[8] Overall, he describes Sagi's work as "direct and unpretencious poetry" in his *Antología de poetas españoles contemporáneos en lengua castellana* (583).[9] Later, in 1931, Sagi reads poetry from her unfinished book *Inquietudes* (published afterward in 1932) at a conference in Madrid. The press will underline her qualities as a poet, athlete, and Republican supporter. And Prada believes this moment to be her "mirage of popularity" and the culmination of her fame in the early 1930s (*Las esquinas* 198).[10] Nonetheless, her short celebrity status as an intellectual was achieved by avoiding a "conceptual entanglement" as described by Prada or by writing sentimental poetry against cold and academic avant-garde poetry, as understood by critic Luis Astrana Marín (*Las esquinas* 180).[11] When interviewed by Carmen Alcade in 1969, Sagi explains her poetry as follows: "My poetry is neither cerebral nor intellectual. My poetry is about zeal, spiritual tension, pain, love and the human heart" (*Las esquinas* 345).[12] And in a 1971 interview with Robert Saladrigas, she asserts that "I have tried to write poetry loyal to our human essence in opposition to dehumanized art" (*Las esquinas* 350).[13] Notwithstanding the complexity and variety of poetry written by so many authors in the early twentieth century, Sagi perceived her own poetry in contrast to a depersonalized or dehumanized type of art mainly outlined and advocated by philosopher José Ortega y Gasset. Regarding sports,

[8] Rafael Cansinos-Asséns, González-Ruano's colleague, also sees an "America's accent" [el acento de América] in Sagi's poems and identifies influences from Ibarbourou, Mistral and Alfonsina Storni (*Las esquinas* 176).

[9] "una poesía directa y sencilla."

[10] "espejismo de notoriedad."

[11] "galimatías conceptual."

[12] "Mi poesía no es ni cerebral ni intelectual. Mi poesía es una poesía de fervor, de tensión spiritual, de desgarradura, de amor y palpitación humana." Sagi further defines her poetry during her interview with Alcalde: [a poet cannot be reduced to mathematical formulas, nor be restricted to reason ... Baroque approaches, linguistic beauty, esoteric rhetoric has nothing to do with the magic of poetry. Such approach gives us intellectual, elitist, heavily dehumanized art ... admirably hermetic and complex, written only for experts [and such poetry] is already an aborted body with the smell of a coming death] "un poeta no se puede reducir a fórmulas lógico-matemáticas, ni bajarlo al nivel de la razón...Artificios barrocos, preciosismos verbales, retórica esotérica, nada tiene que ver con la magia de la poesía. Nos darán, eso sí, una poesía sabia, minoritaria, de arte deshumanizado y lastrado...de un hermetismo admirable y difícil, escrita sólo para sabios iniciados [que] es ya de por sí cosa abortada, con olor a muerte anticipada" (*Las esquinas* 346).

[13] "He procurado que mi poesía...sea...poesía de lealtad humana frente al arte deshumanizado."

Sagi became an active member of the Club Femení I d'Esports, which intended to be a place for women of all social classes to practice sports, discuss political views, and keep abreast of cultural developments. The Club Femení I d'Esports (founded in 1928, defunct in 1936) was heavily critiqued by those who resisted women's emancipation in Barcelona (and in Spain). Its mission was to expose women to their predicament in society and to prepare them to become knowledgeable citizens capable of fighting for their rights. Sagi participated in conferences and national sporting events with great success.[14] In her work *The Lavender Locker Room*, author Patricia Warren describes Sagi as a "LGBT sports pioneer" in her chapter dedicated to Ana María Martínez Sagi (151).

As a female poet in a male-oriented society, Sagi becomes a feminist by developing her intellect and rejecting the pattern of conduct established for her gender.[15] Prada visualizes her during the early 1930s as "a new Eve" who wanted to "represent with her voice a new generation emerging with the Republic which dared to question the traditional role reserved for women, restricted to domestic servitude" and portrays her as a self-assured and confident individual not afraid of transgressing norms (*Las esquinas* 44, 115).[16] As a firm believer in the democratic system as a pathway for social transformation and the emancipation of women, her allegiance to the Republic is unquestionable. In her conversation with González-Ruano, Sagi clearly states that "as a committed republican supporter I

---

[14] Her accomplishments in the world of sports include getting the record for the javelin throw in 1931, participating in national championships and acting as one of the board of Directors for the Barcelona Soccer Club for about a year (1934–1935) becoming the first woman to hold such a position not only in Spain but in the world according to Prada in *La voz sola* (1).

[15] As Caballé argues in her *El feminismo en España. La conquista de un derecho*, the pursuit of education and the access to academic instruction are the fundamental principles that characterize Spanish feminism (29). Contemporary feminist writer Nuria Valera corroborates this idea in *Feminismo 4.0. La cuarta ola* by indicating that "the first demand by feminists, even before defining themselves as such, was access to education" [La primera reivindicación de las feministas, incluso antes de reconocerse como tal, fue la educación] (57). Of course, Sagi's family position as part of a wealthier social class allowed her to cultivate her interests in poetry, sports, and politics. Virginia Woolf reminds us how important is for a woman to "have money and a room of her own if she is to write fiction" (4).

[16] "una nueva Eva [que] quería representar la voz de una nueva generación que emergía con la República y se atrevía a cuestionar el papel que tradicionalmente se había reservado a la mujer, confinado a las servidumbres domésticas."

56   J. SÁNCHEZ

have participated in public events and spoken at meetings" (108).[17] Her views are also published in an article titled "To an aristocratic lady from Madrid" that she publishes in the newspaper *La rambla* in 1931. She declares the following:

> I have always supported the Republic. I am a liberal and a democrat because I believe in our humanity, civility and decency. I believe in liberal people because despotism, feudalism and oppression do not grant justice, civil exemplarity and the social, moral and political rebirth I fully desire for Spain...I support the Republic in order to pursue justice and civility ... and I support the Republic because I am a feminist. (*La voz sola* 240)[18]

Sagi always defended feminism: equality for all, access to education, and voting rights for women.[19] Defending a democratic and inclusive society relates deeply to her personal life. For example, meeting writer Elisabeth Mulder in 1929 is crucial for her. Prada calls it the "central episode of her existence" (*La voz sola* XLI).[20] Surely, author Mulder becomes a clear

[17] "soy republicana, convencidamente republicana, y he intervenido en actos públicos, hablado en mítines..."

[18] "A una señora de la aristocracia madrileña" (republished in *La voz sola*). "soy republicana...de siempre. Soy republicana, soy liberal y soy demócrata por humanismo, por civilidad...y por decencia. Confío y creo en los hombres liberales porque del despotismo, el feudalismo y la opresión no puedo esperar la era de justicia, la ejemplaridad civil, el resurgimiento político, moral y social que deseo con todo mi fervor para España...soy republicana por afán de justicia y de civilidad...y también soy republicana por feminismo."

[19] Approving gender equality norms and voting rights for women became crucial topics of discussion during the early days of the Republic. Once Ana María Martínez Sagi becomes a journalist (1931), she quickly finds herself in a privileged position to reflect opinions about these matters through her contributions. Answering questions for an interview published in the newspaper *La rambla*, Sagi addresses the feminist question: "A feminist? Yes, if we understand feminism as being aware of our rights and responsibilities, and how to acquire and preserve them ... with honor and bravery ... I do not believe neither violence nor compassion is needed, just loyalty and understanding, and that should be enough to triumph when the cause defended is just" (*Las esquinas* 205). Certainly, views varied greatly but Anna Caballé succinctly summarizes predominant perspectives as follows: "from 1914 on in Spain it was discernible a 'radical' feminism defending voting rights and a 'moderate' catholic feminism just trying to secure social opportunities (rights to work, education and decent salary)" (*El feminismo* 24). In the end, voting rights for women were approved in the Spanish parliament and feminist writer Nuria Varela credits politician Clara Campoamor's efforts for it: "Clara Campoamor became a key speaker during parliamentary debates so that the 1931 Constitution would not discriminate against women" (*Feminismo* 147).

[20] "episodio cenital de su existencia."

3 A VOICE IN THE MARGINS: ANA MARÍA MARTÍNEZ SAGI'S POETRY IN EXILE   57

influence on Sagi's work. But their lesbian love affair, albeit short (Mallorca, 1932), will leave a permanent mark on both Sagi's life and poetry. In fact, her deep feelings for Mulder manifest in much of her poetry as one of its central themes even if Sagi never mentions her by name.[21] But, Mulder ends their affair under pressure from Sagi's mother and fearful of social condemnation and repercussions.

Trying to gain independence, Sagi leaves her family abode and procures a job as a journalist. The political turmoil before the advent of the Spanish Civil War allows her to meet historical figures such as Buenaventura Durruti. Loyal to the Republic Sagi joins the antifascist militias as a reporter for various newspapers in 1936. But once Franco's victory was imminent, Sagi understood her political views made her a target for prison or execution. The options for an outspoken journalist were minimal at the end of the civil war as Caballé outlines: "Franco's victory brought three possibilities: exile, jail or silence" (257).[22] Therefore, she crossed the border into France on January 29, 1939.[23] Conscious of the implications of her departure, she laments "I am without country" (*Las esquinas* 496).[24] Critic Shirley Mangini explains the new situation Spanish women had to face: "Women who had defended the Republic suffered a double tragedy at the end of the war: the disappearance of a short-lived democracy in which many had invested their hopes for social equality, and the destruction of further economic, social and political advancement for women" (57). Hence, most intellectuals, including Sagi, chose exile and will have to face rather difficult situations away from their native country.[25] Author Karla Zepeda notes that after the defeat of the democratic government: "the Republican émigrés lost their national soil, community, and material possessions. Furthermore, they had to come to terms with the defeat of

---

[21] Since the topic of exile is central to this chapter, I do not analyze Sagi's love poetry. Yet, I acknowledge the importance of Sagi's poetic body in relationship to Elisabeth Mulder. Prada has analyzed aspects of this topic in *Las esquinas* but it deserves deeper study.

[22] "La victoria de Franco dibujó tres posibilidades: el exilio, la cárcel o el silencio."

[23] As critic María José Porro Herrera indicates, although Sagi continued writing poetry, her exile ended her role with the press: "El exilio cercenó su presencia en la prensa aunque siguió cultivando la poesía" (140).

[24] "haber[se] quedado sin patria."

[25] Nuria Valera provides a short list: "Clara Campoamor, Rosa Chacel, Dolores Ibárruri, Victoria Kent, María Lejarraga, María Teresa León, María de Maeztu, Federica Montseny, Margarita Nelken, María Zambrano..." and many more (*Feminismo* 153). See also list provided by Anna Caballé in *El feminismo en España*, page 257. Michael Ugarte emphasizes: "The diaspora sparked by the war of 1936 to 1939 was above all an intellectual one" (58).

58   J. SÁNCHEZ

their national vision" (6). Surely, Sagi belongs to the diaspora of educated, intellectual, professional women who experienced the collapse of democratic and egalitarian values in favor of conservative, traditional, patriarchal hierarchies. In her case and from now on, Sagi dreams of a potential return to her lost nation, the recovering of a life left behind.[26]

Her first years away from Spain are especially desolate. When she reaches Paris (where she witnesses Germany's victory over France in 1940), obtaining a job proves rather difficult and she faces being homeless. She survives. Later in Chartres, she joins the French Resistance. In a 1977 interview with Karen Robinson for *The Champaign-Urbana News Gazette*, Sagi explains that "All my life I have fought against injustice, dictatorship and oppression. Hence, I decided to join the Resistance ... against the Nazis" (*La voz sola* lvii).[27] Her involvement with this group will be known to the Gestapo from which she narrowly escapes. Around 1947, she moves to Cannes. There, she finds some stability (and money) in her life working as a translator, Spanish teacher, decorator, and selling painted scarfs. She buys a house in Montauroux, a place that she abandons soon after her child (conceived in 1950) dies of disease six years after being born. But in 1959 she decides to travel and settles in the United States as faculty at the University of Illinois (Urbana-Champaign) teaching Spanish and French.[28] She visits Spain briefly in 1969 to publish her *Laberinto de presencias*. Yet, she lives in the United States till 1977.[29] Once retired and the Franco dictatorship over, she finally returns to Barcelona. However, Sagi never feels at home in her own birthplace, as Prada notices: "she never stopped feeling a foreigner in the city" (*La voz sola* lxv).[30] Directly or indirectly reminded of her condition as castaway by older acquaintances, she relocates to Moià and secludes herself in this locality. Sagi's reclusion is easily

---

[26] The work titled *El exilio republicano de 1939 y la segunda generación* (edited by Manuel Aznar Soler y José Ramón López García and based on the fourth international conference on republican exile in 2011) is an example of how people are still dealing with the effects of dislocation and the diasporic experience.

[27] "Toda mi vida he luchado contra la injusticia, la dictadura, la opresión. Así que decidí incorporarme a la Resistencia…contra los nazis."

[28] During 1965–1966, she studies at the Alliance Française in Paris which allows her to join the Department of French at her return to the United States and move up in rank at the same university.

[29] She is 70 years old now, her last academic year at the university was in 1975 according to a letter that Prada recovers and publishes in *Las esquinas* (324–29).

[30] "nunca había dejado de sentirse extranjera en la ciudad."

understood if we consider what scholar Michael Ugarte contends about exile: "Exile, both the phenomenon and the person, always finds itself on the margins of something, in a liminal position between two places, times" (7). The long period spent in different countries solidifies her condition as a permanent exile. She goes to an assisted living facility in Santpedor in 1988. Sagi dies January 2, 2000.[31]

EXILE AND POETIC WORK

As is common during the exilic experience, the forced relocation brings a strong sentiment of homesickness and nostalgia. Cultural critic Edward Said emphasizes that "exile is the unhealable rift forced between a human being and a native place" from where a deep profound sadness and sense of loss, of "something left behind forever," becomes permanent (173). Distance, marginality, and displacement all contribute to the discontinuity of this "state of being" as Said phrases it (177). In Sagi's case, such a separation from her culture and from the inclusiveness promoted by the newly established Republic (granting voting rights to women and offering a new social perspective) damages her sense of belonging regardless of her perseverance to maintain ties to her homeland. According to author Paul Tabori's definition in *The Anatomy of Exile*, the exile is a person "compelled to leave his homeland" for political, social or economic reasons who, despite "efforts at assimilation" and his/her desire to be accepted, s/he might "cling to his original national and spiritual identity" (37). Furthermore, the *destierro* (exile) from the native land foments the attempt to "recover something lost (a land, an identity, a place of origin)" on the part of the exile, who, according to Ugarte, feels "something less than human" (20). The perception of being incomplete as a person forces the individual to be nostalgic. Ugarte defines nostalgia as "a deceptively positive reading of the past in terms of a present which is worse by comparison" (23). Indeed, comparisons between past and present may reinforce the sense of loss and the nostalgic sentiment. The impression that a past is lost or unrecoverable could impede the healing of the exile or his/her coming to terms with the new situation. Said reflects about mourning the past: "it is what one remembers of the past and how one remembers it that determine how one sees the future" (xxxv). Maintaining a constant

---

[31] Biographical data taken from *La voz sola* and *Las esquinas* by Prada.

60   J. SÁNCHEZ

nostalgic view of the past influences the person to see his/her present as inadequate, insufficient, and lacking. At the same time, the return to the idealized nation remains impossible.

Sagi's writing demonstrates her exilic condition through a variety of themes: the sun as absence of country, dehumanization of war, questioning of Christian values, solidarity with the Republican cause, exilic life abroad, and her silence after a disappointing return to Barcelona. At first, under her own circumstances and as Ugarte asserts about intellectuals undergoing expatriation: "Exile … is a catalyst for writing" (4). Indeed, Sagi produces most of her poetry out of a profound sense of loss and acute feeling of absence. Consequently, her poetics reflect her ruptured subjectivity during exile, that is, her lack of bearings, disorientation, uprootedness, and dislocation from her culture and nation. Being forced out and away from a community granting emancipation, voting rights, opportunity, and, the chance for self-realization, her newly acquired condition of outcast creates feelings of incompleteness and insufficiency. In short, her exile and the nostalgia for what is left on the other side of the border drive her to write a poetics of emotion representative of her circumstances. Her work becomes both a sustaining link to her past and a reflection of her pain as an ostracized individual. As is the case with those who are marginalized, what is written, Said explains, "bears a unique freight of anxiety" and therefore "language is about experience and not just about itself" (xv). Far from engaging in experimental poetics, the written word for her signifies mood, experience, and a desire to become part of (melt with) those poetic images as a form of returning to a lost homeland. This is the argument Michael Seidel makes in his *Exile and the Narrative Imagination*. In his work, while following Walter Benjamin, Seidel refers to the term "exilic conjuring" where a fragile and precious reality is created and where the exiled author wishes to return as a way of exercising one's being (5). In other words, "the expression of the desire for home becomes a substitute for home" according to Seidel (11). But, this move toward what is lost simultaneously solidifies a stagnant view of that country. This static notion becomes a distortion when juxtaposed to the present-day reality of the nation, usually after a return takes place. Referring to Sagi, Prada states that she is exposed to the "incongruence between reality and the retrospective reflection of reality" (*Las esquinas* 352).[32] The problem for Sagi,

---

[32] "incongruencia entre la realidad y el retrospectivo reflejo de la realidad"

3 A VOICE IN THE MARGINS: ANA MARÍA MARTÍNEZ SAGI'S POETRY IN EXILE   61

as for many exiles, lies in the contrast between their imaginings of home and the experience of their actual homeland when they return (as further explained below).[33]

Laberinto de presencias (1969) is the work of poetry that best reflects Sagi's experience as exile. This volume is divided into six books: *Canciones de la isla, País de la ausencia, Amor perdido, Jalones entre la niebla, Los motivos del mar* and *Visiones y sortilegios.* Appropriately, Juan Manuel de Prada defines her volume as the "chronicle of a poetic exile" since Sagi indicates the place of composition (a variety of countries) and the date when each poem was written from 1932 to 1968 (*Las esquinas* 354).[34] It is however in both *País de la ausencia (1938–40)* and *Jalones entre la niebla (1940–67)* where Sagi's poems consistently refer to Spain, the civil war, her sense of loss and nostalgia, a languishing hope to return home, and finally the silencing of her voice. *País de la ausencia (1938–40)* was mostly written in France after Sagi leaves Spain when Franco's troops enter Barcelona. The "descriptive impressionism" that Prada identifies with the whole of *Laberinto de presencias* is surely present in *País de la ausencia* (lxi).[35] In addition, however, the verbal images created in her poetry, what I denominate as *estampas,* offer readers a window into Sagi's deep yearning for her lost country. An *estampa* is a short poetic composition that includes a verbal description of a place or geographical location which illustrates a condition or a quality of it and carries emotional overtones. These poems try to convey a relevant characteristic of the location described. They are brief representations of Spanish localities, regions, spaces that provide the poetic persona with a glimpse of the country left behind. Filtered by memory and heavy with emotion, Sagi's linguistic vignettes reconstruct a segment of Spain as a method to staying closer to her origins. These mini portraits of land are a nostalgic recall of a faraway nation and culture. As such, they contain the emotional content of love for country, yearning, and nostalgia. On many occasions, the sun acts as the uniting element between these linguistic vignettes (usually octosyllabic but not always). Her poem "The light" begins by invoking her absent country and proceeds to describe its nature: "In the country of absence, sun on all sides … Sun on the crunchy almond, on the illuminated orange

---

[33] Seidel describes this phenomenon: "the mental energy expended on the image of home in absence proves incommensurate with the reality of home as presence" (78).

[34] "crónica de un exilio poético."

[35] "impresionismo descriptivo."

62   J. SÁNCHEZ

tree, on the luminous pine tree, on the golden and dart-like wheat" (69).[36] The constant reference to the sun allows her to describe her land with a luminous aura that occasionally appears dangerous and harsh. The sun appears in poems such as "The Catalan Farm," "Interior," "August in Sentmanat," "Orense," and "Sentmanat."[37] Also in "Summer" readers find: "Fire. Blonde wheat. Fire. White Flame. Sulphur falls on the fields' skin. Steam from hard hawthorns from scorched forests, from dusty brambles, from fallow lands" (113).[38] Fire and heat permeate nature and the portrayal of summer in Spain. The same approach is found in "Castilla" where we read: "An incandescent sky watches the flames surface from limestone crusts and stone hills" (77).[39] Despite the strong incendiary power, the reference to the sun in her work is a positive force reminiscent of life in Spain.

In her poetry, the sun also suggests a sense of warmth absent in France, Illinois or in other places she resides. In *Jalones entre la niebla* the lack of sun is problematic for the poetic persona and for the exiled in general. The surrounding gloom (darkness and dim light) reflects the feeling of inadequacy, a fall from grace, and the inability to experience life as before. In "Street of a Fishing Cat" the exiled live in "decrepit houses with chipped cornices, rusty leaks which allow a crack of light over the coffin-like sinister street ... and in a sordid hotel ... the exile search for an impossible sky behind blind windows" (203).[40] Aware of the impossibility to return, the sky, the sun, summer, life, and Spain are deeply missed and remembered with deep affection. Contrarily, we read about her surroundings and how "Sewers yawn in a grey morning" and how "An ashy light slides down the

---

[36] "La luz." "En el país de la ausencia:/sol en los cuatro costados/...Sol de la almendra crujiente/del luminoso naranjo/del pino en gomas lucientes/del trigo en dardos dorados..." Sagi frequently uses the octosyllabic structure with an only vowels rhyme in even verses.

[37] "La masía catalana," "Interior," "Agosto en Sentmanat," "Orense" and "Sentmanat."

[38] "Verano." "...Incendio. Trigo rubio./Incendio. Fuego blanco./Cae azufre caliente/ sobre la piel del campo./Vaho de espinos duros/de bosques calcinados/de zarzas polvorientas/de barbechos exhaustos...".

[39] "...Un cielo incandescente mira surgir las llamas/de las costras calizas y los montes de Piedra."

[40] "Rue du Chat qui Pêche." "casas decrépitas [con] desconchadas cornisas/herrumbrosas goteras [que]/dejaron penetrar un resquicio de luz sobre el ataúd de la calle siniestra./...y en un sórdido hotel/...los exiliados buscan un imposible cielo/tras las ventanas ciegas."

3 A VOICE IN THE MARGINS: ANA MARÍA MARTÍNEZ SAGI'S POETRY IN EXILE 63

oozing decrepit walls eaten by moss" in "Fishmonger Square" (209).[41] Again, in "The Jail" the poetic persona notices how the birds "head towards my country's sun" while imprisoned: "I looked at them leave with my fists and forehead hitting the prison bars of the hostile sky" (215).[42] Her restricted freedom as an outcast is reinforced by her inability to reach for her native sunny sky. The lack of sun as synecdoche for the absence of country is also expressed in "Obsession."[43] There, the contrast between the "shaded walls" surrounding Sagi while "thinking about her lost sun" reflects the conflict between her unbearable physical imprisonment (walled out from Spain) and her mental disposition to think about the sun as her only solace, as her effort to transgress her impediments and reduce her pain (217).[44]

The contraposition between light and shadows presents the binary opposite of life and death in much of Sagi's poetry. Against feelings of depression, anguish, and despair the poetic persona juxtaposes the emotion of hope, rebirth, and a communion with clean, pristine, untainted nature in poems such as "May," "April," "Imploration," and others.[45] For example, here is a full poem (*estampa*) titled "Cambados" (locality in Galicia): "A hasty escape of transparent brooks. The mountain's skirt sewn with green stems. A shepherd tanned by the sun sleeps with crossed arms" (99).[46] This bucolic and peaceful image of Cambados allows readers to hear the water, see the colors of the vegetation, and feel the sun. Sagi grants us a communion with an idyllic place. Similarly, the *estampa* "Málaga" denotes heat, luminosity, peacefulness, silence, warmth while playing with the colors white, blue, and red: "Time for a nap and drowsiness in Málaga: saffron on the sea, bars on fire with silent arches against the white wall. On every street the sky opens blue razors" (109).[47] In addition to the already mentioned poems, her representations of land include

---

[41] "Bostezan las cloacas en la mañana gris." "Una luz cenicienta resbala por los muros/ rezumantes decrépitos comidos de verdín." "Plaza de la pescadería."

[42] "La cárcel." "rumbo al sol de mi país." "Yo las miraba partir:/puños y frente golpeando/las rejas del cielo hostil."

[43] "Obsesión."

[44] "muros de sombras." "pensando en el sol perdido."

[45] "Mayo," "Abril," "Imploración."

[46] Una fuga presurosa/de regatos transparentes./La falda de la montaña: cosida con tallos verdes./Un pastor negro de soles/con los brazos en cruz duerme.

[47] La hora de la siesta/y del sopor en Málaga:/azafrán sobre el mar/rejas incendiadas/con arcos de silencio/contra la pared blanca./De calle a calle el cielo/abre azules navajas.

64   J. SÁNCHEZ

"Sevilla," "Pirinieos," "Santiago de Compostela," "Córdoba," and "Jerez de la Frontera," among others. These verbal images or *estampas* are the "exilic conjuring" of a land where she cannot return thus emphasizing a void she wishes to fill. Paraphrasing Ugarte, as the wanderer searches for a home, the exile approaches the desired place with his/her writing (21). This is true in Sagi's case. Overall, the bright light and the luminosity of the sun show the longing for nationhood. Her poems, mediated through memory, portray a deeply missed faraway country and, her only recourse is to "melt with" or to "return" to it via her artistic composition. This fragile sense of belonging created by the simulacrum of unity with her own poetic creation (remembering the sun, sky, light, warmth, heat, colors) mitigates, if only provisionally, her suffering originated by her uprooted condition (shadows, walls, fog, imprisonment) after the war.

Sagi also expresses her sorrow for the loss of life during war while demonstrating the progressive losing of our humanity as well as the abandonment of Christian values in her poems on the lost civil war, the origin of her exile and her grief. In the poem titled "The War" Sagi refers to our destructive nature in association with hate and conflict.[48] Sagi writes in "The Wind of Hate" about how "Hills vomit heavy cannons" (213).[49] We learn about "black wire fences, blood and explosions. A hostile jungle of crushed bodies ... severed heads ... deformed fetuses" (214).[50] The physical dismemberment of bodies profoundly suggests either a deformation or a fracturing of spiritual, human values. As such, the poem ends with "Vultures devour the humans' rotten heart" (214).[51] This final image depicts a corrupted, unsympathetic heart, a polluted, corroded, damaged sense of humanity in its decomposition process only appealing to vultures. This topic is developed in "Bombed School" but with the added reference to God and the questioning of Christian precepts.[52] The horror of war as manifested in broken bodies is part of the poem again: "Shrapnel and gunpowder cut their gut ... severed, rotten heads fall off ... a jungle of legs without bodies stop us" (221).[53] But then the poetic persona calls for

---

[48] "La guerra."

[49] "El viento del odio." "Los cerros vomitan/pesados cañones."

[50] "alambradas negras/sangre y explosiones./Una selva hostil de triturados cuerpos/...cabezas cortadas...fetos deformes."

[51] "Los buitres devoran/el corazón podrido de los hombres."

[52] "Escuela bombardeada."

[53] "La metralla y la polvora/les han tajado el vientre/...las cabezas sesgadas/podridas se desprenden/...una selva de piernas/sin tronco nos detiene."

3 A VOICE IN THE MARGINS: ANA MARÍA MARTÍNEZ SAGI'S POETRY IN EXILE   65

understanding and resolution for such a tragedy by invoking God: "I am sending you this puzzle; Merciful God, you must be getting bored!" (221).[54] Such extreme cruelty, as it is found during any war, leads Sagi to request God to put humanity together (not just bodies). Yet she uses an ironic tone. The suggestion that there needs to be justice, peace, love, understanding requires a merciful God to deliver a response but God remains absent, quiet, and inactive. God is also critiqued in "I Accuse You While Suffering" (*La voz sola*).[55] The poem begins with "It is in my blood, in my body where Spain hurts" (128).[56] After a historical description of how Spain has suffered injustice, pain, ignorance, intolerance, imprisonment, and repression, the voice poses the question "Are there not enough crimes and tombs?" to a God described as "The one who condemned the rich and loved the poor. The one who forgave on the cross" (131).[57] The accusing of God as a being without compassion continues in the poem "God" (*La voz sola*).[58] Here we read: "Lord, you left me defenseless and rebellious ... What do you understand by justice, blind and implacable God?" (136–7).[59] The bond between God and the poetic persona appears broken. At the core of the fractured unity between both are the abandonment, resentment, and anger felt by the poetic voice. This desertion by way of God's inactivity becomes another type of exile for Sagi, it contributes to her solitude.

Sagi, of course, identifies with the Republicans and their plight during the civil war. The language she uses in her poetry connotes great admiration for the lost Republic and all who defended the democratically elected government. She dedicates her poem "Tattooed on the Flesh" to the republican soldier who falls in Belchite.[60] One of the images we are given in this poem describes "a collapsed body in my arms. His bull chest opened ... blood soaks my skirt" (105).[61] The portrayal of the two people

---

[54] "Yo te envío este 'puzzle': ¡Dios [de] misericordia/que estarás aburriéndote!"

[55] "Yo te acuso sufriendo."

[56] "Es en mi sangre en mi cuerpo/donde me dueles España."

[57] "¿No son bastantes las tumbas/...los crímenes cometidos...?" "El que condenó a los ricos/y a los míseros amaba./El que perdonó en la cruz."

[58] "Dios."

[59] "Me dejaste Señor desvalida y rebelde/...¿Qué justicia es la tuya/Dios implacable y ciego?"

[60] "En la carne tatuado."

[61] "...un cuerpo/en mis brazos desplomado./Su pecho de toro abierto./...la sangre empapa mi falda."

66   J. SÁNCHEZ

is reminiscent of *The Pietà* by Michelangelo and therefore carries a religious tone. The poem mainly intends to honor a brave but now dead soldier after fighting for justice. The recognition of soldiers also takes place in "Juan Manuel," killed in action, when he falls "on Spanish soil; his open heart, a red pomegranate, falls" (94).[62] And also in "He Came Down the River" where the militiaman does not have a name and therefore represents all soldiers: "How unlucky you are, the people's soldier, a brave militiaman, a friendly heart" (566).[63] In this way, Sagi's poetry shows her solidarity and unity with the Republican fighter. Her friendship intends to preserve and perpetuate a collective sentiment in these poems after both the soldier and his cause have fallen.

In addition, Sagi offers a representation of her exilic life away from Spain. These poems are mainly found in *La voz sola* and *Jalones entre la niebla*. The despair arising from the lost hope of a potential rebirth is paired with her permanent condition of displacement in "Disheartened Professor" where she acknowledges that "neither ardent heart beats nor fear nor memories nor tangible roots will grow" (329).[64] The impossibility to find a place to belong is enhanced in "You Are Not Awake."[65] She describes herself as a perpetual wanderer without land and people, walking through various landscapes without finding respite: "I walk turned open with an infected wound and carrying a cross. My feet are sored from walking through desert countries and cities. I do not know if I have a face … if forms are true. If I died long time ago. If I am the outline of a dream" (183).[66] Part of her penance, carrying the cross, is the imposed wandering (exilic condition) to find her place in the world. Thus, she feels less than human, a specter, someone who may have already died, a fragile walking dream of a person without belonging anywhere. Indeed, critic Seidel underlines the trope of the exile as "a wanderer by nature" (10). And Said also informs the exile as a person with a "sense of constant estrangement"

---

[62] "sobre la tierra de España;/cae, el corazón abierto,/como una roja Granada" (*La voz sola*).

[63] "Por el río venía." ";Qué muerte la tuya, soldado del pueblo,/bravo miliciano, corazón amigo;" (*Las esquinas*).

[64] "Desalentada profesora." "ni latido ardiente ni temblor ni memoria/ni raíces tangibles arraigarán."

[65] "Tú no despiertas."

[66] "Vengo yo desgarrada/con enconada herida con una cruz a cuestas./Se llagaron mis plantas de caminar países/y ciudades desiertas./No sé si tengo rostro…/Si toda forma es cierta./Si me morí hace tiempo. Si soy perfil de sueño."

3 A VOICE IN THE MARGINS: ANA MARÍA MARTÍNEZ SAGI'S POETRY IN EXILE   67

who "always [feels] out of place" (175, 180). The feeling of homelessness is constantly heightened because "homes are always provisional" and therefore the life of the exile is "nomadic [and] decentered" as Said concludes (185–86).

Away from her native place and culture, any country in which Sagi lives remains at odds with her notion of home. Her *estampas* describing the various places she visits, travels to, and resides in reflect a deep nostalgia of her homeland and her discontent as a marginalized outcast. In "Chartres" the town is a "dead city with narrow and dirty streets," dirty water, and polluted air where the "sky sweats soot" (207).[67] Also, "Montparnasse" is the place where the defeated inhabit: "It is a neighborhood with crazy people, saints, fraternal specters and silenced martyrs" (263).[68] Later in the United States, Sagi dedicates one of her poems to the city of New York. In an approach evocative of Lorca's *Poet in New York*, she writes: "The scattered yellow arrow-like taxis ... crazy elevators ... concrete jungles. Modern Babel ... encouraging the heartbeat of one hundred thriving races ... I salute the people who cut off their roots looking for their heaven in your sky" (313).[69] Her poem depicts the city as the place for the dislocated (whether willfully or not), the location for those coming from anywhere looking for a promised land and the American dream. It is the locus of the diaspora. Migrants put a seed of hope in the city made of concrete to build a home. But Sagi continues her wandering. She portrays her solitude and disorientation in the poem "American Highways": "indomitable. Infinite. Wavering. Dispersed ... I follow you alone and small ... lost in a labyrinth...To which torment or refuge you take me, away from my peaceful routes and from my childhood sky?" (315–6).[70] The nostalgia of her homeland is present in this poem as she reflects on what is left behind. Immersed in an unescapable maze of roads, those *caminos* never lead her to the origin from which she departed. For her, the exilic wandering remains an unending experience, as she intimates in "Vertical Death"

---

[67] "ciudad muerta [con] calles negras y angostas." "cielo rezuma hollín."

[68] "Es un barrio/de locos y de santos/de espectros fraternales/de mártires callados."

[69] "Las saetas amarillas de los taxis desbandados./...los ascensores locos./...las selvas de cemento./Babel moderna.../Del latido pujante de cien razas alientas/...Yo saludo a los hombres que por ti cercenaron/sus raíces buscando en tu cielo su cielo."

[70] "Autopistas americanas." "indomables. Infinitas./Ondulantes. Dispersadas/...Os sigo sola y pequeña/...perdida en un laberinto/...¿A qué calvario o refugio/me conducís separada/de mis sendas apacibles/y del cielo de mi infancia?"

68   J. SÁNCHEZ

where she admits that her condition is "forever … without yesterday nor tomorrow … Walking … Just walking … uninhabited … without yesterday nor tomorrow" (121).[71] Sagi conceptualizes her exile as an eternal traveler cut off both from time and from space.

Silence and the Impossible Return

Her poems, especially her *estampas* of Spain, are a medium through which a return to what is lost seems temporarily possible. Progressively, however, the harsh reality of its infeasibility becomes apparent. In the long term, her voice, rather than soothing her pain, ends up conjuring the agony produced by reliving her expatriation and by the realization of her unreachable goal of recovering her nation. Facing this painful reality, she develops the intention to forget her traumatic past by silencing her poetic voice in order to avoid further suffering. Sagi writes about "a dream of nostalgia and delirium" in "Obsessive Memories" (117).[72] Crafted with her own words, the dream made of yearning becomes a nightmare caused by the same "far away country that I resurrect without pause" (118).[73] Ultimately, Sagi suggests in her poem that such reviving is counterproductive. This truth becomes exposed in "Dialogue."[74] Here, the poetic persona engages in a conversation with herself foregrounding her exilic condition and her solitude: "What are your fixated eyes looking at? A sky which is not mine. What are you listening to? Words that I never understand … this route…It does not go anywhere. Who follows you? Echoes" (119).[75] The reverberation of the past, a reminder of the absence of nation, reinforces an immense sense of solitude for Sagi and underlines her present (and constant) displacement while intensifying her grief. This is the cause for her "herida que no cierra" or the unhealable wound, the main theme in "Resignation," which appears to require forgetting rather than remembering as a probable solution (121).[76] Her suffering is also recorded in "Lost Voice" where we read: "Pain for my dead voice among the rushed clamor of the living.

---

[71] "Muerte vertical." "Por siempre…/sin ayer ni mañana./…Andar…Tan sólo andar…/…deshabitada./…sin ayer ni mañana."
[72] "…un sueño/de nostalgia y delirio." "Obsesionante recuerdo."
[73] "país lejano/que sin cesar resucito."
[74] "Diálogo."
[75] "¿Qué miran tus ojos fijos?/Un cielo que no es el mío./¿Qué escuchas…?/Palabras que nunca entiendo./…esta ruta…/No lleva a ninguna parte./¿Quién te persigue? Los ecos."
[76] "Resignación."

3 A VOICE IN THE MARGINS: ANA MARÍA MARTÍNEZ SAGI'S POETRY IN EXILE 69

My voice is lost around corners made of air and oblivion" (116).[77] Once her voice was silenced by her forced exile and during her wanderings in space and time, her loneliness is further stressed by the noise the living around her make, also suppressing her voice.

A long exile finally produces in her a desire for a self-imposed silenced to avoid more suffering. In her poem "Dread" Sagi writes about her fears to remember, her desire to forget her uprootedness: "In a crucified country I left my dead heart. A desolate landscape made of nostalgia and specters ... tomb of lived dreams and indestructible memories...Don't remove the mud, entombed images and reflected reflections" (201).[78] The obvious religious connotation of the word crucified to describe Spain forges the image of a victimized country. This place, symbolic of a martyr, is a waste land with ghosts who nostalgically remember their broken and suppressed dreams. Only memories remain but those are too painful to live with and, therefore, it is better not to reanimate the experience or to recreate it in a mirror made of images and words. In "The Mask" Sagi confesses the following: "I ordered my words: you will take this course ... be submissive ... I put a subtle gag to my words" (71).[79] This mask she creates for herself to go through life is nonetheless a traumatic tragedy which repeatedly emphasizes the idea of "Vertical Death." In *Visiones y sortilegios (1945–60)* Sagi articulates that she does not speak with her own true voice any longer: "Nobody saw the old wound...Nobody perceives the captive voice" (75).[80] As a form of survival, her later life becomes an attempt to refrain from thinking about her previous existence. This is the main topic in "Give Me Time" where she expresses the difficulty of accomplishing such a task: "I have to build over ruins. I have to sprout in the desert again...It is terrible to bury so many still living people" (*La voz sola* 109).[81] The rebirth that she seeks can hardly take place in the emotional desolation of a wasteland after she tries to entomb her memories. Similarly, Sagi embraces her solitude in "Murky Water" by declaring "the strangled echo

---

[77] "Voz Perdida." "Dolor de mi voz muerta/entre el arrebatado clamor de los vivos./La voz que se ha perdido en la esquinas/del aire y del olvido..."

[78] "Temor." "En un país crucificado/dejé mi corazón muerto./Un desolado paisaje/de nostalgias y de espectros/...tumba de sueños vividos/de indestructibles recuerdos/...No quieras remover légamo/imágenes sepultadas/y reflejos de reflejos."

[79] "La máscara." "Ordené/a mis palabras:/iréis por este cauce/...sumisas.../He puesto/a mis palabras/una sutil/mordaza."

[80] "Ninguno vio/la vieja herida/...Nadie percibe/la voz cautiva."

[81] "Dadme tiempo" "Tengo que edificar sobre las ruinas./Germinar otra vez en el desierto/...Es tremendo enterrar/aún vivos tantos muertos."

of her true, lonely word" (*Jalones entre la niebla* 327).[82] Obviously, her captive voice shows rather than hides her permanent wound as we are aware by reading "Self Portrait."[83] In this poem Sagi describes the poetic persona going through life as follows: "I have walked among all of us as a mute, distant and FOREIGN" (336).[84] The capitals are hers and the intention is to emphasize her banishment, her exile as a form of death amplified by silence. In the final sections of his *Las esquinas* Prada transcribes some of Sagi's memories. There, Sagi (through Prada) confirms how she has voluntarily muted herself: "I have voluntarily turned my voice off" (524).[85] Her yearning for peace instills her to silence herself and stop remembering.

The suppressing of her voice continued when she returned to Spain first in 1969 to publish *Laberinto de presencias* and later when she retired from the University of Illinois and decided to spend her final days in Spain. After long years abroad, Sagi comes back and finds the city from her youth inhospitable. In addition to Barcelona undergoing transformation over time, becoming a bigger metropolis, her friends and acquaintances ignored and avoided her as she was a reminder of the lost civil war to them (*Las esquinas* 347, 352). Moreover, her poetic anthology *Laberinto de presencias* was never appraised as she expected. She explains in her memories to Prada that "it was mainly surrounded by a shroud of silence, the common weapon used to entomb those who had chosen exile" (*Las esquinas* 523).[86] In addition to her poetic work being ignored by the press, the censorship body still functioning in Spain removed certain poems from it (later published in *La voz sola*). All these circumstances enhanced her isolation in Barcelona, a continuation of the exilic experience in her native land. The sentiment of being a foreigner in Spain leads her to define herself as "a perpetual exile" (*Las esquinas* 350).[87]

Her poetry in *La voz sola* also contains evidence of her disillusionment and displacement in her own land. "Return of the Exile" features a description of the people quickly abandoning the company of the exiled who just came back: "Fright. Anxiety. Terror. Run of shame …

---

[82] "El agua turbia." "el eco estrangulado/de la sola palabra verdadera."

[83] "Autorretrato."

[84] "ha pasado entre nosotros/distante muda EXTRANJERA."

[85] "apagado voluntariamente mi voz."

[86] "sobre ella cayó mayoritariamente la mortaja del silencio, que era la común arma que los enterradores empleaban para oficiar el entierro de quienes...habíamos elegido el exilio."

[87] "una perpetua desterrada."

3 A VOICE IN THE MARGINS: ANA MARÍA MARTÍNEZ SAGI'S POETRY IN EXILE   71

rivers of indifference...Cold and bitter faces" (111).[88] The fear of being associated with the exiled (a defender of the Republic) predominates among those who stayed and lived under the military regime. Their indifference hurts Sagi and she resolves to outline the contrast between people in "We Are Not You."[89] We read: "Buried alive. Eternally Banished. Walls of bloody corpses separate us and isolate us from you; you never ate dirt, blood, ashes, humiliation and tears" (113).[90] The separation between what Franco would denominate "winners and losers" is present in the title "We Are Not You." The poetic persona belongs with those who lost the war and ran for their lives out of the country. Death, blood, pain, and tears are not associated with the privileged in this poem. The marginalization she feels, compounded by the lack of understanding from others, is illustrated in "Bitterness:" "I keep turning around and around. Insane. Sick ... I keep turning around and around: I have arrived to my land" (119–20).[91] Such a difficult and disorienting experience is also expressed in "Sad Encounter" where tears resurface again: "Crying for my Lost Land" (135).[92] In fact, in "Hope" Sagi actually demonstrates the lack of hope, disillusionment, despair, and a tremendous disappointment after comparing her dreams of return (crafted by a deep nostalgia) with her surrounding reality: "It was hope that opened the way...Thirty years of exile: you erased our names. Thirty years of exile: you forgot our faces. We are without nation. You buried us alive...Spain stays indifferent, deaf. Hold my legs, my memories, my fists: and put me in this grave" (138–41).[93] All the hardships endured during exile could be surmounted with the hope of returning, recovering a country, a nation, a people. But the failed recognition of her being,

[88] "Retorno del exiliado." "Susto. Zozobra. Pavor./Corrida de la vergüenza./...ríos de indiferencia./...Rostros de hiel y de piedra."

[89] "No somos de los vuestros."

[90] "Sepultados en vida. Desterrados eternos./Murallas de cadáveres sangrientos nos separan/y aíslan de vosotros; los que nunca comisteis/fango, sangre, ceniza, humillación y lágrimas."

[91] "Amargura:" "Doy vueltas/y más vueltas./Enajenada./Enferma./...Doy vueltas/y más vueltas:/he llegado/a mi tierra."

[92] "Triste encuentro." "Lloro 'mi patria' perdida."

[93] "Esperanza." "Era la esperanza la que abría caminos/...Treinta años de destierro: borraron nuestros nombres./Treinta años de destierro: nuestros rostros olvidaron./Ya no tenemos patria. Nos enterrasteis vivos./...España permanece/indiferente, sorda./Sujetadme las piernas, la memoria, los puños:/y echadme en esta fosa."

72   J. SÁNCHEZ

the lack of affirmation for her poetic voice, and the indifference conveyed by her fellow Spaniards breaks her hopeful dream and deepens her exilic experience. Facing this new exile at home, Sagi calls for her symbolic burial and embraces her silence.[94]

Conclusion

Sagi's promising political and lyric voice in the early 1930s is uprooted by a forced exile after the end of the civil war in Spain. Her border crossing and the beginning of her life in transit never become a liberating process. Contrarily, the advent of Franco's authoritarian, conservative, military regime triggers traumatic consequences for Sagi. The termination of the Republic, the abolishing of its democratic institutions and of its nascent liberal culture, affects Sagi's life deeply. Her endeavors as an athlete and her professional life as a journalist end abruptly. Similarly, her role as a poet and her development as an intellectual in her own country are forever altered. Although she continues writing in exile, her poetic work appears impregnated with a profound nostalgia of her native land. Her *estampas*, her descriptive poetics with emotional overtones, suggest a desire to merge with her own written images as a method to shortening the distance between here (France, the United States) and there (Spain). Yet, these efforts appear futile in the long run. The sense of marginality and displacement remain pervasive during her exilic experience thereby producing a serious depression of her self. Frustrated, Sagi complains about the lack of justice from a deaf and mute God in her poems and doing so she questions Christian values. Furthermore, her liminal situation, geographical as well as existential, as expressed in "Vertical Death" for example, leads her to define herself as a perpetual foreigner, a wanderer, another outcast joining the diaspora of the dispossessed. When she briefly returns to Spain in 1969 to publish *Laberinto de presencias*, her anthology is mainly ignored by the literary press and slightly censored. Still under the Franco dictatorship, her voice continues to be repressed because of her political views before expatriation. In fact, she continues to be ostracized not only by government entities but also by older friends and acquaintances in Barcelona after her

---

[94] Please see essay "Laberinto de presencias: *Las esquinas del aire. En busca de Ana María Martínez Sagi*" for a detailed explanation of why Sagi decides to let Prada tell her story and publish her work. Briefly, it is one of her last efforts to avoid literary anonymity and oblivion.

final return in the late 1970s. Her heart's desire for a renewed sense of belonging is never fulfilled. Consequently, her feelings of isolation and of being a stranger prevail in her own country and during her final years. Driven by resentment and by a deep, constant feeling of emptiness, she decides to stop writing, bury her voice, try to forget, and attain peace. This self-imposed silence, another form of exile, dims her voice till Juan Manuel de Prada publishes *Las esquinas del aire. En busca de Ana María Martínez Sagi* in 2000 and an extensive biographical work 22 years later titled *El derecho a soñar: vida y obra de Ana María Martínez Sagi*. Even so, her poetic voice remains in the periphery within the literary world today. She is an exiled, forgotten, non-avant-garde, female poet who nonetheless deserves recognition for her emotional poetics of exile. Her artistic creation is worthy of study and of comparison to other poetic works by exiled Spanish authors under similar conditions.

Works Cited

Caballé, Anna. *El feminismo en España. La lenta conquista de un derecho.* Cátedra, 2013.

De Burgos, Carmen. *La mujer moderna y sus derechos.* Editorial Biblioteca Nueva, 2007.

De Prada, Juan Manuel. *Las esquinas del aire. En busca de Ana María Martínez Sagi.* Planeta, 2000.

———. *El derecho a soñar: vida y obra de Ana María Martínez Sagi.* Espasa, 2022.

González-Ruano, César. *Antología de poetas españoles contemporáneos en lengua castellana.* Editorial Gustavo Gil, 1946.

———. *Caras, caretas y carotas.* Imprenta Helénica, 1930.

Mangini, Shirley. *Memories of Resistance. Women's Voices from the Spanish Civil War.* Yale UP, 1995.

Martínez Sagi, Ana María. *Laberinto de presencias: Antología poética.* Gráficas Celaryn, 1969.

———. *La voz sola.* Edited by Juan Manuel de Prada, Fundación Banco Santander, 2019.

Neuschäfer, Hans-Jörg. "Entre literatura e investigación. La asombrosa carrera de Juan Manuel de Prada." *Juan Manuel de Prada: De héroes y tempestades*, edited by José Manuel López de Abiada and Augusta López Bernasocchi, Verbum, 2003, pp. 352–57.

Pardo Bazán, Emilia. *La mujer española y otros escritos.* Edited by Guadalupe Gómez-Ferrer, Ediciones Cátedra, 2018.

74 J. SÁNCHEZ

Porro Herrera, María José. "Ana María Martínez Sagi y Josefina Carabias: algunos temas recurrentes en la prensa." *Escritoras españolas en los medios de prensa 1868–1936*, edited by Carmen Servén and Ivana Rota, Editorial Renacimiento, 2013.

Said, Edward. *Reflections on Exile and Other Essays*. Harvard UP, 2000.

Sánchez, Javier. "Laberinto de presencias: *Las esquinas del aire. En busca de Ana María Martínez Sagi*." *L'Érudite franco-espagnol*, vol. 13, 2019a, pp. 39–52.

———. "Espejismos de perpetuidad: el leitmotiv de la biblioteca en *Las esquinas del aire* de Juan Manuel de Prada." *Hispanic Studies Review*, vol. 4, no. 1, 2019b, pp. 136–51.

Seidel, Michael. *Exile and the Narrative Imagination*. Yale UP, 1986.

Soler, Manuel Aznar y José Ramón López García, editores. *El exilio republicano de 1939 y la segunda generación*. Editorial Renacimiento, 2011.

Tabori, Paul. *The Anatomy of Exile. A Semantic and Historical Study*. George and Harrap, 1972.

Von Tschilschke, Christian. "Docuficción biográfica: *Las esquinas del aire* (2000), de Juan Manuel de Prada y *Soldados de Salamina* (2001), de Javier Cercas." *Docuficción. Enlaces entre ficción y no-ficción en la cultura española actual*, edited by Christian von Tschilschke and Daymar Schmelzer, Iberoamericana, 2010.

Ugarte, Michael. *Shifting Ground. Spanish Civil War Exile Literature*. Duke UP, 1989.

Varela, Nuria. *Feminismo para principiantes*. Penguin Random House, 2005.

———. *Feminismo 4.0. La cuarta ola*. Penguin Random House, 2019.

Warren, Patricia. *The Lavender Locker Room*. Delta Printing, 2006.

Woolf, Virginia. *A Room of One's Own*. Harcourt, 1929.

Zepeda, Karla. *Exile and Identity in Autobiographies of Twentieth-Century Spanish Women*. Peter Lang, 2012.

CHAPTER 4

Words in Space: The Exile Diary of Zenobia Camprubí

Leonor María Martínez Serrano

Diary Writing and Exile

Married to Juan Ramón Jiménez, one of the master voices of twentieth-century Spanish poetry, Zenobia Camprubí Aymar (1887–1956) led the life of an intellectual in perpetual transit. Since early childhood, her life was marked by travel, mobility and nomadism, particularly after she and Jiménez had to exile themselves upon the outbreak of the Spanish Civil War. When they left Spain for the New World in August 1936, hardly could they imagine they would never return to their homeland. The experience of exile was different for each of them, though. Whereas Jiménez suffered from depression and neurasthenia, Camprubí was a pragmatic, energetic woman who found herself at home in both the Old and New World, used as she was to crossing geographical, cultural and linguistic boundaries. As a child, her English-speaking grandmother and mother made sure she read the classics and received a liberal education, mostly at

---

L. M. Martínez Serrano (✉)
Department of English and German Philology, University of Córdoba, Córdoba, Spain
e-mail: leonor.martinez.serrano@uco.es

© The Author(s), under exclusive license to Springer Nature Switzerland AG 2024
R. M. Silverman, E. Sánchez-Pardo (eds.), *Nomadic New Women*, https://doi.org/10.1007/978-3-031-62482-7_4

76   L. M. MARTÍNEZ SERRANO

home and under the supervision of tutors. In due time, she would become a polyglot—Spanish, English, French, Italian and German were the languages of her voracious mind. Ever since she was a teenager, Camprubí gave ample evidence of a rare intellectual alertness: she would write stories and articles for *Saint Nicholas Magazine*, an American illustrated magazine for young readers, socialise with friends, attend conferences and exhibitions, do physical exercise outdoors and take over domestic responsibilities when her mother was away from home. The most intense writing activity would come with her young adulthood though, after her marriage to Jiménez in 1916. A tireless multifaceted and industrious intellectual in her adult life, at times cultural activist, translator and teacher, she translated many of Rabindranath Tagore's works into Spanish for the first time, became a lecturer at the University of Maryland in Washington and at the University of Puerto Rico, and gave conferences in different academic forums.

From 1936 to 1956, their exile took Camprubí and Jiménez to three different geographical locations—Cuba, the United States and Puerto Rico—where this extremely versatile woman came to terms with space and place, with the more-than-human world, suspended as she was between nostalgia for the lost homeland and a desire for reintegration within the United States. As Anna Caballé claims, it is high time we revisited the lives of Spanish women from the past, not just because it is a moral imperative to make visible their contributions to science, art and philosophy, but also because we need to be aware of the specificity of their own lives.[1] In spite of its fragmentary nature, Camprubí kept a diary for 20 years (2 March 1937–13 September 1956), writing it in English (while in Cuba) and in Spanish (during her stay in the United States).[2] Her three-volume diary remains "a unique exile document" (Acillona López 103), her most accomplished literary work, and a vivid depiction of the life of a woman who was sensitive to (inner and outer) space and to the vibrant materiality

---

[1] "We live in a moment of clear need to recover the history of women in Spain. (...) To know their difficulties, to study them as part of a very long and difficult process of emancipation, is a moral debt that we have contracted with the past" (Caballé 57).

[2] In a diary entry dated 1 February 1937, Zenobia regrets not having started keeping a diary ever since they left Spain: "On Sunday afternoons, I have started to read with real pleasure the notebook of the first diary, reviewing the past months, and regretting very much not having started on 18 July 1936, because I omitted the most interesting parts of my diary, first in Spain, then in France, the United States and Puerto Rico, because from my point of view, the most boring part began after landing in Cuba" (*Cuba* 159).

of the world. Amidst the experience of exile, writing becomes for Camprubí and Jiménez "the inner [and anchoring] "space" of their wandering lives" (Acillona López 105). As such, a diary is a genre in itself, and has its own conventions and tradition. As argued by Lejeune and Bogaert (2006), a diary is a unique work of art—singular, autonomous and unrepeatable—and so the edited and printed version of the text will not do full justice to the original manuscript. Much is lost in the editing process. A diary is a collection of the traces left by time organised into a verbal artefact where the diarist selects relevant data concerning the events of a day or period of time in their life. According to Maurice Blanchot (1959), time is the central element structuring a diary. In articulating a *sui generis* equation between measurable time, historical time and life time, the diary endows the diarist with expressive freedom. It becomes thus "the most vivid form human beings have to express the dialogue they keep with themselves" and "the untransferable space where self-awareness is born" (Caballé 60).

"I've spent the morning writing," says Camprubí in her diary time and again. She was aware that diary-keeping was not merely a ritual, but a life-giving haven. She would devote the first minutes or hours of the day to writing a new diary entry summarising the main events of the previous day, that is, "miniscule and not so minuscule things that define the vital texture of a human, the threads with which she weaves her being and makes sense of her place in the world" (Caballé 60). Life is, after all, woven of small details and gestures, and those are the ones diaries record best. The experience of exile must have enhanced Camprubí's attention skills and raised words to their utmost power, or so appear to suggest her diary pages, written on the spur of the moment, preserving something of the freshness and original impulse that brought them into being in the first place. However, Camprubí is not alone in composing a diary in her exile. As Caballé suggests, "[E]xilic life writing (…) had a feminine voice" ("Memorias" 126). There were other eminent contemporary women exiles, mostly intellectuals, who resorted to autobiographical writing in general and to diary writing in particular to make sense of this traumatic experience. Such was the case of Rosa Chacel (*Alcancía I. Ida* and *Alcancía II. Vuelta*, 1982), Silvia Mistral (*Éxodo. Diario de una refugiada española*, 1940), Victoria Kent (*Cuatro años en París. 1940–1944*, 1947) and Federica Montseny (*Seis años de vida (1939–1945)*, 1978; *Mis primeros cuarenta años*, 1987), among others. Whereas correspondence with the loved ones who had exiled themselves to other countries or who had stayed in Spain represented a kind of umbilical cord with the homeland, diary keeping must have served the purpose of creating a safe space for introspection and deep thinking.

Drawing on the luminous lessons of Karen Barad's landmark *Meeting the Universe Halfway* (2007), Jane Bennett's investigation into vibrant materialism in *Vibrant Matter* (2010) and Stacy Alaimo's notion of transcorporeality in *Bodily Natures* (2010), this chapter looks into how Camprubí responds to the more-than-human world and articulates her sensuous encounters with nonhuman materialities in the form of well-wrought prose descriptions in diary entries that convey the vitality inherent in the world. More specifically, this chapter dwells on the traces of Camprubí's response to space and place, as well as to "the active powers issuing from nonsubjects" (Bennett ix) and to matter as being not "passive stuff, [...] raw, brute, or inert" (vii), but rather as "vibrant materiality that runs alongside and inside humans" (viii), in urban and natural settings alike. Thus, our main aim is to trace the manifold ways in which Camprubí sees, hears and experiences a wide "range of the nonhuman powers circulating around and within human bodies" (ix). After all, she was a sensitive body and an alert mind actively immersed in the vital materiality of the world within and without her. Not surprisingly, given her intellectual alertness and sensitivity, her exile diaries are woven with passages of intense lyricism in which she describes a more-than-human world that serves a therapeutic purpose. Thus, she indulges in "moments of sensuous enchantment with the everyday world—[not only] with nature but also with commodities and other cultural products" (xi). Closely following Alaimo's conceptualisation of "human corporeality as trans-corporeality, in which the human is always intermeshed with the more-than-human world" (2), this chapter focuses on the interconnections and transits between one particular human body (Camprubí's) and nonhuman bodies—that is, natural and cultural objects, organic and inorganic bodies—as captured in her diary entries.

Contours of a Life in Transit

In her "Introducción. El *Diario* de Zenobia Camprubí," the perceptive introduction to Camprubí's three-volume exile diary, Graciela Palau de Nemes characterises this work as being "an intimate work, a monologue that betrays the author's literary skills" (*Cuba* xiii).[3] Not only is Camprubí's

---

[3] Unless otherwise noted, the English translations from the original Spanish texts are by the author of this chapter. The same applies to those diary entries originally written in English by Camprubí and rendered into Spanish by Palau de Nemes.

diary a superb example of life writing by an educated, intelligent and highly articulate woman living in exile at a crucial historical moment in the recent history of humanity, but also a precious sociological document that bears witness to the convulsive period when she happened to live. In Palau de Nemes's words, the diary became "a way to observe one's own survival" (*Cuba* xiii) on account of the traumatic experience of exile Camprubí and Jiménez had to cope with after being forced to leave Spain in August 1936. Her diary is a moving testimony about their life (and about other Spanish intellectuals' lives) as exiles in America, about Jiménez's personality, writing habits and work, and about landmark historical events, including the Spanish Civil War and World War II. Ultimately, Camprubí's diary became "a tool for survival" whereby she tried to "find again the sense of life lost on account of the trauma of the Spanish Civil War. The eloquence, scope and sincerity of her conversation with her own self make the *Diary* a literary text" (Palau de Nemes, *Cuba* xiii).

The author, narrator and protagonist of her diary, Camprubí is a strong, pragmatic and resilient woman who wins the small battles of everyday life and ensures a comfortable material life for both herself and Jiménez throughout their odyssey in Cuba, the United States and Puerto Rico. She started writing her diary in La Habana, on 2 March 1937, which happened to be her 21st wedding anniversary, and kept it until 5–13 September 1956, while hospitalised at the Massachusetts General Hospital of Boston, where she expected surgery to save her life from the uterus cancer that eventually caused her death in Puerto Rico on 28 October 1956. The original text consists of 18 handwritten notebooks and agendas dated on the first page. One of the most fascinating characteristics of the diary is its bilingual nature, written half in English, half in Spanish. As Palau de Nemes (*Cuba* xiv) observes, from 2 March 1937 to 8–9 December 1945, Camprubí writes in English. After a three-year lapse, she resumes her diary keeping on 8 July 1948 and writes in Spanish until shortly before her death, except for a few pages dating back to the 1950s and the last five pages of the 1956 diary, written in English. It is no coincidence that Camprubí should have written her diary in English while residing in a Spanish-speaking country and in Spanish while residing in an English-speaking country. Her goal must have been not only to "ensure their private and personal nature" (Palau de Nemes, *Cuba* xiv), but also to protect them as a space for self-writing and catharsis. If life was a nonstop flux of events, experiences and stimuli coming from all directions, then her diary gave her the chance to verbalise and keep a record of all that mattered to

80 L. M. MARTÍNEZ SERRANO

her—that is, her daily activities, the intensity of her social life, her travels, her readings habits, her constant letter writing, her unwavering support to Jiménez's creative enterprise as his personal secretary, her deepest concerns, aspirations and dreams. In sum, the diary shows a woman responding to life with the maximum of intensity, absorbing every atom and every gift life presented to her along the way despite the provisional and at times precarious existence they led, constantly on the move, from one place to another, trying hard to make ends meet owing to their perpetual financial insecurity.

Camprubí's bilingualism allowed her to keep a diary in both languages, and to do so in elegantly crafted Spanish and English. On her mother's side, Camprubí came from a wealthy bilingual Puerto Rican family. As a child, her grandmother, Zenobia Lucca, was sent to Linden Hall, in Bordentown (New Jersey), by her parents so that she could receive an education in English. Though she could not understand a word of English when she arrived at Linden Hall, she would master the language in almost no time. Zenobia Lucca married Augustus Aymar, a member of a wealthy American family of merchants from New York. Their children (including Isabel Aymar Lucca, i.e., Camprubí's mother) were raised in a bilingual home and spoke English and Spanish since early childhood. Isabel Aymar married the Spanish engineer Raimundo Camprubí in Puerto Rico and then they moved to Barcelona, where the family settled. They had four children: their eldest child was born in Puerto Rico, and subsequent children, including Zenobia, were born in Catalonia. Camprubí was born in Malgrat on 31 August 1887 and was educated at home by her mother, grandmother and tutors, whereas her three brothers were sent to colleges and universities in the United States. (In fact, Camprubí travelled to the United States for the first time at nine, with her mother and eldest brother, who was about to start a degree at Harvard.) Yet Camprubí's mother and grandmother took great care to provide her with a well-rounded education. They taught her languages, especially English, and gave her opportunities to practise it by subscribing her to the children's publication *St. Nicholas Illustrated Magazine for Boys and Girls* and finding her a friend, María Muntadas, from a distinguished family of Catalonian engineers, who could speak perfect English under the supervision of a native tutoress (Palau de Nemes, *Cuba* xvii). At the age of 14, Camprubí was already fluent in English. From 1902 to 1904, the New York *St. Nicholas Magazine* published some of her stories and autobiographical writings in English that testify to her excellent writing skills: "A Narrow Scape" (1902), "The

Garret I Have Known" (1903), "A Dog Hero" (1904) and "When Grandmother Went to School" (1904). In the same period, Camprubí also wrote impeccable Spanish, as betrayed by the autobiographical text "Malgrat," on memories associated with her birthplace, a town on the Costa Brava close to Barcelona.

In 1904, a 17-year-old Camprubí travelled to the United States with her mother and youngest brother (her eldest brothers were already at university in the United States) and would not return to Spain until 1909. They settled in the state of New York, first in Newburg, on the banks of the Hudson River, in a region populated by renowned aristocratic families, including Isabel Aymar's wealthy relatives. Then, they moved to Flushing and eventually to New York City. The four years and a half (from July 1904 to March 1909) Camprubí spent in the United States had a decisive impact on her self, as she enjoyed freedom, social life and outdoor activities in the company of educated, well-off relatives and friends. As pointed out by Cortés Ibáñez, "she discovered a different way of living" (13). It was in America that Isabel Aymar urged her daughter to keep a diary and take note of her everyday activities. In her mother's opinion, "an individual's greatest responsibility was to be of use to other people" (Palau de Nemes, *Cuba* xviii). Therefore, by encouraging her daughter to keep a diary, she hoped Camprubí would realise how most of her daily time was spent on banal, useless things. As the author herself notes in her youth diary: "This diary is not a record of my thoughts and feelings. (…) [T]he aim (…) is simply for me to gain an awareness of how few useful things I do in a day" (*Diario de juventud* 14). Thus, her youth diary, the first she ever wrote, was "a record of her active life and barely of her inner life" (Palau de Nemes I, xviii), a feature which is also discernible in her exile diary. Though the diary genre creates a space for the self's dialogue with itself, the focus is mostly on the outer world, rather than on the inner geographies of the self. Her days are packed with social activity and her eye often turns to the world outside. However, every now and then the record of nonstop activities with which Camprubí filled her days provides a glimpse into her mind and deepest concerns.

In 1909, Camprubí, aged 21, and her mother returned to Spain to join her father, now based in Madrid, where she would spend time with members of the American colony and would come to be known as "La Americanita." In 1911, she travelled once again with her mother to the United States, where they spent a few months travelling from one place to another. The English language was an essential part of her very self and so,

82 L. M. MARTÍNEZ SERRANO

in her early adulthood, she would keep on writing in English for foreign magazines. In 1910, at 23, she wrote an article entitled "A Letter from Palos" for *St. Nicholas Magazine* while living in La Rábida (Huelva), and the article "Valencia, the City of the Dust, where Sorolla Lives and Works," on the famous Valencian painter's works, for *The Craftsman*, another New York magazine. In 1912, she wrote "Spain's Welcome to the Spring," on the Seville Fair, for *Vogue*. In 1916, *St. Nicholas Magazine* published her article "Murillo and the Usurer of Seville" (Cortés Ibáñez 18). In light of her earliest writings, Palau de Nemes (*Cuba* xvi) argues that Camprubí could write well in both English and Spanish and that most of what she wrote about was based on first-hand experiences, her family's past and the places she visited, all of which gave her inspiration to compose her own texts.

In 1913, Camprubí met Jiménez, who fell deeply in love with her. Isabel Aymar did not approve of their relationship and so she and her daughter left Madrid and travelled back to New York in 1915. Jiménez would follow Camprubí to that city, where they married on 2 March 1916. She married the poet not only because she loved him, but also because his job and personality would allow her to develop her own instincts as an active, independent woman and entrepreneur, which would probably have been impossible had her husband been less absorbed in his poetry or had he had a secure income (Palau de Nemes, *Cuba* xxx). Her diary provides evidence that she loved him deeply though, as suggested by the entry dated 26 August 1938: "J. R. can't be left alone at all. He is very dear even if he drives me crazy!" (*Cuba* 254). As Caballé notes, "perfecting her love for Juan Ramón soon became the greatest ethical project of her life" (62). After having spent their honeymoon visiting some cities in the United States, the newly married couple returned to Spain and settled in Madrid, where they lived for 20 years, until the outbreak of the Spanish Civil War on 18 July 1936.

As Palau de Nemes (*Cuba* xviii) points out, upon their arrival in New York in 1936, the new encounter with her mother's family's homeland must have revived in Camprubí the American side to her being and made her start writing a few months later her diary in English, a language which, like Spanish, was an inextricable part of her own identity. For two years (2 March 1937–28 January 1938), they lived first in Puerto Rico and then in La Habana (Cuba) in quite a precarious situation, for they had left all their possessions behind in their home in Madrid, including some of the poet's manuscripts, which would be stolen at a later point. On 29 January 1938, they settled in Miami and then they would move to Washington and Maryland, where Camprubí got a permanent teaching position as a faculty member in 1944. The fact that Camprubí wrote the second half of her diary in Spanish (from 8 July 1948 onwards), immersed in the American lifestyle in the metropolitan area of Washington, may be accounted for by psychological reasons (Palau de Nemes, *Cuba* xix). Having been expatriates for 12 years and having spent seven years in the United States (in Florida, Washington and Maryland), the Spanish language and culture were terribly missed and so "for Zenobia Spanish became once again the language of privacy" (Palau de Nemes, *Cuba* xix). Not surprisingly, the periods of most intense writing are those when Camprubí had to cope with the toughest moments of their exile—at the beginning of their sojourn in Cuba and at the end of her life in Puerto Rico. Unlike during the onset of their stay in Florida, struggling to settle there and making ends meet in 1939–1940, she barely wrote during their stay in Washington and Maryland, where they enjoyed more financial security and could afford better accommodation. After the summer of 1940 she wrote few diary entries, as they had comfortably settled in Coral Gables (Miami) and Jiménez had started collaborating with the Universities of Miami (Florida) and Duke (North Carolina) giving invited lectures to students and faculty members. By the end of 1942, they left for Washington, where the couple's professional relationship with the University of Maryland began in 1943.

As already pointed out, in 1944 Camprubí got a permanent teaching position in the Department of Foreign Languages and Literatures at the University of Maryland, which was her first remunerated job and ensured an income of $2,000 for the couple. In "Una hora de charla con Zenobia Camprubí de Jiménez," an interview with Ángela Negrón Muñoz published shortly after they arrived in Puerto Rico in 1936, Camprubí had confessed that she believed in women's self-sufficiency and self-perfection through study, perseverance and hard work. It seemed to her that not having a job made women waste their precious time.[4] Out of an acute awareness of where the family's fortune came from, Camprubí did not feel comfortable with the idea of living off the fortune amassed by her

---

[4] "She believed that women should be self-sufficient [...], she had faith in the individual improvement of women through study, struggle and work; it seemed to her that not having their own profession made them waste their days, years and lives" (Palau de Nemes, *Cuba* xxviii).

84   L. M. MARTÍNEZ SERRANO

mother's ancestors through hard work and effort.[5] One of the most noticeable aspects about Camprubí's diary is her tremendous "vital energy," her "deep predisposition for life," her "optimistic character" and "her profoundly Calvinist work ethics" (Caballé 65), "an ethics of personal improvement and effort" (Ruano Laparra 177) inculcated in her by her mother. Given her need to feel socially useful and to fill her days with fruitful actions to cultivate herself and other people, she hated spending a full day in complete indolence. She despised the Cuban weather, which she thought favoured physical and mental laziness. Since early childhood, Camprubí's mother had instilled in her a deep sense of responsibility and so, having a job at the University of Maryland may have been a source of joy and self-fulfilment for her, as shown by diary entries dating back to those years. On 25 August 1944, aged 59, she writes: "I have embarked on a professional career" (*Estados Unidos* 244),[6] and, on 6 February 1945, she adds: "I love my double life: one half at university and the other half devoted to domestic life" (*Estados Unidos* 264). Preparing and giving lectures at the University of Maryland became a most important discipline in her everyday life, gave her financial security and a sense of renewed confidence about the future.

In fact, their stay in the United States was a dream come true for Camprubí—"the achievement of one of Zenobia's dearest ambitions" (Palau de Nemes, *Cuba* xx). She felt at home in Washington and Maryland; she loved even the cold weather of Boston and the hectic lifestyle of New York (Caballé 64–65). Living now close to her brothers, settled in New York, less than five hours away by car, her position as a university lecturer was the perfect job for her, a born teacher. Her salary was complemented by her husband's collaborations with Spanish and American journals and the royalties associated with the edition of some of his books in Mexico and Buenos Aires. Their friends included educated people who were conversant with the Spanish language and culture, and she spent time with old friends, literary and artistic celebrities coming from Spain and the Americas to visit them in Washington. Camprubí takes part in a very intense social

---

[5] "She was not satisfied with living off her rents and had a fierce pride and a deep awareness of the fact that her mother's family's capital came from the work of her ancestors" (Palau de Nemes, *Cuba* xxix).

[6] Embracing "freedom of action and choice" (Ruano Laparra 178), the twin pillars of her inner life, the words of her adult life somehow echo a handful of words written decades earlier in her youth diary: "Try, in every place and action, in all external actions, to be free and lord of yourself—everything depends on you" (*Diario de juventud* 55).

4 WORDS IN SPACE: THE EXILE DIARY OF ZENOBIA CAMPRUBÍ   85

life (e.g., she attends conferences, goes to concerts and art exhibitions, and eats with friends in restaurants), while Jiménez lives a secluded life in their Riverdale home, near College Park (4310 Queensbury Road), close to the University of Maryland, surrounded by elms and singing birds that ensured the peace and quiet he needed to compose poetry.

During those years (1948–1950) of bliss and fretful activity, Camprubí writes very few diary entries. In 1948 they travelled to Buenos Aires, which turned out to be a landmark journey in their lives, as Jiménez was received as the great poet he was. However, 1950 was the beginning of a very severe depression that would take him to several hospitals in Washington. Given the poet's deteriorated health, partly aggravated by his missing the Spanish language and culture, a doctor prescribed that they should move to a Spanish-speaking country. At that point, they moved to Puerto Rico, where she would also take a teaching position at the University of the island. Between 1951 and 1953, settled in Puerto Rico, Camprubí writes very few pages, most of them dealing with the couple's precarious health. In November 1951 she is diagnosed with uterus cancer, which she considers "un contratiempo atroz" (*Puerto Rico* 19), a terrible setback, and goes through surgery at the Massachusetts General Hospital in Boston. On 2 March 1952, thinking of the limited time she has in her hands, she wonders whether it might not be a better idea to live in transit, constantly on the move, instead of settling in a fixed place waiting for death. In her original Spanish, she writes: "Tal vez lo mejor es vivir *en marcha* y no pensar en acomodarse en ningún lado esperando la muerte" (*Puerto Rico* 19; emphasis added). In 1953, a year for which there are few diary entries, her illness aggravates and she must combine her lectures at university with radiotherapy sessions. Between September 1954 and September 1956, she resumes her diary writing with great intensity until shortly before her death. Her diary becomes now much more introspective, and most of her time and energy are invested into preparing Jiménez's definitive anthology and securing his material comfort after her final journey.

A Room of One's Own

Ever since the onset of their exile in America, Camprubí's dream was to have a home of her own, a private space where she could do as she pleased. For years, the need for a home becomes "an obsessive need that fills the pages of her notebooks" (Acillona López 105). In fact, a home represents

86 L. M. MARTÍNEZ SERRANO

"the space of identity par excellence" and "'the place' in the middle of a crossroads of places not of one's own" (105); it stands for "inner space, a closed space, protection" (106). In this regard, Camprubí's diary becomes a home of sorts, "a home where she can analyse her self" (106) and spend time with her thoughts. In an early entry dated 23 August 1937, sharing a hotel room with her husband in La Habana, she dreams with having "a small, compact house where I could possibly travel light through life, without earthly attachments that may damage the peace of the final moment" (*Cuba* 85). About one year later, on 3 May 1938, fed up with living in such a cramped place with Jiménez and thinking of moving to the United States, Camprubí considers renting two rooms in the hotel where they were staying so that she could have one for herself, to do such simple things as sitting, walking, standing, reading and writing (*Cuba* 198). After moving to Miami in January 1939, she still dreams with having a private room. On 25 July 1939, she writes: "I want a room to myself to do whatever I want, throw the windows wide open, put cream on my hands when the scrubbing makes my skin hard, and move around in bed if I feel like it" (*Estados Unidos* 93). On 27 November 1939, after having spent a good portion of her life in rented rooms, she writes: "I am seriously considering sheltering in a house of my own in my old age" (*Estados Unidos* 157). Now it is not a room but a home that she wishes to acquire so that she can spend old age in a place she can call her own. Having spent a whole lifetime in transit, in rented lodgings, it was only natural for her to desire to have a place of her own—a space of warmth, comfort and protection where her spirit could flourish unimpeded.

Ten years later, in a house she and Jiménez had bought at long last, she ponders upon the rooms of her life. In an enlightening entry dated 5 August 1949 written in Riverdale, in words reminiscent of Virginia Woolf's apropos the importance of having a private space where one could thrive personally, she devotes over 13 pages (*Estados Unidos* 318–31) to describing the different rooms she has enjoyed over the course of her life in Malgrat, Barcelona, Sarriá, Tarragona, Valencia, Newburgh, Flushing, Amity St., Madrid, Cuba, Coral Gables, Washington, Riverdale and Buenos Aires (her last room was in Hato Rey, Puerto Rico.) The whole entry is a dexterous constellation of words *in* and *on* space. Space is not synonymous with place, though. Like time, space is vast, boundless and undomesticated—one of those elemental axes that frame human experience. In contrast, place has boundaries—it is clearly demarcated and closely connected with the specifics of a life. Camprubí's entry embodies

4 WORDS IN SPACE: THE EXILE DIARY OF ZENOBIA CAMPRUBÍ   87

an autobiographical meditation on life and the places where it comes into full bloom. Those places described by the diarist represent the geography of her life and her untiring struggle with the financial difficulties and economic precarity that marked her existence during her exile.

Camprubí's first room in Malgrat was a room that looked onto a big garden surrounding a huge colonial house where she was born and which her parents would then rent for their summer holidays. The author associates this room with "the immense serene security of [her] mother's large hospital bed" (*Estados Unidos* 319) and the warmth of her childhood paradise. In Barcelona, Camprubí shared her room with her grandmother, Zenobia Lucca; her small bed was placed next to hers. It was a sun-infused room that looked onto the Paseo de Gracia in Barcelona and that the little girl enjoyed immensely. The adult Camprubí reminisces about how "the room was filled with infinite colours that, if there was a breeze, moved softly along the walls and ceiling, reflected by the crystal prisms of the chandeliers" (*Estados Unidos* 320). In intensely lyrical prose, Camprubí records with great precision the effects of sunlight on the walls and ceiling of the room, which is indicative of her keen eye for chromatism and the vitality running through the objects populating the domestic world. A most special bond united Camprubí and her grandmother, who installed the girl's first library in their shared room and would read Homer's *Iliad* and the *Odyssey* aloud to acquaint her with the Greek myths and the Olympian gods even before her eighth birthday (*Estados Unidos* 320–1). In her second room, Camprubí also had her first experience of death. The last time she got to see her grandmother, she was "lying very serene and calm on her large bed, but she did not open her eyes or speak, and on the sides of the bed there were large lighted candles" (*Estados Unidos* 321). Sunlight was replaced this time with lighted candles and one of the two women central to her life had inexplicably vanished forever.

Aged 9 to 12, Camprubí enjoyed a small room of her own in the family's home in Sarriá that looked onto a smaller beautiful garden. It was adjacent to another room for the girl's use alone where she would take piano lessons. In this room she gains an awareness of her sense of responsibility and independence for the first time in her life. As Epi, her youngest brother, suffered from diphtheria and her mother had to isolate herself with her son, she had to be in charge of home management, making decisions concerning their cook, the two servants and the domestic budget (*Estados Unidos* 322). Then, the family would move to Tarragona, where his father had been transferred to a new position. From her beautiful

88   L. M. MARTÍNEZ SERRANO

bedroom, Camprubí could see the sea far away in the distance: "The night lights of the harbour filled me with nostalgia" (*Estados Unidos* 323), she writes in words expressive of her alertness to nuances of the outer world and their impact on her states of mind. Later on, they moved to Valencia, as her father was transferred to that city. Camprubí barely remembers her fifth room, which she must have shared with her mother. To her mind, the two years she spent in Valencia were years of utter *ennui*: she felt annoyed, sad, weird (*Estados Unidos* 324). She remembers her music, French, Italian, History and Literature lessons with private tutors and with her own mother, as well as daily one-hour walks outdoors with her father to keep fit. As Yolanda Ruano Laparra observes, in late nineteenth-century Spain it was not common at all for a girl to be able to "speak five languages, [and] have an education in literary, historical, mathematical, musical, philosophical and social matters" (174). On Sundays, she would go to mass with Bobita, the mulatto servant who had been presented to her mother as a gift when she was a kid and would become one more family member. Camprubí summarises those two years in the story of her life in eloquent words: "I didn't know a single girl my age. An inward-looking life, and for only companions, mom, Epi and books" (*Estados Unidos* 325). It seems that a nearby river she could not even see afforded her an opportunity to let her imagination fly (*Estados Unidos* 325). Interestingly, in the description of most of her rooms the natural world appears to loom somewhere in the background as a subtle, barely audible or visible, yet powerful presence. At any rate, Camprubí is aware of the vitality of the more-than-human world and senses that she is a tiny thread in the vaster scheme of things.

In Newburgh, Camprubí shared the sixth room of her life with her mother. There was a world of a difference between this and her previous rooms in Spain. Two big windows looking onto the Hudson River allowed her to experience a deep sense of communion with the green world: "my room was nothing more than the four temporary walls where one thinks everything outwards. The vast meadow in front of the house and the river, frozen in winter, blue in summer—that was the best thing about the room" (*Estados Unidos* 326). The ubiquitous presence of the natural world floods her rooms. Now the river is not a murmuring presence like in Valencia, and the exuberance of the meadow whose views she seems to enjoy immensely stands for everything that is not human-made. In Newburgh, 17-year-old Camprubí was taking private lessons to get ready to enter university, whereas her brother Raimundo was already taking a degree and her brother José had already finished his at Harvard and was working as an engineer in New York at the time. Shortly afterwards, Camprubí and her mother moved to Flushing, a place she simply loved. For the first time in her description of the rooms, Camprubí dwells on arboreal beings in passing. Trees are a prominent presence in her seventh room:

> Everything was clear, concise, useful and harmonious. My room was a small corner room and both white-curtained windows overlooked the trees and meadows of a quiet, modern town, full of young people who came home daily asking us to play tennis or dance. (*Estados Unidos* 326)

Her eighth room was on Amity St., in Flushing, too. The house was sad, a bit dark, located in a much less attractive neighbourhood. Her mother insisted on giving her the biggest room in the house, the one with more sunlight, though. Light is dear to Camprubí. Her diary provides ample evidence that she was alert to daylight and the way it enhanced the texture of objects across its journeying on the surface of the world. In 1909, Camprubí and her mother moved first to New York and then back to Spain, to join her father, "whom at no time in my life do I remember loving" (*Estados Unidos* 327), she writes in sharp words. Back in Spain, the young lady settled with her parents in Madrid, where they lived in a house on the Paseo de la Castellana, a distinguished neighbourhood in the city centre. Her ninth room afforded her a view of the Castellana and "a nightingale sang in the garden" (*Estados Unidos* 328) opposite their house. Once again, the natural world enters her room unannounced in the form of a singing nightingale in a nearby garden. She missed her brothers, who had stayed behind in America, and the lifestyle marked by freedom and outdoor activities she had enjoyed in Newburgh and Flushing for four years. Her most rewarding moments were now the ones she spent with her mother travelling to "the ancient cities of Spain" (*Estados Unidos* 328), interested as she was in the history and monumental architecture of the country. She kept herself busy, writing, reading, attending courses and conferences, going to art exhibitions and concerts, but she was afraid she might meet someone and get married, which would prevent her from going back to America (*Estados Unidos* 328).

Camprubí's tenth room, on Conde de Aranda Street in Madrid, was her first room as a married woman. On 2 March 1916, she had married Jiménez in New York. "My next bedroom was not completely mine. I had got married and life had changed completely for me" (*Estados Unidos* 328), she writes in seemingly unemotional words. A sad bedroom with an en-suite bathroom looking onto an interior patio, it was a practical and comfortable room, though. They would soon move with her own mother to a beautiful apartment in a modern house on Velázquez Street, where she shared a bedroom with her husband: "the view from our bright bedroom overlooked the Guadarrama, sometimes snowy and sometimes blue" (*Estados Unidos* 329). This time it was a room with a view of mountains on the horizon, but the tram noise was so unbearable that they had to leave the place and move to a more spacious flat on Padilla Street, where she would have a room of her own at last: "It had a large window overlooking the city gardens at noon, but the Plaza de Salamanca could be seen in the background" (*Estados Unidos* 329). Upon the outbreak of the Spanish Civil War, they had to leave Spain in August 1936 and cross the Atlantic Ocean to settle in a hotel in La Habana, where they lived for almost two years (1937–1938): "Our hotel bedroom overlooked the blue Caribbean Sea, and from the sunset sea rose cumulus clouds set ablaze by the west that I will never forget" (*Estados Unidos* 329). The sea was an overwhelming presence in her life during their stay on the Caribbean island. A decade later, writing in Riverdale, she could still remember the beautifully sun-infused clouds floating above the sea at sunset. In fact, Camprubí's diary entries dating back to their stay in Cuba are interspersed with references to atmospheric phenomena—winds, clouds, rain, storms, thunder and so on—that show her responding to the agency of inanimate forces with great articulateness.

Camprubí's fourteenth room was in Coral Gables, Miami, where they stayed in a rented house from 29 January 1939 to 19 November 1942. It was a fully equipped modern American house, with clean, white, hospital-like bedrooms, a bathroom, a shower and an electric stove (*Estados Unidos* 330), which turned out to be very practical and comfortable for the couple. Though the house had limited views, Camprubí and Jiménez were within walking distance of the sea and would go for long walks to enjoy the neighbourhood and scenery. Afterwards, from November 1942 to May 1950, they lived in Washington. From September 1946 to February 1947, owing to Jiménez's severe depression they stayed at the beautiful Washington Sanatorium and Hospital, where her room looked onto gardens, parks, trees and distant horizons (*Estados Unidos* 330). The poet had been depressed for the summer, since the idea of being left behind alone at the beginning of a new academic year at the University of Maryland, where Camprubí was now a full-time lecturer, caused him extreme anxiety. The description of her sixteenth room, that in Riverdale, is written in terse, lyrical language:

> In Riverdale, my bedroom is a luminous corner room, with windows framed (while the trees keep their leaves on) by the leafy oaks through whose tops the sun sometimes shines in and the moon sometimes plays hide-and-seek, but it is in a house that is a puzzle. I dream with building a single large room with a fireplace and many windows that will be mine and free me from everything else. (*Estados Unidos* 330)

The last room Camprubí describes is a hotel room in Buenos Aires, where she and her husband travelled in 1948. Jiménez was welcomed as the great poet he was. On the eighth floor of the Hotel Alvear, they would enjoy "[a] view that expanded the soul day and night" (*Estados Unidos* 331), with the river looming large far away in the distance. Camprubí's retrospective description of the rooms where she lived for some period of time in her life is expressive of a nomadic existence, in perpetual transit from one place to another, between childhood, adolescence and adulthood, between singlehood and marriage, between the Old and New World. Yet reading her description of all the places she lived in, readers cannot help being under the impression that she somehow succeeded in feeling at home, if only temporarily, in all the rooms that accompanied her throughout her life. Camprubí's life-long search for a home of her own runs parallel to the construction of a private space for self-scrutiny and self-expression in her diary. The home is, in fact, a metaphor that represents the desire for stability as well as "an unconscious plurisemic symbol which betrays their castaway condition" (López Acillona 110). Writing provided her with a different kind of room, one where she could keep a record of the intensity of her daily life and, every now and then, dig deeper into her concerns and aspirations. At any rate, what makes Camprubí's description truly fascinating is how she responds to the vibrant materiality of the world around her in prose that turns out to be highly articulate and registers the small motions implicit in the flux of life. As shown in the next section, this seems to be a ubiquitous feature of the diary entries where she paints with words the landscapes surrounding her life—or rather the landscapes with which her life happens to be deeply intermeshed at specific moments in time.

Responding to a Vibrant World

Camprubí's exile diary offers massive evidence of her sensory-intellectual alertness to the overwhelming presence of the natural world, regardless of whether she happens to have her living quarters in a rural or urban setting. In many of her diary entries, she captures nuances of the more-than-human world and moments with the texture of transcendence in prose marked by intense lyricism. Painting landscapes and seascapes with dexterously chosen words, Camprubí displays a special, enhanced sensitivity to chromatism and soundscapes, to the vitality of matter. In and through her writing, she uncovers a universe populated by vibrant entities endowed with a sort of will of their own. As Barad argues, matter is "not little bits of nature, or a blank slate, surface, or site passively awaiting signification (…). Matter is not immutable or passive. Nor is it a fixed support, location, referent, or source of sustainability for discourse" (*Meeting* 151). Quite on the contrary, matter is vibrant, communicative and alive, as claimed by Bennett in her homonymous book, where she acknowledges that matter is not "passive stuff" or "raw, brute, or inert" (vii). By 'vitality' Bennett means that nonhuman bodies or things have the capacity "to act as quasi agents or forces with trajectories, propensities, or tendencies of their own" (viii). This is what she calls *thing-power*; the universe is full of entities intra-acting with each other on an unimaginable scale. *Homo sapiens* is part of that vast web or gigantic mesh of subtle interconnections.

Building on Barad's and Bennett's insights, Alaimo (2008; 2010) has posited the notion of "trans-corporeality" to emphasise the fact that the human body is porous and open to a world of material beings. Most importantly, in light of the porosity of our bodies and the permeability "between our flesh and the flesh of the world" (Tuana 188), Alaimo's core insight is that "the corporeal substance of the human is ultimately inseparable from the environment" ("Trans-corporeal" 238). As an open space, the body is exposed to and absorbs sense impressions coming from the outer world it is *a part of*, not *apart from*. Thus, the act of perception is expressive of trans-corporeality, that is, a palpable proof of the participation of our porous flesh in the larger flesh of the Earth. Because humans are literally embodied beings intra-acting with other (in)animate entities populating the world, "sensory perception is the environmental engagement of every organism at its most basic" (Sullivan 81). In her exile diary, Camprubí reveals herself to be *an embodied self* responding to the world and recording that sensuous encounter with the nonhuman with verbal clarity, simplicity and elegance.

In this regard, a close reading of Camprubí's diary shows how she stays alert to and responds to the vitality of the more-than-human world through her senses and keeps a record of her sensuous immersion in it in highly articulate language. Most of the time, the pre-eminence of sight over the remaining senses reveals her to be a sort of Emersonian "transparent eye-ball" (39) looking at the world from multiple perspectives, her self being part of a continuum of life ranging from grass, flowers and trees to the sea, clouds, sky and mountains on the horizon. At any rate, the natural world filters through the interstices of her record of her daily activities, even when these happen to be quite mundane routine actions. Her scrutinising eye registers subtle differences in the landscapes of her life as an exile in Cuba, the United States and Puerto Rico, not as a mere backdrop to her existence, but as a pervasive presence in which her everyday life is inextricably enmeshed. Thus, the diary entries written in Cuba show her responding to and capturing the exuberance of the native, Caribbean landscapes. As in her earliest articles written in English, Camprubí's prose becomes intensely lyrical in those passages where she describes the natural world. This is a description of a sunset on a Cuban beach originally written in English by Camprubí and then rendered into Spanish by Palau de Nemes:

> 11 July 1937
> On our return the clouds in the northeast had broken and the sunset glow was only visible through that gap which lighted us from such an extraordinary quarter that the world seemed made anew. The sea shellrose-tinted opened a glorious path toward the unreal light and all of a sudden made all one's child dreams true and the hope became intense that all the time of non-belief had been a waste of joy. ("Introducción," *Cuba* xix)

An assemblage of clouds, sea and light suffices to catch the diarist's full attention. To Camprubí's mind, the different parts of a house are all places from which she can observe the sea and the horizon. She looks at the beauty of the sea from her window, the house hall or the rooftop: "windows and the sea are my only solace" (*Cuba* 215), she admits. Her soul rejuvenates "when in contact with nature and the open horizons. The sea, the walks, the bay are not a "place" for her, but allow her to set herself free from the anguish that derives from a sense of physical and spiritual

94   L. M. MARTÍNEZ SERRANO

closure" (Acillona López 109), like the one she experienced sharing the small hotel room with Jiménez. The Caribbean Sea holds endless fascinations for Camprubí, who seeks hard to depict its protean nature in multiple diary entries like the following one:

> 30 August 1937
> As the sun set, the sea was pink and purple at one end like a trail of deep blue and gold, where the golden disc of the sun was hidden behind the waters. What perfect peace and harmony and the deep hope that one day we may all march with perfection towards total union. (*Cuba* 87)

The tropical weather gives Camprubí countless opportunities to experience wind, rain, storms and thunderstorms, which she transcribes into words the best way she can to convey a sense of the awe-inspiring power inherent in nature. Thus, on 2 May 1937, she writes: "It has been a long time since I last saw a thunderstorm like tonight's. Rain and lots of lightning, the fiery lightning cracking the canopy above the houses" (*Cuba* 35). And on 10 August 1938, she writes on rain again, invoking a confederation of vibrant elements in her lyrical prose: "the continuous downpour and the long, wet arcades and the rain-heavy palms and banana trees reflecting on the tiles, the fragile Japanese pines caressing the windows" (*Cuba* 245–6). Camprubí listens closely to the polyphony of the natural world and captures it through poetic prose where every single word falls exactly into place. She also has a keen eye for the observation of the flora native to the place. This is how she responds to palm trees and bamboos in an entry dated 28 May 1937: "the beautiful row of royal palms on the sides and in the centre the bridle path lined with pale green bamboos that almost touch at the top" (*Cuba* 47).

Observing nature affords Camprubí moments of joy, bliss and communion with the green world that she seeks to freeze through the medium of words before they vanish for good. On 6 August 1937, she writes: "I feel I am in intense communication with the unseen" (*Cuba* 77), acknowledging a deep connection with the invisible forces of which she feels herself to be participant. Her ecological sensibility compels her to experience the relationship between her sentient, embodied self and other nonhuman materialities more horizontally. On 12 May 1938, she feels a kind of calm happiness that she ascribes again to a deep communion with nature: "This afternoon I am content with the extraordinary joy that transcends all sadness and comes from that deep communion with nature" (*Cuba* 202). On

15 June 1938, she confesses that she wishes to make the most of "this beautiful communion with nature, which can be experienced here [in Cuba] more than anywhere else" (*Cuba* 219). As a porous, material body herself, she experiences the thrill of what it means to be literally immersed in the flesh of a vibrant world as she swims in the sea in Cuba for the first time. Thus, on 22 May 1937, she writes: "I spent the most joyful morning, immersed in air and sea. (...) [T]he wonderful sensation of water on my skin gave me an almost forgotten emotion" (*Cuba* 44). Transcorporeality is at stake in Camprubí's depiction of this sensuous experience. The sea water is perceived as a prolongation of her own body, or rather the porous membrane separating her body from the sea becomes increasingly blurry to the point of indistinction. Not long before leaving La Habana for Miami, Camprubí stumbles upon a fundamental truth that seems to capture the philosophy of her own life: "Mientras más vivo más creo en la sencillez" (*Cuba* 238), she writes on 26 July 1938. Her epiphany amounts to embracing utter simplicity, the one she experiences when in close contact with nature: "The more I live, the more I believe in simplicity." Time and again, her diary entries provide evidence of attentive encounters between the materiality of her own bodily existence and other thing-materialities, ranging from (in)animate entities in the more-than-human world (e.g., trees, breezes, birds, clouds, flowers, mountains) to artefacts, shades of light, melodies, paintings and books.

Camprubí was a widely travelled intellectual, a deeply read woman and an avid music and painting lover. Among her most precious belongings was a radio, which she and Jiménez enjoyed listening to in the solitude of their hotel room in La Habana. It gave them countless opportunities to listen to concerts and to foreign radio channels (London, Paris, Berlin, Rome) that brought them news about the Spanish Civil War and World War II. In other words, the vibrant cosmos of Camprubí and Jiménez is made of cultural artefacts that they treasure deeply. Thus, her diary displays an abundance of references to books as being a ubiquitous presence in Camprubí's life and to reading as a daily practice that was inculcated in her by her English-speaking mother and grandmother. On 19 January 1939, Camprubí and Jiménez moved to Miami. Descriptions of urban landscapes or cityscapes as such are almost non-existent in her exile diary, particularly in those entries written during her stay in the United States, mostly in Miami and Washington, but she dwells on visits to museums and art exhibitions and she somewhat captures the vibrancy of the American lifestyle. There are innumerable references to shopping centres, cafés,

96   L. M. MARTÍNEZ SERRANO

restaurants, concert halls, skyscrapers and the prototypical urban spaces of American cities. Reading her diary entries on her intense social life and commitments in America, readers are likely to experience something akin to what happens on the canvases by the well-known realist painter Edward Hopper, who immortalised cityscapes of the America of the 1930s and 1940s. In an eloquent diary entry dated 2 May 1939, having settled in Coral Gables (Miami), Camprubí—a lover of lists—makes plans about acquiring a car and a house of their own. She writes on her dreams: "a three-year plan: first year, a car; second year, a house; third year, make the house bigger" (*Estados Unidos* 55). If the home represented roots and bonds with a place, the car represented "the conquest of public and open spaces" (Acillona López 122) and gave Camprubí and Jiménez mobility opportunities and a greater sense of freedom to travel around and explore new geographies. Her diary entries feature numerous references to her visits to the MoMA and to art exhibitions, and at that point her exquisite sensibility turns to the language of an art critic or connoisseur to express her aesthetic experience. In her 24 September 1939 entry, she dwells on Picasso's blue period and harlequins, on Tintoretto's "Christ at the Sea of Galilee" and on El Greco's painting of Christ's head in the Virgin's arms (*Estados Unidos* 124–5). The language of domestic chores prevalent in previous entries gives way now to multiple references to books and readings, musicians and painters, for this is after all an intellectual's diary. They are the characters in which her domestic cosmos is written and as such they are not inert, but rather perceived as embodying thing-power.

However, even if Camprubí is deeply immersed in a literate culture—one made of music, books and art objects—and in a largely urban setting, during her stays in the United States she remains alert not just to inorganic matter, but also to the organic vitality and alphabet of nature: to clouds and sky, breeze and air, birds and trees, mountains and prairies, the sun and the moon, and the sea. She experiences the thrill of freedom in open spaces, outdoors, in touch with the green world. Listening closely to the soundscapes surrounding their rented home in Coral Gables, she is not oblivious to a bird singing nearby. On 11 May 1939, she writes: "The birds here are an extraordinary thing. I would like to know what kind of bird sings near us almost all day long with such a prolific, varied and melodious trill" (*Estados Unidos* 59). Her curiosity prompts her to wonder what bird species sings such a sweet song for them. Camprubí's mind is made of all the natural elements she attends to, including the ubiquitous sea. On 1 April 1939, she writes: "the sea is no artifice" (*Estados Unidos*

41), which is an accomplished eulogy of a powerful force of nature that seemed to be central to her life. In Miami, the sea exerts the same fascination upon her imagination it did in Cuba. Time and again, she goes for long walks and sits on a bench for hours just to absorb a rejuvenating breeze and the views of a majestic sea in solitude, as happens to be the case in an entry dated 28 May 1939: "[I] looked out over the wonderful green waters, until the sun went down and a portentous high cloud of salmon pink came up and was casting strange bright reflections on the sea, illuminating a passing ship" (*Estados Unidos* 68). No less powerfully lyrical are the descriptions of trees Camprubí crafts in her American diary. She possesses a keen eye for observing the trees native to the place (mostly fir trees and pine trees) and how they fit in the larger picture of the landscape. Painting them with words, Camprubí resorts to simple, precise language to describe their majestic existence. Because trees know best how to simply exist, they appear to offer her a temporary haven in the midst of her busy life, in summer and winter time alike. Thus, on 19 August 1939 she writes about a fine day when she and her husband walk to "a forest of fir trees, full of shadows, with the rocks and the stream in the middle. Still and bare, it was like a great open-air cathedral surrounded by greenery" (*Estados Unidos* 103). On 8 December 1939, they walk to the University of Miami after sunset and discover "a beautiful grove of dark green velvet-like trees, with different pine trees, which looked like cedars" (*Estados Unidos* 162).

After moving to Puerto Rico, Camprubí's diary becomes more reflective and introspective. On 27 December 1951, she writes alone in her room at the Massachusetts Hospital: "Por fin estoy 'sola con mis pensamientos'" (*Puerto Rico* 11), in the hope that surgery might give her some extra time. During the last years of her life, Camprubí seeks a final reconciliation with the poet and with herself in the face of impending death. Every day reveals itself to be a precious gift. Her diary becomes her true home at long last. There are still eloquent references to the green world, which remains a source of calm and solace. On 2 January 1954, she writes: "The natural beauty of this island should suffice to calm my spirit" (*Puerto Rico* 40), emphasising the therapeutic effect nature had on her body and mind. Camprubí did not finish her diary; she simply stopped writing when the moment of her final departure came and she gave herself over to silence. Paying attention was the labour of a whole lifetime, the true purpose of her life. "The simple perception of natural forms is a delight" (42), says Emerson. Camprubí taught herself the discipline of looking at and

98   L. M. MARTÍNEZ SERRANO

listening to thing-power. That was possibly what she could do best of all. The fruit of a life lived avidly and the record of her amazement at the more-than-human world with all its gifts and presences, the three-volume exile diary remains a literary monument—one that testifies to the experience of a woman who lived in transit, constantly on the move, with her eyes and ears wide open to the nakedness and vitality of matter.

CONCLUSION

Camprubí's exile diary is, on one level, the precious testimony of one extraordinary life, that of an intellectual who led a nomadic existence, in transit across cultures and tongues (her native English and Spanish plus the languages she learnt in the formative years of her early life) and different spaces, both literal (continents, countries, cities, rooms) and figurative (home vs. exile, financial security vs. precarity, past vs. present, health vs. illness). In her transit between the Old and New World, and then between one country and another, she probably ended up making uprootedness into a virtue. What seems to be out of the question is that her three-volume diary became much more than a tool for survival. Composed in English and Spanish, it became a spacious room of her own when she was forced to leave her home and exile herself after the outbreak of the Spanish Civil War in 1936, living in rented rooms with Jiménez. Most importantly, it offered her a safe space for introspection where tessellating words in the early hours of a new day became an opportunity to make sense of the events fashioning her life and identity.

However, on yet another level, the diary entries offer a view of Camprubí's attentive encounters with the materialities of nonhuman entities. Faced with landscapes of the green world, atmospheric phenomena, details of the domestic world, books and other artefacts, she comes up with accomplished descriptions that successfully communicate the vitality they seek to capture through the medium of words. Hers is an ecological mindset—one sensitive to the common substratum that brings together people-materialities and objects-materialities. Running through all (non) human bodies populating this world, she senses the presence of what Barad calls "desire" in this enlightening reflection: "Eros, desire, life forces run through everything ... (...) [F]eeling, desiring and experiencing are not singular characteristics or capacities of human consciousness. Matter feels, converses, suffers, desires, yearns and remembers" ("Interview" 59). Whether it is trees, the sea, a breeze, a stream, a mountain or the horizon, matter in its manifold manifestations reveals itself to be ultimately vibrant, communicative, expressive of something larger that transcends the self. That Camprubí responds to the physical world with the maximum of attention is revealed by the very texture of her language, by her perception of the minutest details and by how her massive diary is ultimately a moving celebration of life.

WORKS CITED

Acillona López, Mercedes. "Espacios del exilio en los *Diarios* de Zenobia Camprubí." *Revista de Escritoras Ibéricas*, vol. 3, 2015, pp. 101–31.

Alaimo, Stacy. *Bodily Natures. Science, Environment and the Material Self.* Indiana UP, 2010.

———. "Trans-corporeal Feminisms and the Ethical Space of Nature." *Material Feminisms*, edited by Stacy Alaimo and Susan Hekman, Indiana UP, 2008, pp. 237–64.

Alaimo, Stacy, and Susan Hekman, editors. *Material Feminisms*. Indiana UP, 2008.

Barad, Karen. *Meeting the Universe Halfway: Quantum Physics and the Entanglement of Matter and Meaning.* Duke UP, 2007.

———. "Interview with Karen Barad." *New Materialism: Interviews and Cartographies*, edited by Rick Dolphijn and Iris van der Tuin, Open Humanities P, 2012, pp. 48–70.

Bennett, Jane. *Vibrant Matter. A Political Ecology of Things.* Duke UP, 2010.

Blanchot, Maurice. *Le livre à venir.* Gallimard, 1959.

Caballé, Anna. "'Pasé la mañana escribiendo': el diario de Zenobia Camprubí (1937–1956)." *RILCE*, vol. 28, no. 1, 2012, pp. 57–73.

———. "Memorias y autobiografías en España (siglos XIX y XX)." *Breve historia feminista de la literatura española (en lengua española)*, vol. 5. *La literatura escrita por mujeres (del siglo XIX a la actualidad)*, edited by I. Zavala, Anthropos, 1998, pp. 111–37.

Camprubí, Zenobia. *Diario 1. Cuba (1937–1939).* Translation, introduction and notes by Graciela Palau de Nemes, Alianza Editorial/La Editorial, Universidad de Puerto Rico, 2006a.

———. *Diario 2. Estados Unidos (1939–1950).* Translation, introduction and notes by Graciela Palau de Nemes, Alianza Editorial/La Editorial, Universidad de Puerto Rico, 2006b.

———. *Diario 3. Puerto Rico (1951–1956).* Translation, introduction and notes by Graciela Palau de Nemes, Alianza Editorial/La Editorial, Universidad de Puerto Rico, 2006c.

———. *Diario de juventud. Escritos. Traducciones,* edited and introduced by Emilia Cortés Ibáñez, Fundación José Manuel Lara, 2015.

100 L. M. MARTÍNEZ SERRANO

Chacel, Rosa. *Alcancía I. Ida.* Seix Barral, 1982a.

———. *Alcancía II. Vuelta.* Seix Barral, 1982b.

Cortés Ibáñez, Emilia. "Introducción." *Diario de juventud. Escritos. Traducciones,* by Zenobia Camprubí, Fundación José Manuel Lara, 2015, pp. 9–27.

Emerson, Ralph Waldo. "Nature." *Nature and Selected Essays,* edited with an introduction by Larzer Ziff, Penguin Classics, 2003, pp. 35–82.

Kent, Victoria. *Cuatro años en París. 1940–1944.* Sur, 1947.

Lejeune, Phillipe, and Catherine Bogaert. *Le journal intime: histoire e anthologie.* Textuel, 2006.

Mistral, Silvia. *Éxodo. Diario de una refugiada española.* Minerva, 1940.

Montseny, Federica. *Seis años de vida (1939–1945).* Plaza y Janés, 1978.

———. *Mis primeros cuarenta años.* Plaza y Janés, 1987.

Palau de Nemes, Graciela. "Introducción." *Diario 1. Cuba (1937–1939),* by Zenobia Camprubí, Alianza Editorial/La Editorial, Universidad de Puerto Rico, 2006, pp. xiii–xxxvi.

Ruano Laparra, Yolanda. "Los géneros autobiográficos rescatan a las grandes eruditas de la época." *La Querella de las Mujeres en Europa e Hispanoamérica.* Vol. 2, edited by María Dolores Ramírez Almazán et al., Arcibel, 2011, pp. 173–88.

Sullivan, Heather I. "The Ecology of Colors. Goethe's Materialist Optics and Ecological Posthumanism." *Material Ecocriticism,* edited by Serenella Iovino and Serpil Opperman, Indiana UP, 2014, pp. 80–94.

Tuana, Nancy. "Viscous Porosity: Witnessing Katrina." *Material Feminisms,* edited by Stacy Alaimo and Susan Hekman, Indiana UP, 2008, pp. 188–213.

CHAPTER 5

"A Gem of Many Colors": Articulating Migration in Isabel de Palencia's *I Must Have Liberty* (1940)

Lisa Nalbone

Born in Málaga to a Spanish father and Scottish mother, Isabel Oyarzábal Smith (1878–1974) grew up in a progressive, upper-class household and would later embrace Republican ideals that in broad terms reflected her support of and sympathies toward the working class with the undercurrent of respecting humanist ideals and basic human rights.[1] The themes of liberty and justice are constants in her writing, and her loyalty to family, friend, and compatriot showed her to be an ardent defender of basic human rights. Her accomplishments rank her among the most influential women of her time in the public arena where she was active in literary and

[1] Understood broadly, humanist ideals consist of a set of principles that guide individuals to uphold tenets of respect and dignity to denounce injustices. In the context of this essay, we read humanism as explained by Edward Said: "humanism is the only, and, I would go as far as saying, the final, resistance we have against the inhuman practices and injustices that disfigure human history" (xii–xiii).

L. Nalbone (✉)
University of Central Florida, Orlando, FL, USA
e-mail: lisa.nalbone@ucf.edu

© The Author(s), under exclusive license to Springer Nature Switzerland AG 2024
R. M. Silverman, E. Sánchez-Pardo (eds.), *Nomadic New Women*, https://doi.org/10.1007/978-3-031-62482-7_5

101

102   L. NALBONE

political endeavors alongside such prominent figures as Carmen de Burgos (1867–1932), Clara Campoamor (1888–1972), Victoria Kent (1898–1987), María Lejárraga (1874–1984), and Margarita Nelken (1896–1968).

Palencia's socioeconomic privilege, including her multilingual upbringing, positioned her within elite intellectual, cultural, and political circles in Spain and, later, abroad. Her political engagement and social activism began with her journalistic writing in 1907 as an international correspondent for London's *Laffan News Bureau* and also *The Standard*. That year she also founded and edited the *La Dama y La Vida Ilustrada* (1907–1911), a periodical publication of 38 issues that conveys a sense of burgeoning feminist ideals.[2] She discusses this time of her life as one of an intellectual awakening (81–82) that set the course for her future, public-facing role in politics. Her writing and activism continued throughout the remainder of her life.

Palencia's activism took root in the latter decades of Spain's Silver Age, a period coinciding with the turn of the nineteenth to the twentieth century, marred by political turmoil and social class conflict in the face of the country's transition to modernity. Her efforts spanned marginalized sectors as well as international geographies. Throughout the 1910s, 1920s, and early 1930s, she actively promoted women's rights in the workplace and advocated for women's suffrage, speaking frequently in the Ateneo de Madrid. She joined associations and organizations that advocated for gender equality. One the earliest displays of her commitment to social justice was her membership in 1918 with the Asociación Nacional de Mujeres de España, holding the elected role as vice president. She advocated for workers' rights, especially those of women and children following the miners' strikes in Asturias in 1936 (Lizarraga Vizcarra 52), efforts she had begun earlier in that decade through her involvement with the Partido Socialista

---

[2] For Paz Torres, the publication served a dual purpose: "Behind the descriptions of social reality there exists a revealing intrahistory of events, occurrences, and news with the author's marked awareness of gender. Social criticism is present, and beneath that, the discovery of a moral and social feminine innocence and an encounter with a brutal reality" ("Detrás de las descripciones de la realidad social, existe la intrahistoria reveladora de sucesos, acontecimientos y noticias con una marcada conciencia de género por parte de la autora. La crítica social está presente y, por debajo de ella, el descubrimiento de la inocencia moral y social femenina, y el encuentro con una realidad bruta") (113).

5 "A GEM OF MANY COLORS": ARTICULATING MIGRATION IN ISABEL DE... 103

and the Unión General de Trabajadores as well as her participation in the Spanish delegation at the Conferencia Internacional del Trabajo de la Sociedad de Naciones (1931). Palencia advocated for better working conditions for women, including pregnant women, and for the prohibition of child labor (Eiroa San Francisco, "Una vision"). Her humanitarian work also included her participation in the Slavery Commission of the League of Nations, in support of its mission to ensure "the complete suppression" and "securing the abolition of slavery and the slave trade" a declaration signed in Geneva in 1926 (United Nations Human Rights). In addition, the ideological underpinnings of justice and liberty also surface in her participation in 1934 in the Comité Nacional de Mujeres contra la Guerra y el Fascismo. Further, one of the pillars of Palencia's writing, including her journalistic, fiction, and non-fiction pieces, was her advocacy of literacy as a vehicle of empowerment.

Her indefatigable commitment to working for the causes of liberty and justice was the cornerstone of her numerous speeches, writings, and radio addresses to promote the missions of groups such as the Círculo de la Unión Mercantil, Centro de Hijos de Madrid, Agrupación Femenina de Acción Republicana, and Asociación Femenina de Educación Cívica, including national and international conferences, for example, those at the Casa del Pueblo (Madrid), the Sociedad Abolicionista, and at the Conferencia sobre el Desarme (Geneva). These examples of Palencia's endeavors reveal a deeply committed activist who crossed political borders to advocate for socially marginalized populations.

In 1909, she married Ceferino Palencia (1882–1963), writer, artist, and political figure, and with him had two children: Ceferino (Cefito) (1910–1990) and María Isabel (Marissa) (1914–1977). Her autobiographical writing constitutes an inextricable link between family happenings and her professional work, especially following the outbreak of the Spanish Civil War that pulled her family apart for most of its duration. Palencia writes through the lens of femininity as wife, mother, grandmother, and sister to elucidate her experiences of joyous union and woeful separation as she lives in Sweden during the devastation in her country conflicted by civil war.

Uprooted from her homeland in the aftermath of the Spanish Civil War, Oyarzábal Smith—writer, political activist, journalist, diplomat—became one of the many who represented the Spanish Republican

104   L. NALBONE

diaspora in the Americas. Also known as Isabel de Palencia, her most popular works of fiction were her two novels, *El sembrador sembró su semilla* (1923) and *En mi hambre mando yo* (1959) and a collection of nine short plays titled *Diálogos con el dolor* (1944). She contributed to newspapers both within and outside of Spain, notably in *El Heraldo de Madrid* and the *Daily Herald* in London before the Civil War and a multitude of political periodicals during and after the war.

She published an autobiography and a memoir under the name of Isabel de Palencia, written in English with the purpose of drawing attention to key events in her life with nuanced representations of the political climate of her native Spain that focus primarily on the pre-Civil War and war period, the first of which is *I Must Have Liberty* (1940). Then, with a focus on the first five years of her life in exile in Mexico, she published *Smouldering Freedom* (1945).[3] *I Must Have Liberty*, one of Palencia's most enduring works, is a vivid autobiographical account that traces the significant happenings in her life to the time of publication that coincided with the conclusion of the Spanish Civil War and the migration of 20,000 Spaniards away from their war-ravaged country to avoid death or persecution. Her clamoring for freedom echoes throughout *I Must Have Liberty*, most saliently epitomized in her comments relating to the end of 1930 at a time when Miguel Primo de Rivera's dictatorship had transitioned to the leadership of Dámaso Berenguer: "I could not ignore the call for freedom nor forget the hardships that I had seen the people endure. Neither could I submit to the indignity of being ruled by an irresponsible and arbitrary power. Life without liberty was not worth living. All Spain was awakening to that fact. It was our duty to help her" (189–90).

This essay provides context to Palencia's life begun in exile in April 1939 when she moved to Mexico, by identifying her post in the Spanish Legation (embassy) in Sweden as the turning point of migration out of Spain three months after the outbreak of the Civil War, in October 1936. In this intermediate period, she was forced to reconcile that returning to Spain during the war was dangerous, even life-threatening, so that by the time the political climate became untenable toward the conclusion of the war, her only thoughts were trained on where to begin a life outside of

---

[3] Pilar Nieva-de la Paz undertakes a study of Palencia's professional life in exile in Mexico as relayed in *Smouldering Freedom* as a way to vindicate the accomplishments of exiled Spanish intellectuals, writers, and artists ("Isabel Oyarzábal Smith, una republicana exiliada en México" 121).

Spain rather than if she should return to her home country. I posit that her diplomatic posts and the travel associated with her ambassadorship that placed her on the international stage contributed to her gradual displacement from Spain, an uprooting culminating with the definitive rupture from her homeland as she began a life of exile in Mexico, never to return to Spain after she left Sweden in 1939. While her diplomatic post evinced her willingness to work with full support of Republican Spain's leadership, political imperatives imposed her status of exile that marked her alterity in the totalitarian structure of governance emerging during—and then taking hold after—the Spanish Civil War. In this way, Tisha M. Rajendra's interpretation of migration systems theory may be applied to elucidate the "social, political, historical and economic context" surrounding Palencia's experiences (363). This multifaceted perspective roughly intersects with Josebe Martínez's estimation of Palencia's autobiography as "written in exile by one of the vanquished, a woman, and in a foreign language" (131),[4] as Palencia navigated her circumstances intent on informing her English-speaking audience of the legitimacy of Spain's second Republic and the injustices her country suffered both due to the war and to the international reaction that jeopardized the Republic's chances for victory. For her convictions, Palencia "chose" to live in exile rather than remain in peril under dictatorial Spain's totalitarian rule.

In order to elucidate the trajectory in Palencia's life, his essay traces the period in Palencia's life from the beginning of her professional career as a journalist in 1907 through her departure from Stockholm where she was serving as Ambassador of Spain and concludes with her arrival and taking up residence in Mexico City in 1939. From the standpoint of social privilege, she narrates a journey of international border crossings preceding her migration, during a period that runs parallel to world events most geographically proximal to the European continent. Through the clamorous title in English, she articulates her experience of disjunction and fusion, through the ephemeral liminality of her passages by land, air, and sea to the tangible geographies that span about a dozen countries. This study echoes Pilar Nieva-de la Paz's assertion that Palencia "should be recognized as one of the female pioneers from Spain who offered the legacy of her personal testimony of Spanish history during the first half of the 20th century and of the protagonism that women had in historical milestones"

---

[4] "escrita en el exilio por uno de los vencidos, una mujer, y en una lengua extranjera" (131).

106   L. NALBONE

("Isabel Oyarzábal" 121).[5] For Shirley Mangini, Palencia is in the company of fellow generationally grouped compatriots Concha Méndez (1898–1986), Federica Montseny (1905–1994), María Teresa León (1903–1988), María Zambrano (1904–1991), and the above-mentioned Victoria Kent, all of whom wrote: "women-woven texts, fused together to form a historical quilt" (56). Indeed, Palencia's writing is imbued with signifiers construed by gender that serve as a reminder of her most prominent roles outside her professional career as wife and mother. As such, by examining Palencia's work, life, and accomplishments not only in Spain but in the international arena, this analysis contributes to "combatting the silence imposed by the victors of the Civil War" (Paz Torres, 396).[6]

Before tracing Palencia's trajectory of migration, a clarification of terms that characterize her life and work abroad aids in the discussion. When referring to her diplomatic efforts while serving as a Plenipotentiary Minister for Spanish Legation in Stockholm, Sweden, I view Palencia as an expatriate, through historian Justin M. Jacobs's succinct definition of the term as "someone who resides outside the borders of their country of citizenship but retains cultural, social, economic, and sometimes political ties to their homeland" (69). Expatriation, further, implies a temporal construct, in that living and working outside one's home country is intended as temporary, rather than permanent. This label aptly pertains to Palencia's experience as living and working in Stockholm from 1936 to 1939 as she evinces her close connection with Spain through constant concern for the well-being of her family members who still live in her home country, with the objective of returning home. She displays this close connection also

---

[5] "Debe ser reconocida como una de las pioneras españolas en ofrecer el legado de su testimonio personal de la historia española de la primera mitad del siglo XX y del protagonismo que las mujeres tuvieron en hitos históricos" (121). Furthermore, Raquel Conde Peñalosa signals the need for further study on writing by women in exile, identifying a gap in scholarship on works published outside of Spain or influenced by the exile experience. Notable exiled authors Conde Peñalosa places in this group include, in addition to Isabel de Palencia and Carlota O'Neill, Rosa Chacel, Maria Teresa León, María Zambrano, María Rosa Alonso, Cecilia De Guilarte, Felisa García Rata, María Dolores Boixadós, Luisa Carnés, Aurora Betrana, Concha Castroviejo, and Carmen Mieza (153). Several foundational sources on this topic are Joaquin de Entrambasaguas's "Las novelistas actuales," Josebe Martínez's *Exiliadas: escritoras, guerra civil y memoria*, Paul Tabori's *Anatomy of Exile*, and Paul Ilie's *Literatura y exilio interior: escritores y sociedad en la España franquista*. Publications by Grupo de Estudios del Exilio Literario (GEXEL), beginning with the proceedings of their first conference in 1995 published in 1998 under the editorship of Manuel Aznar Soler titled *El exilio literario español de 1939*.

[6] "...combatir el silencio impuesto por los vencedores de la Guerra civil" (Paz Torres 396).

5 "A GEM OF MANY COLORS": ARTICULATING MIGRATION IN ISABEL DE...

through careful consideration of her county's wartime news items as well as regular contact with friends and acquaintances who were committed to the Republican cause. During this almost three-year period, she maintained her ties with Spain through her diplomatic as well as her culturally and politically engaged speeches and periodical publications on behalf of the democratically elected Spanish Second Republic.[7] She at times refers to her experience or status as a refugee in the political sense, but I move away from the term refugee in the context of an economic immigrant to characterize Palencia's life in Mexico because its implicit nexus with economic struggles and insecurities does not apply in sustainable measure to Palencia's experience of displacement; as she portrayed it, her displacement did not entail significant financial hardships.[8] Further, the term *asilada política* (individual in political asylum) appears on her emigration documents (Paz Torres, 342)[9] although Palencia does not use this term to describe her circumstances. The term exile, however, not only refers to an individual. In the context of the Spanish Civil War, Mary S. Vásquez considers that exile, "with its etymological weight of banishment, is a severing, and even if voluntary, even if sought, carries the connotation of an impetus of some urgency that propels one away, not toward" (14). Further, exile, the experience Sebastiaan Faber characterizes as one of "expulsion and exclusion" (15), constitutes an event, one of displacement—as applied to Spanish exile to refer to the migratory movement of Spaniards away from their homeland as a result of the Civil War. The term exile also describes, in the sense that Edward Said explains, those who are displaced as a result of belonging to a minority population (258).[10]

---

[7] Palencia worked tirelessly to support the Republican cause throughout much of Europe and especially in the Nordic countries when she served as Spain's ambassador to Sweden. In 1937 she organized in Oslo the "Semana de ayuda a España." She contributed to left-leaning periodicals in Sweden directed toward women and working rights such as *Arbetarkvinnornas Tidning* and *Morgonbris* in defense of her ideals cultivated in and linked to Spain.

[8] Nor does Palencia portray herself as the victim of a humanitarian crisis—"hungry, desperate and ragged in appearance" as often seen in publicity campaigns of charitable organizations (Rickett 18).

[9] Paz Torres undertakes an exhaustive study of Palencia's personal archive held in the Arxiu Nacional de Catalunya, which includes in part tracing the trajectory of her writing both fiction and non-fiction, her speeches, personal correspondence, and travel records. This biographer sheds light on Palencia's life events by recovering these archival contents in the ANC that have been forgotten and collecting dust (396), which in 2015 were only just beginning to be inventoried and catalogued.

[10] For Rickett, the term exile "evokes particular psychological traits—a lack of belonging, alienation, frustration" (18).

108   L. NALBONE

In the context of Palencia's experience, the minority population was defined ideologically as belonging to those vanquished as a result of the Civil War. Downtrodden and persecuted, facing loss of life, they felt the immediacy to leave Spain. Following Myron Weiner's concept of migration theory, his five-part classification of entry rules as pertinent to Palencia's experience point to the category of the "selective entry rule" (444), since the government of President Lázaro Cárdenas opened his country's borders to Spanish exiles without limitation. Implicit in the departure from her home country via Sweden was the difficulty she would have encountered had she tried to leave directly from Spain, difficulties her husband, son, and several members of her extended family experienced, which in the context of Weiner's exit rules falls under the classification of the "prohibition exit rule" (444), as the newly formed government in Spain consolidated under Franco effectively shut down international borders.[11] Further, "totalitarian states do not grant their citizens [the right to leave], since the mechanisms of political control that characterize totalitarian states would be eroded were such a right granted" (Weiner 445). For instance, with the complicity of the French government, those caught crossing the border to France were almost exclusively and immediately held in concentration camps.[12]

Ahead of her exile to Mexico, Palencia's travels throughout Europe and North America served as an intermediary experience to her time away from Spain, markedly different from her postwar life because these travels, sanctioned by Republican leadership, positioned her in the midst of diplomatic circles that emblematized a deep connection with her home country. Moreover, she accepted the terms of this travel, whether short or long term, on behalf of her democratically elected government, to promote the Republican ideals it represented. Two of her early trips were crucial to fostering awareness of and gaining support for the Republican cause. In October 1936, she addressed British Parliament in Edinburgh, in her mother's native Scotland, to advocate not only for the reversal of the Non-Intervention Pact but to inform her European compatriots of the deleterious effects of non-intervention in democratic Spain. Palencia vehemently criticized the pact, entered into by France and England, for its banning of

---

[11] The five entry rules include unrestricted, promotional, selective, unwanted, and prohibition (444), while the five exit rules include prohibition, selective, permissive, promotional, and expulsion (444–45).

[12] For a summary of the migration waves of Spaniards to Portugal, see Ángel Rodríguez Gallardo.

these countries to support the legitimately elected Spanish Republic by providing arms and other war materials to the Republican forces. The pact could be considered an implicit endorsement of the German and Italian support that the Nationalist troops were receiving. One of her most famous remarks shows just how practical yet charismatic she was about advocating for change at an international level: "You had the excuse that you did not know before but '*ye ken noo*'" (*I Must* 247). She employs the popular phrase as a display of linguistic solidarity with her audience of Labour Party members and as a way to emphasize that ignorance of the ramifications of non-intervention could not be an excuse for upholding its enforcement. Although the pact remained in effect for almost the entirety of the Civil War, Palencia's criticism of it stands out as a hallmark of her tireless efforts on the international stage to seek justice for her home country.

Palencia stood firmly on the grounds of supporting the Republican cause in the months between her speech in Edinburgh and beginning her diplomatic assignment in Sweden. Palencia's geographic separation from Spain continued between October and December 1936 in the context of her trip to Canada and United States. Visiting such cities as Toronto, Quebec (McGill University), New York (Madison Square Garden), Edmonton, Vancouver, Seattle, Portland, San Francisco, Denver, Tampa, St. Louis, Chicago, Boston, and Washington, D.C. (White House) (250–58), she raised over $200,000 to support her country's officially elected government (260). After her 53-day tour where she spoke in 42 cities, she sailed to France and then immediately took up her diplomatic post as Plenipotentiary Minister (in essence, ambassador) for Spain in Sweden with no time to see her family in Madrid as she had intended. A small consolation was that she was able to see her two sisters in their convent in Liege, where she quickly came to understand that the elder of the two, in her eighth year of the sisterhood, condemned the Republican government, while the other who had just recently entered the convent had a better understanding of recent Spanish polity and was more sympathetic to the Republican cause. The visit with her sisters is yet another example of displacement that marks Palencia's life defined by separation rather than union with her family.

Nieva-de la Paz explains that Palencia is attuned to the notion of conceiving feminist ideals in the context of the normative roles of mother and wife. These roles exist in tandem with women's social undertakings and thus her writing endeavors "to encourage her contemporaries to put their 'maternal' qualities in the service of advocating for justice and peace, while

110   L. NALBONE

at the same time understanding that the responsibilities of caring for their children implies taking on the role of properly educating them" ("Cambios y permanencias" 45).[13]

Throughout *I Must Have Liberty*, Palencia exhibits an awareness of holding the roles of wife, mother, aunt, grandmother, sister, and friend to other women.[14] These roles exist not in conflict with masculinity but serve as a reminder that she took very seriously her responsibility toward others, specifically in terms of caretaking. Interactions she describes relating to her two children, Cefito and Marissa, are imbued with a deep sense of concern and worry, whether they are ill or in harm's way. While she exhibits concern for both children's well-being, she references most often her daughter, who was a frequent companion on her travels and life abroad. One memorable event in particular conveys the danger of travel throughout Europe during the Civil War. In transit with her daughter Marissa from Amsterdam to Copenhagen, she insisted on traveling directly between the cities by air to avoid the dangers of land passage through Germany where she would surely be "sent back to Franco. Several Spaniards had suffered that fate and, of course, it meant death" (262). She deliberately boarded a scheduled non-stop flight and was horrified when the plane made an unexpected mid-flight landing in a German airfield decorated with planes and a station house all bearing swastikas (263). Once the only other passengers—a small group of young, uniformed pilots—deplaned, she instructed her daughter to deny their relationship should they be questioned by the German police, for fear of worsening the outcome if the plane were to be inspected. The moments were fraught with a danger that intensified when Palencia revealed she was also carrying numerous politically sensitive documents that would have been impossible to make disappear.

Another narrative articulation of Palencia's separation from Spain appears in the context of the 1937 Christmas season when Ceferino visited

---

[13] Her writing endeavors "empujar a sus contemporáneas a que pongan sus cualidades 'maternales' al servicio de la lucha por la justicia y la paz, al tiempo que deben cobrar conciencia de que los deberes del cuidado a los hijos implican asumir la responsabilidad de su correcta educación" ("Cambios" 45). Nieva-de la Paz further elaborates that Palencia's posture aligns with an anthropological approach that does not consider the reality of working-class women who do not have the financial means or social freedoms to raise children on their own ("Cambios" 46).

[14] Palencia established meaningful friendships with other women who also held diplomatic posts in Sweden, most notably, with Russian diplomat and revolutionary Alexandra Kollontay (1872–1952) and Swedish politician and women's rights activist Elizabeth Tamm (1880–1958). In 1947, Palencia published *Alexandra Kollontay: Ambassadress from Russia*.

5 "A GEM OF MANY COLORS": ARTICULATING MIGRATION IN ISABEL DE... 111

her in Stockholm. Christmas nostalgia accentuates her separation from Spain when she reminisces about the celebrations and decorations typical of many Spanish homes. The overlay of devastating wartime events surrounding the Battle of Teruel in December 1937 and air bombardments her children would likely experience on Christmas Eve mar the tranquility Palencia might have felt.[15] Although she is elated to learn of what would ultimately be a temporary turn in battle favoring the Republican troops, the December 24th festivities meld the yearning for the past with the devastation afflicting her home country. Through food, gifts, decorations typical of both Spain and Sweden, and friendly chatter with her party guests, Palencia recreated the customary joyous holiday atmosphere. Tempering the mood, however, was the radio programming about the Teruel Battle. Palencia's conversation with her husband after the guests' departure turns to reminiscence of Christmases past, celebrated with *villancicos*,[16] music with guitars and castanets, Guadarrama mountain fir trees, wintery fragrances, and *nacimientos*.[17] Their exchange offers only momentary respite before their thoughts return to the present day in which the trees are now resting vertically, used as reinforcements to blockade the streets, and night-time bombardment would surely ensue (388–89), to replace the melodious sounds of Christmas carols. Palencia cannot reconcile the "angel's message to men" and "the little Child in the manger who was to preach brotherly love" with the bombs that would "destroy little children; and on that night of all nights" (389). The reality became more apparent later that night when they read a letter from Marissa that detailed the destruction of Madrid due to heavy air raids, where people endured scarce resources to battle cold and hunger.

Ever mindful of her role as caretaker, Palencia articulates the intersection of maternity and migration as a gender-inscribed experience with the war as a backdrop. When she learned in March 1938 that her daughter, living in Spain at the time, was pregnant, her physical remove accentuated

---

[15] The Battle of Teruel (December 1937–February 1938) took place in the harshest of wartime winters in which soldiers from both sides, especially those with the Nationalist band, were ill equipped to deal with subzero-degree temperatures, and many suffered loss of limbs due to frostbite. Weaponry and machinery froze and freezing temperatures temporarily halted fighting. The eventual Nationalist victory consolidated Franco's ability to reach the Mediterranean and cut Republican territory in two.

[16] The *villancico* is a Christmas carol. The term originally referred to a poetic and musical form popular from the fifteenth to nineteenth centuries.

[17] Nativity scenes, or *nacimientos*, are commonly displayed in homes during the Christmas season to represent the birth of Jesus.

112   L. NALBONE

her state of worry: "My little girl. I trembled to think of her under bombardments and without food. I knew that shortly after she returned to Spain after the summer, she had had nothing to eat for twenty-three days but mushrooms boiled in water" (394), and her worries also extend to "so many other expectant mothers going through all the privations of war" (394). She bridged the geographic divide by arranging for her daughter to relocate to Stockholm and spend the remaining months of her pregnancy out of harm's way. The overlay of maternity with war emerges in the timing of Marissa's travel to Sweden that roughly coincided with March 16–18, 1938, air bombardment campaign on Barcelona that left 1300 people dead and another 2000 injured (Thomas 785). The attacks by Italian aviation forces occurred every two to three hours and heavily damaged the city. Palencia's description of the devastation appears through the maternal lens, in which she recounts a story she heard of a mother kneeling, reeling with grief as she clutched the dismembered arm and hand of her young son, still clasping his book as he was in school at the time one of the bombs was dropped (397). The image of war's devastation Palencia paints here evokes the suffering of the mother depicted in the upper left quadrant of Pablo Picasso's *Guernica* (1937) as an indelible reminder of the fragility of human life. Upon learning of this story, she "thought sadly of the longing for culture that [her] people had shown, of the efforts that had been made by the republic to satisfy their hunger, of the ruthless destruction of that culture the Fascists were carrying on" (397). Then, in one of the most poignant moments of her narration, she miscalculates the war's outcome with phrasing that would only point to a symbolic rendering of ideological victory: "But I knew now that they [Franco's factions] would not succeed. The people, like that little child, would hold on to their treasure in spite of fire, in spite of bombs, in spite of death. The tiny hand was the emblem of the new Spain that might be temporarily beaten but would not let go what she had prized above all things" (397).

Palencia's thoughts on her soon-to-be-born grandchild's sex coincide with her daughter's, that they both wish for a girl to spare a son from having to go to war so as not "to be used as cannon fodder in war" (428). Even though she was at safe physical remove from the dangers of war, the ever-present threat of death or injury as a result of war could not escape her thoughts.[18] The tangible reminder of a worrisome newspaper headline

---

[18] Palencia's reaction to her daughter's pregnancy was also one of elation at becoming a grandmother and prompted her to recall her own experience of motherhood. Through the maternal lens she conveys a sense of stoic wisdom about what it means to move into the roles

announcing "The Spanish War" muted the joy she experienced at the birth of her grandson. Palencia marks the physical remove of the family as an implicit consequence of war—more so than of her assignment in the Swedish legation—by commenting that she announced the baby's birth (in August of 1938) to her husband and son-in-law not in person but by telephone. In addition to the overlay of political events in Spain that frame the circumstances of her grandson's arrival, the baby's birth evinces questions of identity that are common to children born away from their parents' homeland. Although named after his paternal grandparents, Juan Enrique, "since he had been born in Sweden we got into the way of calling him Jan, and Jan he probably will always be" (430).

These months away from her country and family (husband, son, and son-in-law) were fraught with angst. Palencia's husband at that time was serving Spain's representative to the legation in Riga, Latvia, but the political climate in Spain in the early fall of 1938 necessitated his departure. Before returning to Spain, he went to Stockholm for a four-day visit to spend time with his wife, daughter, and newborn grandson. Palencia again must negotiate the terms of family separation and the despair this causes her when he takes leave, knowing the hardships her husband will have to endure upon his return to a war-torn Barcelona, compounded by realizing "it was my own loneliness I dreaded and my anxiety that would naturally be increased a hundredfold" (433). She longed to return to Spain, a trip that her government would not authorize, to experience life and its dangers with her husband and son: "It was much worse to be up in Sweden all alone, hungering for news and knowing that they were going to be bombed continually, that they might be killed while we were safe in Stockholm" (434). Her only recourse was to try to distract herself by keeping busy, occupying her mind with the latest news in Europe, including events surrounding Germany's rise to power following the annexation of Austria and the imminent fracturing of Czechoslovakia following the September 1938 Munich Agreement. This is an important juncture in Palencia's life abroad, which I argue is the turning point in the transition from expatriate to exile that becomes cemented once she leaves Sweden the following spring. Palencia's experience illustrates that a confluence of events contributed to her exile, as she did not foresee that the diplomatic assignment in Sweden would result in a permanent separation from her

of mother and grandmother, concluding that "you become a mother yourself and are made a grandmother by someone else" (430).

114 L. NALBONE

homeland.[19] Except for limited, brief return trips to Spain while in Sweden, Palencia's diplomatic assignment effectively ended her residence on Spanish soil, though she would not truly understand this until years later. Even at the time of writing *I Must Have Liberty*, she could not anticipate that she would never again return to her homeland once she arrived in Mexico in 1939, evoking Rajendra's premise that migration systems operate on an intertwined thread of social, political, historical, and economic contexts. Her social status as associated with the intellectual elite and the economic favor this status granted her, combined with the support of her work as ideologically aligned with the Republican government, position Palencia as part of the migration system leading to the Spanish diaspora.

As the situation in Spain deteriorated for Republican Spain in the final months of the war, in tandem with the German Reich's rise to power, the Swedish government gradually started showing signs of recognizing the Franco-led factions as the prevailing ones, jeopardizing Palencia's stay in the capital city. Her concomitant, yet sparse, updates from Spain revealed to her the imperative for the vanquished Republican sympathizers to escape Spain despite myriad dangers of "the incessant bombing, as plane after plane pelted the ambulances carrying the wounded and the cars and the trucks and the lorries loaded with ammunition, and the people! The helpless famished people as they scurried up the roads or lay dying in the ditches, compact masses of men, women, and children, fleeing for safety and pursued by those merciless instruments of war right up to the very limits of republican Spain!" (448).[20] The life and death situation affects her directly because some of the bombings take place where her husband (ultimately safely in France) and son-in-law Germán Somolinos may have

---

[19] Rajendra does not view migrants as deprived of agency, but rather considers that "the push of need and the pull of a promise of a better life—often for their children or families—lured them away" from their homeland (364). The distinction is an important one as it establishes that the migrant is a rational, decision-making being rather than a victim of "historical forces and social networks" (364). This was the case of Palencia, who weighed her options and deliberately selected Mexico as her destination as the best option for her as well as her family.

[20] Palencia quotes her friend George Branting, Swedish left-leaning political figure, to lend credence to the stark images of death and dying on the route to exile from Spain to France: "'I do not believe Dante's *Inferno* would be an adequate description,' he said. 'It was so terrible, so inconceivably terrible, that at times I thought I must be looking at a film, that nothing so frightful could be really happening'" (451), which Palencia would also reference five years later in *Smouldering Freedom* (39), her moving essay intended to inform the English-reading public of the atrocities and injustices Spain had been forced to endure over the previous decade, from the time of the Civil War to the postwar period.

5 "A GEM OF MANY COLORS": ARTICULATING MIGRATION IN ISABEL DE... 115

been located. Indeed, Somolinos and his wounded younger brother were detained in a concentration camp upon crossing into France.

Tensions augmented as well due to the spatial divide that separated her from her son. Mediated through the maternal lens, this tension emerges at the close of the Civil War when Palencia tries to determine Cefito's whereabouts, previously in Figueras where a bombing had just occurred. Over an eleven-day period she is fraught with anxiety, worrying that he is in harm's way or worse, dead: "I could not sleep or rest. [...] Could he have been caught? The thought was maddening. I kept on thinking that if he had not managed to escape he would be shot, tortured like all those that fell into the insurgents' hands" (449–50). When faced with the possibility of his death, she was relieved to learn he was alive, though interned in a concentration camp, and she set the process in motion for her husband to intervene on his behalf and secure his release.

With the catastrophe that marked the fall of Republican Spain, Palencia experiences a defining moment in her own self-identity as someone displaced from her homeland yet resolute in defending the downtrodden; she remains a vocal proponent of continuing her fight to preserve the liberties of her fellow citizens. The work leads her to the following rhetorical questions as she begins to reassess her situation. She experiences a feeling of "unreality" and becomes unrecognizable to herself:

> What has happened to me? [...] Am I the same person that I was? Or by some strange transformation am I someone else? Why should I be doing all these things? And then the urge of business, the daily calls on my time brought with them the imperative necessity of doing, not dreaming, and of applying myself body and soul to the task before me. [...] What bigger surprise could life ever offer us than what had happened and what was happening to our country? We had believed and trusted and had wakened to find we were deceived and betrayed. Should we as human beings never be able to give credit to anyone again? A dismal outlook, indeed. (375)

Her sentiments echo the existential angst that had begun to permeate writing in Spain in the previous decades as the country grappled with the aftermath of the loss of the Spanish American War and the ensuing social and political unrest that plagued much of the country. Existential motifs that resonate with Palencia's essay, and pointedly to the quote above, reflect despair, the quest for freedom, sense of duty relating to the choices one makes, and anguish (Palley 21). Palencia's attempt to consider these

116   L. NALBONE

questions without answering them is testimony to the issues she grapples with as she takes stock of her work that has separated her from her family and homeland.

At war's end, the Franco government confiscated the home Palencia shared with her husband in Madrid (Eiroa San Francisco, "Isabel de Palencia" 266). Complicating matters was the complaint that the Sociedad General de Autores (General Society of Authors) filed against her in the Tribunal Regional de Responsabilidades Políticas (Regional Court for Political Responsibilities) for her left-leaning rhetoric while in Stockholm that resulted in the sanctions of a fine and of removal from the society (Eiroa San Francisco 266–67).[21] The convergence of social, political, economic—and now historical—relationships that Rajendra references in terms of migrations systems constituted the environment that definitively forced Palencia's migration. Hers was not a personal choice, nor did it "arise spontaneously [but was] the result of these pre-existing relational structures" to borrow from Rajendra (363). The migratory shifting was facilitated—in the case of the Spanish diaspora in México—by President Lázaro Cárdenas's insistence that "To those who have fought in favor of a legally constituted government, we are not going to offend them with an interrogation. We must welcome them all" (qtd. in Abellán 20).[22]

Unable to return to Spain, she carefully arrived at her decision of where to take up residence. Her foremost goal was to keep her family intact while at the same time expressing concern for her children's livelihood, which led her to discount the possibility of living in Europe due to the language barrier as well as "most counties' immigration laws, particularly in the case of Spanish refugees, the 'reds' as we were called" (460). Further, she sensed a palpable tension in the months preceding the outbreak of World War II and deduced that future reunions with her family would be difficult if the family were to disperse across Europe (461). She understood the risks of returning to Spain and was therefore motivated to embark on a transatlantic journey so as to bridge the spatial divide that has previously

---

[21] Eiroa San Francisco states that the General Society of Authors falsely accused Palencia of conducting public pro-Republican meetings. Additional infractions brought forth before the tribunal included her membership with the Partido Socialista Obrero Español (Spanish Socialist Workers' Party, PSOE) and holding private meetings with prominent Republican leaders. The sanctions—in place until she was officially pardoned in 1960—were not carried out, as she never returned to Spain ("Isabel de Palencia" 267).

[22] "A los que han luchado en su país a favor del Gobierno legalmente constituido, no les vamos a ofender con un interrogatorio. Hay que recibir a todos" (qtd. in Abellán 20).

5 "A GEM OF MANY COLORS": ARTICULATING MIGRATION IN ISABEL DE... 117

separated her from her family. Thus, her departure from Sweden on April 1, 1939, constituted her definitive separation from Spain.

After an emotional farewell, her reflections during transatlantic crossing aboard the *Drottingholm* filled her with unease related to the uncertainties and mysteries surrounding what her future would hold, yet she mediated her unease with the knowledge that she would be free from persecution: "It might be a happy and prosperous [life], it might hold nothing but sorrow. [...] Only one thing was sure, that although we were all together, the ship was taking us farther from Spain, from the Spain we had loved, from our people who were now prisoners in Franco's hands or in French concentration camps. We, ourselves, might come up against all kinds of unexpected difficulties, but at least we were free" (463). The symbolic sigh of relief she articulates for the first time in her essay conveys a sense of hopefulness that had eluded her over the course of the previous three years, yet her solidarity with fellow compatriots left behind serves as a bold reminder of the continued suffering and injustice.

On June 13, 1939, Palencia and her family set foot in Veracruz, Mexico—one of the more than 20,000 who arrived between 1937 and 1946 (Fagen 37)—making their way soon thereafter to the capital city. The terminology around migration Palencia uses at this point in her narration is telling in that she indirectly refers to herself as a refugee when narrating the difficulties she might encounter in finding a place to live because "House owners are as a rule suspicious of refugees" (465–66) for both financial and political reasons. She continues that refugees in her current day "are considered outlaws of a sort when, as in the case of the Spanish refugees, they have had to go into exile because they observed and defended the law of their land. This is all very confusing but attention ought to be called to it if we do not want future generations to think that we have been quite mad" (466). Nonetheless, she and her family found housing and purchased basic furnishings within the first few days. Palencia's descriptions initially elide financial hardships: they rented "an apartment that was big enough, and cheap enough, and pretty enough, and healthy enough, to satisfy the needs of an artist, a housekeeper, two doctors and a baby" and paid "several months in advance" (466).

However, they soon understood that the nuances of day-to-day living would be more problematic to negotiate, such as the minimal financial resources they had to purchase all the items needed to run a large household, especially kitchen items and linens. The realization sunk in that they were living in a foreign environment and chose to adapt to the best of

118   L. NALBONE

their abilities, with her son and son-in-law eventually setting up modest medical practices, and with Palencia resuming her writing.

Though at times her displacement saddened her, Palencia chose to marvel at her new surroundings, not for what she lacked but for what she had gained: "I saw only the Mexican sky lit up by the rising sun and being turned into a gem of many colors—colors of rubies and emeralds and opals and topaz. I have had this same sensation every day since. It has never failed me nor have I grown weary of it. I expect I never shall" (466–67).

The initial stages of her time in Mexico exemplify Kyle E. Lawton's observations of the Spanish exile experience:

> More than temporary asylum from the persecutions of the Francisco Franco dictatorship or escape from the indignities of French concentration camps, many Spanish exiles saw Mexico as a location where they could transplant important aspects of their earlier lives and continue the fight to reconquer their lost home. Mexico, more than anything else, was imagined as a place where the exiled Spaniard could feel at home again and continue being "Spanish." (19)

Indeed, Palencia yearned for the return of Spain's democratic rule under which freedom in the broadest sense reigned. In the concluding lines of her essay—"thinking of Spain, sure of Spain, and with my heart full of gratitude for Mexico" (472)—Palencia melds nostalgia for the past with the hope for the future, mindful of her present circumstances.

The circuitous route Palencia followed from Spain to Mexico, predicated upon the coalescence of political circumstances surrounding the election of Spain's democratically elected Republic, the Civil War, and its aftermath, represents one person's experience of migration that is emblematic of other Spanish Republican exiles' experiences. Within the collective experience in the context of migration systems, we read Palencia's journey as unique in the sense that diplomatic post buffered her transition away from her homeland, whereas others endured the harsh conditions of the concentration camps in southern France before their migration. Of the estimated 500,000 Spaniards who fled their country as a result of the war and its aftermath, their experiences are shaped by social, political, historical, and economic contexts. The exigencies of the ideologically driven exodus relies on a system that first permitted them to migrate, while considering the political agreements in place that granted them access to starting a life in a new country, recalling the negotiation of Spain's prohibition exit rule and Mexico's selective entry rule. Social and economic forces required adapting to life in exile, which Palencia embraced through her continued activism aimed at highlighting the plight of the Spanish exile and also through her publishing about the exile experience.

Works Cited

Abellán, José Luis. "El exilio de 1939: la actitud existencial del transterrado." *El exilio cultural de la Guerra Civil: (1936–1939)*, edited by José María Balcells and José Antonio Pérez Bowie, 2001, pp. 19–28.

Aznar Soler, Manuel. *El exilio literario español de 1939: actas del Primer Congreso Internacional.* Associació d'Idees-GEXEL, 1998.

Conde Peñalosa, Raquel. *Mujeres novelistas y novelas de mujeres en la posguerra española (1940–1965): catálogo bio-bibliográfico.* Fundación Universitaria Española, 2004.

Eiroa San Francisco, Matilde. *Isabel de Palencia: diplomacia, periodismo y militancia al servicio de la República.* Universidad de Málaga, Publicaciones y Divulgación Científica, 2014a.

——. "Una visión de España en la obra de Isabel Oyarzábal de Palencia." *Bulletin Hispanique*, vol. 116, no. 1. 2014b, pp. 363–80.

Entrambasaguas, Joaquín de. "Las novelistas actuales." *El libro español*, vol. 17, 1959, pp. 286–94.

Faber, Sebastiaan. "The Privilege of Pain: The Exile as Ethical Model in Max Aub, Francisco Ayala, and Edward Said." *Journal of Interdisciplinary Crossroads*, vol. 3, no. 1, 2006, pp. 11–32.

Fagen, Patricia W. *Exiles and Citizens: Spanish Republicans in Mexico.* U of Texas P, 1973.

Ilie, Paul. *Literatura y exilio interior: escritores y sociedad en la España franquista.* Fundamentos, 1981.

Jacobs, Justin M. *Xinjiang and the Modern Chinese State.* U of Washington P, 2016.

Lawton, Kyle E. "Navigating Ambiguity: Narratives of Spanish Exile in Mexico by Simón Otaola and Max Aub." *Cincinnati Romance Review*, vol. 49, 2020, pp. 18–35.

Mangini, Shirley. *Memories of Resistance: Women's Voices from the Spanish Civil War.* Yale UP, 1995.

Martínez, Josebe. *Las Intelectuales: De la Segunda República al exilio.* Ayuntamiento de Alcalá de Henares, 2002.

Nieva-de la Paz, Pilar. "Cambios y permanencias en la maternidad en *Diálogos con el dolor* (1944), de Isabel Oyarzábal Smith." *Estreno*, vol. 37, no. 1, 2011, pp. 42–56.

120   L. NALBONE

———. "Isabel Oyarzábal Smith, una republicana exiliada en México (*Rescoldos de libertad*)." *Hispania*, vol. 100, no. 1, 2017, pp. 114–24.

Palencia, Isabel de. *Diálogos con el dolor*. Leyenda, 1944.

———. *El sembrador sembró su semilla*. Rivadeneyra, 1923.

———. *En mi hambre mando yo*. Libro Mex, 1959.

———. *I Must Have Liberty*. Longmans, 1940.

———. *Smouldering Freedom: The Story of the Spanish Republicans in Exile*. Longmans, 1945.

Palley, Julian. "Existentialist Trends in the Modern Spanish Novel." *Hispania*, vol. 44, no. 1, 1961, pp. 21–26.

Paz Torres, Olga. *Isabel Oyarzábal Smith (1878–1974): una intelectual en la Segunda República española: del reto del discurso a los surcos del exilio*. Universitat Autònoma de Barcelona, 2015.

Rajendra, Tisha M. "The Rational Agent or the Relational Agent: Moving from Freedom to Justice in Migration Systems Ethics." *Ethical Theory and Moral Practice*, vol. 18, no. 2, 2015, pp. 355–69.

Rickett, Rosy. *Refugees of the Spanish Civil War and Those They Left Behind: Personal Testimonies of Departure, Separation and Return since 1936*. Dissertation, U of Manchester, 2014.

Rodríguez Gallardo, Ángel. "Un modelo poco explorado de refugiado político: gallegos en Portugal durante la Guerra Civil Española y la primera posguerra." *Cahiers de civilisation espagnole contemporaine*, vol. 18, 2017.

Said, Edward W. *Orientalism*. Penguin, 2003.

Tabori, Paul. *Anatomy of Exile: A Semantic and Historical Study*. Harrap, 1972.

Thomas, Hugh. *The Spanish Civil War*. Modern Library, 2001.

Vásquez, Mary S. "The Grammar of Contested Memory." *Female Exiles in Twentieth and Twenty-first Century Europe*, edited by Maureen Tobin Stanley and Gesa Zinn, Palgrave Macmillan, 2007, pp. 13–29.

Viswanathan, Gauri, editor. *Power, Politics, and Culture: Interviews with Edward W. Said*. Pantheon, 2001.

Weiner, Myron. "On International Migration and International Relations." *Population and Development Review*, vol. 11, no. 3, 1985, pp. 441–55.

CHAPTER 6

María Zambrano's Caribbean Imaginings: Philosophy from Island to Continent and Back

Esther Sánchez-Pardo

Through the word we make ourselves free, free from the moment, from the besieging and instantaneous circumstances.
—María Zambrano, *Hacia un Saber sobre el Alma*, 35

INTRODUCTION

This chapter will focus on María Zambrano's (1904–1991) rich Caribbean work, especially on a selection of her texts written or published in Puerto Rico and Cuba, where she developed valuable philosophical and aesthetic ideas, in an inquiry into and a hybridization of several traditions. I will be tracing Zambrano's thinking in a series of texts from "Island of Puerto Rico" to *The Agony of Europe* and "Time and Truth" which have proved invaluable to gain a sense on her meditations upon the future of Europe from her exilic condition in the Caribbean. Moved from her experience on

---

E. Sánchez-Pardo (✉)
Department of English Studies, Complutense University, Madrid, Spain
e-mail: esanchez_pardo@filol.ucm.es

© The Author(s), under exclusive license to Springer Nature Switzerland AG 2024
R. M. Silverman, E. Sánchez-Pardo (eds.), *Nomadic New Women*,
https://doi.org/10.1007/978-3-031-62482-7_6

121

122   E. SÁNCHEZ-PARDO

these islands, I argue that these writings constitute crucial meditations on the prospect of a hopeful horizon for the old European continent and a utopian regeneration after the war. These meditations tinged with the melancholy of loss and the hope of recovery move from ideology (loss of a Europe of democratic values) to the personal domain, always from her position as an engaged Republican intellectual.

In part, the underlying idea of this chapter is to approach how Zambrano created across borders, working cross-culturally, or against the grain of the dominant culture or philosophical tradition, at times suffering the absence of Spanish as her mother tongue, even if her close intellectual and emotional milieu used mostly Spanish. I will explore, among other issues: the creation of singular philosophical and aesthetic responses to exile; the development of innovative and hybrid essayistic forms; and the role of the intellectual and her relation with community and truth. I intend to investigate the way in which crossing the Euro-American divide responds to a traumatic exilic experience, as well as how writing across borders can be construed as a strategy to manage the anxiety and psychic instability that comes as trauma's aftermath.

In 1939, in the aftermath of the Spanish Civil War, María Zambrano (1904–1991) went into exile. Her 45 years spent in Mexico, Cuba, Puerto Rico, Italy, France, and Switzerland allowed her to produce her distinctive philosophical and creative work, as much as to develop an intense existential awareness on the "exilic condition." As part of a generation of Spanish Republican exiles who were fleeing the Spanish Civil War (1936–1939) and the regime of the dictator Francisco Franco, Zambrano lived a nomadic existence, shared with her generational peers, in a variety of geopolitical locations.[1] Their work gave rise to the most impressive cultural production that Spain had to offer to the twentieth century.[2]

For the Spanish Republican exiles, relocating to America represented an "extremely selective emigration. Without ignoring the presence of working class emigrants, still the majority of Spanish who fled to Latin

---

[1] A large number of Spaniards crossed the border into France during the tragic winter of 1939. In Latin America, Mexico, Chile, and the Dominican Republic were the only three American countries willing to officially welcome the Spanish republicans.

[2] After the collapse of 1898, with the loss of Cuba and the Philippines, in the aftermath of this epochal disaster for the nation, a generation of writers and critics, known as Generation of 98, such as Unamuno (1864–1936), Ángel Ganivet (1865–1898), Pío Baroja (1872–1956), Antonio Machado (1875–1939), and Ramón Menéndez Pidal (1869–1968) made substantial progress in questioning the Spanish mindset. The Generation's mythical resurrection of a "tragic" way of life (Unamuno) only reconfirms the concepts of crisis, decay, and loss related to Spain's essence.

6 MARÍA ZAMBRANO'S CARIBBEAN IMAGININGS: PHILOSOPHY FROM ... 123

America belonged to the leader levels of society" (Vilar 360).[3] The exile in the American countries was then characterized by a large number of exiled people connected to a range of professions in the fields of politics and intellectual and liberal arts.

Throughout their intellectual journey, the group of Spanish Republican exiles produced a body of work crucial for any approach and attempt at understanding the cultural reality of Spain after the Civil War. Writers, politicians, historians such as, Antonio Machado (1875–1939), Manuel Azaña (1880–1940), María de Maeztu (1881–1948), Salvador de Madariaga (1886–1978), Claudio Sanchez Albornoz (1893–1984), Dolores Ibárruri (1895–1989), María Enciso (1908–1949), and Max Aub (1903–1972), among others, contributed immensely to the project of rereading and reconsidering Spain's endemic flaws and the country's sense of historical failure. Years later, from the poetic "Generation of 27" and its milieu, Luis Cernuda, Rafael Alberti, Pedro Salinas, Concha Méndez, Manuel Altolaguirre, Ernestina de Champourcin, Emilio Prados, María Teresa León, and Rosa Chacel, bearing the generational burden of having outlived their brutally repressed fellow nationals, and the aftermath of Federico Garcia Lorca's assassination at the hands of the Franco militia, took the legacy of their elder fellow émigrés and built upon the remnants of a country devastated by a fratricidal civil war. They had to negotiate their own survivors' traumas as well as their painful deracinated existence. In Zambrano's view, the country's historical debate over "What is Spain?" would continue to generate the battles between brothers and sisters so that "the Spaniard dies in order to live, in order to recuperate its history" (*Los Intelectuales* 142).[4]

María Zambrano was also an important member of a unique generation of women thinkers and intellectuals who radically confronted rationalism and the continental philosophical tradition from within. With their unique contributions, Rosa Luxemburg (1871), Edith Stein (1891), Hannah Arendt (1906), Simone de Beauvoir (1908), Simone Weil (1909), and Zambrano herself, introduced women into philosophical, political, creative, and academic circles and offered a solid body of work with far-reaching insights into a crucial period of political turmoil in European history. A true diaspora of modernist women philosophers and artists

---

[3] "emigración extremadamente selectiva. Aún sin ignorar la presencia de inmigrantes de clase obrera, la mayoría de los españoles que escaparon a Latinoamérica pertenecía a las capas dirigentes de la sociedad." Almost none of Zambrano's works have been translated into English and, unless indicated otherwise, all translations from Spanish are mine.

[4] "El español muere para vivir, para recuperar su historia."

124   E. SÁNCHEZ-PARDO

decided, or saw themselves forced, to go beyond frontiers. Many of them remained permanently "in transit" across national and other sorts of boundaries, experiencing the trauma of exile.

Zambrano's Writings: From Island to Continent

Can we speak of a specific kind of hybrid essay, one in which the experiential, the epistemological, the documentary, and the lyrical interact and fuse into a new form? I am arguing in support of the appraisal of the philosophical hybrid essay in Zambrano's work. It goes beyond the strictures of genre taxonomy within philosophical writing and opens up to more flexible modernist literary elaborations, in an attempt to interrogate and to understand the human condition in moments of crises. In my attempt at crossing the "transcultural" frontier with the inspiration provided by Zambrano's writings, I would like to posit the existence of a movement back and forth in several of her texts which is based on repetition, iteration, and the movement back and forth between the location of the philosopher in exile and the old Europe.

During her time in Cuba and Puerto Rico, Zambrano would carry her travel journal as an acute observer of the realities that surrounded her. In an attempt to recreate a portrait of the remote foreign land, so far unknown to an audience largely from Spain and its politically repressed diaspora, she conveyed her sense of defamiliarization as much as her feelings of complicity and identification with the plight of the islanders. Far from mirroring other realities to legitimize the European ethos, Zambrano rather wove her own narrative in order to understand the place and the historical experience of the Other as well as the events of political history which crystallize on the Caribbean societies she visited and where she became a temporary resident.[5] Zambrano not only became a keen observer and

---

[5] This sense of wonder and pure inquiry is a time ripe for philosophy in which she was refining her thinking about liberalism, current democracy, and the political situation in Europe. According to Mariátegui, in the Puerto Rican context, "the philosopher's writings '...' affected the cultural and political landscape into which she was inserting herself" (*To Reach the Isle* 74). In his view, Zambrano's "Isla de Puerto Rico" forms part of her quest to renovate the liberalism she examined in her first book, *Horizontes del liberalismo* (1930). In Avilés-Ortiz's research, it remains clear that "The island [was] a hotbed of political passions" ("La isla [era] un hervidero de pasiones políticas," "Una filósofa en la 'red Benítez'" 120) and Zambrano was not exempt from watching developments taking place in Puerto Rican (and largely Caribbean) geopolitics. The philosopher was trying to make sense out of the intellectual life, university environment, and Puerto Rico's position vis-à-vis neighboring countries, the US, and the Spanish heritage.

6 MARÍA ZAMBRANO'S CARIBBEAN IMAGININGS: PHILOSOPHY FROM ... 125

analyst of the Caribbean societies she visited, she became integrated within intellectual groups such as the Orígenes in Cuba or the group of professors and researchers from the University of Puerto Rico. Some scholars hold Zambrano was a participant in the "networks"[6] of intellectual exchange active within many Latin American institutions at this moment in time. From letters to pieces in periodicals or fragments of memoirs, and as a complement to her published more canonical works, these pieces allow us to better understand all elements, influences, and crucial factors that had an impact on the trajectory of her work. These networks also allow the researcher to explore more in depth the connections operating among different scientific and academic communities, and their relations with ongoing political projects (Avilés-Ortiz, "Una filósofa" 101).

In this new hybrid genre, the aforementioned travel journal, Zambrano uses both narration and the essay form, and a range of other smaller genres that critically contribute to its expansion, as both a meditative and an imaginative outgrowth of the writer's capacities to comprehend human reality. In the Zambranian writings in exile that appear as proper to an insular setting, one finds an impressive fusion of genres mostly from narrative and essayistic ventures, such as: public lecture, newspaper or journal article, academic paper, letter, short story, piece of (historical) research, petition, complaint, and confession. These are all among the most frequently used and crucial as far as the overall design of the essays is concerned.

There is also an abundance of marginal or lesser known genres such as the micronarrative, the anecdote, the maxim, the aphorism, the epigram, the proverb, and the piece of popular wisdom that take us both to a Spanish and to a larger European context, and also to creating bonds with her new personal and intellectual horizons in exile. As it is amply known, during her exile in Cuba, the philosopher came to be associated to the

---

[6] Iliaris A. Avilés-Ortiz has recently demonstrated that Zambrano, during her stay in Puerto Rico, 1940–1945, was a 'participant' in Jaime Benitez's intellectual "network," the Chancellor of U. Puerto Rico. She draws from Eduardo Devés Valdés in his *Redes intelectuales en América Latina*. In Devés' view, an intellectual network is "a group of people engaged in intellectual pursuits who contact each other, meet, exchange written pieces, write to each other, collaborate in joint projects, improve the extant channels of communication and above all, create ties of mutual trust" ("el conjunto de personas ocupadas en los quehaceres del intelecto que se contactan, se conocen, intercambian trabajos, se escriben, elaboran proyectos comunes, mejoran los canales de comunicación y, sobre todo, establecen lazos de confianza recíproca" *Redes intelectuales* 18).

126   E. SÁNCHEZ-PARDO

Orígenes poetry group whose leader, José Lezama Lima (1910–1976), became a life-long friend and correspondent.[7]

In her insular essays, Zambrano manages to imagine the city (San Juan, Havana) as a point of destination and also to introduce the broad social and individual force field that both constrains and enables the writer to create under specific historical and contextual circumstances. Her real-life journey into exile is transformed into a meditative essay and, finally, into a philosophical elaboration which takes place in the Caribbean (Cuba and Puerto Rico) and the Latin American mainland (Santiago de Chile, Mexico DF, Morelia—Mexico) including New York, with intermittent trips to Europe (south of France, Paris, Rome, Trélex-sur-Lyon—Switzerland—La Pièce, Greece, Geneva), and back to Spain in 1984. In her rich philosophical pieces, Zambrano reflects upon the phenomenological, the historical, the political, the ethical, the spiritual, the anthropological, the rational, and the poetic.

It is important to note that we should understand Zambrano's exile in the Caribbean as a continuum, the majority of which she spent in Cuba (1940–1946) with short periods in Puerto Rico (1940, 1941, 1943, 1945) and sporadic and very occasional trips to other locations.[8] This was probably the most creatively fruitful and philosophically rich period in her life. Specifically, "Isla de Puerto Rico" (1940), is a central piece in Zambrano's personal, philosophical and political exploration that occurs in transit. Dedicated to her friends, Luz Martínez and Jaime Benítez—the president of UPR—this text was written upon Zambrano's returning to Havana after a visit to San Juan. This "document" in which the philosopher, nurtured by the spirit of the island, inspires hope, and advocates for a better world, ends up including some sort of Pan-Americanist manifesto. "Isla de Puerto Rico" was first published in the Puerto Rican newspaper "El Mundo" in 1940, and later in the same year in Cuba in "La Verónica" publishing house as a book.[9] In Puerto Rico, the Spanish philosopher

---

[7] The rich correspondence between Zambrano and Lezama has been beautifully edited by Javier Fornieles Ten (Lezama Lima and Zambrano, *Correspondencia*). It also includes the correspondence between the Spanish philosopher and María Luisa Bautista, Lezama's wife, after Lezama's decease in 1976.

[8] Zambrano left for good for Europe in 1953 after spending time in Cuba, Puerto Rico, Chile, and Mexico (Ortega Muñoz, *María Zambrano* 20).

[9] "La Verónica" was founded by the Spanish poet, editor, and critic Manuel Altolaguirre (1905–1959). As a young Republican intellectual, he was forced into exile in 1939. He lived in Cuba and Mexico. A member of the "Generation of 27," he was also the editor of a collection devoted to Spanish poets in his publishing house.

6 MARÍA ZAMBRANO'S CARIBBEAN IMAGININGS: PHILOSOPHY FROM ... 127

joined another group of intellectuals invited by Jaime Benitez. It is interesting to note that this small book was dedicated to her friend, José Lezama Lima, "whom also felt and thought about the islands" ("Isla de Puerto Rico").[10]

Like other Caribbean and Latin American societies, after the Great Depression of the 1930s, Puerto Rico went through difficult times.[11] Only after World War II a period of economic reconstruction and political transformations would bring about significant changes. In the early 1940s Puerto Rico was economically dependent on the US, and the colonial state saw migration to the mainland as a leeway to ease off the unemployment situation of the island. All through the twentieth century, most Puerto Rican writers and intellectuals have problematized the purported breach between major 'opposed parties' such as those of "islanders" and "mainlanders." Politically, the Partido Popular Democrático held legislative dominance between 1940 and 1968 and supported Puerto Rico's status intact as "non-incorporated" territory to the US up until the beginning of the Cold War period.

Crucial to reaching a more accurate understanding of the Puerto Rico Zambrano appraised, and to assess the fundamental shifts in cultural, socioeconomic, and political terms the island underwent, are Antonio Pedreira's ideas on *Insularismo* (1934). In Pedreira's view, Puerto Rico's future must privilege the university-educated youth who will end up taking a similar position to those supporters of *autonomismo* in the nineteenth century (in favor of home rule but without independence from Spain) in relation to the US. Puerto Rico's underdeveloped potential should not expect to gain full autonomy until it achieves a certain level of cultural development. Pedreira's rhetoric and ideas would pave the way for a renewed insularity, at the basis of the Partido Popular Democrático's ideology, for the decades to come.

---

[10] "quien también ha sentido y pensado sobre las islas." Lezama dedicated to Zambrano his poem, "Noche insular, jardines invisibles." As it is well known, Lezama created his own "Poetic System of the World," his idiosyncratic ideas on metaphor and the image support a sophisticated philosophical-poetic system based on an Orphic-Pythagorean basis. His whole cosmogony constitutes a solid attempt to substantiate his ideas and *Weltanschauung*.

[11] In the Caribbean region of the so called Lesser Antilles, Puerto Rico exhibits the particularity of its territorial status as a "non-incorporated territory" of the US. A good number of monographs by legal scholars have charted the history of non-incorporation under US law up until now (see Duffy Burnett and Marshall, *Foreign in a Domestic Sense*, and Rivera Ramos, *American Colonialism*).

128   E. SÁNCHEZ-PARDO

Zambrano's—and later on Juan Ramón Jiménez's—understanding of insularity will not take her far from the ideas entrenched in 'institutional' political circles in the decades of the 1940s and 1950s. The philosopher, as many of her acquaintances finally failed to see in what ways insularity would have been instrumental in developing alternatives to the political status quo, to for instance, foreground issues of class and race, and to integrate the island with its Caribbean neighbors and gradually separate it from the US and the Global North.

In "Isla de Puerto Rico," Zambrano's rhetoric, in her descriptions of her Puerto Rican idealized "homely" environment, in her affect-laden discourse, takes us with a trope to a paradisal[12] scene of origins, an idyllic place where she could think and write and be free. Zambrano moves from the solitude of the island to the nostalgia of today, to the political conundrum of her ideas on person and democracy (*Person and Democracy*) and to the origins of the Pan-Americanist proposals by several contemporary intellectuals and politicians (Bolívar, Martí, Rodó, Mariátegui). Zambrano's encounter with "the island," with Cuba and Puerto Rico, was for her a long journey of arrivals and departures, an intellectual pilgrimage that connected her to people and places, that opened up new far away friendships and comradeships, that immersed her deep into her thinking and enriched her experience with the benefits of collaboration with poets and intellectuals, with artists and politicians. She was able to penetrate deep into the "island-world," reaching finally for a sensible rationale to her understanding of poetry and poetic reason.

CARIBBEAN LOCALITIES

Zambrano's sojourn in Puerto Rico has recently been researched and approached from different angles: from a philosophical and biographical perspective (Moreno Sanz, "Ínsulas extrañas"), from our philosopher's ideas on Pan-Americanism (Cámara and Ortega, *Caribbean*), and from her teaching, lecturing, and intellectual activities on the island (Avilés-Ortiz, "Zambrano in Puerto Rico"). We have been fortunate with what

---

[12] *Paradiso* (1966), Lezama's major and only completed and published novel during his life time, is considered to be one of the most accomplished texts in Cuba's history. The novel's structure, inspired by Dante's *Divine Comedy*, can also be discussed as an allegory dealing with creativity, homosexuality, death, and regeneration. *Paradiso* is certainly a product of Lezama's insular, Pythagorean-gnostic imagination.

seems a recent scholarly interest on Zambrano's Caribbean work, with the publication of volumes by Arcos (Zambrano, *Islas*) and Cámara and Ortega (*Caribbean*) as well as with recent papers on her Caribbean period (Sánchez-Gey, "Relaciones personales;" Sedeño, "Viaje iniciático;" and Burgos-Lafuente, "Ruinas, islas y escritura").

During her stay in Cuba and Puerto Rico, Zambrano reflected upon alternative ways of philosophizing such as through poetry, music, and painting rather than through the usual structures of logical and onto-epistemological thought. Checking the limits of impermanence, precariousness,[13] and solitude, but also of bodily resilience and speech, Zambrano constructs her philosophical meditation. For Zambrano it is the notion of style that gives cohesion and binds together disparate elements. Nothing, not even an experiential sensuous item, when it responds to a style, to another way of life, remains loose, nor could it exist without deep connections to other elements.

The island acts in Zambrano as a mirror that gives us the nostalgic image of our solitude. In the case of Puerto Rico, the island inspires love and tenderness, she describes it as a "flake of land on water that miraculously floats, but so incredibly light for such beauty" ("Isla de Puerto Rico" 9).[14] The island, in which "every corner of its land is full of beauty",[15] exhibits a "flourishing" ("floreciente") solitude, and Zambrano associates it with femininity, perhaps by what she understands as "humble fecundity, overflowing with her presence, this perpetual overflow without tiredness or pride" (9).[16] Puerto Rico represents "The miracle of integrity, in equilibrium" (9).[17] Zambrano weaves her essay as a conversation, "with you,

---

[13] Even during their very intellectually fruitful exile in Cuba and Puerto Rico, Zambrano and her husband, the historian Alfonso Rodriguez Aldave, lived a very difficult life. They never had financial security, a university position, or any stable source of income. Judith Butler first introduced the concept of precarity in *Precarious Life*, defined as a type of precariousness by which human life can be understood from a collective, communal, and interdependently political point of view. Whereas all lives are born precarious—vulnerable and hence finite—precarity refers to a politically induced condition derived from (in)action on the part of social and economic systems, which fail to protect human lives from physical impairment and extreme situations of poverty or political violence.

[14] "copo de tierra sobre el agua en que milagrosamente flota, paso tan leve para tanta belleza."

[15] "cada rincón de su tierra está cargado de belleza."

[16] "fecundidad humilde, de este desbordar de su presencia, de este rebasar siempre sin cansancio, ni soberbia."

[17] "El milagro de la integridad, en equilibrio."

130 E. SÁNCHEZ-PARDO

friends of Puerto Rico whose names will always be intertwined with this nostalgia and this hope of mine, in the present terrible hour" (10).[18] At present, in the terrible hour,[19] she writes "from the failure of our past as Spaniards and from the anguish of our present as Europeans" (10)[20] to revitalize hope, "The hope of a past better off if it turned into the future" (11).[21] Hope must arise from the present moment, and reunite past and present in order to get away from the slavery to which reason has subjected us. Reality—historical, social, political—is far from rational, and the events of the War are a clear demonstration of this.

A sense of continual itinerancy can be perceived from the opening lines of "Isla de Puerto Rico." She addresses previous conversations she had entertained with colleagues and friends "in the best moments in long walks across the island watching the twilight" (3).[22] Her addressees are thus her friends, and she wants her writing to work as a "testimony of profound friendship, creative friendship that unites us, and of those joyful days of my stay on this gorgeous island" (3).[23] Her piece shows a dialogical nature and it is, thus, presented as a gift of friendship to her peers. This piece opens with Zambrano's thoughts around islands: "For the imagination, an island holds always a promise (3).[24] From early on, the island is associated to daydreaming, whereas the continents and mainland are the land of work. The islands appear as the "expected compensation, true compensation beyond justice, where grace plays its part" (3).[25] The islands occupy a place between daydreaming and dream (3–5), "The islands are the gift made to the world on days of peace for their enjoyment" (3).[26]

---

[18] "con vosotros, amigos de Puerto Rico cuyos nombres irán siempre entrelazados con esta nostalgia y esta esperanza mía, en la terrible hora presente."

[19] It is important to remember that it was precisely in Puerto Rico where Zambrano received the terrible news of the fall of Paris. The Nazi occupation of Paris was an imminent danger, and a great risk for her mother and sister who were, at the time, in exile in Paris (see Avilés-Ortiz, "Zambrano in Puerto Rico" 7).

[20] "desde el fracaso de nuestro pasado de españoles y desde la angustia de nuestro presente de europeos."

[21] "La esperanza de un pasado mejor convertido en porvenir."

[22] "en los mejores momentos en largos paseos por la Isla mientras mirábamos el atardecer."

[23] "testimonio de la honda amistad, amistad creadora, con que me siento unida a ellos, y del recuerdo de los días venturosos de mi estancia en esta Isla maravillosa."

[24] "Una isla es para la imaginación de siempre una promesa."

[25] "la compensación esperada, compensación verdadera más allá de la justicia, donde la gracia juega su papel."

[26] "Las islas son el regalo hecho al mundo en días de paz para su gozo."

6 MARÍA ZAMBRANO'S CARIBBEAN IMAGININGS: PHILOSOPHY FROM … 131

The islands appear to our imagination as a gift, and in parallel, as a residue of something, the remains of a better world, a sense of lost innocence. Out of the island we always expect the prodigy of life in peace, of a life in harmony, of an age in which no word had been prostituted, when the work was joyful and there was no envy (4). Puerto Rico was to Zambrano, in maximum degree, "a place of evasion of this present dreadful world" (4).[27] In Puerto Rico, she lived outside the usual coordinates of space and time, in a pure space of wonder, and in a "time outside time" in which she remained in contact with something alive and pure (4).

Zambrano wonders about the role of islands in history, from the Greek islands of the Aegean to the islands of the Antilles. In her view, Spain has rather been an island more than the Iberian Peninsula (4–5). The island is the sign and prelude for a better world, a better life. This is an idea of a life enmeshed in pure nostalgia, for "Man is the creature that is defined by his nostalgia more than by his treasures, so he misses so much or more than by what he has" (5).[28] From Columbus' times, the Antilles were islands containing the rare and exquisite, the highly coveted species and, associated with them, all things related to the refinement of the senses. The islands had a landscape "of trees miraculously flowered, of heaven unalterable …" (6).[29] The island always belonged to another realm, far from the madding crowd.[30] Many inland Europeans were nostalgic for the mere vision of freedom traditionally evoked by the islands. The emotion of nostalgia has no clearly defined object, but in Zambrano's words "Whenever nostalgia is directed at something, it becomes hope" (6).[31] At present, nostalgia is a pervasive sentiment; the nostalgia of Europeans today is a nostalgia for what now seems a bygone way of life. Zambrano argues that Europeans have snatched a certain way of life, a "style" from us: "a system of attentions and disdain, a unity of reason and sensitivity, a conscious and flexible measure" (7).[32]

---

[27] "lugar de evasión de este pavoroso mundo actual."

[28] "El hombre es la criatura que se define por sus nostalgias más que por sus tesoros, por lo que echa de menos tanto o más que por lo que tiene."

[29] "de los árboles milagrosamente florecidos, del cielo inalterable…"

[30] I am certainly alluding to Thomas Gray's 1751 "Elegy Written in a Country Churchyard," and to Thomas Hardy's homonymous novel, *Far from the Madding Crowd* (1874) and their ironic pastoralism.

[31] "Toda nostalgia cuando se dirige a algo se transforma en esperanza."

[32] "un sistema de atenciones y de desdenes, una unidad de razón y sensibilidad; una medida consciente y flexible."

132   E. SÁNCHEZ-PARDO

In Zambrano's section devoted to "The failure of the Spanish Empire" the philosopher speaks about the "peculiar pain" (11) and bad conscience that a Spaniard feels upon arrival in America. All the "incapacities" and "terrible evils" (12) of the old imperial Spain are patent when confronting the realities of America. The most serious evil of those endemic to the Spaniards is "their lack of communication with the past, their lack of self-knowledge, and their ignorance about origins" (12).[33] These important problems appear even more acutely in their offspring in the America Hispana. It is thus a question affecting all Spaniards and all Spanish-speaking peoples, those that the Northerners have called "Spanish"—"Spanish" is the national and place name that appears in Zambrano's paper. Their unity is more profound than what it might seem, "The great unity of language, origins and culture, the hidden and poorly known unity ... of a whole way of life, of facing all the questions that decide upon life, even death itself" (12).[34]

At this very moment in time, Puerto Rico plays a distinctive role regarding culture and values (13), and "The destiny of the little island enters, we believe, a decisive phase in which man ... (this upright creature, the remnant of a better world) must muster all his treasure ... to arrive at the understanding of something more transcendent..." (13–14).[35] In Zambrano's view, the destiny of the people of Puerto Rico will be to serve a mission universal in scope, showing the island's Spanish tradition and its American present (15). This mission will be one of pacification and "reconciliation of the two Americas" (16). This is a crucial, critical moment, "It is the terrible time of danger, of anxiety, despair, and hope. It is the moment of truth" (16).[36]

For Zambrano, at the root of the failed Spanish imperial origin lies the fortitude which must take over the noble heritage of Western culture, namely, human creation. This Western heritage, consisting essentially of objectivity of thought and love, makes possible the existence of a livable

---

[33] "su incomunicación con el pasado, su aislamiento de la tradición, su tremenda ignorancia acerca de sí mismo, de sus orígenes."

[34] "La gran unidad de idioma, de orígenes y de cultura, la unidad oculta y mal conocida ... de todo un estilo de vida, de un encararse con todas las cuestiones que deciden la vida, hasta la misma muerte."

[35] "El destino de la islita nos parece que entra en una fase decisiva en que el hombre ...(Esa criatura íntegra, intacta, como residuo de un mundo mejor) se ve forzado a poner en juego todo su tesoro ... para llegar a la comprensión de algo más trascendente..."

[36] "Es la terrible hora del peligro, de angustia y desesperación y esperanza. Es la hora de la verdad."

6 MARÍA ZAMBRANO'S CARIBBEAN IMAGININGS: PHILOSOPHY FROM ... 133

world. This livable world is made by free men and for the benefit of free men, by the human person and for the benefit of the human person. At present, "[The human person] is the victim, sentenced to death, enslaved and persecuted, marked for annihilation" (16).[37] This person opts always first for dignity and justice rather than for her own individual life, and believes in essential freedom. It is in line with the best Spanish tradition, the Stoic and the Christian. In her view, the Spanish-speaking American man should be able to go back to this Spanish-European root in order to face his "inalienable heritage" (17).[38]

North America has in its root something very noble inherited from old Europe, its tradition in the autonomy and freedom of the human being. North America is a colossus brimming with strength and "the wide space of history ahead" (18).[39] Finally, Zambrano points out that the greatest evil afflicting America is its present cult of success, what she calls "the religion of success" (18). America has come of age, and the cult of success, of results, and of achievements must yield in favor of principles—ethical, democratic, principles of respect and peaceful coexistence. This new cult demands "much more effort and heroism than the previous one" (19).[40] Everything points to the fact that the small and graceful island of Puerto Rico might be the place where the encounter between the South and the North occurs, "Reconciliation between the powerful man of the North; the clear understanding of the work to be performed, awareness and enthusiasm for the acceptance of the difficult destiny" (19).[41]

Zambrano's philosophical essay defies any taxonomical imperative, the systematicity of any philosophical or literary corpus. She proceeds in a palimpsestic mode, superimposing layers that get adhered to a fragile surface which remains scratched and encrypted as if written on a sand bank— from the failure of the Spanish Empire to Europe at war, from democracy imperiled to a present-day man, unaware of his past and unresponsive to the demands of these times of crisis. She insists upon the trope of origins, of the lost and irretrievable past that is nostalgically evoked, on the erosion of ethical and social principles, and on the decay of a way of life.

---

[37] "[La persona humana] es la víctima, la sentenciada a muerte, la esclavizada y perseguida, la que se pretende aniquilar."

[38] "herencia inajenable."

[39] "el ancho espacio de la historia por delante."

[40] "mucho más esfuerzo y heroismo que el anterior."

[41] "La reconciliación entre el hombre poderoso del Norte; la comprensión clara de la obra a realizar, conciencia y entusiasmo para la aceptación del difícil destino."

134   E. SÁNCHEZ-PARDO

In my view, Zambrano generates an encounter between some of the ways in which islands have been imagined and used from without, primarily in the interest of the advancement of the West, and from within, as can be gathered from the experience of Cubans and Puerto Ricans. This perspective from within, an affirmative and creative counter-imagination on islands emerges from works by José Lezama Lima, Cintio Vitier, Fina García Marruz, and the poets from the Orígenes group, as much as from Zambrano's reading of Juan Ramón Jiménez or Luis Cernuda—both of them in exile in the US and spending time, Cernuda mostly in Cuba, and Jiménez in Puerto Rico. In her work on the islands, Zambrano reflected upon some key concepts associated with insularity—the light, the coast, and the ocean—and the ways in which they force a rearrangement of crucial philosophical concepts: respectively, vision and sense perception, time, space, and history. The epistemological problems posed by the islands open up several lines of enquiry for a different understanding of history and the imagination inspired by Caribbean texts, whose singularity precludes us from an easy classification that exhausts their differences.[42]

HEMISPHERIC CONNECTIONS

Certainly, the pressing situation in Europe with the advent of WWII did not have much to do with the specific situation in Puerto Rico and Cuba. Zambrano had come to a Puerto Rican scenario of modernity to lecture with a well-deserved aura of knowledge and prestige—at the university and at a series of institutions (the PR Athenaeum, the Professional School of Social Work) where she was welcomed as one of the disciples of Ortega who soon became well-known and gained respect and the admiration of intellectuals, professors, and critics. In any event, Zambrano was addressing audiences, speaking of subjects as varied as Seneca and stoicism, Greek ethics, Ortega, or Antonio Machado, but she was also living as an exile and had a reputation for being a "red." This was certainly a big obstacle for her candidacy to be hired as a university professor of philosophy.

During the difficult times of continuous travel back and forth to San Juan, Zambrano maintained a fluid correspondence with Waldo Frank

---

[42] During her Caribbean exile, Zambrano was extremely prolific. She wrote many hybrid texts moving between philosophy, literature, painting, and the other arts. For an exhaustive account of her Puerto Rican and Cuban intellectual activities, see Moreno Sanz, *La visión más transparente*, and Zambrano, *Islas*.

(1889–1967). Frank had become an important referent in the relations between the US and what he himself called the "America Hispana."[43] They both benefitted from this friendly intellectual exchange and Frank tried to help Zambrano gain a stable position with his contacts, but to no avail. Even though Frank's ideas about the reconciliation of the two American hemispheres were influential on Zambrano—and the most telling instance is precisely her elaboration in "Isla de Puerto Rico"—the philosopher remained cautious in relation to the incipient Puerto Rican nationalism that arose in the 1940s as a counterpart to the American colonial regime.

Zambrano was clearly in a position of vulnerability, identified as a leftist political exile. She spoke of exile as an experience lived by those faithful to their ideals. Exiles went through a long and painful process of loss of the mother country, fellow nationals, and an immense solitude. Exiles also became refugees who, watching the future, hoped to recover as soon as possible their lost existence. Finally, the exiled became aware that what they longed for did not exist anymore, and, personally, they did not completely adapt to their new societies. Many of them ended up having two mother countries, the one of origin and the other of stay, a double identity, and a form of identification.

Zambrano suffered from a double exile, a political and physical exile, a forced eviction from her home and homeland, and also a philosophical exile. As F. J. Martin has noted:

> Hers was also a philosophical exile, in a double and complete sense. Her work grows independent and strong on the margins of schools and academies ... and above all she strengthens ties, through the vindication of poetic reason and her choice for the knowledge of the vanquished and humiliated by the weight of history, with all the tradition of thought in exile and with the exiles of the Great Philosophy.[44]

[43] Frank published a book entitled *America Hispana. A Portrait and a Prospect* (1930). Dedicated to Peruvian intellectual José Carlos Mariategui (1894–1930), this was one of the first volumes that presents us with a cultural history of North and South America.

[44] "Exilio filosófico también, el suyo, y en un doble y fuerte sentido, pues su obra se gesta y crece al margen de las escuelas y de las academias (téngase presente que fueron los poetas antes que los profesionales de la filosofía los que primero reconocieron el valor de su pensamiento), y, sobre todo, se hermana, a través de la reivindicación de la razón poética, de su abrazo integrador, de su opción por los saberes vencidos y humillados por el peso de la historia, con toda la tradición del pensamiento exiliado y de los exiliados de la Gran Filosofía" (Martín, "Presentación").

136   E. SÁNCHEZ-PARDO

In "Island of Puerto Rico," Zambrano's prospect is, to a great extent, her dream for America, both halves of the hemisphere integrated into one people, a new spiritual synthesis where the ethical ideas of person, community, and democracy will regain momentum. With her views, the philosopher challenges a transimperial history of global power relations between the English and the Spanish (Mignolo) with an idiosyncratic philosophical-literary language that exceeds canonical traditions. She also brings to the fore a vein of avant-garde ideas of her Cuban milieu and the Spanish Republican diaspora. Zambrano meditates upon the literary as a locus of thought. She introduced poets who uniquely ventured into broadly comparative and international terrains, including Lezama, Cernuda, García Marruz, Cabrera, whose work straddles trans-American literary traditions, engaging Latin American history as well as a global poetics of dissent and non-complicity with the old Empires.

Finally, Zambrano elaborates on exile and cultural borders in ways that distance her from more established and "neutral" ways to think about displacement and deracination. Her philosophical, critical, and creative work is a celebration of a hybrid Spanish of the Republican diaspora, a Mexican, Cuban, and Puerto Rican Spanish in conjunction with the English spoken in Puerto Rico and N.Y. as well as the legacy of other Native American languages that question cultural and literary traditions.

BACK TO EUROPE

At the aforementioned historical conjuncture, it is imperative to revisit Zambrano's thought in the 1940s. At that moment, as a Spanish Republican philosopher in exile in Cuba she engages in a sustained meditation on the future of a Europe besieged by war with an essay that will give title to her book, *The Agony of Europe*, published in Buenos Aires in 1945. In that book, a collection and reworking of articles rewritten between 1940 and 1944, Zambrano wrote:

> Europe is not dead, Europe cannot entirely die; it agonizes. Because Europe is perhaps the only thing – in History – that cannot entirely die, the only

6 MARÍA ZAMBRANO'S CARIBBEAN IMAGININGS: PHILOSOPHY FROM ...   137

thing that can come back to life. This principle of resurrection will also be the principle of its life and of its transitory death. (*Agony* 42)[45]

Zambrano certified the disaster of Europe. She experienced that only through nostalgia do we encounter the unity of Europe—unity composed of all the diversities of its rich life; her experience was so strong that she surrendered to her suspicion that Europe was truly dead." However, in her view, utopian obstinacy was stronger. Unable to believe in a definitive death for Europe, the profile of utopia was held within the very reality of Europe (82). Based on the assumption of the new man that takes shape in the Augustinian *Confession*, Zambrano outlined a paradigm for the European man and his way of living history:

> ... from his hope of resurrection here on earth, a revolutionary need sprang up for a world, for an ideal city always there on the horizon. It is man's historical anxiety, that of wanting to substantiate his dreams, of somehow believing in them. For this reason, history is more history in Europe than elsewhere because of this definitive importance of the horizon, because of the belief in one's dreams that corresponds with an aspiration to go beyond oneself. ... The European man's effort has been his tireless straining to reach toward a world, a city forever on the horizon, unreachable. The European landscape is pure horizon... (80–81)[46]

Europe exhibited a dual profile: an unreachable horizon, and the utopia of an impossible hope whose necessary failures give way to the real history, history itself as a failure. Thus, the Augustinian City of God is equivalent to a final paradigm for all European culture, even in its bloodiest nightmares:

---

[45] "Europa no ha muerto, Europa no puede morir del todo; agoniza. Porque Europa es tal vez lo único –en la Historia– que no puede morir del todo; lo único que puede resucitar. Y este principio de su resurrección será el mismo que el de su vida y el de su transitoria muerte."

[46] ... de su esperanza de resurrección aquí en la tierra, ha brotado la exigencia revolucionaria de un mundo, de una ciudad ideal siempre allá en el horizonte. Es su ansia histórica. El querer substantivar sus sueños, el creer en ellos de alguna manera. / Por eso la historia es más historia en Europa que en otra parte, por esta importancia definitiva del horizonte, porla creencia en los propios sueños que corresponde al afán de salir de sí. ... El esfuerzo del hombre europeo ha sido la infatigable tensión de tender a un mundo, a una ciudad siempre en el horizonte, inalcanzable. El paisaje europeo es puro horizonte..."

138   E. SÁNCHEZ-PARDO

> In every European struggle, someone is pushed by this impossible hope, in defense of the invisible city, having made sure that the visible cities rise; at the entangled base of the nightmare and among the terrible tension between two worlds, a longing for the kingdom of God on earth still lives, and solely by the virtue of that image, Europe has inflamed itself with nostalgia and hope, in search of its permanent utopia, its final and definitive resurrection, its transfiguration. (84)[47]

The disaster, the sickness of Europe will thus be weariness that can no longer bear the tension between the two worlds, it will be the desire to shatter the horizon, to erase the line of the unreachable, to abolish the distance, nullify the yearning for utopia—"to destroy the horizon so that everything is nearby" (84);[48] "monist barbarity, false mysticism"[49] writes Zambrano, and "weariness of the lucidity and of love for the impossible" (85).[50] If we take the utopian tension out of what Europe is, the old continent belongs to the time of that which is not. And in the space of this paradox, nostalgia intertwines with utopian sentiment. Nothing living can reach unity if not through death (once again echoing Zambrano): this unity in which Europe shows up in our nostalgia plunges us into the suspicion that it is truly dead. The condition of possibility, of our looking back in time to the turn of the nineteenth century and the consequences of the Great War is perhaps nostalgia for a lost Europe, a Europe that we have learned to perceive precisely in our suspicion of its death. We know however that the other side of suspicion is hope, the hope to return to utopia, the lucidity of the European man who learns to live history as a failure.[51]

Zambrano's words in *The Agony of Europe*, when she herself walked across the Franco-Spanish border and into exile in January 1939, are a

---

[47] Pero sí cabe decir que toda lucha europea hay alguien que ha ido a ella lanzado por esta imposible esperanza, en defensa de la ciudad invisible, y que ha hecho levantarse a las visibles. Que siempre en el fondo intrincado de la pesadilla y en la terrible tensión entre los dos mundos se encuentra vivo todavía el anhelo del reino de Dios en la tierra, por cuya sola imagen Europa se ha incendiado de nostalgia y de esperanza, en busca de su permanente utopía, de su resurrección última y definitiva, de su transfiguración."

[48] "destruir el horizonte para que todo esté al alcance de la mano."

[49] "barbarie monista, falsificada mística."

[50] "cansancio de la lucidez y del amor a lo imposible."

[51] In the aftermath of the ravages of the Spanish Civil war and the dispossession of exile, Zambrano remained determined to counter the "truth of necessity" ("verdad de la necesidad") with the "truth of hope" ("verdad de la esperanza" *Delirium and Destiny* 103).

most telling testimony of the trauma of exile, disenfranchisement, and deracination.[52] The efforts that she made in supporting the Republican cause appear all through her life and work. Unfortunately, learning to live history as a failure was not a clear outcome of the somber times of WWII. The indelible mark of colonial history and its implications remained visible in Latin America and the Caribbean, and certainly became a shameful reminder of the past into the present and the future.

THE EMERGENCE OF TRUTH IN TIME, OR WAKING UP TO REALITY

Zambrano worked indefatigably on what was to be one of her major contributions to the history of thought, that of "poetic reason." Her stay in Cuba and Puerto Rico constituted a true laboratory for the generation and articulation of this crucial concept. Far from giving rise to a similar quasi-utopian elaboration as in "Isla de Puerto Rico," Zambrano resumes her indefatigable roaming around the Caribbean and ends up writing another central piece for the completion of her Puerto Rican sojourn, namely, "Time and Truth" ("El tiempo y la Verdad" publ.1963). At this point, her essay becomes a genuine heterotopia[53] where temporality and truth are at stake.

From the tendency in continental philosophy to the abstraction of temporal consciousness, Zambrano posits time as the substance of our existence, and it is a crucial element in any consideration of her ideas on "person" and "democracy." In her view, democracy is oriented toward building a community, and "democracy ... is the society in which to be a person is not only a requirement, but a must" (*Persona y democracia*

---

[52] In *Las Palabras del Regreso*, she writes, "We had to cross the border of France one by one ... And the man who preceded me was carrying a lamb on his back, a lamb whose breath reached me and for an instant, of those indelible ones, of those that are always worthy, for all of an eternity, looked at me. I looked at it ... then I saw that the lamb was I" ("Tuvimos que pasar la frontera de "Francia uno a uno ... Y el hombre que me·precedía llevaba a la espalda un cordero, un cordero del que me llegaba su aliento y que por un instante, de esos indelebles, de esos que valen para siempre, por toda una eternidad, me miró. Y yo le miré ... entonces vi que el cordero era yo," 70–72).

[53] From the beginning of her career, in the late 20s and early 30s, Zambrano was already a student of temporality. She even planned to write a modernist novel tentatively called, *The Multiplicity of Temporalities* (see Rodríguez García, "Two Essays on Ruins" 99).

140   E. SÁNCHEZ-PARDO

169).[54] In *Person and Democracy* (1958) Zambrano alludes constantly to the human condition, humankind, "must humanize its history, making it his, assuming it from the person" (100).[55] Almost simultaneously, in "Time and Truth," we hear Zambrano's lament for a bygone way of life, that of democracy in Europe.

In Zambrano, time occupies a double dimension, the historical and the transcendental. The first dimension addresses the time of a specific community, from the past and into the present. The transcendental dimension is one in which the "person" conceives of her relation to the community as a part of her own relationship to the future. It is important to note that not only time passes, we also pass with time, and time is certainly the medium of human existence, and, in Zambrano, time is even figured as the space where the person is born. Time, the word, and the creative action are three essentials—"notas esenciales" ("Tiempo y verdad" 63)—of the human condition. In "Time and Truth," Zambrano foregrounds the convergences between being in exile and being born, since "to live entails getting into a 'situation'...that the exile, as soon as he is away, must procure for himself" (63).[56] Still there is a dramatic difference between exile and biological birth.

"Time and Truth" opens with the trope of a birth scene, a scene of origins in which the human being senses the unique feeling of "coming out of a dark place which contains us" (63).[57] Time is already there, assisting the human. In Zambrano's mythical account, it is Cronos, the first agent and "efficient cause" of the liberation of human life. With recourse to mythical time, to Hesiod's Theogony,[58] she ushers us into her account of time and truth. Zambrano poetically states that "The encounter with time will be the awakening of the dream" (67)[59] and argues that man only discovers himself over time. At this point, it is important to note that, in

[54] "la democracia ... es la sociedad en la cual no sólo es permitido, sino exigido, el ser persona."

[55] "ha de humanizar su historia, hacerla suya, asumirla desde su persona."

[56] "vivir implica asumir una 'situación' ... que el exiliado, tan pronto como se va, debe cuidar de sí mismo."

[57] "salir de un lugar oscuro que nos contiene."

[58] As it is well known, Hesiod's Theogony (eighth—seventh century B.C) is a poem and the first Greek mythical cosmology in which an explanation is given of the origin of the Cosmos with the Greek gods, their deeds, and offspring. It tells how Cronus overthrew Uranus, and how in turn Zeus overthrew Cronus and his fellow Titans, and how Zeus was eventually established as the final and permanent ruler of the cosmos.

[59] "El encuentro con el tiempo será el despertar del sueño."

the philosopher's view, our knowledge of time does not start with a question, "it was, no doubt, a poetic and experimental knowledge, a knowledge of suffering that corresponds to the first awakening of consciousness" (68).[60] She claims, "To wake up to reality is to wake up to time. But one does not wake up to reality without others having awakened to the truth" (69).[61]

Zambrano speaks from her position of exile, and speaks about "the truth of the vanquished" (72).[62] She also speaks of "passivity" and how passivity is also a major way of action which resides in suffering, suffering for the truth (72). In *La Confesión, género literario*, she goes on to argue that "[confession] deals with finding the point of contact between life and truth" (31–32).[63] And we should not forget that confession is a genre that, in her view, appears mostly in times of crisis. While we may feel entitled to question Zambrano's own self-representation, the philosophical essay she cultivates is an opaque and democratic form of self-writing. What literature does rhetorically and discursively, philosophy does inquisitively as a continuous quest—here, both gestures attempt to reveal the mystery of the writer's identity. Could this identification of writing and selfhood then make the confessional, as defined by Zambrano, into one of the crucial paradigms of her oeuvre?

For Zambrano, "Truth occurs firstly in speech" ("Tiempo y verdad" 71)[64] and if it were not for the word one would tend to think that time is all that exists. Throughout her work, Zambrano speaks frequently of the poet's role in connecting the people to the word—in her view this was best represented in Antonio Machado's poetry (see her crucial "La guerra de Antonio Machado")—and in his engagement with community and truth. She considers both poetry and philosophy as based on the love for knowledge and on the love and admiration for the world. Her notion of "Poetic reason," which announces as "This reason for reintegrating love of the rich substance of the world" (*Senderos* 69)[65] comes out of what she calls "the deep root of love" (*Senderos* 68).[66]

---

[60] "fue un saber poético y experimental sin duda, un saber de padecimiento que corresponde al primer despertar de la conciencia."

[61] "Despertar a la realidad es despertar al tiempo. Mas no se despierta a la realidad sin otras haber despertado a la verdad."

[62] "la verdad de los vencidos."

[63] "[la confesión] trata de encontrar el punto de contacto entre la vida y la verdad."

[64] "La verdad se da primeramente en el decir."

[65] "esta razón de amor reintegradora de la rica substancia del mundo."

[66] "honda raíz de amor."

142   E. SÁNCHEZ-PARDO

It seems to me there is an aporia in the midst of the philosophical essays examined in this chapter: the crisis in experience parallels the unsurmountable obstacles the individual faces in any attempt at reconstructing memory, community, and homeland. In Zambrano, the writing of philosophy becomes a mediation between the historical demands of her intellectual project and those realities that were, in her view, traditionally excluded by Western philosophy. In her Caribbean essays, as much as in her philosophical practice Zambrano works with all that exists beyond the limits of intelligibility as established by the dominant idea of Reason: affect, emotions, the immaterial, and the excluded (friendship, love, time, democracy, hope). Throughout this chapter, I have attempted to show how the recursive movement back and forth, from the insular space to the mainland, from the Caribbean to Europe, present at the level of the form and content of her work, functions not only internally as a trope for the nascent writing process but also externally as a mirror image of the issues strategically addressed.

In her hybrid philosophical essays, Zambrano's journey goes from the island to the continent and back to the island. Throughout her journey, she reveals new insular topographies, exploring with genuine interest the role of the other—interlocutor, friend, poet, artist—in sustaining life and democratic ideals. Upon writing "Isla de Puerto Rico," and "Time and Truth" (1948),[67] Zambrano touches upon a geographic imaginary and concurrently presents us with her major latent ideas on love, loss, temporality, history, and truth. Her exile status gravitates around the conditions of the known world and the horizons of possible worlds (Daniels 183), and within her real-cum-imagined geographies, she piles up perceptions, reflections, and analyses related to a largely unmappable world. It is through her emotional attachments and memorable experiences linked to specific places and times that past and present prove to be interconnected through her epistemologically rich involvement. For our thinker, Puerto Rico and Cuba came to be promised and promising lands to engage in creative activities and do philosophy. Both islands came to be "clearings in

---

[67] "La Cuba Secreta" (1948) is a central text in which Zambrano speaks about her engagement with Cuba and with the Origenistas: Lezama, Cintio Vitier, Eliseo Diego, Fina García Marruz, Lidia Cabrera, among other writers and artists. They were the aesthetic and intellectual basis that nurtured Zambrano. Their gatherings, conversations, shared readings and life, were instrumental in the philosopher's work, as well as in the evolution of many of their oeuvres.

the woods,"[68] where her own philosophical system, in touch with the new insular realities, was drawn to the intimate, solitary, and meditative spaces of the islands.

Zambrano's legacy of modernity, feminism, and democratic ideals shows in "Isla de Puerto Rico" and "Time and Truth" as a response to the pressing concerns that assail the person, then and now, in times of crisis. From the heterotopia of her enchanted Caribbean islands to the heart of Europe, her words resonate with the rhythmic insistence of the abiding human.

WORKS CITED

Anderson, Benedict. *Imagined Communities. Reflections on the Origin and Spread of Nationalism.* 1983. Verso, 1991.

———. *The Spectre of Comparisons: Nationalism, Southeast Asia and the World.* Verso, 1998.

Anzaldúa, Gloria. *Borderlands/La Frontera: The New Mestiza.* Spinsters/Aunt Lute, 1987.

Appadurai, Arjun. "Here and Now." *Visual Culture Reader*, edited by Nicholas Mirzoeff, Routledge, 2002, pp. 173–79.

Avilés-Ortiz, Iliaris A. "María Zambrano in Puerto Rico: Chronicles of an Extraordinary Journey." *Aurora*, vol. 17, 2016, pp. 6–19.

———. "María Zambrano. Una filósofa en la "red Benítez." *Devenires*, vol. 44, 2021, pp. 97–132.

Benítez-Rojo, Antonio. *The Repeating Island: The Caribbean and the Postmodern Perspective.* Translated by James E. Maraniss, Duke UP, 1997.

Bhabha, Homi. "DissemiNation: Time, Narrative, and the Margins of the Modern Nation." *Nation and Narration*, Routledge, 1990, pp. 291–322.

———. *The Location of Culture.* Routledge, 1994.

Bonilla, Alcira B. "Razón Poética y Género. Arquetipos Femeninos." *Philosophica Malacitana. Monográfico sobre M. Zambrano*, vol. 4, 1991, pp. 49–64.

Burgos-Lafuente, Lena. "¿Qué es entonces una isla? Ruinas, islas y escritura en el Caribe de María Zambrano." *Journal of Spanish Cultural Studies*, vol. 16, no. 4, 2015, pp. 375–96.

Butler, Judith P. *Precarious Life: The Powers of Mourning and Violence.* Verso, 2004.

---

[68] Zambrano published *Clearings in the Woods* (1977) as a sustained philosophical-literary meditation on mysticism, poetry, and the unveiling of the hidden and the occult that is in Nature.

144   E. SÁNCHEZ-PARDO

Cámara, Madeline, and Luis Ortega, editors. *María Zambrano. Between the Caribbean and the Mediterranean.* Juan de la Cuesta Hispanic Monographs, 2015.

———, editors. *María Zambrano. Palabras para el Mundo.* Juan de la Cuesta Hispanic Monographs, 2011.

Carens, Joseph. "Aliens and Citizens: The Case for Open Borders." *Theorizing Citizenship*, edited by Ronald Beiner, SUNY Press, 1995, pp. 229–55.

Daniels, Stephen. "Geographical Imagination." *Transactions of the Institute of British Geographers*, vol. 36, no. 2, 2011, pp. 182–87.

Del Moral, Solsiree. "Modern Puerto Rico: A First Reading List." *Puerto Rico: A US Colony in a Postcolonial World*, special issue of *Radical History Review*, vol. 128, May 2017, pp. 13–25.

Devés Valdés, Eduardo. *Redes intelectuales en América Latina. Hacia la constitución de una comunidad intelectual.* Santiago de Chile, Instituto de Estudios Avanzados de la Universidad de Santiago de Chile, 2007.

Duffy Burnett, Christina, and Burke Marshall, editors. *Foreign in a Domestic Sense. Puerto Rico, American Expansion, and the Constitution.* Duke UP, 2001.

von Flotow, Louise. "Gender and Translation." *A Companion to Translation Studies*, edited by Piotr Kuhiwczak and Karin Littau, Multilingual Matters, 2007, pp. 92–105.

Friedman, Susan S. *Planetary Modernisms. Provocations on Modernity across Time.* Columbia UP, 2015.

García Marruz, Fina. "María Zambrano, entre el alba y la Aurora." *Zambuch*, vol. 2, 1998, pp. 5–58.

Habermas, Jurgen. *The Inclusion of the Other. Studies in Political Theory*, edited by Ciaran Cronin and Pablo De Greiff, MIT Press, 1998.

Jameson, Fredric, and Masao Miyoshi, editors. *The Cultures of Globalization.* Duke UP, 1998.

Kristeva, Julia. *Strangers to Ourselves.* Translated by Leon S. Roudiez, Columbia UP, 1991.

Kuhiwczak, Piotr, and Karin Littau, editors. *A Companion to Translation Studies.* Multilingual Matters, 2007.

Lezama Lima, José, and María Zambrano. *Correspondencia.* Espuela de Plata, 2006.

Lowe, Lisa. *Immigrant Acts. On Asian American Cultural Politics.* Duke UP, 1996.

Mariátegui, Juan Diego. *To Reach the Isle: Poetics of the Island in Puerto Rican Literature of the 20th Century.* 2021. U Chicago, PhD dissertation.

Martín, Francisco José. "Presentación. María Zambrano en su centenario. Los años de Roma." *Zambrano: los años de Roma (1953–1964)*, 2004. cvc.cervantes.es/literatura/zambrano_roma/presentacion.htm. Accessed 12 Dec. 2022.

Mignolo, Walter. *Local Histories, Global Designs: Coloniality, Subaltern Knowledges and Border Thinking.* Princeton UP, 2000.

6 MARÍA ZAMBRANO'S CARIBBEAN IMAGININGS: PHILOSOPHY FROM ... 145

Mirzoeff, Nicholas, editor. *The Visual Culture Reader*. Routledge, 2002.

Mohanty, Chandra Talpade. *Feminism Without Borders. Decolonizing Theory. Practicing Solidarity*. Duke UP, 2003.

Moreno Sanz, Jesús. "Insulas extrañas, lámparas de fuego. Las raíces espirituales de la política en Isla de Puerto Rico." *María Zambrano: la visión más transparente*, edited by Juan Antonio González Fuentes and José María Beneyto Pérez, Trotta, 2004a, pp. 209–86.

———. *María Zambrano. De la razón cívica a la razón poética. Catálogo Exposición*. Publicaciones de la Residencia de Estudiantes, 2004b.

Ortega Muñoz, Juan F., editor. *María Zambrano. El exilio como patria*. Anthropos, 2014.

Pedreira, Antonio S. *Insularismo. Ensayos de interpretación puertorriqueña*. San Juan, Biblioteca de autores puertorriqueños, 1942.

Rivera Ramos, Efrén. *American Colonialism in Puerto Rico. The Judicial and Social Legacy*. Markus Wiener, 2007.

Rodríguez García, José M. "María Zambrano: Two Essays on Ruins." *Modernist Cultures*, vol. 7, no. 1, 2012, pp. 98–131.

Said, Edward W. *The World, the Text and the Critic*. Harvard UP, 1983.

Sánchez-Gey Venegas, Juana. "María Zambrano. Sus relaciones personales y su aportación a Cuba." *Escritos* (Medellín, Colombia), vol. 19, no. 43, 2011, pp. 423–39.

Sedeño, Kevin. "Viaje iniciático de María Zambrano a la isla secreta. Pensamiento insular y vivencia caribeña del exilio en Cuba y Puerto Rico." *María Zambrano: Palabras para el mundo*, edited by Madeline Cámara and Luis Ortega Hurtado, Juan de la Cuesta Hispanic Monographs, 2011, pp. 91–104.

Soysal, Yasemin. *Limits of Citizenship. Migrants and Postnational Membership in Europe*. U Chicago P, 1994.

Vilar, Juan B. *La España del exilio. Las emigraciones políticas españolas en los siglos XIX y XX*. Síntesis, 2006.

Zambrano, María. "El tiempo y la verdad." *El Exilio como Patria*. Anthropos, 2014, pp. 63–74.

———. "Isla de Puerto Rico. Nostalgia y esperanza de un mundo mejor." *Islas*, edited by Jorge Luis Arcos, Verbum, 2007a, pp. 3–19.

———. "La guerra de Antonio Machado." *Senderos. Los intelectuales en el drama de España. La Tumba de Antígona*, Anthropos, 1986a, pp. 60–70.

———. *Claros del bosque*. Seix Barral, 1977.

———. *De la aurora*. Edited by J. Moreno Sanz, Turner, 1986b.

———. *Delirium and Destiny: A Spaniard in Her Twenties*. Translated by Carol Maier, SUNY Press, 1999.

———. *El hombre y lo divino*. Siruela, 1992.

———. *Islas*. Edited by Jorge Luis Arcos, Verbum, 2007b.

———. *La agonía de Europa*, Trotta, 2000.

146   E. SÁNCHEZ-PARDO

———. *La confesión. Género literario.* Siruela, 2004a.

———. *La visión más transparente.* Edited by José María Beneyto and Juan Antonio González Fuentes, Trotta, 2004b.

———. *Las palabras del regreso.* Edited by Mercedes Gómez Blesa, Cátedra, 2009.

———. *Los bienaventurados.* Siruela, 2004c.

———. *Los intelectuales en el drama de España y Escritos de la guerra civil.* Trotta, 1998.

———. *Obras completas II, 1940–1950.* Edited by Jesús Moreno Sanz, Galaxia Gutenberg, 2016.

———. *Persona y democracia. La historia sacrificial.* Anthropos, 1988.

———. *Senderos. Los intelectuales en el drama de España. La Tumba de Antígona.* Anthropos, 1986c.

CHAPTER 7

The Scene of the Firing Squad: Zambrano's *Delirium and Destiny* and Goya's *The Third of May*

Juli Highfill

Writing in exile in 1952, María Zambrano produced an anguished, poetic meditation on the tragic loss of life and of democracy in Spain.[1] *Delirium and Destiny: A Spaniard in Her Twenties* focuses on the years 1929 to 1931, when Zambrano and her fellow university students were intensely engaged in the movement to establish a democratic republic. In a lyrical and often delirious narration—interwoven with philosophical reflections—she expresses her ardent hopes, shared by her comrades, for a collective awakening by the Spanish people, such that they might breathe an atmosphere infused with a restorative, egalitarian spirit. Yet her re-creation

---

[1] Zambrano penned the book in a four-week period in 1952, while still living in Havana; it was not published until 1988. As she explains in her introduction, she submitted it to the Institut Européen Universitaire de la Culture, for the Prix Littéraire Européen, and received an Honorable Mention.

J. Highfill (✉)
Department of Romance Languages and Literatures at the University of Michigan, Ann Arbor, MI, USA
e-mail: highfill@umich.edu

© The Author(s), under exclusive license to Springer Nature Switzerland AG 2024
R. M. Silverman, E. Sánchez-Pardo (eds.), *Nomadic New Women*,
https://doi.org/10.1007/978-3-031-62482-7_7

147

148   J. HIGHFILL

of that moment of solidarity and hope is haunted by violent deaths—those of the past and those that would come—in particular, death by firing squad. Zambrano repeatedly invokes Francisco de Goya's powerful painting, *The Third of May* (1814), which portrays an anonymous fighter in the War of Independence, as he faces a firing squad. Lit by a bright lantern and wearing a white shirt open at the chest, he throws his arms outward and looks directly at his executioners. By dwelling on Goya's painting, Zambrano is bearing witness to the massive numbers of executions by firing squad during and after the Civil War. And in doing so, she attempts to fathom the meaning of those deaths, among them dear friends. Zambrano describes that white-shirted figure as at once cursing and blessing the world, issuing a "scream of life," thereby affirming that in that instant of death, he delivers himself to life.

Her re-creation of those years of solidarity and hope is thus a work of mourning. In a letter to Rosa Chacel, sent from Rome in 1953, Zambrano describes her life in exile, confessing the "great, immense pain that is now like a void without shorelines, a vast ocean in which our heart keeps on beating, the ocean of our blood and of our thought" (43).[2] She tells Chacel of the book she wrote the previous year, *Delirium and Destiny*: "It's not a novel. What is it?" (45).[3] From an objective, academic viewpoint, she adds, it is a history of the origins of the Republic—a personalized account that ends on April 14, 1931—the date of the proclamation of the Republic. The second part of the manuscript, she explains, is an epilogue comprising "Delirios" that represents "the skeleton of truth," so named because "skeletons that are obliged to live become delirious" (46).[4] "That is why I don't know if I've transmigrated to the world of blood or to the world of bones," she adds (46). Throughout the letter, as she recounts both tragic and trivial details of her life, she repeats the phrase— "That is why I haven't died" (46).[5] Her purpose in writing to her friend, she admits, is to explain why she has not died, why she is still alive. She is casting herself as one of those skeletons of truth, obliged to go on living

---

[2] "[E]l grande, inmenso dolor que es ya como un vacío sin riberas, piélago sobre el que ha de seguir latiendo nuestro corazón, el de nuestra sangre y el de nuestro pensamiento" (43). (My translation)

[3] No es una novela. ¿Qué es? (45).

[4] "[L]a verdad en su esqueleto. Y los esqueletos obligados a vivir deliran" (46).

[5] "Por eso no he muerto [...]. Me doy cuenta que lo que quiero decirte es por qué no me he muerto, por qué estoy viva todavía" (44).

7 THE SCENE OF THE FIRING SQUAD: ZAMBRANO'S *DELIRIUM...* 149

in a state of delirium, obliged to adopt the anguished, phantasmal narrative voice that we hear throughout *Delirium and Destiny*.[6]

In the first chapter, titled "Adsum" (I am Here), the narrator begins with a startling assertion—"She had wanted to die, not the way a person wants to die when death is a long way off, but by going toward it" (5).[7] By writing in third person, Zambrano might seem to be distancing herself from her own lived experience; yet the intimate, confessional language draws the reader into a deeply felt, disorienting experience of being newly born after nearly dying from a prolonged illness—in this case, tuberculosis:[8] "She had decided to be born, but she would have to continue being born. Actually, she was living a prenatal state, in which she inevitably found herself a prisoner of deliriums, and she would traverse dark corridors, pushing on half-open doors, her small, motionless being unfurling" (14).[9] The feverish stream-of-consciousness narration gives voice to these deliriums, alternating between childhood memories and philosophical meditations. In fits and starts "she" emerges, at times sinking back, but gradually reawakening to life, to consciousness, and to a "dreamed destiny" she calls history. She is now here, "simply, as a wisp of being, a speck of dust, eager

---

[6] Delirium operates throughout the text as an ambivalent and fluid term. Early in the book, the young student activists are intent on "rejecting the delirium that had devoured Spanish life in the nineteenth century. They were escaping from delirium and the resultant suffocation" (28) ["renunciaban al delirio que devoró la vida de los españoles en el siglo XIX. Huían del delirio y de la consiguiente asfixia"] (57). But after the tragic defeat of the Republic, after all the losses of friends and loved ones, delirium becomes Zambrano's lifeline, her only consolation.

[7] "Había querido morir, no al modo en que se quiere cuando se está lejos de la muerte, sino yendo hacia ella" (21). For in-text quotations, I rely on Carol Maier's translation of *Delirium and Destiny*. For the original Spanish text provided here and in subsequent notes, I draw from the 2011 edition of Zambrano's *Delirio y destino*.

[8] In this chapter, Zambrano interweaves several live experiences of birth and rebirth: First, in a general sense, she recaptures her early infancy and coming to consciousness in the patio in Vélez-Málaga, with its lemon tree and swallows circling above—there where her father engendered her from his forehead (as Zeus engendered Athena). Second, she recalls scenes in Madrid, where the family lived briefly in 1908, and where she was convalescing after nearly dying from typhoid fever at age three or four. Third, and more extensively, she recounts her reemergence into life after being bed-ridden for several months in 1929, suffering from tuberculosis. For biographical studies of Zambrano's early life, see: Marcet, Moreno Sanz, and Tellez.

[9] "Se había decidido a nacer, pero tendría que ir naciendo. Vivía, en realidad, un estado prenatal en el que inevitablemente había de ser presa de delirios, y recorrería galerías oscuras empujando puertas semiabiertas; su pequeño ser inmóvil se despegaba" (34-35).

150   J. HIGHFILL

to enter the light, to receive it in her poverty, to vibrate in harmony" (10).[10] Now (re)born and committed to being born as often as necessary, she has arrived naked to the world, impoverished, stripped of her self-image, and utterly alone. But in a strategic move, she pledges to keep faith with that nakedness, poverty, loneliness, and with that very absence of a coherent self, or *persona*.

In so doing, she pivots to an affirmation of shared poverty and intimate comradeship with others, with her brothers and sisters: "Poor and alone, all of them" (10).[11] She affirms her immediate historical moment as well, referencing Ortega y Gasset's famous statement, "I am I and my circumstance" (Ortega 322). Bed-ridden and delirious, she gazes through the window at the clouds above and reads her circumstance as "sky-writing," as destiny, and as history (13–14):

> Madrid's blue sky was full of white, bluish, and gold-tinged clouds; suddenly they had turned into figures: horses, ancient kinds, armies, monsters in combat, and there below, level with the horizon, a glorious wreath, a promise that seemed to frame everything, to bind heaven and earth [...]. It was the history of Spain awakening at that very hour, projecting itself on Madrid's implacably blue sky in 1929. Yes, all life and all history seemed to await her. It gave her time, it would give her time for everything: yes, I am here. (13–14)[12]

As she attempts to decipher the images drawn upon that garland of clouds binding heaven and earth, she confesses that her circumstances remain malleable, lacking any definite meaning. Only later, she muses, when she could truly enter into the future, would she be "forced by circumstances"; but for the moment, everything remained suspended (14).[13] Even so, "the dream of Spain seeped into her and she began to live this dream

[10] "[Simplemente], como una brizna de ser, un poco de polvo, ávido de entrar en la luz, de recibirla, en su pobreza" (29).

[11] "Pobres y solos, todos" (29).

[12] "El cielo azul de Madrid, estaba lleno de blancas, azuladas y semidoradas nubes; de pronto habían cobrado figura; caballos, reyes antiguos, ejércitos, peleas de monstruos, allá abajo a ras del horizonte, una guirnalda de gloria, una promesa que parecía enmarcarlo todo, sujetar cielo y tierra [...]. Era la historia de España que se despertaba en aquella hora precisa [...], se proyectaba sobre el cielo implacablemente azul de Madrid, 1919. Sí, toda la vida, y también la historia parecía aguardarla. Le daba tiempo, le darían tiempo para todo: sí estoy aquí" (34).

[13] "[L]as circunstancias la forzarían" (35).

7 THE SCENE OF THE FIRING SQUAD: ZAMBRANO'S *DELIRIUM...* 151

alone"—not only her country's dream but also "the world's dream, Europe's dream" (15).[14] And as she waits to rejoin life and history, she affirms, "I am here"—*adsum* (14).[15]

Throughout this initial account of birth and rebirth, Zambrano enacts a movement from the solitary, vulnerable, and destitute inner being, toward the outside, toward the circumstances she shares with others who also face that historical moment with all its promise and peril. This "autobiographical gesture," according to Rose Corral, consists of two intimately connected "gestations"—her own birth and Spain's birth during those years, culminating in the proclamation of the Second Republic (59). The meaning of "Dreamed Destiny," the title of the first half of the book, thus becomes clear: "In this dreamed destiny her own life becomes fused with the life of the anonymous collective, with 'the pulse of Spain'" (Corral 59).[16] Also manifest in this metaphoric double birthing—of herself and of the collective—is the function of the third-person narration; for it enables Zambrano to avoid the unitary I of traditional autobiography. As Roberta Johnson points out, the pronoun "she" works as a provisional "social mask that shields the central consciousness of the work from a radical individualism and moves it towards the communal social self that is increasingly implied as the narrative progresses" (233). It is evident, however, that the text conforms to the autobiographical mode; for as in all autobiography, we have an older, wiser "narrating self" who places herself back in time and focalizes through a younger "experiencing self."[17]

As readers, we partake in the narrator's gaze as she recreates the experiences of her younger self, the "Young Spaniard in Her Twenties," referenced in the book's subtitle. After that initial moment of rebirth, we observe her reentry and immersion in her social and political circumstances. She joins the University Student Federation (FUE, la Federación Universitaria Escolar) and pours her energies into political activities in opposition to the dictatorship of General Primo de Rivera, who, since

---

[14] "[E]l sueño de España se le fue entrando y comenzó a vivir sola ese sueño. Y el sueño del mundo, de Europa" (35–36).

[15] "Estoy aquí" (34).

[16] "En este destino soñado se funde la propia vida con la de colectividad anónima, con 'el pulso de España'" (59).

[17] I draw these terms, "narrating self" and "experiencing self" from Franz Stanzel, *A Theory of Narrative*. Similarly, Philippe Lejeune in *On Autobiography* famously coined the phrase, "the autobiographical pact" to refer to the identity of author, narrator, and reader. This three-fold identity emerges as an implicit contract between the reader and author.

152   J. HIGHFILL

seizing power in 1923, had ruled with the consent of the King, Alfonso XIII.[18] What emerges powerfully in these early chapters is a sense of comradeship; the students take very seriously Ortega's dictum—"Vivir es convivir" ["living is living with others"] (27). And together they affirm a "shared life," as they engage in efforts to revive communality and to rebuild Spanish life, "flagging now, after centuries of inertia" (27, 22).[19] Whereas they support a democratic republic, the young activists resist joining a political party or defining a revolutionary, moral, or esthetic program. Instead, they aim to be the "vehicle" of a generalized change in attitude, an awakening (28); for in that moment, Zambrano asserts: "Spain was still not visible, we felt Spain more than we saw her, and we were yearning to see her, and it was necessary, absolutely necessary, that she become visible to the world once more, healed, whole, and self-possessed; she must be young and awake after her centuries-long sleep, whole despite her history, beyond her history, real, present" (22).[20] In conveying this intense longing to *see* an awakened, rejuvenated Spain, Zambrano turns to metaphors of redemption, evoking images of crystalline waters that will cleanse and heal the country. She characterizes the students' first secretive projects "as something whose birth had just begun, like a silent spring under the stones" (23); and she likens their work in transmitting "the new attitude" to "melt-water born at last in the rocky heights of the Guadarrama, from the thaw that became cascades, streams, and rivers running down from the mountains to revitalize all of Spain" (28).[21]

---

[18] In actuality, Zambrano began her student activism in 1927 and experienced two periods of serious illness and seclusion, in 1928 and 1929. In *Delirium and Destiny*, she admits to "wanting only to give herself completely, not knowing what she was doing, exhausting herself in a passion for knowledge and action focused on one point: Spain. In this she was not alone" (21); ["buscando tan sólo darse enteramente, sin saber que lo hacía, quemándose en una pasión de conocimiento y de acción atraída hacia un foco: España. No estaba sola tampoco aquí" (46)].

[19] "[L]a convivencia"; "renovación de la convivencia, [...] renovación de la sociedad; hay que construir la vida española que viene arrastrándose desde siglos de inercia" (47).

[20] "España no era todavía visible, la sentíamos más que la veíamos y teníamos ansia de verla, era necesario absolutamente necesario que se hiciera de nuevo visible al mundo, recobrada, entera, dueña de sí: joven, despertada desde su sueño de siglos; intacta, a pesar de su historia, más allá de su historia, real, presente" (48).

[21] "[D]e lo que comienza a nacer como los manantiales silenciosos cubiertos por las piedras" (50); "de esta nueva actitud, el hielo de agua nacido, al fin, en las alturas pétreas del Guadarrama, del deshielo, que bajase hecha cascada, arroyos, ríos a vivificar toda España" (57).

7 THE SCENE OF THE FIRING SQUAD: ZAMBRANO'S *DELIRIUM...* 153

Similarly, poetic images of the sky and air abound throughout the text—metaphors for the deeply felt communal purpose shared by these students: "they wanted to breathe easily, deeply, in unison—not only the pulse but also the rhythm, the rhythm of a common breathing" (24).[22] She returns to "sky-writing," echoing that image of the garland of clouds that bound heaven and earth, which earlier she had seen through her window. Now, seated with a comrade on the wall outside the Residencia de Estudiantes, on a hill above Madrid, she intensely feels the new "fraternal understanding" they shared: "the concave sky dipped down to embrace the city, and in that air it was possible to sense the breath of the city, a human breath, full of life" (21).[23] The students' principal aim was not political, at least not in the generally accepted sense, but rather, to "facilitate an opening up of Spanish life" (21). Through innovative thought and thoughtful deeds, they would create a "vital, breathable space" and make Spain "a habitable country for all Spaniards" (28–29).[24] The poetic, affective effect of these images—of cleansing waters and of bracing air—works not only to recreate that moment of intense and intimate commitment among the youths but also to immerse readers in that very atmosphere, casting us too as their comrades.[25]

Indeed, later in the narration she characterizes the actions of the FUE as "poetic, totally invented"; for rather than direct political actions, they were engaged in something she regards as more serious and enduring: "an ambience was being created, an atmosphere that was gradually enveloping

---

[22] "[Q]uerían respirar ancha, profundamente, al unísono; no sólo el pulso sino el ritmo, el ritmo de una común respiración" (51).

[23] "[E]l cielo cóncavo bajaba a abrazar la ciudad y en su aire se sentía la respiración de la ciudad, una respiración humana, plena de ida" (46).

[24] "[A]brir paso o hacer que se abriera esa vida de España" (46-47); "un espacio vital, respirable" (58); "un país habitable para todos los españoles" (57).

[25] See Roberta Johnson, "The Context and Achievement," for a concise discussion on how Zambrano reconceptualizes Ortega's concept of "vital reason" by positing the notion of "poetic reason" (228–29). First posited in the essay, "Hacia un saber sobre el alma" (1934), "poetic reason" affirms the crucial role of emotion, affect, dreams, and even delirium in the political and social domain. The intimate, lyrical narration of *Delirio y destino* with its account of a subject's immersion in the collective can be understood as a consummate enactment of poetic reason. For a useful overview of the copious scholarship on poetic reason: refer to Enquist Källgren (13–19; 163–73); and for further scholarship on the concept, refer to: Bundgaard, Caballero Rodríguez, *Maria Zambrano*; Lapiedra Gutiérrez; Parente, and Revilla Guzmán.

154   J. HIGHFILL

the life of the city and of other Spanish cities" (87).[26] Toward this end, these youths adopted a humorous tone in their communications. They embraced sports, cinema, jazz, and café life; they felt themselves "floating in a sort of slight intoxication," part of "a great upsurge in the life of the city" (87).[27] In their interactions between the sexes, they adhered to "an initial creed, or rather an unformulated promise," expressing "horror and aversion" toward coquetry and conquest; the young men made fun of "donjuanismo," and the girls disdained prissiness (27–28).[28] While these youths did not regard themselves as revolutionaries, they were fully committed to "convivencia"—shared life: "with their elders, with their equals, with the illiterate, with the peasants, with the workers" (27).[29]

As of yet, the authorities paid them no mind, but something was changing, the rhythm was quickening, an irrevocable force was building. The students would eventually turn to direct action—organizing strikes, mass protests, and occupying university buildings—as agitation for a Republic heightened in the years 1929 to 1931, but even in the early stages of mobilization, their activities were not solely cultural.[30] In 1928, the students divided into small groups, each assigned to approach several "elders," the most illustrious writers and thinkers in Spain at the time, among them Ramón de Valle Inclán, Gregorio de Marañon, Luis Giménez de Asúa, Ramón Pérez de Ayala, Manuel Azaña, and many others left unnamed. The students hoped to awaken these intellectuals to the common task that they had not yet recognized (21). Zambrano provides vivid accounts of the interviews she conducted, in some cases, revealing the elders' initial reluctance to joining the students' cause.[31] Azaña, who would later become President of the Republic, reacted dismissively at first, regarding their

[26] "[E]sta acción era poética, enteramente inventada. Y por ello más constante. No se proyectaban actos políticos. Era algo más grave: se estaba creando un ambiente, una atmósfera que iba envolviendo a la vida de la ciudad y de otras ciudades de España" (143).

[27] "[S]e sentían flotar en una especie de embriaguez ligera" (144); "desbordamiento en la vida de la ciudad" (143).

[28] "[E]specie de credo inicial, de promesa más bien no formulada [...]: había horror y repugnancia de la coquetería, de la conquista: se burlaban ellos del donjuanismo, ellas de las remilgadas" (56).

[29] "[C]on los mayores, con los iguales, con los analfabetos, con los campesinos, con los obreros. Vivir es convivir" (55).

[30] For more on this student mobilization, see González Calleja (31–37).

[31] For more detail on these interviews and the meetings with elders that followed, refer to Bundgaard (105–16); Johnson, "Context and Achievement" (219–22); and Moreno Sanz, "Síntesis biográfico" (39). Whereas in *Delirium and Destiny*, Zambrano leaves most of the

7 THE SCENE OF THE FIRING SQUAD: ZAMBRANO'S *DELIRIUM...* 155

project as impractical and undefined. But in the end, nearly all the elders agreed to attend a meeting with the students, where together they formed the League for Social Education (Liga de Educación Social). As the struggle against the regime intensified over the next few years, the young activists and elder intellectuals would maintain this intergenerational solidarity, which would become a key factor in the fall of the monarchy and the advent of the Republic.

Among the activities of the League for Social Education were efforts at outreach to labor unions, the Socialist Party, and the Anarchist Confederation (CNT). Their aim was to approach the workers "respectfully and in solidarity [...] with a longing to understand" (31).[32] Zambrano herself spoke before the *cigarreras*, members of the Cigar Workers' Union, who represented "the heart of working-class Madrid traditionalism," and she describes the experience in musical terms:

> [T]here was no struggle, no imposition, no "pedagogy"; it was a moment of "pre-established harmony," as in music. The tone was set from the beginning; it pre-existed. There was perfect harmony among all those present: the men—the most illustrious men of the sciences, the Spanish university, Spanish letters; the cigar workers; and the young people. Words had merely provided the cadenza in a concert improvised by a Mozart-like musician. (32)[33]

In Zambrano's account of this "concert," she describes the sense of sheer happiness she felt afterwards—the joy of having experienced a perfect harmony, a deep, mutual understanding with the women workers, akin to "a beam of light flooding her mind," the same joyful feeling she experienced "those few times she understood something in philosophy" (32).[34] She

---

elders unnamed, decades later, in an article about Gregorio de Marañon, "Un liberal," she offers a frank and more detailed account (in *Las palabras del regreso*, 85–95).

[32] "[C]on simpatía y respeto; con anhelo de comprender" (62); "este gremio, corazón del casticismo madrileño" (63).

[33] "Y no hubo lucha, ni imposición, ni 'pedagogía', fue un momento de 'armonía preestablecida', a la manera musical; el tono estaba dado ya desde el principio; la consonancia fue perfecta entre la presencia de aquellos hombres, los más ilustres de la Ciencia, de la Universidad española, de las letras, las cigarreras y ellos, los jóvenes; las palabras habían sido solamente la cadencia en aquel concierto improvisado por un músico a lo Mozart" (63). Note that I have slightly changed Maier's translation.

[34] "[U]n rayo que iluminase la mente"; "las pocas veces que había entendido algo en filosofía" (63).

156   J. HIGHFILL

felt she had spoken not *to* these women but *with* them, "with the heart of Madrid": "The pulse of Spain, its very heartbeat, had created that harmony, that living silence where words fell like music; meaning was expanding, the horizon was opening, breathing" (32).[35]

As Zambrano continues to recount her growing political engagement, this pulse steadily quickens. Increasingly, she invokes *el pueblo* (the people)—understanding them as an "alive and organic" force, a reservoir of lived history, in contrast with the anonymous, undifferentiated masses (120).[36] For centuries the people had suffered from hunger and unrealized hope; now they were awakening to "dreamed destiny," to history: "Before Spain could make demands as a people, it had to dare to hope, and hope was now breaking free" (50).[37] The experience of hunger, as bodily need, cannot allow for hope, she asserts; the people must have enough to eat before they can sense all that they lack. Only sometime after that point, can they begin to feel "that transcendent hunger that is hope, the hope that is total hunger—the non-being that becomes apparent to itself in a positive way because it is located in the future" (52).[38] The Republic, now on the horizon, came to embody that transcendent hunger. During an interregnum of uncertainty—the months that elapsed between the end of Primo de Rivera's dictatorship and the end of the monarchy (January of 1930 to April of 1931)—the groundswell of hope and expectation continued to build: "The new constitution of the Republic was roughed out, and you could see the Republic, the way you sense the presence of an awaited guest who's approaching your door. The Republic was visible now" (117).[39] The "beloved Spain of anonymous villages hungry with every hunger, was emerging from its hell—hope throbbing" (153).[40] As Tania Gentic has argued, Zambrano powerfully casts the Republic "as a

[35] "[C]on el corazón de Madrid"; "el pulso de España, su latir, había creado aquella armonía, aquel silencio viviente donde caían las palabras como música; el sentido se ensanchaba el horizonte se abría, respiraba" (63).

[36] "[V]iviente y orgánico" (191).

[37] "Y el pueblo español, antes que a exigir, tenía que atreverse a esperar, y la esperanza se estaba ya desatando" (88).

[38] "[E]se hambre trascendente que es la esperanza. La esperanza que es el hambre total, el no-ser que se manifiesta a sí mismo de modo positivo porque se sitúa en el futuro" (92).

[39] "[S]e esbozaba la nueva Constitución de la República, que se sentía … como se siente la presencia del huésped que se espera cuando se aproxima a nuestra puerta; que era visible ya" (187–88).

[40] "España, la España entrañable, la de los pueblos anónimos, hambrientos de todas las hambres, salía de su infierno—esperanza palpitante" (242).

7 THE SCENE OF THE FIRING SQUAD: ZAMBRANO'S *DELIRIUM...* 157

processual, affective experience of the *pueblo*," in striking contrast with the "static structure of the state" (60).

In recapturing that intensely felt experience of mass coalescence around the Republic, Zambrano turns once again to atmospherics, employing metaphors of light, air, and common breath.

> The autumn air was weightless; it vibrated with an incitement to live [...] At that historic moment the light of Madrid was more vibrant than ever, weightless and fleshy, a luminous body. Madrid is a city of few trees, but the trees there were, now gilded with autumn, turned the city's atmosphere into a golden ember, and a golden rain seemed to be falling over this gold sprung from earth like an offering to the light. (125–26)[41]

The heightened atmosphere of the city emerges as an expression—indeed, a creation—of the people's hopes and desires, and as such it acquires a certain substance; that golden autumnal light becomes "a luminous body," a palpable body politic, the *demos* mobilized around the promise of democracy. The Republic, as the vehicle for realizing that promise, was "the creation of a work of art or of thought" that had taken form and solidified into an imminent possibility (122).[42] Reiterating the idea of common breath, Zambrano emphasizes that "all the efforts to revitalize Spain made by the renewed generations of thinking individuals had finally gotten 'the whole of Spain' breathing" (121).[43] Their intellectual and creative efforts had radiated and cohered over time, such that the people at large were now ethically and vitally attuned to this historical moment. The young Zambrano, after a period of some distance from public life, began "to form part of the 'atmosphere' of that diffuse body," thinking and breathing with others, "part of the soul and conscience of the history occurring at that moment" (127).[44]

---

[41] "El aire del otoño era ligero, vibrante de incitación para vivir. [...] En aquella hora histórica la luz de Madrid vibraba más que nunca; era ligera y carnal, se hacía presente, era un cuerpo luminoso. No es ciudad de muchos árboles, pero los que había dorados del otoño convertían la atmósfera de la ciudad en ascua de oro; y una lluvia de oro parecía caer sobre este oro salido de la tierra como ofrenda a la luz" (201).

[42] "[L]a creación de una obra de arte o de pensamiento" (194). I made a slight change to Maier's translation, from "thinking" to "thought."

[43] "[L]as renovadas generaciones de gentes de pensamiento, todos los esfuerzos de revitalización habían logrado por fin que 'toda España' respirase" (194).

[44] "[H]abía entrado a formar parte de 'la atmósfera', de este cuerpo difuso [...] formaba parte [...] del alma y de la conciencia de la historia de aquella hora" (202).

158   J. HIGHFILL

In early spring, 1931, Zambrano joined efforts to mobilize the people before the pending municipal elections, giving speeches in provincial towns and cities. After speaking in a bull ring in La Mancha, she stood before an "immense chorus that filled the plaza, waiting so soberly for its freedom" (152).[45] The local elections, to be held nation-wide on April 12, 1931, were intended as a limited reform, a means of appeasing the masses' desire for freedom. However, in the context of growing republican sentiment, it became a referendum on the monarchy. On April 13, the results showed an overwhelming victory for the broad coalition in support of the Republic; and on April 14, throughout the morning and early afternoon, the populace awaited the outcome of negotiations taking place in the Royal Palace. "There were no perceptible signs of fear," Zambrano observes; nevertheless, "'everything was possible,' no one knew anything, rumors, rumors" (160).[46] In Madrid, people in small groups begin filling the streets, not yet a crowd, tense but calm, still waiting. Then, "[i]n an instant something like an electric spark shook everything, and all the people crammed into the cafes were hurled into the street," she vividly recounts (161–62).[47] Above the Plaza of Cibeles, a lone man in the tower of the Palace of Communications raised the flag of the Republic, and from the vast crowd below, arose the cheers: "¡Viva la Republica!" (162). The news that the king had abdicated spread through multitude like a "resounding wave," like "wind in a wheatfield"; some of them had witnessed his black "gondola" gliding along the streets carrying him into exile (162).[48] "It was the hour of crime, and he avoided crime," Zambrano respectfully observes, "May he rest in peace!" she adds.[49] Violence was averted; he had not wanted the blood of Spaniards to be spilled on his behalf.

"[H]istory does have ecstatic moments," Zambrano had asserted earlier; and here she represents that peaceful advent of the Republic as a collective outburst of joy (130).[50] The diffuse body politic that had been

---

[45] "[A]quel inmenso coro" que llenaba la plaza esperando tan sobriamente su liberación" (240); "[E]l aire vibraba" (239).

[46] "No se percibían señales de temor, sin embargo, 'todo era posible', nada se sabía, rumores, rumores" (249).

[47] "En un instante, una especie de chispa eléctrica sacudió a todos y arrojó a la calle a los que se apiñaban dentro de los cafés" (251).

[48] "[C]omo el viento en un campo de trigo, se extendió la onda sonora" (253).

[49] "Era la hora del crimen; y lo evitó. ¡Descanse en paz!" (254).

[50] "Y la historia tiene sus momentos extáticos" (208).

coalescing over the past few years, propelled by transcendent hope, had now fully materialized before her eyes.[51] Initially, the crowd was composed of groups—of family members, neighbors, friends, or fellow workers—who had poured into the streets at the same time. Rather than a uniform crowd, it was made up of "close-knit units," interacting amongst themselves, as defined social circles within the massive sea of people; hence, a "single happiness was reflected differently, according to the situation, social class, character, or style of each group" (162).[52] By early evening, the shape of the crowd had changed:

> The groups were still visible, but there were hands extended between them, people were exchanging witty remarks, and the crowd was now like a garland of human circles nestled one in the other like a gigantic circle turning round and round, breaking and closing again. There were never more people than would fit in the space—not bunched together but joined—and the men and women, stars forming constellations, formed discernible patterns, as if they were reproducing the map of the heavens here below, as if that ring were the center of the earth. (163)[53]

With this image of intersecting, nestled circles—turning, opening to let others in, then closing once more—Zambrano underscores the extraordinary intimacy within the massive crowd. Employing two striking metaphors, she likens the human circles first to interlinked garlands of flowers and then to multiple, adjoining constellations, whose patterns taken together create a map of the heavens on the plaza below. This lyrical language hearkens back to a key moment in the first chapter, "Adsum," when bed-ridden and in a pre-natal state, she had gazed out the window at a

---

[51] According to Moreno Sanz, on April 14, Zambrano joined the crowds earlier in the day, in the company of several leading intellectuals, among them Juan Panero, Arturo Serrano Plaja, Antonio Sánchez Barbudo, José Antonio Maravall, and Enrique Ramos Ramos. Later, in the afternoon, she was joined by her father, sister, and Carlos Díez Fernández, a doctor and specialist in tuberculosis, who had attended her while she was bed-ridden with tuberculosis and who later married her sister, Araceli ("Síntesis biográfica" 41–42).

[52] "[U]nidades de intimidad [...]. Una alegría única y reflejada de modo distinto en cada grupo según su condición, su clase social, su carácter o estilo" (252).

[53] "Seguían visibles los grupos, pero de unos a otros se extendían las manos se cruzaban los dichos, y era ya como una guirnalda de corros engarzados unos a otros, como un gigantesco corro que daba vueltas, se rompía y se volvía a unir; no estaban siendo más de los que cabían en aquel espacio, no agolpados, sino unidos, y se distinguían las figuras formadas de hombres y mujeres, estrellas que formaban constelaciones, como si se repitiese abajo el mapa celeste" (253).

160   J. HIGHFILL

"glorious wreath" of clouds that revealed "the history of Spain reawakening, while offering a promise that bound heaven and earth" (14).[54] If earlier she had presented herself as newly (re)born, emerging from solitude into "the circumstances [that] resembled the semicircle of clouds that arose from her bed," now *el pueblo* was being born, imbued with political consciousness and hopes for the new democracy.[55]

Zambrano continues to evoke the jubilation of the people in this ecstatic moment—the apotheosis of all that the young activists and the entire republican movement had struggled for. The cries of "¡Viva la República!" arise "in different tones, in a hundred registers as from a gigantic organ never heard before, as in a chorale intoned by an entire people, the voice," rising toward the clouds and falling again, filling the air (163).[56] Amid that chorus of repeated cheers—"¡Long live the Republic! and ¡Long live Spain!"—one voice in particular stands out. Zambrano, standing in the Puerta del Sol, observes a man nearby, who in a flash of anger, raises his fist and shouts, "and long die! …"; then abruptly, he stops himself: "But no, death to no one, life to everyone. Yes, long live the world, long live everyone, everyone in the world" (165).[57]

With this dramatic affirmation of life, Zambrano ends her account of those years of youthful political commitment culminating in the joyful and peaceful proclamation of the Republic. An abyss opens between this chapter and the next, between two moments in time, April of 1931 and January of 1939; and in that interim, as her readers well know, some hundreds of thousands have died in Spain. In the chapter that follows, "Towards a New World," the young Zambrano is crossing the Pyrenees in the bitter winter of 1939, heading into a long and painful exile, accompanied by her mother, two young cousins, an elderly servant, and thousands of other Spaniards. She has not yet fully grasped the tragic defeat of the Republic— the loss of the "dreamed destiny" that she and her comrades had so ardently struggled to realize. She tells us nothing of the intervening eight years, a period of intense intellectual and political activity in support of the

---

[54] See note 12 for the text in Spanish.

[55] "[L]as circunstancias eran como ese semicírculo de nubes que venía desde la cama" (35).

[56] "[E]n tonos diferentes, en cien registros como en un gigantesco y nunca oído órgano en una coral, que entonaba todo un pueblo, subía la voz a las nubes, y volvía a bajar, y así el aire estuvo lleno de esos gritos" (254).

[57] "¡Y muera! … pero no, que no muera nadie, que viva todo el mundo. Sí, viva el Mundo, que vivan todos, todo el mundo" (256).

7 THE SCENE OF THE FIRING SQUAD: ZAMBRANO'S *DELIRIUM*... 161

Republic, even as she avoided party affiliation.[58] She relates nothing of her participation in the Pedagogical Missions: how she traveled to remote rural areas along with other intellectuals and students; how they conveyed to the citizenry their new rights under the Republic, established libraries, and held performances of classical plays and traditional music. Nor does she recount her increasing radicalization after the failed Revolution in Asturias in 1933, her support for the Popular Front in the elections of 1936, nor her ceaseless work in defense of the Republic during the Civil War.[59] As readers, having been enveloped in an atmosphere of hope and solidarity, we now stare into a chasm of horror and immeasurable loss. What follows are three brief chapters, situated, respectively, in 1939, 1941, and 1946—bare sketches of the agony of her years of exile in the midst and in the aftermath of a World War. The remainder of the book, as Zambrano explained to Chacel in her letter, is composed of a series of "Deliriums"—short stories and philosophical reflections—that she had written in the darkest times after the death of her mother in 1946.

Before arriving at this moment in her narration—at this abyss of inexpressible pain and loss—we have shared the narrator's gaze as she recreates those exhilarating years of youthful struggle and all the hopes invested in the new Republic. However, Zambrano's narrating self, in focalizing through her younger self, leaves occasional hints of the catastrophe to

---

[58] Zambrano had resisted party politics since the early days of her student activism in the F.U.E. Shortly after the proclamation of the Republic, she declined a request to be a Socialist Party candidate as a delegate to the Constituent Assembly, assigned to drafting the new constitution. She became more adamant in her aversion to formal party participation after what she would later call her "gravest error" (Moreno Sanz, "Síntesis"). In 1932, she, among other disciples of Ortega, co-founded an organization, el Frente Español (Spanish Front), which was to be grounded in the *maestro's* principles; however, it soon took a turn toward fascism, and she immediately disbanded the organization. For more information on the formation of the Frente Español, see: Soto Carrasco (188–93).

[59] During the war, Zambrano served as a leading member of the Alianza de Intelectuales para la Defensa de la República, she served on the Consejo Nacional de la Infancia Evacuada, which oversaw the network of refuges for children evacuated from cities subject to bombardment, and in collaboration with other anti-fascist intellectuals, she published regularly in key journals of the war-time years, *Hora de España* and *El mono azul*. For detailed accounts of Zambrano's activities during the Republic and war years, see: Mangini; Moreno Sanz ("Síntesis biográfica," 42–52); Robles Carcedo, and Tellez. It bears mentioning that in the 1930s, Zambrano published some of her most important works: *Horizonte del liberalismo* (1930); "Por qué se escribe" and "Hacia un saber sobre el alma" (1934); and *Los intelectuales en el drama de España* (1937). Also early in the war, she prepared and published *Antología de Lorca* and *El romancero de la guerra civil española* (1937).

162   J. HIGHFILL

come.[60] We have seen how, early in the narration, she likened the young activists' "change in attitude" to melt-water flowing from the heights of the Guadarrama, becoming "cascades, streams, and rivers" to revitalize all of Spain (28).[61] Their vocation, as they defined it was: "to be a pulse, a deep breath that teaches how to breathe freely and confidently. Flowing water and pulse, in other words, blood. New blood, purified by the free air that had just freed the Spaniards from their obsessions, their laziness, and their pride" (28).[62] Strikingly, water—the revitalizing, fluid substance that would cleanse and heal Spain—metamorphoses into new blood that would likewise revitalize through the body politic. For Zambrano and her comrades, "the words they used with increasing frequency, all the words they emphasized, outlined one metaphor—the metaphor of clean blood that before long would be spilt" (28).[63] It is precisely here where, for just an instant, we find a leap forward from the "narrated moment" of transcendent hope to the "narrating moment" and an intimation of the bloodbath soon to come.

Immediately after this ominous hint, Zambrano launches into a reflection on how "thought apparently tends to become blood"; that is, "why thinking is so serious" (28).[64] At certain points in time, when thought crystalizes, blood, as the essence of life, "finds that it must answer for thought's transparency"; it must "pay for, or at least authorize" thought, which she considers the most pure, free, and disinterested activity of humankind (29).[65] Here the "physio-logic" behind her recurrent atmospheric and respiratory metaphors becomes clear; for it is through breath that blood receives oxygen and nourishes the body: "[B]reathing requires

---

[60] Caballero Rodríguez, in "The Cathartic Exercise of Memory," discusses these hints of catastrophe as symptoms of trauma—the pain locked in memory; see pp. 145–46.

[61] "Cambio de actitud"; "cascada, arroyos, ríos a vivificar toda España" (57).

[62] "Vocacíon de ser pulso, respiración profunda que enseñase a respirar libre, confiadamente. Agua que corre, y pulso, es la sangre. Una sangre nueva, purificada por el aire libre, que acabase de liberar a los españoles de sus obsesiones, de su pereza y de su orgullo" (57).

[63] "[T]odos los vocablos que empleaban con mayor reiteración, todos los que acentuaban, diseñaban una metáfora; la metáfora de una sangre limpia que no habría de tardar mucho en derramarse" (57).

[64] "El pensamiento, por lo visto, tiende a hacerse sangre. Por eso, pensar es cosa tan grave" (57).

[65] "[C]uando un pensamiento se formula cristalinamente encuentra enseguida la sangre que ha de responder de su transparencia, como si lo más 'puro', libre, desinteresado que hace el hombre hubiera de ser pagado, o a lo menos autorizado, por aquella 'materia' preciosa entre todas, esencia de la vida, vida misma que corre escondida" (57–58).

7 THE SCENE OF THE FIRING SQUAD: ZAMBRANO'S *DELIRIUM...* 163

the right environment. Breathable air. Thought that reveals reality creates vital, breathable space. One of thought's vital roles is to make the atmosphere breathable, to free human beings from suffocation" (29).[66] Citing Aristotle, she asserts that "the act of thinking is life," which explains "the terror, and the hatred of intelligence, the desire to kill intelligence because it is life"—a clear reference to the fascist aversion to free inquiry; hence, "thought becomes blood; it enters blood and insists on bloodshed" (29).[67]

Zambrano's own process of thought is struggling to understand and explain all that happened in Spain in the 1920s and 1930s—how the expansive surge of innovative thought, how the struggle for a revitalized Spain would be "answered" by massive bloodshed. In so doing, she differentiates criminal violence (implicitly fascist terror), from honest or heroic action, because in the latter instance,

> its desire for something to become reality is united with love—is a joyful desire for something to exist. And this is how their group of young people [...] felt desire for Spain, joyfully; they wanted Spain to exist, to completely exist. Was this criminal, was this a crime? They would have to pay for it as such, with their blood, with their deaths, with their lives [although] at the time they could foresee none of this. (30)[68]

Once more we encounter a shift in the narrative lens—from that narrated moment of ardent struggle (in 1929) to the anguished moment of writing (in 1952), after so many of her companions had indeed paid the fatal price.

Other intimations of tragedy appear during her re-creation of those years of youthful comradeship—before they were all "wounded by our

---

[66] "Respirar requiere un medio adecuado, un aire respirable. El pensamiento que revela la realidad crea un espacio vital, respirable. Una de las funciones vitales del pensamiento es hacer respirable el ambiente, librar a los seres humanos de la asfixia" (58).

[67] "[E]l acto del pensamiento es vida [...] Y de ahí, también el terror a la inteligencia, el odio, el querer matarla, por ser vida" (59). "Y así sucede que el pensamiento se hace sangre; entra en la sangre y la obliga a derramarse" (58).

[68] "Y la diferencia entre la acción criminal y la honesta o la heroica es por querer la realidad de algo en el amor que es querer la existencia de algo con alegría. Y aquel grupo de muchachos [...] querían a España así, con alegría; querían que existiese, que acabase de existir. Era, fue un crimen. Como tal habrían de pagarlo; con su sangre, con su muerte, con su vida" (59–60). (I slightly changed Maier's translation for "acabase de existir"; I believe "to completely exist" is more faithful than "to finish with existing.")

164   J. HIGHFILL

contemporary history" (126).[69] She shares with her friend, Carlos, a sense that they're on the "edge of an abyss," that another military conflict will soon consume Europe (72).[70] Carlos contends that "we're a sacrificed generation," and he warns Zambrano, "[D]on't get yourself thrown into the bonfire before you have to; you're a woman, and you might be able to escape" (72).[71] Her mother, too, senses that a catastrophe "was hovering over Europe and would first hover over Spain, in spite of how well everything was going" (78).[72] For the young Zambrano, fear erupts into her moments of greatest joy and hope. When she attends a concert of Beethoven's Fifth Symphony, she feels the utter happiness of those rare moments "when you realize that you and others are breathing together" (98).[73] Yet she returns home upset and dares not explain, "It's because I've felt happy, mother ... we all seemed about to enter Paradise together; we were all one soul, and I'm afraid, I'm afraid" (99).[74] Later, in a reflection on how humankind engenders history, she recalls the full participation, "the unity of time and soul, this 'ecstasy'" she had felt at the symphony, and it is here where she asserts that "history does have ecstatic moments" (130).[75] Albeit unnamed, the proclamation of the Republic is clearly in the back of her mind, as she asks: "What measures will be necessary to ensure that something engendered in such exceptional 'ecstatic' processes will be permanent? Won't anything born this way be most

---

[69] "La luz del Mediterráneo tiene su historia permanente, tan maternal cuando estamos heridos de la nuestra de hoy. No había llegado la herida" (201).

[70] "[A]l borde del abismo" (122). Carlos Díez Fernández was a pulmonologist who treated both María and her sister, Araceli. He married Araceli, but they separated several years later. A close friend of María, he was active in the student movement in opposition to Primo de Rivera's regime. During the Civil War, he held important leadership positions in the military medical corps. After the war, he went into exile, first in the Soviet Union and later in Venezuela, where he committed suicide in 1952. See Marco Igual, "Médicos republicanos," pp. 6–7.

[71] "[S]omos una generación sacrificada [...] Y tú mira a ver lo que haces, no sea que te quemes en la hoguera antes de tiempo, eres mujer y quizá te libres" (122).

[72] "[U]na catástrofe que se cernía sobre Europa, y antes sobre España, a pesar de lo bien que marchaba todo" (131).

[73] "[E]n ese raro momento en algo que respira a la vez" (161).

[74] "Es que he sido feliz, madre mía ... parecía que fuéramos a entrar en el Paraíso todos juntos; todos éramos un alma y tengo miedo tengo miedo" (162).

[75] "[L]a unidad de tiempo y alma, aquel 'éxtasis' [...] Y la historia tiene sus momentos extáticos" (207–08).

7 THE SCENE OF THE FIRING SQUAD: ZAMBRANO'S *DELIRIUM...*   165

threatened when ecstasy is most pure and participation most intense?" (131).[76] Haunting this latter question is an affirmative answer; for the Republic would not survive those threats, and those who so joyously participated in its birth would pay dearly for their ecstasy.

But aside from these occasional, brief allusions, only in one instance does Zambrano (or strictly speaking, her narrator) directly address the catastrophe to come by inserting into her narration a true prolepsis—a leap forward in time. This interruption occurs in the chapter, "Inspiration," when she is recounting a moment of intense political commitment amid increasing tension and uncertainty. It is the year 1930; the dictator, Primo de Rivera, has stepped down, and the King has installed a general charged with finding a path to restore the constitutional monarchy. Meanwhile, an already mobilized republican coalition is developing plans for the Constituent Assembly that will draft a new constitution. Zambrano and her closest comrades have declined requests by their political elders that they serve as delegates in that Assembly. Their refusal to participate in official partisan politics prompts her to reflect on the next critical decision five years hence when: "That No, at a different time was Yes, to the definitive hour when we met again briefly. The first days of the 'Madrid front' consumed many of those lives, and you were sown forever in the places we had walked during the weightless hours on the last of our ritual excursions, along the banks of the Manzanares in the Sierra" (145).[77] In a stunning break with the third-person narration, she now writes in first person, referring to "my friends," and to all of "you" whose remains lie along the Madrid front (144–45). She pays homage to other friends she lost in the war—those who died without ever considering it "sacrifice," because it "was something so natural"—among them "the boy who attended my classes" and the "sculptor of Guadarrama granite" (145).[78] She remembers those

---

[76] "¿Y qué modos habrá de seguir para que aquello que se engendre en tales procesos especialmente 'extáticos' sea permanente? Y cuanto más puro sea el éxtasis, la participación más alta, ¿no estará lo que nazca más amenazado?" (208).

[77] "Aquel no, que fue otra vez Sí, a la hora definitiva en la que volvimos a encontrarnos por poco tiempo. Los primeros días del 'frente de Madrid' consumieron muchas de aquellas vidas, sembrados os quedasteis para siempre en aquellos lugares por donde habíamos pasado en aquellas horas sin peso, a orillas del Manzanares, en la Sierra" (230).

[78] "¡[C]osa tan natural que era!"; "aquel muchacho que escuchó mis 'clases'"; "el escultor del granito del Guadarrama" (230).

166   J. HIGHFILL

shot in distant provinces and at crossroads, like the beautiful girl, so full of life, who had collaborated in Pamplona; like her husband, governor for only two weeks, which was nevertheless long enough to make him keep fighting until he fell, riddled with bullets, in the courtyard of the governor's palace. And like Fe, cut in two by bombs right at the border, holding her little girl by the hand (145).[79]

She goes on to list the "suicides of exile," among them the "doctor brother" (Carlos), who "had stopped her at the very threshold of death," and she acknowledges those who remain in internal exile, "the torture without any imaginable end that was in store for the defeated who remained inside. Yes, I understand you, I understand you" (145).[80] In this heartrending elegy, Zambrano cries out from her own locus of exile as she expresses the unending pain from the loss of life and of the hope for Spain they had all shared. At that point, she breaks away entirely from her narration of the past and speaks from her moment of writing in the aftermath, directly addressing the dead:

> But now I cannot relive that hour, enter it through the corridor of my memory without naming all of you. A person does not weep when she's writing. That's a rhetorical figure, and besides, I don't want to weep for you. I'm just calling to you, because that way I call to myself, so I can feel your voices mixed with mine and answer that I am still here, and so you can call to me from the silence into which you have fallen, from the life of what we could have been. (146)[81]

This statement—"I am still here"—echoes the *ad sum* that began the narration, when, after a long illness, the young Zambrano evokes her rebirth

---

[79] "Y los fusilados en lejanas provincias y en las encrucijadas de los caminos, como aquella muchacha bella y llena de vida que había colaborado desde Pamplona, como su marido, quince días de Gobernador, lo preciso para sostener la lucha, hasta caer en el patio del Palacio del Gobierno, acribillado. Y Fe, cortada en dos por las bombas, al borde mismo de la frontera, con su niña de la mano" (230–31).

[80] "[L]os suicidas del destierro"; "su médico hermano"; "aquel que la detuvo en el umbral de la muerte"; "la tortura sin fin inimaginable que había para los vencidos que quedaron dentro. Sí; os comprendo, os comprendo" (231).

[81] "Y ahora no puedo revivir aquella hora, entrarme en ella por la galería de mi memoria sin nombraros. No se llora cuando se está escribiendo. Es figura retórica, pero además no quiero lloraros, os llamo tan sólo, porque así me llamo a mí misma, para sentir vuestra voz mezclada con la mía y poder contestaros que estoy aquí todavía, para que me llaméis desde ese silencio en que habéis caído, desde esa vida que de él que pudimos ser" (232).

7 THE SCENE OF THE FIRING SQUAD: ZAMBRANO'S *DELIRIUM...* 167

into her vital circumstances. But now this *ad sum* is a keening call to her dead comrades, asking them to speak through her from that abyss of silence they inhabit, so that she might mix their voices with hers. Ultimately, "[t]he dead have no voices," she concedes:

> We can hear them within ourselves, in the music that erupts when we're most oblivious, as if we could never be alone. Faltering words come to us, syllables from the land of the dead. A voice, choking as it tries to speak, wants to tell us its history, its story. Anyone who has died prematurely, who has died violently needs to have his story told, because a person can sink into silence only after everything has been said. (146–47)[82]

Thus the silence that envelops her dead comrades is not absolute; nor is it the harmonious silence of "reason fulfilled"; rather, it is the "dissonant silence that leaves a faltering word in the air, reason turned to scream [...], the silence enveloping inspiration that has been murdered" (147).[83]

Let us return now to that void in the text—that chasm that opens after the ecstatic moment of the proclamation of the Republic, leaving untold Zambrano's experiences during the Republic and the Civil War. Zambrano's call to her dead comrades suggests that we read that void as an enactment of a dissonant silence, implicitly filled with choking, faltering voices that want to speak, that emit the mute scream of the victims of that historic catastrophe. But something else implicitly inhabits that abyss— Goya's well-known work, *The Third of May* (1814)—an image that Zambrano repeatedly evokes in the text [see Fig. 7.1]. This painting memorializes the executions of Spanish citizens who revolted against Napoleon's Army on May 2, 1808, the beginning of the War of Independence that would last six years. Before dawn on May 3, forty-four *madrileños* were shot by firing squad on this site, Príncipe Pío, and many more in other parts of the city (Joaquín Murat, the Commander of the Napoleonic forces in Spain had ordered that all the rebels be shot). Goya

---

[82] "Los muertos no tienen voz [...] Se les oye dentro de uno mismo, en esa música que por instantes brota cuando más olvidados estamos, como si ya nunca pudiésemos estar solos. Y llegan palabras entrecortadas, sílabas de ese país de la muerte. Una voz, ahogada en el esfuerzo para hablar, quiere contar su historia. Todos los muertos prematuros, los muertos por la violencia, necesitan que se cuente su historia, pues sólo debe ser posible hundirse en el silencio cuando todo quedó dicho" (233). Nearly a decade later, in "Carta sobre el exilio" (1961), Zambrano reflects on the "voz inaudible" of the exiliado (67).

[83] "[L]a razón cumplida"; "el silencio disonante que deja en el aire la palabra entrecortada, la razón convertida en grito [...] El silencio que envuelve a la inspiración asesinada" (234).

Fig. 7.1 Francisco de Goya y Lucientes. *The Third of May in Madrid*. 1814. Prado Museum, Madrid

has made one of those rebels the focal point of the painting, captured in the instant before certain death. Illuminated by a large lantern, his white shirt open at the chest, he raises his arms and stares directly at the troops before him, a monolithic block, their bodies in identical poses, their rifles raised in a parallel, receding row. Behind the victim wait other captive rebels, bowed down with fear, some covering their faces so as not to see what awaits them. Before him lies a pile of bodies in a pool of blood. This resonant image—a visual enactment of the defiant and mute scream of a condemned man—recurs at key points in *Delirium and Destiny*, standing in for the tens of thousands shot at crossroads, against cemetery walls, and buried in unmarked common graves all over Spain.[84]

---

[84] Historians concur on the impossibility of determining exactly the number of those executed behind the lines during the Civil War. However, according to Paul Preston in *The Spanish Holocaust*, executions of rebels in Republican zones are more reliable—49,272,

7 THE SCENE OF THE FIRING SQUAD: ZAMBRANO'S *DELIRIUM...* 169

Zambrano makes her first direct reference to the painting, when recounting a visit to the Prado Museum with a comrade, Ulysses, who recently began attending the meetings of Zambrano's circle of student activists.[85] An athlete, studying to be a sailor, Ulysses had spent "forty blessed days in the Modelo prison" the year before, after an incident during the student strikes (100).[86] Zambrano recounts in great detail their extended conversation on politics and on their hopes and fears for Spain— at one point touching on the question of their willingness to give their own lives. As they walk through the galleries, viewing paintings by Zurbarán, Velázquez, and Goya, they discuss questions of art, Spanish history and their own critical moment, while also contemplating what lies ahead.[87] At one point, after praising Ortega's book, *The Revolt of the Masses*, Ulysses comments on the facelessness of modern-day citizens: today "everything gets carried away by the crowd, and you can't see the individual" (105).[88] Zambrano argues that when they see before them "unhidden faces—whole persons—they will no longer be masses and become a people," and Ulysses responds, "Yes, that's why it will be tragic" (105).[89] Afterwards, walking home alone, Zambrano wonders how her companion could be so sure—why did what was coming have to be tragic? She thinks of Seneca, the great Stoic, and how he went willingly to his death; and she feels certain that "the *pueblo* when its turn came would die

based on existing records (xvi). By contrast, estimates of Republican victims of rebel violence are much less trustworthy; many records were deliberately destroyed during the Franco regime, while many deaths were never registered at all (xvi–xvii). Extensive recent research, however, indicates that the repression by military insurgents and supporters "was about three times greater than what which took place in the Republican zone" (xvii–xviii). The current most reliable, yet still tentative, figure is 130,100, but Preston thinks it unlikely that such deaths were fewer than 150,000 (xviii). For the numbers of those executed after the war, under the Franco Regime, he cites 20,000. Many more died of malnutrition and disease in prisons, concentration camps, and in forced-labor battalions (xi).

[85] The friend who accompanied her, "Ulysses," is likely José Troyano de los Ríos, nephew of the renowned socialist intellectual and politician, Fernando de los Ríos. Troyano de los Ríos was an officer in the Spanish Navy during the Civil War. In exile afterwards, he lived in the Dominican Republic, Puerto Rico, and Venezuela.

[86] "[F]ue a pasar cuarenta hermosos días a la Modelo" (163).

[87] Zambrano published this segment separately as an essay, "Una visita al Museo del Prado" in *Cuadernos del Congreso por la libertad de la cultura* in 1955. The same essay is included in an anthology of her writings on art, *Algunos lugares de la pintura* (1989).

[88] "[L]a multitud se lo lleva todo y al individuo no se le ve" (171).

[89] "[S]i ellas tienen ante sí rostros que no se esconden, personas enteras, no dejarán de ser masas, serán pueblo" "Sí, por eso será trágico" (171).

170   J. HIGHFILL

innocently like the man in the white shirt who figures at the center of Goya's painting, *The Third of May*" (108).[90] They had just seen the painting and walked by it without saying a word, Zambrano recalls. Then, in a remarkable passage, she translates that image into language, evoking

> the man opening his arms in a cross, instead of pressing them to his defenseless chest, responding to the rifles with an unnatural gesture, beyond the instinctive fear felt by all animals as they face death; giving up his soul, which leaves his body before the bullets reach it; holding his entire soul—which cries out to heaven—in his arms, embracing the world, cursing, blessing; and in his eyes, which also leave his body before the bullets reach them, and in that scream ... What is that Celtiberian in the immaculate white shirt forever screaming to us as he gives up his soul? That scream, my Spain, of your animal, of its soul pouring out beyond death, a soul that will not stop at death's banks but empty into life? The scream is one of life! (108–09)[91]

This man—this vulnerable, brave "animal" staring at death, while embracing and blessing the world—implicitly conjoins that earlier moment in the narration, when Zambrano suddenly spoke in first person, calling out to her dead comrades, to all those sacrificed in the Civil War. "The dead have no voices," she had written; yet "we hear them within ourselves as "a dissonant silence," as "faltering words," a "voice choking," "reason turned to scream" (146–47).[92] That resonant image of the condemned man standing before the row of rifles, represents her attempt to rescue and render meaning to all the deaths she has lived through. His "scream of life" unleashed at the moment of death, arises from the abyss of all that Zambrano does not and cannot recount.

---

[90] "[E]n cuanto el pueblo, moriría inocentemente como el hombre aquel de la camisa blanca, figura central del cuadro de Goya, 'Los Fusilamientos de la Moncloa'" (176).

[91] "[A]quel hombre que abre los brazos en cruz, en lugar de apretarlos sobre su pecho desamparado, frente a los fusiles, en un gesto antinatural, más allá del miedo instintivo de todo animal frente a la muerte; dando esa su alma que se le sale antes de que las balas le alcancen; el alma entera en sus brazos clamando al cielo, abrazando al mundo, maldiciendo, bendiciendo; y en sus ojos, que se salen también antes de ser alcanzados, y en ese grito .... ¿Qué nos grita siempre ese celtíbero de camisa inmaculada que da su alma, ese grito, España mía, de tu animal, de su alma volcándose por encima de la muerte, esa alma que no va a parar al mar del morir, sino a verterse en la vida! ¡ese grito es de vida!" (176–77). I have slightly changed Maier's translation of "por encima" from "over" to "beyond," which, I believe, better captures Zambrano's meaning.

[92] See note 82 for the text in Spanish.

7 THE SCENE OF THE FIRING SQUAD: ZAMBRANO'S *DELIRIUM...*   171

Another haunting reference to the firing squad appears soon after her visit to the Prado, as Zambrano recaptures an ominous moment one year before the proclamation of the Republic. Along with her father and a close friend, she is walking through a city enveloped in an eerie silence. It is December 14, 1930, and on "that terrible Sunday in the very dark of winter," an execution has taken place in the north of Spain, just two days after Captains Fermín Galán Rodríguez and Angel García Hernández, had led a military uprising in Jaca with the intent of establishing a Republic (136).[93] Plans to coordinate with troops stationed in other cities had failed, and the two officers were soon arrested, hastily court-martialed, and sentenced to death. According to reports, Galán himself gave the order to shoot, then shouted out, "¡Viva la República!," as he fell. Galán and García Hernández would become martyrs to the republican cause, but in the moment when Zambrano is walking through Madrid, the city is paralyzed by uncertainty and fear. She thinks of the many public executions, the "legal" crimes that had taken place on those same streets, in those same plazas—whether by gallows, firing squad, or *garrote vil* (136). Notably, she evokes Rafael del Riego, who was hanged in 1823 for rising up against the absolutist monarch Fernando VII, and whose "anthem of hope" would become the hymn of the Second Republic (136).[94] With horror, she reflects on the mob that tore Riego's body apart, acknowledging the potential of a *pueblo* to become degraded, to be governed by "viscera" in the absence of thought, and driven to commit horrendous crimes (136). "[W]hen dusk fell that sinister afternoon," she recounts, "a different hellish viscera, the machines, the murder machines, appeared instantly"; for on "each deserted corner, a group of soldiers was assembling a machine gun—the image of viscera mechanized" (137).[95] Then implicitly citing Goya's painting, Zambrano remarks: "The soldiers seem mechanical too, the way soldiers in the firing squad must seem to the eyes of the one about to fall, wrapped in his own warm blood"; [...] "Cold viscera. Could that be how they feel to a person condemned to death?" (137).[96] Standing in

---

[93] "[A]quel terrible domingo del más negro invierno" (215).

[94] "Himno de la esperanza" (215).

[95] "[E]sas otras entrañas infernales que son las máquinas, las máquinas de matar, hicieron su aparición en aquel instante del siniestro atardecer"; "en cada esquina desierta un grupo de soldados montaba una ametralladora, imagen de las entrañas mecanizadas" (216–17).

[96] "Los soldados parecían mecánicos también, como deben de parecer los que forman el pelotón de fusilamiento ante los ojos del que va a caer envuelto en su propia, cálida sangre. [...] Las entrañas enfriadas, ¿las sentiría así el condenado a muerte?" (217).

172   J. HIGHFILL

perfect alignment with rifles raised, the soldiers are "de-brothered men who lack any bond of community at all, who are mechanisms, men who are also condemned—to be machines, to be turned into men possessed by a trigger" (137).[97] She feels pity and disgust for the soldiers, and a scream catches in her throat, "the scream that arises irrepressibly from the bottom of one's heart in the presence of any dictated death [...]: 'Don't shoot!'" (137).[98] Yet, she asserts, that is never the cry of a condemned man facing a firing squad; "No, what you hear are opposite screams: 'Shoot, aim right for my heart!' This is understandable. It's what the victim screams as he rushes for dear life toward death, as he allows himself the final luxury of dying voluntarily, of dying alive" (137).[99] On that dark Sunday, as it turned out, the soldiers assembled on the streetcorners of Madrid did not shoot. But in capturing this tense and fearful moment, Zambrano implicitly evokes Goya's painting of the firing squad, as she turns the victim's defiant acceptance of death into a proclamation of life.

Zambrano's final and most compelling reference to Goya's *Third of May* appears once more in narration, precisely at its most ecstatic moment—the proclamation of the Republic. Earlier, I touched upon an anonymous man whom Zambrano singles out amidst the jubilant crowd. It is twilight, shortly after the Republican flag was ceremoniously unfurled from the balcony of the Government Ministry above the Puerta del Sol. She notices a group of jubilant workers, one of whom breaks away and cries out to a man passing by, "¡Viva la República!" as his comrades continue dancing and shouting, "¡Viva España!" (165). The passerby, in turn, responds to that chorus of "¡Vivas!" with his own "long live Spain!" In an instant, however, his mood darkens; he raises his fist and starts to shout— "¡Y muera! ..." (And long die!)—only to stop and reverse himself again, turning his curse into a blessing: "But no, death to no one, life to everyone. Yes, long live the world, long live everyone, everyone in the world" (165).[100] Zambrano recasts him as the figure in Goya's painting: "Raising his arms to the sky, exposing his chest, offering it as if he were facing the

---

[97] "[H]ombres des-hermanos, sin lazo alguno de comunidad, mecanismos, aquellos hombres condenados también a ser máquinas, a convertirse en poseídos de un gatillo" (217).

[98] "[E]se grito que nace irrefrenable del fondo del corazón ante toda muerte al dictado [...]: ¡No disparéis, no disparéis!" (217–18).

[99] "No; se escuchan gritos contrarios: '¡Disparad, apuntadme bien al corazón' ... Y se comprende. Es el grito de la víctima que se precipita viviente a la muerte, que se da el lujo final de morir voluntariamente, de morir viviendo" (218).

[100] See note 57 for the text in Spanish.

7 THE SCENE OF THE FIRING SQUAD: ZAMBRANO'S *DELIRIUM*... 173

universe all by himself, he kept shouting, 'Long live the whole world!' The beam from a spotlight bathed him from head to toe and was reflected in his white, white shirt, one so white it was whiteness itself" (165).[101] It is precisely here where Zambrano ends her narration of those years of impassioned political struggle and shared hope. It is here where we as readers encounter the void of all that she leaves untold about the years of the Republic and Civil War; here she leaps abruptly to that moment of defeat, of absolute loss, in the winter of 1939, when, after so many of her fellow citizens have died, many shot summarily by firing squad, she is crossing the Spanish border into France.

* * *

I began by citing Zambrano's letter to Rosa Chacel, penned in 1953 soon after completing *Delirium and Destiny*, in which she refers to the "great, immense pain" that envelops her—"like a void without shorelines, a vast ocean in which our heart keeps on beating, the ocean of our blood and of our thought" (43).[102] Her profound and persistent pain could only have deepened through the 1940s with the conflagration in Europe and the ongoing brutal repression in Spain, as the regime continued to execute thousands of citizens, deemed guilty for having struggled for democracy. Much later in life, after the death of Franco, she would write:

> I have lost, perhaps forever, my patria, that word that is uttered with so much fear and more often remains unsaid. I have lost my life, the life that I could have had in Spain, the life of my friends and my comrades. I have lost, at the very moment it started, what we didn't yet know would be a civil war. I have lost a large part of the people of my generation, which we call the generation of the bull for their sacrifice, which they foresaw, beings very dear to me, victims. (*Palabras* 110)[103]

---

[101] "Y alzando los brazos al cielo, dejando el pecho al descubierto, ofreciéndolo como si estuviese frente al Universo, él solo, aún gritó: '¡Viva todo el mundo!' La luz de un foco eléctrico le bañaba de arriba abajo; se reflejaba en su camisa blanca, blanca, de tan blanca, la misma blancura" (256).

[102] See note 2 for the text in Spanish.

[103] "¿Nada? He perdido, tal vez para siempre, mi patria, esa palabra que con tanto temor se dice y que se calla más que se dice. He perdido mi vida, la vida que yo hubiera tenido en España, la de mis amigos, la de mis compañeros. He perdido, no más iniciada, lo que ni siquiera sabíamos si iba a ser una guerra civil. He perdido a gran parte de la gente de mi generación, a la que llamo la del toro por su presentido sacrificial, seres muy queridos, vícti-

174   J. HIGHFILL

In *Delirium and Destiny* Zambrano vividly recaptures the incandescent hope, the heartfelt solidarity that she had shared with her comrades as together they struggled to make the Republic a reality. And in so doing, the immensity of this loss—of friends, comrades, of democracy, of the life she could have had—becomes palpable, indeed excruciating for her readers. Even more so because she conveys that loss by pointing to an abyss of all that she cannot recount, but instead expresses by evoking the scene of the firing squad, Goya's *The Third of May*. Throughout her life, as she mourned the deaths of her comrades, fellow citizens, and of democracy itself, Goya's valiant figure, facing down death, must have served as a touchstone, a lifeline.[104] Indeed, it was only months after fleeing Spain, when she first referenced the painting in a lecture she presented in Mexico in 1939:

> [A]ll his humanity pours outward in an exuberant expression of life on the precipice of death. The shirt is torn, perhaps from the immense, vital impetus of his chest, which the cloth cannot cover or contain. A white strip of cloth is indeed a very small thing for covering the chest of a man. And this is how he faces death—so vibrant, bursting with blood and life-force, such that it seems impossible, impossible, that death could seize that overflowing abundance of blood and thus chill that incandescent fire contained and concentrated in him. He is a man, fully a man of flesh and bone, in soul and spirit, in overwhelming presence that absorbs everything. A whole, true man. (*Pensamiento* 44–45)[105]

mas" (*Palabras* 110). Here Zambrano recounts how she responded to friends and acquaintances who had reproached her for not rejoicing after the death of Franco. They had suggested that living in exile, she had suffered much less that those who remained in Spain under the long dictatorship. This statement appears in "La muerte apócrifa," a column Zambrano published in *Diario 16* in 1985 after her return to Spain (anthologized in *Palabras del regreso*) (My translation).

[104] In 1985, Zambrano once more evokes Goya's scene of the firing squad in a column, "Aquel 14 de abril," published in *Diario 16* (anthologized in *Palabras del regreso*, 105–08). She recalls the man in the white shirt, who on the evening of the proclamation of the Republic had shouted—";¡Que no muera nadie! ¡Que viva todo el mundo!"—"el grito del que van a fusilar, del fusilado" (108–09).

[105] "[T]oda su humanidad se vuelca hacia fuera en un gesto pletórico de vida al borde mismo de la muerte. La camisa está desgarrada, diríase que por el inmenso ímpetu vital del pecho que no alcanza a cubrir. Es muy poca cosa un guiñapo blanco para cubrir el pecho de un hombre. Y así se enfrenta a la muerte, tan palpitante, tan rebosante de sangre y empuje, que parece imposible, imposible, que la muerte cuaje aquel caudal arrollador de sangre y enfríe tan ardiente fuego como se aprieta en él, concentrado. Es el hombre, el hombre ínte-

Here, she represents this man as the consummate emblem of life in that instant of imminent death, as she will again in *Delirium and Destiny*. And in so doing, she dwells on his vibrant physicality; he is at once mortal and immortal, bursting with a life-force that cannot be quelled. As she goes on to affirm: "The entire universe is inside him—all its elements and its plenitude; he alone gives us the idea of the infinity of the world and of its cohesion and its fire" (*Pensamiento* 45).[106]

Ekphrasis is, of course, the term for such evocations of a work of art in a literary text. When appearing in narrative, ekphrasis works to still the linear progression of time, making us contemplate an image in all its simultaneity. That "stilled movement," Murray Krieger has argued, is "'still' moving, as a forever-now movement, always in process, unending" (268). In *Delirium and Destiny* those repeated instances of ekphrasis, require us to halt and contemplate the scene of the firing squad with that singular figure in the white shirt, who represents all the victims of the countless atrocities of wars and dictatorship past and present. As readers, we are thus compelled to witness that scene of horror as a "forever-now movement," as an unending reenactment of all the men and women standing before those rifles—that "cold viscera"—and the mechanized, "debrothered" men who hold them. And in bearing witness, we are called upon to respond to that "scream of life," as a "forever-now" affirmation of life-force itself. Zambrano, after reflecting on her visit to the Prado, puts it plainly: what is most important "at the present historical conjuncture was, is, to find the possibility of life equal to this dying," that is, "to find the way of living that our death deserves" (*Delirium* 109).

Works Cited

Bundgaard, Ana. "Etica y estética de la razón poética." *Filosofía y literatura en María Zambrano*, edited by Pedro Cerezo, Fundación José Manuel Lara, 2005.

Caballero Rodríguez, Beatriz. "The Cathartic Exercise of Memory in María Zambrano's *Delirio y destino*." *Memory and Trauma in the Postwar Spanish Novel: Revisiting the Past*, edited by Sarah Leggott and Ross Woods, Bucknell UP, 2014, pp. 141–53.

---

gro, en carne y hueso, en alma y espíritu, en arrolladora presencia que todo lo penetra. El hombre entero, verdadero" (44–45). (My translation)

[106] "El universo entero está en él, en sus elementos y en su plenitud; él sólo nos da idea de la infinitud del mundo y de su cohesión y de su fuego" (45). (My translation)

176   J. HIGHFILL

———. *Maria Zambrano, a Life of Poetic Reason and Political Commitment*. Wales UP, 2017.

Corral, Rose. "Memoria y exilio en Delirio y destino de María Zambrano." *Actas del XII Congreso de la Asociación Internacional de Hispanistas*, vol. 4, edited by Derek W. Flitter, Dept. of Hispanic Studies, U of Birmingham, 1998, pp. 57–63.

Enquist Källgren, Karolina. *María Zambrano's Ontology of Exile: Expressive Subjectivity*. Palgrave Macmillan, 2019.

González Calleja, Eduardo. "Rebelión en las aulas: un siglo de movilizaciones estudiantiles en España (1865–1968)." *Ayer*, vol. 59, no. 3, 2005, pp. 21–49.

Goya y Lucientes, Francisco de. *El 3 de mayo en Madrid*. 1914. Oil on canvas. Prado Museum, Madrid.

Johnson, Roberta. "The Context and Achievement of *Delirium and Destiny*." *Delirium and Destiny: A Spaniard in Her Twenties*. By María Zambrano, translated by Carol Maier, SUNY Press, 1999, pp. 215–35.

Krieger, Murray. *Ekphrasis: The Illusion of the Natural Sign*. Johns Hopkins UP, 2019.

Lapiedra Gutiérrez, Guillermo. "Una comparación entre Razón Vital y Razón Poética: María Zambrano y la Filosofía de la Religión." *Ilu. Revista de Ciencias de la Religiones*, vol. 2, no. 63, 1997, pp. 63–74.

Lejeune, Philippe. *On Autobiography*. Translated by Katherine Leary, U of Minnesota P, 1989.

Mangini, Shirley. "María Zambrano's Enduring Drama: Remembering the Spanish Civil War." *Spanish Women Writers and Spain's Civil War*, edited by Maryellen Bieder and Roberta Johnson, Routledge, 2016, pp, 15–34.

Marco Igual, Miguel. "Los médicos republicanos españoles exiliados en la Unión Soviética." *Medicina e Historia*, no. 1, 2009, pp. 1–15.

Marset, Juan Carlos. *María Zambrano: I. Los años de formación*. Fundación José Manuel Lara, 2004.

Moreno Sanz, Jesús. "Razón armada a la razón misericordiosa." Introduction to *Los intelectuales en el drama de España y escritos de la guerra civil*, edited by Jesús Moreno Sanz, Fundación María Zambrano, 1998, pp. 9–41.

———. "Síntesis biográfica." *María Zambrano, 1904–1991: De la razón cívica a la razón poética*, edited by Jesús Moreno Sanz, Residencia de Estudiantes, 2004, pp. 37–80.

Morey, Miguel. "Estoy aquí todavía." *Delirio y destino: Los veinte años de una española*. By María Zambrano, Alianza, 2021, pp. 9–40.

Ortega y Gasset, José. "Meditaciones del Quijote." *Obras completas*, vol. 1, Editorial Revista de Occidente, 1966, pp. 311–400.

Parente, Lucia. "El texto vital: Ortega y Zambrano." *Aurora*, no. 17, 2016, pp. 78–90.

7 THE SCENE OF THE FIRING SQUAD: ZAMBRANO'S *DELIRIUM...* 177

Pittarello, Elide. "Sentir y conocer: *Delirio y destino* de María Zambrano." *Actas del XIV Congreso de la Asociación Internacional de Hispanistas,* vol. 3, edited by Isaías Lerner, Robert Nival, and Alejandro Alonso, Juan de la Cuesta, 2004, pp. 419–26.

Preston, Paul. *The Spanish Holocaust: Inquisition and Extermination in Twentieth-Century Spain.* W.W. Norton, 2012.

Revilla Guzmán, Carmen. "Sobre el ámbito de la razón poética." *Revista de Hispanismo Filosófico,* no. 9, 2004, pp. 1–13.

Robles Carcedo, Laureano. "María Zambrano en la 'Guerra InCivil.'" *Las mujeres y la Guerra Civil Española: III Jornadas de Estudios Monográficos, Salamanca, Octubre, 1989,* Ministerio de Cultura, Dirección de los Archivos Estatales, 1991, pp. 158–64.

Rodríguez-Fischer, Ana, editor. *Cartas a Rosa Chacel.* Versal Travesías, 1992.

Stanzel, Franz K. *A Theory of Narrative.* Translated by Charlotte Goedsche, Cambridge UP, 1986.

Tellez, Juan José. *María Zambrano y la República Niña.* C&T Editores, 2011.

Zambrano, María. "Carta del exilio." *Cuadernos del Congreso por la Libertad de la Cultura,* no. 49, 1961, pp. 65–70.

———. *Delirio y destino: Los veinte años de una española.* Editorial Horas y Horas, 2011.

———. *Delirium and Destiny: A Spaniard in Her Twenties.* Translated by Carol Maier, SUNY P, 1999.

———. *Las palabras del regreso.* Edited by Mercedes Gómez Blesa, Cátedra, 2009.

———. *Los intelectuales en el drama de España.* Alianza, 2021.

———. *Pensamiento y poesía en la vida española.* Casa de España en México, 1939.

———. "Una visita al Museo del Prado." *Algunos lugares de la pintura,* edited by Amalia Iglesias, Espasa Calpe, 1989, pp. 47–60.

———. "Una visita al Museo del Prado." *Cuadernos del Congreso por la libertad de la cultura,* no. 13, 1955, pp. 36–40.

PART II

Border-Crossing: Displacement and Creativity

CHAPTER 8

Gertrude Stein Off Center in Spain (1901–1916)

Anett K. Jessop

Act so that there is no use in a center.
—Gertrude Stein, *Tender Buttons* (63)

In a 1937 article for the newly established journal *Hispania*, Stanford professor John Reid reported on "Spain as Seen by Some Contemporary American Writers." He profiles three American male writers and selected works: Waldo Frank (*Virgin Spain*, 1926; *America Hispana*, 1931), John Dos Passos (*Rosinante to the Road Again*, 1922; *In All Countries*, 1934), and Ernest Hemingway (*The Sun Also Rises*, 1926; *Death in the Afternoon*, 1932). Reid searches for Spain's attraction—what he calls a "comparatively unimportant corner of Europe"—and concludes that the Spanish pace of life and customs offer "a welcome antithesis to the industrial chaos of American life" (139, 150). Reid determines that his authors identify with characterizations they have of Spain that mirror their own preoccupations: for Frank, religious mysticism; for Dos Passos, nostalgia for the

---

A. K. Jessop (✉)
The University of Texas at Tyler, Tyler, TX, USA
e-mail: ajessop@uttyler.edu

© The Author(s), under exclusive license to Springer Nature Switzerland AG 2024
R. M. Silverman, E. Sánchez-Pardo (eds.), *Nomadic New Women*,
https://doi.org/10.1007/978-3-031-62482-7_8

181

182   A. K. JESSOP

pastoral; for Hemingway, rituals of violence. At core, their notions of Spain portray a singularly masculine ethos: the "natural dignity, self-control, and sincerity" of the Spanish peasant (143–4); the spirit of "lo flamenco"—in Dos Passos's words, "The tough, swaggering gesture, the quavering song well sung,…the back turned to the charging bull" (146); for Hemingway, "a compendium of the manly virtues: probity, courage, self-respect, and pride" as illustrated in the bullfight (149). The mystical, romantic, and aesthetic mores of a perceived culturally unified and traditional Spain countered the dynamism of an industrializing world at the start of the twentieth century. As Reid notes, "We are, of course, not surprised to learn that Don Quijote, that poor knight…becomes…a symbol of Spain. Like his native land, Quijote, guided by a set of noble, medieval ideals, meets in unequal battle a world of reasoning and materialism"—or, as Waldo Frank describes it, "a multiverse of fragmentary facts which is the modern crisis" (143).

The only woman mentioned in Reid's article is Gertrude Stein and, then, only as a footnote credit for her phrase the "Lost Generation." In fact, to correct the record, Hemingway was directed to Spain, and the bullfight specifically, by Stein, who was by 1937 an acclaimed modernist in her own right as well as a seasoned traveler and longer-term resident in Spain, well before Frank, Dos Passos, or Hemingway set foot in the country. Also relevant to Reid's assignment but ignored were other American women writers who had travelled to and written about Spain by the date of Reid's publication: Edith Wharton, Laura Riding, Muriel Rukeyser, to name but several. As feminist revisionist scholarship has demonstrated, omissions like Reid's confirm the androcentrism of the academy and an attempt to canonize a majority-male modernist vanguard. Spain's role in modernist studies has been likewise reassessed, though still with unequal coverage of women's literary contributions; even so, recent cultural histories are adding balance to our knowledge of the engagements of Anglophone women writers crossing Hispanic divides. And while the American expatriate Gertrude Stein is more often associated with France for her enormous literary influence and associations brought together in her Paris salon, this chapter will assert the ways in which Stein's acquaintance with Spanish artists and culture significantly influenced her fiction and experimental style at critical junctures in her development. In Stein's work, Spain becomes a multivalent motif in her quest for an organizing structure through which to channel her literary explorations in pursuit of knowledge of, in particular, domestic intimacies. As Reid notes, the figure of the idealistic and questing Don Quixote was an ubiquitous "symbol of Spain" in the Western imagination, well represented in the visual arts from the eighteenth and nineteenth centuries (Charles-Antoine Coypel, Gustave Doré, Honoré Daumier, Cézanne) and just as relevant into the twentieth (Picasso and Salvador Dalí). As Stein was an avid art collector, with particular interest in French and Spanish painting, she was well aware of such depictions. In literature, the picaresque novel was elevated by such luminaries as William Dean Howells, who recommended every American novelist "study the Spanish picaresque novels; for in their simplicity of design he will find one of the best forms for an American story" (*My Literary Passions* 143).[1] Increasingly, early twentieth-century women writers were rewriting romance conventions, particularly those derived from, in Reid's words, "noble, medieval ideals" in the face of "unequal battle" in the social, political, and literary domains within which they existed. Through the character of the *pícaro*, I argue, Stein found for her protagonists (and arguably herself) an exemplar for exploration and inquisition. And while Reid's writers sought sanctuary and confirmation in Spain's patriarchal traditions, Stein embraced Frank's "multiverse of fragmentary facts" through her increasingly innovative poetics. Furthermore, as shall be discussed, Stein's Spain was entirely more queer than the androcentric and heteronormative versions promoted by Reid's writers.

In Gertrude Stein studies, scholars have largely discussed Spain as a refuge and aesthetic reference introduced through her friendship with Picasso. David Owens's "Gertrude Stein's 'Lifting Belly' and the Great War" considers Stein's year (1915–1916) in Mallorca as reprieve from the European war. "'Baptized Spanish': Gertrude Stein and the Making of a Spaniard," by David Murad, credits Picasso with influencing her through his developing abstract method to shift from the romanticized narrative style of her earlier novel, *Q.E.D.* (c. 1903), toward the experimental steam-of-consciousness prose in *Three Lives* (1909). Murad joins María De Guzmán and others to challenge modernist studies' privileging of Paris, London, and New York as the cynosures of modernism. Murad posits that Stein's friendship with Picasso and other Spanish artists influenced her to deem Spain the seedbed for modernism. In similar vein, Mary

---

[1] As Michael Schmidt details, Cervantes's *Don Quixote* was "not tied into the Spanish language" (128) and quickly took root in literary traditions across Europe and America to influence many writers, to include Lewis Carroll, Conrad, Dickens, Dostoyevsky, Faulkner, Fielding, Flaubert, Joyce, Kafka, Melville, Proust, Scott, Stendhal, Sterne (128–31).

184   A. K. JESSOP

Gossy's "The Stain of Spain in Some of Stein" offers a rhetorical analysis of "What is Spain" from "Lifting Belly" as a cubist envisioning. While these articles highlight Picasso and Spain as significant stylistic inspirations, these critics fail to recognize the more specific generic indebtedness Stein's work owes to Spanish literature: that is, the ways the picaresque permeates her narratives, as well as her radical transformation of generic conventions. Ambitious literary surveys such as Gayle Rogers's *Modernism and the New Spain: Britain, Cosmopolitan Europe, and Literary History* (2012) and *Incomparable Empires: Modernism and the Translation of Spanish and American Literature* (2016) propose reconsiderations of Spain's contributions to the global modernist project; still, these histories focus on predominantly male modernists (including Reid's trio)—with Stein given only passing reference. Encouragingly, some cultural historians have trained more interest on earlier twentieth-century women writers (Richard Kagan's *The Spanish Craze: America's Fascination with the Hispanic World, 1779–1939*, 2019). Stein, in her essay "Picasso" (1938) asserts: "America and Spain have this thing in common, that is why Spain discovered America and America Spain, in fact it is for this reason that both of them have found their moment in the 20th century" (514). Stein is explicit in tracing a symbiotic relationship of discovery between Spain and the United States, Spain and herself—and ultimately their historical "moment" when incipient literary and artistic innovations become "modernism."

The *Autobiography of Alice B. Toklas* famously states that Stein's creative transformation occurred during a 1912 trip to Granada, Spain; however, Stein's *hispanophilia* goes back further. During her childhood Stein travelled widely with her family throughout Europe and the U.S. and, in adulthood, toured within and settled for extended periods in Spain across the first two decades of the twentieth century, first in the company of her brother Leo and later with her partner Alice Toklas. So, too, do Stein's literary avatars wander through similar locations in search of experience. Wandering and wondering, as it were, comprise the plot trajectories of Stein's two early novels and foreground her later experimental compositions drafted in Spain. The Cervantean-styled picaresque and, in particular, the character of the *pícaro* associated with travel, nomadism, and quest—the hallmarks of this collection—offered a fitting generic template for her narratives of search and discovery. This chapter advances a chronological reading of key early works by Stein (*Q.E.D.*, "Melanctha" from *Three Lives, Tender Buttons*, and "Lifting Belly"), written during the period of her travels in Spain and influenced by those experiences, what I think of as her Spanish Period. I focalize Stein's early fiction through the perspective and development of the wandering woman, the *pícara*, whose romantic adventures challenge the time-period's social conventions of courtship, love, and sexuality. Quixotic fancies, disillusionments, and subsequent awakenings provide the scaffolding of my method for reading Stein. Further, I contextualize Stein's work in light of Mikhail Bakhtin's early twentieth-century narrative theory and philosophy of language. Finally, recent scholarship by Maite Zubiaurre on erotic subcultures in Spain during the early twentieth century rebalances the depiction of Spain as hyper-masculine: to wit, Spanish culture was entirely more erotically fluid than previously represented. My purpose is to highlight the ways in which "Spain," as a category, intersects with Stein's aesthetic evolution and must thereby serve as a critical locus for Stein studies. In Spain—off center, as it were—Stein innovates her signature literary style, grounded in part in Spanish precedent then stylized in original ways. These several reconsiderations bring together new contexts and perspectives for a deeper understanding of the range of influences that Spanish culture wielded on Stein's work as well as a more balanced appraisal of Spain's contributions to international modernism.

Wandering Women and the Picaresque (1901–1907)

Stein's early novels are replete with wandering women, and, indeed, twentieth-century Anglo-American women's literature offers many examples of women in transit, from Virginia Woolf's Rachel Vinrace in *The Voyage Out*, Djuna Barnes's Robin Vote in *Nightwood*, Kate Chopin's Edna Pontellier in *The Awakening*, to name but a few protagonists. That early twentieth-century women writers were unclear about their cultural, social, and political identities and status is no surprise; these anxieties, questions, and explorations are the core concerns of many women writers' works. The most notable wanderers in Stein's early novels are the characters Adele, from *Q.E.D.*, and Melanctha, from *Three Lives*, who wander in search of direction and understanding, particularly in matters of desire, sexuality, and love. The picaresque offered a genre well suited for the quest narrative represented in Stein's first novels. As defined by critic William Harmon, the picaresque novel (*picaresca* in Spanish; from *pícaro*, "rogue") is

186   A. K. JESSOP

a chronicle... presenting the life story of a rascal of low degree engaged in menial tasks and making his living more through his wits than his industry. The picaresque novel tends to be episodic and structureless. The *picaro*, or central figure—through various pranks and predicaments and by his association with people of varying degree—affords the author an opportunity for satire of the social classes. Romantic in the sense of being an adventure story, the picaresque novel nevertheless is strongly marked by realism in petty detail and by uninhibited expression. (*Handbook to Literature* 362–3)[2]

Cervantes's *Don Quixote* (Part One 1605, Part Two 1615) follows the adventures and misadventures of Don Quixote, self-appointed knight-errant who, accompanied by his peasant-squire Sancho Panza, ranges across the Spanish countryside in search of challenges to bring honor to Quixote's Lady Fair, a local farm girl. Sancho Panza is the pragmatic and earthy foil to Quixote's fantastical conceits about love, idealism, and glory, lunacies spurred by reading chivalric romances. The novel ends with Quixote returning to his town and falling ill—during which time he dreams and wakes with sanity restored. His "awakening" allows him to see his earlier illusions such that he revokes his "title," apologizes for injuries he has incurred, dictates his will, then dies. In its most general sense, the picaresque is an episodic recounting of adventures on the road, and, in Stein's iteration, the wandering hero—rendered female—leaves home, travels freely, and follows her heart. With Adele and Melanctha as *pícaras* (the feminine form implies deviant behavior, often sexual), wandering in search of comprehension and connection invert (echoing sexologist Havelock Ellis) the heteronormative dramatic plot and generic courtly conventions.[3]

Q.E.D. is the story of a love triangle enmeshing three "college bred American women of the wealthier class" (3): Adele, the main protagonist, Helen Thomas, and Mabel Neathe. The novel follows their peregrinations crossing the Atlantic, through Europe, and back to the United States. The

---

[2] I choose Harmon's definition, taken from a relatively recent 2012 issue of his handbook, as a contemporary example of the continued masculinizing of the picaresque protagonist.

[3] While *Don Quixote* is the best known example of the Spanish picaresque in English, having been translated by Thomas Shelton around 1612 (Part Two, 1620), those deeply read in Spanish literature would know earlier cases of the picaresque (*Lazarillo de Tormes*, 1554; *Guzmán de Alfarache*, 1599; *El Buscón*, 1626), as well as examples of the *pícara*, the questing female protagonist, in works such as Francisco López de Úbeda's *La pícara Justina* (1605), later translated into English as *The Spanish Jilt*, 1707. I thank Dr. Esther Sánchez-Pardo for these important references.

three women are mere acquaintances at novel's start before Adele slowly falls in love with Helen who is involved with Mabel. Intrigue and contestation ensue, and, in the end, the ultimately incompatible Adele and Helen are unable to forge a long-term commitment and the increasingly jealous Mabel wins out. While not a "rascal of low degree," Adele is certainly the fool ("'Of course I am not logical,...logic is all foolishness,'" 5), opining regularly and confidently on her theories of social and economic class, stridently in favor of middle-class stability and custom. She is, however, unschooled in the arts of love and falls under the spell and tutelage of Helen. Instead of threatening windmills, Adele encounters the rocky terrain of courtship and, in the tradition of chivalric literature, is by turns repulsed, attracted, elevated, and disciplined by her experience of desire and love. In her parodic turn on the picaresque, Stein reorients romantic convention to set Mabel and Adele as male-typed suitors of Helen, styled as a late nineteenth-century New Woman. Mabel, on the other hand, is described as having the "unobtrusive good manners of a gentleman" (15) while Adele often refers to herself with a masculine pronoun and early exclaims, "I always did thank God I wasn't born a woman" (6).

The prospect of conflict between explorations and internalized constrictions is forecasted from the start, as the novel opens with the three women sailing across the Atlantic for Europe. Adele voices her reservations about the unknown: "Heigho it's an awful grind; new countries, new people and new experiences all to see, to know and to understand; old countries, old friends and old experiences to keep on seeing, knowing and understanding" (3). How to integrate "new experiences" with past (self-) conceptions is one of the novel's primary conundrums. Adele's contemplations on "seeing, knowing, and understanding" will comprise the narrative subtext—but only after much effort spent refusing to see, acknowledge, and accept. Stein early signals Adele's pervasive sense of imprisonment, even as she travels the expansive Atlantic: "One hears so much of the immensity of the ocean but that isn't at all the feeling that it gives me....it is the most confined space in the world....Being on the ocean is like being placed under a nice clean white inverted saucer. All the boundaries are so clear and hard. There is no escape from the knowledge of the limits of your prison" (6–7). Adele alludes to the domestic nature of her confinement in the image of the saucer, emblematizing the restrictions on a middle-class woman's experience in the world.

Stein structures *Q.E.D.* in the picaresque mode with wandering and questing as both plot structuring and stylistic modes of peripatetic

188 A. K. JESSOP

narrative designed to move the characters, Adele in particular, toward better understanding of their conditions and motivations. Likewise in the picaresque genre, the novel's satire occurs in the dismantling of Adele's attitudes on class and gender as well as in parody of the chivalric romance. The novel's antagonist would seem to be late nineteenth-century middle-class and patriarchal strictures as the dramatic action and conflicts occur between conventional social stability and a woman's desire and independence. Adele proudly promotes herself as a member of the middle class and proponent of propriety, decency, and motherhood (5). When the three women socialize, Adele and Helen routinely provoke each other through intellectual jousting during which occasions Adele "vehemently...explained her views and theories of manners, people and things, in all of which she was steadily opposed by Helen who differed fundamentally in all her convictions, aspirations and illusions" (8). In particular, the two clash over the profits of education over experience. Adele initially argues that education should be undertaken only to achieve "definite future power" while experimentation is "both trivial and immoral" (7); Helen counters by noting Adele is "cutting passion quite out of [her] scheme of things!" (7), to which Adele retorts that, as to "physical passion," she has "an almost puritanical horror and that includes an objection to the cultivation of it in any of its many disguised forms" (7–8). In accordance with her privileged upbringing and indoctrination (sexual aversion included), Adele represents Thorstein Veblen's nineteenth-century leisure-class status quo to Helen's incipient modernist spirit of exploration. Clearly, their arguments mask attraction and Adele soon capitulates her severe stances: "I could undertake to be an efficient pupil if it were possible to find an efficient teacher" (8).

Stein deploys allusions to wandering (whether physical or emotional, on land or sea) to describe Adele's contemplations on her attraction to Helen: "Of course Helen may be just drifting as I was, or else she may be interested in seeing how far I will go before my principles get in my way" (9). Adele and Helen are character foils, with Adele as rational and Helen emotional. During one interchange Helen asks, "Haven't you ever stopped thinking long enough to feel?" to which Adele responds, "I always think. I don't see how one can stop it"—at which point Helen abruptly stands to leave: "In that case I had better leave you to your thoughts" (12). In a particularly Steinian turn of phrase, when Adele asks Helen to "tell me how much do you care for me," Helen replies: "Care for you my dear...more than you know and less than you think" (12). Knowing and thinking are concepts that Stein interrogates both playfully and philosophically across the novel.

Granada, Spain, is the setting for prehension when Adele is attracted to a local girl. Their memorable communication, for Adele, rests in sitting together, though not speaking as they do not know each other's language, then strolling for a time before "part[ing] as quiet friends" (14). Adele feels a connection to this shared experience and her yet unarticulated emotions for Helen: "No it isn't just this, it's something more, something different. I haven't really felt it but I have caught a glimpse" (14). Adele considers the tacit and nonphysical intercourse with the Spanish girl to be the perfect intimate encounter while any other expression, she notes, "rather annoyingly gets in my way and disturbs my happy serenity" (14). Following the meeting, Adele indulges in Dante's *Vita Nuova*, the tale of unrequited romantic love as spiritual refinement. Upon her return to the U.S., Adele complains in sentimental fashion: "what's the use of anything as long as it isn't Spain?" (16). In this scene, Spain represents fantasy fulfillment even while the dynamics between Adele and Helen push for a more physical level of communion.

In the novel's final two chapters, the three women negotiate their relationships, which Stein narrates in episodes depicting shaded moods and contestations. Back in New York, during "interminable walks in the long straight streets," they "continued their homeless wanderings" (19). The romantic struggle between Helen and Adele is strained even as their longing for each other intensifies. Adele believes Helen is bound to Mabel by economics, as Mabel supports Helen financially in the manner of a man his mistress. Adele several times describes Helen as a "prostitute" (53, 58) and the competition between herself and Mabel as a struggle for "stolen…property" (45). When Helen first kisses her, Adele is incapable of describing what is happening. When they finally consummate their physical relationship, Adele experiences "very real oblivion. Adele was aroused from it by a kiss that seemed to scale the very walls of chastity. She flung away on the instant filled with battle and revulsion" (39). Stein resists explicit description of physical love in *Q.E.D*, while in works later written in Mallorca she will invent ways to codify the body and love play. Likewise, there are gaps in the novel's narrative time when Adele and Helen are alone together and when sleepovers are suggested. Adele continues to swim in remorse, fear, and denial, often wishing instead for "peace and a quiet life!" (21). At novel's end, in a final stolen moment before Helen and Mabel leave for Europe, Helen and Adele meet, however, "[t]here

190   A. K. JESSOP

was no ardor in their reconciliation, they had both *wandered* too far" (italics mine 48). After their many equivocations, Adele and Helen have frayed the filaments of romantic attraction in the face of the longer-term stability that Mabel represents for Helen.

Q.E.D. is a quest chronicle of Stein's *pícara*'s adventuring in the world and growing apprehension of her desires in the face of bourgeois conformity. Stein resists conventional plot schema: following Adele's "awakening," there is no climactic resolution nor dénouement to speak of. Consummation does not lead to marriage or harmony—only agitation, disappointment, and (one expects) more wandering. While the long-suffering knight loses her lady, she does gain some spiritual perspective: Adele "had proved herself capable of patience, endurance and forbearance" (56). Still, the novel's title, *Q.E.D.*—abbreviation for "Quod erat demonstrandum," that which was to be demonstrated—is an ironic seal for a circumambulating series of episodes with no closure, that, instead, end in "dead-lock" (63).

The Cervantean picaresque is widely considered the prototype of the modern novel,[4] particularly for its juxtaposition of high and low generic conventions and for the diversity of peoples, classes, and ideologies portrayed—what modernist-period theorist Mikhail Bakhtin terms, in "Discourse in the Novel," its linguistic and contextual heteroglossia: the way meaning is conveyed in the narrative (*Dialogic Imagination* 263). According to Bakhtin, "Cervantes excelled in describing encounters between a discourse made respectable by the romance and vulgar discourse—in situations fundamental in both novels and life" (384). The picaresque novel winds through the everyday and commonplace, "one's native territory," and thereby more graphically exposes "vulgar conventions and, in fact,...the entire existing social structure" (165). Bakhtin points to the ways the device of the quixotic fool allows the author to expose prejudices, inequities, and injustices. By means of the innocent and ignorant protagonist, the author can further reveal "all unofficial and forbidden spheres of human life, in particular the sphere of the sexual and of vital body functions...as well as a decoding of all the symbols that had covered up these processes" (165–6). As such, *Q.E.D.*'s opinionated yet unworldly Adele is the reader's companion into the veiled world of turn-of-the-century lesbian culture as well as victim of the period's

---

[4] See Harold Bloom's "Don Quixote, Sancho Panza, and Miguel de Cervantes Saavedra," xxi–xxxv.

8 GERTRUDE STEIN OFF CENTER IN SPAIN (1901–1916) 191

heteronormative and patriarchal systems. Equally productive is Bakhtin's identification of "not understanding" as a literary topos: "The device of 'not understanding'—deliberate on the part of the author, simpleminded and naïve on the part of the protagonists—always takes on great organizing potential when an exposure of vulgar conventionality is involved" (164). Adele's agonizing coming-to-terms with her sexuality (through transitory "glimpses") into a more authentic and liberated experience of herself bypasses homophobic rejection of "sexual inversion" to allow the reader a vicarious embrace of social and cultural alternatives. As Marianne DeKoven observes, Stein alludes to Cervantes in the scene when Helen and Adele recognize their feelings for each other, by calling their attitudes and reactions "quixotic."[5]

Q.E.D. was not published during Stein's lifetime—not until 1950 when released by a small press in limited edition—for, as Richard Bridgman notes, "The subject of the book was a dangerous one in 1903" (*Gertrude Stein in Pieces* 40). Nonetheless, by depicting sexual orientations and social relations rarely represented in fiction, *Q.E.D.* was pioneering in its content and would soon be joined by other modernist women writers' works deploying lesbian subjects and themes. Broadly, Stein's contribution in *Q.E.D.* was to off-center the Cervantean picaresque by introducing a lesbian twist into the chivalric tradition. What Bakhtin extols as *Don Quixote*'s "artistic possibilities of heteroglot and internally dialogized novelistic discourse" (*Dialogic Imagination* 324) will be more innovatively styled in Stein's subsequent quest tale "Melanctha," from *Three Lives*, wherein the dilemma of marginalized women (African-American and immigrants) takes textual wandering to a compelling and original level.

Three Lives, another collection with a tripartite structure, is organized according to its principal female protagonists: "The Good Anna," "Melanctha," and "The Gentle Lena." "Melanctha," the longest and most complex portrait, depicts the young adulthood of Melanctha, a "graceful, pale yellow, intelligent, attractive negress" who is "complex with desire" (125–6). The plot is built on the examination of four key love relationships—two with women (Jane Harden and Rose Johnson) and two with men (Jeff Campbell and Jem Richards)—through which she seeks the oppositions of excitement and safety during her relatively short life. As scholars note, there are many parallels between the relationship dynamics in this work and *Q.E.D.*, even to closely styled episodes and

[5] See *Norton Critical Gertrude Stein*, footnote no. 9, 201.

192 A. K. JESSOP

dialogue exchanges; still Stein expands her repertoire of romantic types to include the erotic, courtly, gambler, and service. The theme of power and sexuality is pervasive and more explicit in "Melanctha" than in *Q.E.D.*, as lovers negotiate desire, conquest, and submission. The tropes of wandering, learning, teaching, and knowing that surface in *Q.E.D.* are now clearly inflected with sexualized meanings.

Beginning in *medias res*, with Melanctha Herbert caring for Rose Johnson as Rose prepares to give birth, the narrative quickly circles back to recounting Melanctha's childhood to show key episodes when she forms opinions about the relationships around her and develops strategies for how to navigate the world. Melanctha's youth was neglectful and chaotic: she disliked her parents (and they her, having wanted a son), with particular hatred toward her father, through whom, nevertheless, she gains her early sense of her own power. While her mother was likewise "mysterious and uncertain and wandering in her ways" (128), her father was violent during the occasions when he would show up at the home. Melanctha identifies "successful power" with her father, and men more generally, while "[t]he things she had in her of her mother, never made her feel respect" (133). Melanctha learns that, while she could not match her father for physical strength, she can use her intellect against his ignorance to intimidate him and she can endure pain (in one case, a broken arm) and not let him see her suffering. The narrator underscores that Melanctha's ability to stand up to her "virile and unendurable black father" is a sexual coming-of-age experience for her: "Melanctha now really was beginning as a woman. She was ready, and she began to search in the streets and in dark corners to discover men and to learn their natures" (132). Melanctha rightly observes that, in a patriarchal society, authority rests in the hands of men while women have subordinate position. Melanctha's sexuality is one aspect of herself that she recognizes could command attention from men and might thereby make her successful.

With little supervision at home, Melanctha begins her wandering early: from age twelve to sixteen "she wandered, always seeking but never more than very dimly seeing wisdom. All this time Melanctha went on with her school learning" (133). As with *Q.E.D.*, this passage sets experiential learning against academic education in terms of the protagonist's pursuit of a kind of knowledge that will most profit her. Intelligence is often discussed in this work, and it is more often evaluated as to its practical applications: Melanctha is accused by several characters of not using her

8 GERTRUDE STEIN OFF CENTER IN SPAIN (1901–1916)   193

intelligence well. Melanctha, however, wants to practice "how to use her power as a woman" (131) and so:

> she strayed and stood, sometimes by railroad yards, sometimes on the docks or around new buildings where many men were working. Then when the darkness covered everything all over, she would begin to learn to know this man or that. She would advance, they would respond, and then she would withdraw a little,.... It was a strange experience of ignorance and power and desire. Melanctha did not know what it was that she so badly wanted. (132–3)

Melanctha's campaign of approach and retreat, her excitement and fears, parallel Adele's. And while she "wandered on the edge of wisdom" (136), the subtext suggests she remains a virgin. Ultimately, at the end of her first campaign for "knowledge and power," "[i]t was not from men...that Melanctha learned to really understand this power" (133): it was from a woman.

At age sixteen Melanctha discovers her first teacher and initiator into the arts of love: Jane Harden is seven years older than Melanctha and better educated. Melanctha's "sweetness" is matched by Jane's worldliness and hedonism, and Melanctha respects Jane because she "had power and she liked to use it" (139). The attraction to each other is mutual and, at first, the two "wandered" (138) together before becoming a couple. Over the course of their two-year affair, Jane, the libertine, instructs Melanctha in the amatory arts: "Jane had many ways in which to do this teaching. She told Melanctha many things. She loved Melanctha hard and made Melanctha feel it very deeply. She would be with other people and with men and with Melanctha, and she would make Melanctha understand what everybody wanted, and what one did with power when one had it" (140). With Jane, Melanctha first experiences love's "joy" and "suffer[ing]" (140)—the cardinal tropes of romantic love conventions. However, their relationship deteriorates as the power dynamic between the two shifts, with Melanctha growing dominant. Finally, Melanctha decides she "did not really need [Jane] any longer. Now it was Melanctha who was stronger and it was Jane who was dependent on her" (141). The early intensity of the relationship when control is negotiated is what excites Melanctha. Once she gains leverage over Jane, she loses interest: she is no longer "learning." The lesson for the lover is that excitement is to be pursued, dependency avoided. As with a newly minted knight, her training now complete, Melanctha embarks with confidence upon new conquests,

194   A. K. JESSOP

"ready now herself to do teaching. Melanctha could do anything now that she wanted. Melanctha knew now what everybody wanted" (141).

Jefferson Campbell, a young country doctor, is Melanctha's new mark. This heterosexual courtship and eventual coupling is the longest in textual length though not, in the end, the most important in Melanctha's life. Nevertheless, it is the most extensively explored, perhaps because its heteronormativity was more acceptable to an early twentieth-century readership. The "good and strong and gentle and very intellectual" Jeff Campbell was slow to advance their friendship which makes Melanctha "want him very badly" (142); in the fashion of literary romance, resistance always makes the lover's quest seem more worthy. Jeff, however, is more attracted to Jane Harden, whom he admires for her intelligence and her "power." While he is treating Jane for her excessive drinking, she continually disparages Melanctha, claiming she "didn't use her mind enough" (145). There are many parallels across the interactions between and espousings of *Q.E.D.*'s Adele and Helen and Jeff and Melanctha, now translated into the dialect Stein imagines for her African-American characters. For example, Jeff—Stein's representation of African-American middle and professional class—expresses his preferences for traditional family and community stability over experiences and "excitements": "to live regular and work hard and understand things,...that's enough to keep any decent man excited" (148). Jeff's service to community as a medical doctor is countered by Melanctha's romanticized notions of closeness and her advocacy for "real, strong, hot love...that makes you do anything for somebody that loves you" (152). Jeff explains that he is "always so busy with my thinking about my work I am doing and so I don't have time for just fooling" (152). Melanctha counters: "Don't you ever stop with your thinking long enough ever to have any feeling Jeff Campbell" (159–60). When Jeff questions her affection for him, Melanctha replies "Care about you Jeff Campbell....I certainly do care for you Jeff Campbell less than you are always thinking and much more than you are ever knowing" (160). It comes as no surprise when Jeff finally appeals for a "teacher" (Stein's shibboleth for erotic awakening): "Perhaps I ought to know more about such ways Miss Melanctha....perhaps I could learn a whole lot about women the right way, if I had a real good teacher" (154).

At the climactic point, the lovers come together to be fully satisfied before the inevitable dénouement. Stein is fairly explicit (in early twentieth-century terms) when describing their lovemaking:

And Jeff took it straight now, and he loved it, and he felt, strong, the joy of all this being, and it swelled out full inside him, and he poured it all out back to her in freedom, in tender kindness, and in joy.... Every day now, Melanctha poured it all out to him, with more freedom.... Every day now more and more Melanctha would let out to Jeff her real, strong feeling. (176–7)

The rhetorical styling of tidal feeling and response is strongly conveyed in Stein's experimental prose. At first, Jeff delights in her "teaching" and "learning to be real bright, just like my teacher" (181), however, Jeff cannot square the medieval trope of woman as "more wonderful than a pure flower, and a gentleness, that is more tender than the sunshine, and a kindness, that makes one feel like summer" (165) with what he mistrusts in Melanctha (her sexual appetite and physical enjoyment) as well as the revelation from Jane Harden that she and Melanctha were once lovers. As the chivalric trope of love as devotion to the Beloved disintegrates, Jeff is overwhelmed with confusion, shame, and disgust. He exclaims that Melanctha "never had deserved a reverence from him," and that she was no longer "a real religion to him" because she was "just made like all us others" (203, 204). Melanctha's ordinariness, frank and full expression of her sexuality, and past sexual experience leave him "bitter" because "he had let himself have a real illusion in him" for "what was good and had real beauty" (204). Metaphysical notions of The Good and Beautiful could not survive the carnality of human sexual expression. Through lengthy exposition, Stein's narrator charts the breakdown of their emotional bonds until there is little left. Eventually the two stop seeing one another and Melanctha resumes her wandering.

Rose Johnson is Melanctha's Sancho Panza with her commonsense scolding and arguments against Melanctha's fantasies of love. Rose believes in the practicality of marriage—not romanticized delusions—as the cornerstone of a stable life for women and she questions why "Melanctha with her white blood attraction and her desire for a right position had not yet been really married" (125). Rose is also Melanctha's most significant love relationship (238). Melanctha finds comfort in Rose's constant maternal reprimands which provide Melanctha some oversight and sense of security. Melanctha's expression of her love for Rose is service to her: "Melanctha now always wanted to be with Rose,.... Melanctha Herbert always was doing everything for Rose that she could think of that Rose ever wanted" (211). However, once Rose marries, Melanctha returns to wander.

196   A. K. JESSOP

Melanctha's final lover, Jem Richards, is Jeff Campbell's foil: he is fast and flashy where Jeff was cautious and traditional. Jem is a gambler and skilled in the amatory arts: "Jem Richards was more game even than Melanctha. Jem always had known what it was to have real wisdom. Jem had always all his life been understanding. Jem Richards made Melanctha Herbert come fast with him.... Now in Jem Richards, Melanctha found everything she had ever needed to content her" (225). The refrain across this episode is that loving Jem made Melanctha "mad and foolish" (228). When Jem gives her an engagement ring (something Jeff never did), Melanctha becomes besotted, for, at this point, "Melanctha needed badly a man to content her" (226). In time, Jem encounters gambling trouble and his attitude toward Melanctha shifts toward distance even while she reacts by grabbing on more tightly. In desperation, Melanctha returns for comfort to Rose who is preparing to have her baby (and to the initiating event of the story). Soon, however, both Rose and Jem condemn Melanctha, claiming that the town is gossiping about her exploits. Where once Melanctha was independent and powerful in pursuit of her desires, she is now dependent and needy of assurance and protection. The very dependency she once rejected in Jane Harden becomes her frailty and defeat: without a lover, she is "lost" (237). In the end, solitary Melanctha suffers several illnesses before dying of "consumption" (239). The closure is emblematic of the forces of desire and need that pursue Melanctha across her short life. Unlike Don Quixote, however, Melanctha does not appear to have awakened from a final dream into full understanding of her life.

In the progress of *Three Lives*'s "Melanctha," Melanctha is increasingly styled the *pícara*, a person "of low degree," living by her "wits," and ever more the "mad fool" in love. Melanctha's character is largely to blame: her personality admixture is insoluble: Stein brings qualities of temperament together that cannot easily coexist, at least within the perimeters of story-line: "Melanctha Herbert was always seeking peace and quiet, and she could always only find new ways to get excited" (129). These oppositions in Melanctha's personality are repeated across the narrative, ascribing them resolutely and permanently to her character until Melanctha is debilitated by the contradictions. Under the narrator's insistence, there is no opportunity for maturation. Moreover, while several modes of romantic intimacy are explored, there is little significant development in the relationships themselves, to the point where all of Melanctha's intimates denounce her before wandering off themselves while Melanctha dies alone in a sanitarium "consumed" by her travails.

In addition to the picaresque quest, Stein insinuates two other European romance conventions into "Melanctha": The Romance of the Rose and Philosophy in the Bedroom—conventions set by the medieval French poem, co-authored by Guillaume de Lorris and Jean de Meun, and the 1795 treatise by the Marquis de Sade—a marriage of the courtly and the coarse. The chivalric courtship, with its preoccupations with purity, reverence (love as a religion), and aspiration parallel the sexual awakening of the protagonist at the hands of a libertine-teacher, who instructs the neophyte in the erotic arts until she is ready to initiate her own conquests. (And, to state the obvious, there is a romance with a Rose.) The recurring questions seem to be: what do women and men—lovers generally—want from each other? What exists past the excitement of courtship, arousal, and eventual consummation? What exactly are we in search of? In Stein's modernist rendition of romance literature, the crux of the lovers' dissonance and suffering hinges on mutual mistrust and misunderstanding of what each partner wants and says. Stein dwells upon the existential suspicion whether one can really know our intimates' needs or the meanings of their utterances: "Melanctha never could make out really what it was Jem Richards wanted" (229); Jeff Campbell exclaims: "I certainly do wonder, Miss Melanctha, if we know at all really what each other means by what we are always saying" (157). "Melanctha" begins with the solipsistic epigraph "Each One As She May" and, in the end, both "Melanctha" and *Q.E.D.* depict romance as an adversarial landscape.

While Stein's early novels are innovative, they still evidence a commitment to an American realism promoted by William Dean Howells and others. William Harmon's definition posits that the picaresque is realistic in its inclusion of "petty detail and...uninhibited expression." As befits turn-of-the-twentieth-century American fiction, "Melanctha" does indeed reference industrial sites (railroad yards, shipping docks, construction zones), and, in its styled social naturalism, *Three Lives* represents the ordinary lives and challenges of its poor and marginalized female protagonists: African-American Melanctha and German immigrants Anna and Lena. Stein attempts realistic characterization of African-American Vernacular English dialogue in "Melanctha" as well as English as Second Language sociolects in the portraits of "The Good Anna" and "The Gentle Lena." Her earlier studies in human psychology at Johns Hopkins bring an additional level of realism to Stein's modeling of interior dialogue as evidenced in her renderings of rumination, thought-looping, self-questioning, even dysphoria. As Bakhtin theorized in "Discourse in the Novel," the

198   A. K. JESSOP

picaresque genre reveals linguistic and cultural heteroglossia—defined as "*another's speech in another's language*" (324)—as well as prevailing social structures. Multivalent and often contesting meanings comprise what Bakhtin terms "double-voiced discourse" which "serves two speakers at the same time and expresses simultaneously two different intentions: the direct intention of the character who is speaking, and the refracted intention of the author" (324). According to Bakhtin's paradigm, in the novel, "[o]ppositions between individuals are only surface upheavals of the untamed elements of social heteroglossia, surface manifestations of those elements that play *on* such individual oppositions, make them contradictory, saturate their consciousness and discourses with a more fundamental speech diversity" (325–26). At the time Stein is writing her novels, the social and gender identities of women and men are in dispute as are issues of class, race, and rank across the nation. The hierarchical stability of white, land- and resource-owning men was increasingly challenged by the flood of emancipated African-Americans as well as new immigrants coming to the U.S. from around the world.[6] In "Melanctha," racialism surfaces in its narrative biases as well as accounts of violence against African-Americans in the American South (135). Stein's (presumed white) narrator's racism is apparent from the start, proclaiming, on the one hand, the "earth-born, boundless joy of negroes," then, one paragraph later, condemning the "simple promiscuous unmorality of the black people" (124, 125). Melanctha's sincere affection for Rose is contrasted with the narrator's snide asides: "this coarse, decent, sullen, ordinary, black, childish Rose and now this unmoral promiscuous shiftless Rose" (220). Even as Stein attempts to highlight and lend sympathy through her depictions of the lives of poor and marginalized women, her narrator's bigotry persists.

The lack of conventional plot structure, characters' endless wanderings from episode to episode, and minimal closure in Stein's prose works—outside of, perhaps, the death of a protagonist—are representative of the picaresque genre and can be further examined within the context of Bakhtin's "double-voicedness" in the novel:

> The internal dialogism of authentic prose discourse, which grows organically out of a stratified and heteroglot language, cannot fundamentally be... dramatically resolved (brought to an authentic end);...it is not ultimately

---

[6] William Dean Howells's *A Hazard of New Fortunes* wrestled with these shifting social and political conditions.

8 GERTRUDE STEIN OFF CENTER IN SPAIN (1901–1916)   199

divisible into verbal exchanges possessing precisely marked boundaries. This double-voicedness in prose is prefigured in language itself... as a social phenomenon that is becoming in history, socially stratified and weathered in this process of becoming. (326)

Language drives narrative and, in "Melanctha" in particular, it is the polyphonic texture of the dialogues—entreaties and responses; action and reactions—that comprise plot as story. Additionally, double-voiced discourse that "serves two speakers"—each with their own motivations—results in a competition that ensures the lack of narrative resolution and almost guarantees that some characters (particularly the female and marginalized) are held in check, unable to make progress or prosper. Wandering, in Stein's novels, happens at the textual and lexical levels, as many scholars have observed. In *Curved Thought and Textual Wandering*, Ellen Berry explicates Stein's distinctive narrative approach: "textual wandering describes an intratextual strategy whereby the organization of a work is generated by the convergence and dispersal of moments of significance, a dynamic process that stops but does not end" (9). Wandering is similarly a cross-cultural migrancy as represented through Stein's immigrant and disempowered characters: Priscilla Wald remarks that "[i]mmigrants, for Stein, were selves in transit, between narratives as much as between geopolitical locations" ("Immigration and 'The Anxiety of Identity'" 441). For Stein's female protagonists, migrancy might mean resident "alien" designation and certainly disenfranchisement—the status into which all women in the U.S. fell in the early twentieth century. Wandering is attempting a new course, often pushing against restrictions, conformity, and convention, even at the syntactic level, as Wald notes: "authorship entails struggling with *sentences*, with the compulsory regulations of conventional grammatical units and the culture they reflect" (*Constituting Americans* 242). Additionally, wandering in Stein's works occurs at the lexical level: To Wander (intransitive) is to ramble, meander, stray, and even to err. Stein tests and resets lexical meanings across *Q.E.D.* and *Three Lives* wherein the denotative drifts into connotative terrain. The infinitives "to learn," "to know," "to understand," and "to wander" become energized with sexual significance.

Finally, wandering is a symptom of and precursor to becoming, as Bakhtin suggests: "The revitalizing of linguistic consciousness, its crucial participation in the social multi- and vari-languagedness of evolving languages, the various *wanderings* of semantic and expressive intentions...,

200   A. K. JESSOP

the inevitable necessity for such a consciousness to speak indirectly, conditionally, in a refracted way—these are all indispensable prerequisites for an authentic double-voiced prose discourse" (326–27; my emphasis). Becoming is a distinctively modernist trope. In "Composition as Explanation," Stein describes the prose style of "Melanctha" as "a constant recurring and beginning...in the direction of being in the present" (524)—that is, becoming. There are ways in which Bakhtin's theories of genre and narrative forecast Stein's experimental projects drafted in the next decade during her travels with Alice Toklas across the Spanish mainland and from her residence in Mallorca. In *Tender Buttons* and other works, Stein explores language's ability to make meaning by testing its grammatical and definitional flexibility. The *pícara*'s practice of questing will evolve into Stein's compositional system for pointing and refraction, where meaning is queried and sentences are queered.

LOVE OFF CENTER IN SPAIN (1908–1916)

Stein's relationship with Picasso plus her many travels through Spain proved to have "transformational" effect on her work (Kagan 412). However, Spain's culture of gendered extremes would not have been lost on Stein: the masculine bravado and violence of the bullfights (celebrated in Reid's *Hispania* article) as well as the social conservatism and patriarchy of the Catholic Church. These were also values espoused by Spain's literary vanguard. While the Generación del 98 embraced some of the revolutionary zeal of European experimentalism, intellectuals were still contending with injuries to the national pride brought about by defeats in the Spanish American War of 1898, evidencing its waning power as an empire. In essays and tracts, the majority male avant-garde cautioned against depravities that weakened the Spanish national spirit, including homosexuality, and decried "señorita men" over "macho men."[7]

Paralleling the High Art movement was another, equally dynamic, popular culture movement trafficking in new theories of sexuality and the psyche. Maite Zubiaurre's *Cultures of the Erotic in Spain, 1898–1939* reveals an archive of recovered erotica long censored under the Franco dictatorship. Zubiaurre accounts for Spain's growing consumer culture, eagerly importing "technology and sex" (16); she claims that Spain "embraces foreign technology and its inventions to an extent rarely seen

[7] As quoted in Zubiaurre, 9–10.

in high-cultural art and literature" (2). Through new printing technologies, sexual and erotic content was distributed in pamphlets, magazines, postcards, stereograms, and pornographic films. The link between sexuality and the project of modernism is ubiquitous in the visual, literary, and performative arts: Picasso's *Les Demoiselles*; Mina Loy's "Feminist Manifesto"; Luis Buñuel's *L'Age d'Or*. "Techno-eros" was, according to Zubiaurre, good for women (2), and the turn-of-the-century Spanish word for erotic and pornographic works, *sicalíptico*, reveals a female-pleasure-centered etymology: Greek *sykon* (vulva) and *aleiptikos* (arousing) (4). Sexual indeterminacy and androgyny become leitmotifs across visual culture, particularly images of "effeminate" metropolitan men and the "androgynous *moderna*," women sporting short hair and riding bicycles (12). Thus, in the annals of "eroto-historiography"—a more general application of the concept coined by Elizabeth Freeman in *Time Binds: Queer Temporalities, Queer Histories*—early twentieth-century Spain offered residents and visitors an eroto-tourist subculture within which to wander.

Into this environment of permissiveness and accommodation, Stein and Toklas came and went, traveling to Spain on holidays and living in Mallorca for extended periods. *The Autobiography of Alice B. Toklas* states that Stein's aesthetic vision shifted during their 1912 trip to Spain: "We enjoyed Granada,... and it was there and at that time that Gertrude Stein's style gradually changed. She says hitherto she had been interested only in the insides of people, their character and what went on inside them, it was during that summer that she first felt a desire to express the rhythm of the visible world" (119). While traveling, Stein drafted a number of Spain-inspired pieces, including "In the Grass (On Spain)." Following their return to Paris she continued to ply her breakthrough approach to new subjects, "describe[ing] rooms and objects" (119), in works subsequently collected in *Tender Buttons* (1914). Finally, during the long stay in Palma, Mallorca, from May 1915 to June 1916, Stein further evolves her innovative style in works, including the erotic sequence "Lifting Belly," later published in *Geography and Plays* (1922).

Stein's new method produces a generic shift and hybrid styling. As earlier proposed, *Q.E.D.* and "Melanctha" explore the subjectivity of their protagonists ("the insides of people, their character and what went on inside them"), particularly in their pursuit of desire and knowledge, a strategy well in accordance with Cervantes' novel, as Georg Lukács observed in *The Theory of the Novel* (written during this period,

202   A. K. JESSOP

1914–1915): "*Don Quixote* is the first great battle of interiority against the prosaic vulgarity of outward life, and the only battle in which interiority succeeded" (104). In *The Outside Thing: Modernist Lesbian Romance*, Hannah Roche argues that Stein's use of the romance plot (particularly as reminiscent of courtly traditions) allows her an acceptable genre through which to explore a woman's desire. Stein's interpretation of the picaresque—the quixotic protagonist, the quest for love deployed in plot as well as textual wandering—evolves from prose fiction to what might be called experimental poetic prose focused on cubist-styled still lifes, portraits, and social vignettes, now refracted to include multiple angles of animating description ("the rhythm of the visible world") and channeled through a nonspecific narrator.

"In the Grass (On Spain)," for example, continues the themes of *eros* and control present in *Q.E.D.* and "Melanctha," declaring "culture is power, Culture is power. Culture" (*Geography and Plays* 75).[8] Culture includes social and sexual relations, and this work contrasts gendered images in a striking collage of associations. There are intimations, in images and references, of a male presence:

> All of it cucumber.
> Cup of lather and moan moan stone grown corn and lead white (75)

which prefaces the "culture is power" passage. It is not improbable to see phallic substitutions in the vegetables, which are in the act of hardening and enlarging, in conjunction with the implied beard awaiting shaving—perhaps suggesting a "snake" "In the Grass"? The exact nature of the "moan" is unclear: a groan (suggested in the homophone "grown")? Pleasure or complaint? Then, there is a clandestine interlude implied in the playful pairing and reshuffling of words:

> Whispers, whispers. Whispers not whiskers, whiskers, whiskers and really hair. Hair.
> Hair is when two are in and show gum.
> > Kiss a turn, close.
> Suppose close is clothes, clothes is close. (80)

---

[8] According to Zubiaurre, the color green, "verde," is "associated with sex in Spanish" (27). Stein's proximal joining of "Grass" and "Spain" in the poem's title invites the connection.

The tryst sketches an encounter where "whispers" and "whiskers" are vetted—the simple exchange of the "p" and "k" makes the difference—substituting a woman for a man. The flashing image, "show gum," implies the mouth opening to "kiss a turn, close." The musing line, "Suppose close is clothes, clothes is close," alternates "close" for "clothes"—where, with the removal of the "th," nothing stands in the way of complete physical intimacy (close-ness)—while the verbal "close" asserts privacy. Soon a couple reemerges in the "we" who are now "wet"—"A wet syllable is we are, a wet syllable is we are we in" (81)—evidencing (by the addition of "t") the *sicalíptico* of sexual excitement. Language itself, not plot, is the foremost agent of the composition's action, that is, words' proximity to lexical and syntactic meaning-making as well as skillful obfuscation, here exemplified toward the end of "In the Grass (On Spain)": "next to between, next to between in intend intender. In tender" (81). The somersaulting wordplay juxtaposes positions and intentions and augurs Stein's next publication, *Tender Buttons*.

Upon their return from Spain, "Alice," in the *Autobiography*, records that Stein soon launches a new project in order to further refine her aesthetic method: "Hitherto she had been concerned with seriousness and the inside of things, in these studies she began to describe the inside as seen from the outside" (156). Stein's earlier "seriousness" in her fiction now turns to experimentation and play even as she transitions from subjectivity to objective distance. The format and style of *Tender Buttons* are indeed original. Organized under the categories of "Objects," "Food," and "Rooms," thus continuing her penchant for tripartite structure, the collection's first two sections resemble dictionary or textual glosses, while the final section comprises a lengthy discourse. In "Objects" and "Food," the entry headings are configured as punctuated statements: for example, "Eyeglasses." and "A Piece of Coffee." These two sections pose domestic references to cleaning, cooking, dressing, eating, and socializing. "A Purse." illustrates one of the more accessible entries:

> A purse was not green, it was not straw color, it was hardly seen and it had a use a long use and the chain, the chain was never missing, it was not misplaced, it showed that it was open, that is all that it showed. ("Objects" 21)

The "definition" offers a collage of associations, tangentially and idiosyncratically ascribed to the title. The purse is described by its availability and use while the visual account states what colors it is not. Here, as elsewhere,

204 A. K. JESSOP

all sentimentality has been removed along with expressive punctuation cues, such that every line (whether declarative, interrogative, or dialogue) is given the force of facticity. As such, the methodology presents as forensic and Stein seems to be asking whether saying more about what an object isn't might be equal to attempting to represent what it is—a modernist reformulation of John Keats's negative capability. According to Virgil Thomson, Toklas once remarked that Stein's ambition in *Tender Buttons* was "to describe something without mentioning it" (*Virgil Thompson* 173). Critic Juliana Spahr characterizes Stein's approach as "definitional desire," a resurfacing of desire in new materialization ("Afterword" 110). Stein's cataloguing format proposes a kind of order even while the "definitions" undermine prescription in their kaleidoscope of associations and deflections. The remnants of picaresque wandering now transmute to linguistic and imagistic wandering. The collection's title captures the spirit of incongruous combinations: an affective attribute (Tender) and an object (Buttons)—both words fluidly nominal and verbal—formulate an affective-objective as mode of definition.

As many scholars note, Stein now privileges language above all literary conventions: In *Time Binds*, Elizabeth Freeman claims that Stein "strips the dominant language down to a bare minimum; parataxis, repetition, and pronominal ambiguity" (xix). Stein additionally emphasizes intertextuality within her own word/world-building, as Ulla Dydo observes: "Always one Stein piece engenders the next, so that each becomes a context for the next" (*Gertrude Stein* 78). Indeed, in the matrix of congruencies, the reader discovers surprising correspondences: the "cucumber" passage cited above from "In the Grass (On Spain)" finds footholds in *Tender Buttons* under the entry of the same name and with reference to shaving: "Not a razor less, not a razor, ...rest in in white widening" ("Cucumber" 55). *Tender Buttons* also deploys alternative patterning as a form of meaning-making: for example, the auditory: Another way to "hear" *Tender Buttons* is homophonic: "Tend her buttons," which admits suggestive connotations. Whether by sense or sound, Stein is now more focused on the relationships between words and works than her human protagonists. Stein's intertextuality both contributes to a modernist idiom and presages the postmodern.

"Rooms" shifts format in its long decanted discourse on the cogent and obscure. It, too, contains keywords but these are more abstract: "center," "change," "place," "time," suggesting stability and instability, locus and temporality. The opening imperative, "Act so that there is no use in a center" (63), is a call to advance across arenas bridging "[a] whole center and a border" (63). Importantly, what is occurring off-center or at the margins ("Any change was in the ends of the center," 63), be it geolocations or aesthetic innovations, is "spreading" (63). Together, Stein suggests, the center and margins make a more fulsome and expansive mapping. Of course, to wander is precisely to "act so that there isn't a center" (to paraphrase). The text indicates that the important action occurs away from the "miserable center" where there wanders over "hills" and gradients the intrepid "pink tender descender" (67–68). What is a center? In truth, the center moves with the curious seeker: "A fact is that when the place was replaced all was left that was stored and all was retained that would not satisfy more than another. The quest is this, is it possible to suggest more to replace that thing. This question and this perfect denial does make the time change all the time" (64–65). Riddled through the rhetoric, Stein offers discernments of degrees—spatial, logical, aesthetic. In discourse like this—double-voiced and lexically shifting—questions and answers entwine: "All the time that there was a question there was a decision" (65). Further, this section disserts on education ("Why is there education," 71), religion ("Why is there so much useless suffering. Why is there." 75), and the human condition writ large ("Harmony is so essential." 65). "Rooms" presents kōan-type statements:

A sack that has no opening suggests more and the loss is not commensurate. (67)

Giving it away, not giving it away, is there any difference. Giving it away. Not giving it away. (69)

Tender Buttons' final feverish Quixotic dream in "Rooms" prompts awakening: "The author of all that is in there behind the door and that is entering in the morning. Explaining darkening and expecting relating is all of a piece" (64). This is the terrain of modernist wisdom literature where puzzlement might spur enlightenment. Stein's propositions defamiliarize conventional language, what Russian formalist Viktor Shklovsky termed *ostranenie* ("Art as Technique" 1917), as a means to distinguish poetic language from the prosaic. Stein's friend Sherwood Anderson records, in his introduction to *Geography and Plays*, that her language has "an oddly new intimate flavor and at the same time makes familiar words seem almost like strangers" (5). Stein's language does not make meaning through commonsense constructions, rather she disrupts expectations for what words mean and how in order to highlight interpretive possibilities. Her

206   A. K. JESSOP

Dada-styled mysticism harkens to the Spanish mystics she read (and several of whom she commemorated in her *Four Saints in Three Acts* libretto, 1925): St. Teresa of Ávila, Ignatius of Loyola, St. John of the Cross, Ramon Llull of Mallorca.[9] Through *Tender Buttons'* linguistic "Cloud of Unknowing"—referencing the late-medieval Christian prayer book—the reader/seeker surrenders to the illogic and half-glimpsed understandings that make up the phenomenal and epistemological realms. In this way, Stein's literary deconstruction of "knowing" and "understanding" moves to transcendental planes of meaning.

Germane to this study, there needs be one final interrogation into work from Stein's Spanish period. In the private and revealing "Lifting Belly" (not published during Stein's lifetime), "the inside as seen from the outside" acquires a voyeuristic gaze. Coy, flirtatious, disclosing, "Lifting Belly" is a love story and amalgam of the many attributes of desire explored in this chapter: romance, gender, pleasure, and mutuality. "Lifting Belly" is also a litany of definitions, an inquest into what exactly the title references without naming it. Intimacies are sketched onto the page, reminiscent of those erotic leaflets in Spanish bookstalls, as Stein indicates: "A magazine of lifting belly. Excitement sisters" (423). In the presence of desire, the "inside as seen from the outside" is the essence of *scopophilic*—couched in coded references and playful significations. In "Lifting Belly" the reader peers at arousing intimate interludes:

> Kiss my lips. She did
> Kiss my lips again she did.
> Kiss my lips over and over and over again she did. (425)

Elements of the chivalric romance are embedded in the work, such as the profession of "love as religion": "Lifting belly is so strong. I love cherish idolise adore and worship you. You are so sweet so tender and so perfect" (424), and expressions of gallantry: "I say that I need protection./You shall have it./After that what do you wish./I want you to mean a great deal to me" (440). "Lifting Belly" interrogates gender ("What is a man./What is a woman." 436) through a styling of double-voiced discourse:

---

[9] "Among the saints there were two saints whom she had always liked better than any others, Saint Theresa of Avila and Ignatius Loyola, and she said she would write [Virgil Thomson] an opera about these two saints," (*The Autobiography of Alice B. Toklas*, 229).

8 GERTRUDE STEIN OFF CENTER IN SPAIN (1901–1916)   207

Please be the man.
I am the man.
Lifting belly praises.
And she gives
Health.
And fragrance.
And words.
Lifting belly is in bed. (455)

In "Lifting Belly" the lover comes home to discover repose and fulfill-ment, benefits denied to Adele and Melanctha. The Beloved luxuriates in the Cervantean geography of the body: "The hill above lifting belly" with its "windmill" (417). Ultimately, "Lifting belly is a language" (422), and the text reminds us of pleasure in reading, the profits of decentering, delight, and re-awakening to the corpus lingua, as celebrated in the final line: "In the midst of writing there is merriment" (458).

"Spain," for Stein, served as a destination, an aesthetic category, as well as vehicle for larger themes, including gender, culture, power, even the metaphysical. Through the template of the picaresque, Stein adopts a leg-acy genre but dismantles the romance quest in order to reveal the hidden contemplations of her protagonists. Well-chosen, the picaresque embodies the spirit of exploration that is modernism, and, underneath the pen of a woman writer, the genre is significantly altered. Stein's focus on narrative in *Q.E.D.* and "Melanctha" moves increasingly to narration as linguistic utterance and lexical play in *Tender Buttons* and "Lifting Belly." When reading Stein, the estrangements of modernist semantic innovations bring the reader back to language, even while that language destabilizes expecta-tions that grammar and syntax will provide a foundation and predictable center for meaning. Reading Stein is a textual/lexical excursion and it is fair to ask: To what do we awaken after reading Stein? I'd suggest that her experimental language of process and presence, with its emphasis on the phenomenological, is, in fact, effecting "becoming" (as Bakhtin describes), an ontological "coming out." In tandem with her protagonists, Gertrude Stein is modernism's *pícara*, boldly pursuing meaning while, at the same time, testing the means to it. Textual wandering is thinking in writing and in the spirit of this volume's anchoring Virginia Woolf and Theodor Adorno quotation: for a female expatriate journeying through the Spanish world, "writing becomes a place to live."

WORKS CITED

Anderson, Sherwood. "The Work of Gertrude Stein." *Geography and Plays*, Dover Publications, 1999, pp. 5–8.

Bakhtin, M. M. *The Dialogic Imagination*, translated by Caryl Emerson and Michael Holquist, U of Texas P, 1981.

Berry, Ellen E. *Curved Thought and Textual Wandering: Gertrude Stein's Postmodernism.* U of Michigan P, 1992.

Bloom, Harold. "Don Quixote, Sancho Panza, and Miguel de Cervantes Saavedra." *Miguel de Cervantes' Don Quixote*, translated by Edith Grossman, Ecco, 2003, pp. xxi–xxxv.

Bridgman, Richard. *Gertrude Stein in Pieces.* Oxford UP, 1970.

DeKoven, Marianne, editor. *Norton Critical Edition Gertrude Stein: Three Lives and Q.E.D.* W. W. Norton & Company, 2006.

Dydo, Ulla E., with William Rice. *Gertrude Stein: The Language That Rises, 1923–1934.* Northwestern UP, 2003.

Freeman, Elizabeth. *Time Binds: Queer Temporalities, Queer Histories.* Duke UP, 2010.

Gossy, Mary S. "The Stain of Spain in Some of Stein." *Empire on the Verge of a Nervous Breakdown*, Liverpool UP, 2009, pp. 18–23.

Harmon, William. *A Handbook to Literature.* 12th ed., Longman, 2012.

Howells, W.D., *My Literary Passions: Criticism and Fiction.* Harper and Brothers, 1891.

Kagan, Richard. *The Spanish Craze: America's Fascination with the Hispanic World, 1779–1939.* U of Nebraska P, 2019.

Lukács, Georg. *The Theory of the Novel.* MIT P, 1990.

Murad, David. "'Baptized Spanish': Gertrude Stein and the Making of a Spaniard." *Interdisciplinary Literary Studies*, vol. 18, no. 4, 2016, pp. 524–44.

Owens, David M. "Gertrude Stein's 'Lifting Belly' and the Great War." *Modern Fiction Studies*, vol. 44, no. 3, Fall 1998, pp. 608–18.

Reid, John T. "Spain as Seen by Some Contemporary American Writers." *Hispania*, vol. 20, no. 2, May 1937, pp. 139–50.

Roche, Hannah. *The Outside Thing: Modernist Lesbian Romance.* Columbia UP, 2019.

Schmidt, Michael. *The Novel.* Harvard UP, 2014.

Shklovsky, Viktor. "Art as Technique." *Russian Formalist Criticism*, translated by Lee T. Lemon and Marion J. Reis, U of Nebraska P, 2012, pp. 11–16.

Spahr, Juliana. "Afterword." *Tender Buttons: The Corrected Centennial Edition*, City Lights Books, 2014, pp. 109–25.

Stein, Gertrude. *The Autobiography of Alice B. Toklas.* Harcourt, Brace, 1933. Reprint Vintage Books, 1990.

8 GERTRUDE STEIN OFF CENTER IN SPAIN (1901–1916) 209

———. "Composition as Explanation." *Gertrude Stein: Writings 1903–1932*, edited by Catharine R. Stimpson and Harriet Chessman, The Library of America, 1998a, pp. 520–29.

———. *Geography and Plays.* Dover Publications, 1999. Facsimile of The Four Seas Company 1922 edition.

———. "Lifting Belly." *Gertrude Stein: Writings 1903–1932*, edited by Catharine R. Stimpson and Harriet Chessman, The Library of America, 1998, pp. 410–58.

———. "Melanctha." *Gertrude Stein: Writings 1903–1932*, edited by Catharine R. Stimpson and Harriet Chessman, The Library of America, 1998b, pp. 124–239.

———. "Picasso." *Gertrude Stein: Writings 1932–1946*, edited by Catharine R. Stimpson and Harriet Chessman, The Library of America, 1998c, pp. 497–533.

———. "Q.E.D." *Gertrude Stein: Writings 1903–1932*, edited by Catharine R. Stimpson and Harriet Chessman, The Library of America, 1998d, pp. 1–63.

———. *Tender Buttons: The Corrected Centennial Edition*, edited by Seth Perlow, City Lights Books, 2014.

Thompson, Virgil. *Virgil Thompson.* Knopf, 1966.

Wald, Priscilla. *Constituting Americans: Cultural Anxiety and Narrative Form.* Duke UP, 1994.

———. "Immigration and 'The Anxiety of Identity.'" *Norton Critical Edition Gertrude Stein*, edited by Marianne DeKoven, W. W. Norton & Company, 2006, pp. 440–47.

Zubiaurre, Maite. *Cultures of the Erotic in Spain, 1898–1939.* Vanderbilt UP, 2012.

CHAPTER 9

La Americanita: Janet Riesenfeld's Nomadic Crossings of the Spanish Civil War and Exile

Maria Labbato

The life of US-born Janet Riesenfeld (1914–1998) was one in transit. Professionally trained in the USA, she danced flamenco in Madrid during the first months of the Spanish Civil War (1936–1939). She crossed the closed border from France to Spain in July of 1936, just days after the outbreak of war when the self-proclaimed Nationalists staged a coup. While dancing for six months with Madrid's *gitanos* (Spanish for *gypsies*), her new friends affectionately called her *la americanita*.[1] Riesenfeld arrived in Spain with the hope of marrying her Catalan fiancé and dancing professionally, but she departed with a profound awareness of the Spanish conflict and the ideological battle between fascism and democracy in Europe. Her memoir, *Dancer in Madrid*, passionately called on Americans to aid Spain. She moved to Mexico in 1937 or 1938 and contributed to a flourishing industry, the Golden Age of Mexican cinema. She deliberately rejected US job offers, choosing instead to move to Mexico City, and in

---

[1] While the term *gitano* bears a history of marginalization, racism, and discrimination, referring to people of Roma descent in Spain and subject to discriminatory policies since the fifteenth century, I use it where Riesenfeld used it and where popular folk attributes much of modern flamenco to *gitano* culture in Spain. Translations are my own.

M. Labbato (✉)
UNC Charlotte and Providence Day School, Charlotte, NC, USA

© The Author(s), under exclusive license to Springer Nature
Switzerland AG 2024
R. M. Silverman, E. Sánchez-Pardo (eds.), *Nomadic New Women*,
https://doi.org/10.1007/978-3-031-62482-7_9

212   M. LABBATO

the process forged a successful career as a foreign woman in Mexican cinema. Riesenfeld constantly traversed Anglo-Hispanic borders and boundaries, electing a volunteer exile against the context of war and global displacement between the 1930s and 1940s.[2] Despite her participation in these well-studied events, the American dancer is nearly invisible in the historical record.

This study demonstrates Riesenfeld's nomadism that crosses Anglo-Hispanic and national boundaries. Feminist theory applied to women's biography provides practical historical examples through life stories. Riesenfeld embodied what theorist Rosi Braidotti calls the "nomadic subject"; that she bore witness to the war and moved across literal and symbolic borders reveals a personal and historical identification with and empathy for the "other" (3). The nomadic subjectivity is a feminine identity that is multiple and layered, permitting the transgression of various boundaries. In applying Braidotti's theory to Caribbean writers, literary scholar Sandra Pouchet Paquet points out that shifting social or geopolitical conditions facilitate that mobility of position and subjectivity: "Nomadic thought with its implied open-endedness" offers an intellectual tool to value the creative agency of the writer or artist *and* the place of the nation with political, economic, and cultural transnationalism (66). The addition of women's voices in the Spanish Civil War and exile reveals the gendered dimension to that participation. The Spanish conflict offered Riesenfeld, and others, a political awakening and a lens for us to see into the Popular Front's promise for breaking down divisions.

The dancer belonged to a community of liberated, artistic women on the left who were coming of age just before the European struggle between fascism and democracy, which first unfolded in Spain. The war sparked political and personal awakening and anti-fascist activism for women seeking independence, including Riesenfeld. Helmut Gruber and Pamela Graves trace women's experiences in socialist movements during the interwar period when leftist parties and trade unions attained "prominence." Socialist organizations were more equipped to ask and deal with the "woman question" and the increased autonomy of the new, modern woman (Gruber and Graves 4). Studying women artists or writers during this period illuminates women's increased mobility, limits on challenging gender norms, and these women's attraction to the Spanish Civil War.

---

[2] Although Germany and Italy also signed the Non-Intervention pact, they ignored it and aided the Nationalists.

While positivist reasoning and fervent nationalism helped to ignite the traumatic conflicts of the twentieth century, volunteers and intellectuals were attracted to the global Popular Front's defense of democracy in Spain. For many women, this coalition of leftist interests also offered liberation, political and sexual independence, and political participation. Despite official Non-Intervention (a 1936 pact signed by several governments with the stated goal of avoiding a second world war), Riesenfeld and other volunteers and activists, many of them women, took up the cause of a democratic Spain.

This nomadism and empathy with the "other" enabled a kind of *Hispanism*, producing multiple forms of Anglo-Hispanic transculturation in creative works. Riesenfeld's *Hispanism* presents an alternative to professional academia. Downplayed by "professionals," this form of personal and feminist politics is an example of women's consciousness-raising decades before the 1960s feminist movement. Situating women's creative works vis-à-vis academic writing offers new light on institutional Hispanic studies or *Hispanism* that transcends discipline, party, or nation. Riesenfeld's cultural and gender crossings and outsider perspective add what many archival sources lack: the ordinary experiences, conditions, and emotions of war. Despite affection toward Spanish people and culture, at critical moments the dancer's empathy acted as a solvent for historical and contemporary differences and marginalization. Such shortcoming of the Anglo nomad still provides scholars the opportunity to explore the privileges inherent in Anglo-Hispanic crossings. Cuban anthropologist Fernando Ortiz offered that rather than *acculturation*, indicating the "transition from one culture to another," *transculturation* more accurately captures *mestizaje* (racial and cultural mixing) in Latin America, and in Cuba more specifically for Ortiz, the varied and "extremely complex transmutations of culture" (Ortiz 98). This definition allows us to see that through film analysis, the evolution of folk occurred into the twentieth century and was a process participated by Hispanic and non-Hispanic outsiders. In Mexico, the screenplays she co-wrote challenged gendered social and cultural ideologies and parodied notions of national authenticity.

Moving to Mexico, Riesenfeld started acting and screenwriting during the Golden Age of Mexican cinema. A film analysis exposes Riesenfeld's nomadic subjectivity and proximity to Spanish Republican exiles, which results in critical engagement with notions of Anglo-Hispanic cultural and gendered authenticities in Mexico. Her remarkable life and achievements as an international dancer, actress, and writer are demonstrations of the

214   M. LABBATO

complex ways women maneuvered Anglo-Hispanic divides in the twentieth century. They further suggest how war and dislocation produced trauma while also generating opportunities for personal, professional, and creative expression and liberation. The dancer traversed and worked in different countries, which illuminates more porous national borders and helps to fill the lacuna in the foreign participation of women in the Spanish Civil War and exile. Her nomadism generated an empathy with diverse experiences but, paradoxically, can also run the risk of further essentializing the "other."

THE DANCER AND THE CIVIL WAR

Artistic and creative works, such as memoirs and dance, illuminate alternative forms of political expression and activism that for Riesenfeld were developed in Spain. Published in 1938, in its original print, and unanalyzed by historians until now, Riesenfeld's memoir recounts the experience of being a foreign witness to the siege and defense of Madrid during the Civil War. She was only twenty-one when she followed her love of flamenco and Jaime Castanys to Spain. Daughter of Jewish Austrian composer Hugo Riesenfeld, she learned Spanish from her Spanish governess. She also began studying dance at a young age, but she did not care much for ballet. In the Rivoli Theater, Riesenfeld had the pleasure of watching a Spanish dancer perform and became enamored with the style, a tradition woven into Spanish historical identity. She then secured permission from her father to learn the art. Riesenfeld studied with Maestro Ortega for two years, moved with her family to California where she continued learning the dance originated in Andalusia, and met a Catalan man, Jaime Castanys. This first romantic meeting in Hollywood was brief and the American woman married another man. Years later, the nearly divorced Riesenfeld crossed paths with Jaime again in Mexico City while she performed flamenco under the name Raquel Rojas. They fell deeply in love this time—her divorce would become finalized during her stay in Spain—but when Jaime's family business required that he return to Spain, he requested she wait before joining him across the Atlantic. Enthusiastic and ignoring his direction, Riesenfeld left the USA to meet Jaime in Madrid and pursue a career in dance and fulfill a concert engagement. It was July 1936, and she did not have a political or party leaning; instead, she was draped with the cultural idealization of a beloved, yet exoticized, Spain. On the eve of the Civil War, this was to change (Riesenfeld 13–19). The war ignited when a right-wing coalition, led by military officers with the support of the fascist Falange party, the Church, wealthy industrialists, and many landowners, revolted against the democratically elected, left-leaning Popular Front of the II Republic (1931–1939).

Sitting on a train from Paris hurrying toward the Spanish border, Riesenfeld felt the overwhelming anticipation of an outsider's fantasy of a "mad mixture of fiestas, sunshine, *manzanilla*, gypsies, music, and dancing" (8). In her memoir she recalled a warning, "There is a revolution in Spain." Fellow travelers seemed to know as little of the events in Spain as she. "A revolution in Spain? I'm glad it's nothing more serious. A matter of two days, maybe three," said a Dutchman. When the border was pronounced closed, due in fact to a military-led coup, and Riesenfeld and the other foreigners could not cross, Riesenfeld's main concern was to find a way to her fiancé, Jaime, even expressing irritation at "the whole business." After two weeks stuck in Hendaye, the dancer finagled her way across the Pyrenees border by posing as a Spanish translator for a newspaperman from New York. Already during those weeks of waiting, Riesenfeld experienced the first emotional effects of the revolutionary atmosphere. She remembered camaraderie with strangers, "everyone, including myself, was united in the vast brotherhood of the beret, regardless of age, sex, or station in life" (31–33). Spain and the Civil War provided a space to realize a sense of equality and liberation. Once in Madrid, Riesenfeld was exposed to an array of groups, including ordinary residents of Madrid (*Madrileños*), flamenco dancers, bullfighters, a circle of government bureaucrats through the Press Building, and Jaime.

Riesenfeld's personal relationships in Madrid exposed her to strong Loyalist sentiments that defended the II Republic. She quickly made close acquaintance with the leader of the Militia of the Press, war correspondents, and Loyalist fighters, as well as a wide circle of dancers and artists. To keep her cover in Madrid as a press translator, she visited the Press Building regularly; she was asked to "report frequently to offset suspicion, explaining that because of the extensive spy system, any dissimulation was dangerous." The dancer received and disseminated such information, however. Riesenfeld observed that the press presented a skewed image of the supporters of the Popular Front. She recognized that this coalition, voted in during the February 1936 elections, consisted of leftist Republicans, anarchists, trade unions, the Social Party, and the Republican Union, all with various leanings, "When you read that the Government was radical, red, you did not read that it was a coalition of all the democratic parties, some radical, it is true, others more conservative, but all of them with one purpose—to eradicate the Fascist terror." Further, she had some insight into the ordinary motivation:

> You did not read that the average man who took up his gun to fight not only was not a radical but probably did not even know what the word meant. But he did know that the people did not want any regime, no matter what it was called, that catapulted him back into the misery and oppression that had been his lot in Spain until a few short years ago. (Riesenfeld 67, 68)

Through such friendships with Madrileños of different backgrounds, Riesenfeld was attuned to various perspectives of the conflict. Riesenfeld learned alongside some Spaniards of the will of the people and their capabilities under conflict; an elderly friend confessed, "Sometimes it seems to me that even I, a Madrileño, did not know the depths of my own people until now" (68).

Riesenfeld adored the *gitano* culture, mimicking and adopting it to support democracy in Spain. At the start of the Spanish generals' coup on July 18, 1936, Riesenfeld was uneducated on the politics of the electoral forces of the Popular Front in the 1936 February elections, but her affinity toward flamenco facilitated her political awakening. In the Albaicin dance studio and family home in Madrid, Riesenfeld was known by a large network, or what she would often lovingly call "a real gypsy *juerga* (spree)," as "*la americanita*, who was going to try to dance *flamenco*" (76, 77). While her affection served as a steppingstone for cultural exchange and political activism, she essentialized the Romani people in Spain. The "gitano" and flamenco traditions of resistance have roots in the inherently nomadic Romani community in Spain and their persecution or marginalized status by the state over centuries. Riesenfeld's nomadic subjectivity is quite different and removed from the transnational history and essence of "gypsy" culture and identity. Despite being Jewish-American at a time of extreme anti-Semitism, her US, middle-class privilege of continuous movement permitted a silencing of her Jewishness in Spain and may have contributed toward an exoticized vision of Spanish cultures. Yet, she came to understand the flamenco performers and their politics in Spain.

While still disconnected from the historical and lived experiences of many impoverished and discriminated Romani people in Spain, Riesenfeld personalized and rooted her romantic visions. Her friendships with flamenco performers in Madrid illuminated the nature of resistance inherent in the tradition. At first, the American is surprised to find a fellow dancer,

Enrique, draped in the volunteer soldier uniform of the *miliciano* one day: "What did Enrique and the others have to do with all this? Their comprehension, their world, never went beyond the four walls of a studio and all that it meant." She realized the "injustice" of her ignorance that tried to reduce the "gypsy" artists to their "thoughtless generosity, their *juergas*, their fiestas, the clapping of hands, the sounds of guitars and stamping of feet." Despite not knowing how to use a gun, Enrique felt compelled to do something (205). The realities of war de-romanticize Riesenfeld's vision over time; she recounted that his truck, with fellow artists, leaving for the front was bombed by the Rebels. Her subjective and emotional reporting provides the insight needed to understand the convictions and actions of ordinary Madrileños, artists, and writers.

Dance is an intentional expression of feeling and its performance becomes a dialogue between the artist and an emotionally responsive audience. The flamenco performer is an active agent, as its history is one of marginalization, resistance, and cultural hybridity. The dancer is defiant in their movement and boisterous in their heelwork; the dance transfigures the dancer. Flamenco scholars aptly synthesize, "The flamenco body is a kinetic site of ideological resistance, its embodied articulation carries the cruel burden of marginalization and nomadism" (Goldberg 124). Riesenfeld affectionately exoticized what she perceived as Spain's authentic character. That the American exemplifies Braidotti's nomadism is not to conflate this metaphorical nomadic figuration with the lived stigma and historical persecution of Romani peoples. Still, the flamenco body communicates with an audience, while choreography might serve as a cultural map in the spatial metaphor for movement into other cultures and subjectivities (Braidotti 16, 17). Dance historian Mark Franko explores Martha Graham's ballet, most notably the explicit and implicit anti-fascist message of her 1938 *American Document*, for its creative value, but more significantly "reevaluate[s] her work from the perspective of politics and world events, literary modernism, and major trends in anthropology, psychoanalysis, and criticism" (3).[3] Considering dance as a "nomadic aesthetic" and as historical text highlights the American's creative modes of activism

---

[3] Martha Graham (1894–1991) was an American modern dancer and choreographer, traveler, and cultural ambassador. Graham created a lifelong profession in dance, founding a dance company, The Martha Graham Dance Company, and many of her works served as social and political expressions of her contemporary moment, whether the Spanish Civil War, World War II, or inspired by American history.

218   M. LABBATO

and forging alternative, political accounts, and subjectivities. Through dancing flamenco to support the II Republic, Riesenfeld demonstrated the nomadic subject's "critical consciousness that resists settling into socially coded modes of thought and behavior" (Braidotti 1, 5). As argued by Braidotti, one cannot "separate the question of style from political choices" (16). In defiance of the official US policy, Riesenfeld publicly used her body to resist Non-Intervention, the embargo of arms against the II Republic, and fascism by dancing in fundraising benefits alongside hundreds of Loyalist artists, writers, and poets in Spain.

Indeed, Riesenfeld's growing political and social consciousness began not at the front or within militarized, international volunteer units but in the common, everyday spaces of civilian life. During the American's early weeks in Madrid, Riesenfeld observed that while there were some notable changes, the "normal way of life" persisted despite that the "enemy was only some sixty miles away." This business-as-usual extended to the arts and entertainment: movie pictures ran, "people still sat four hours over a cup of coffee in a café," and the gala theatrical season was in full swing (Riesenfeld 97). Her desire for—or perhaps evidence of the more limited space for women's involvement during times of war—a more emotional connection peers into the ways average people experience traumatic threats, a perspective often blurred, or absent, in political histories.

Riesenfeld's reporting echoes researchers who compiled evidence of the expositions, arts, and propaganda organized and continued through the Civil War. The first couple of months of the war witnessed the greatest outpouring of banquet concerts in support of the II Republic (Gómez 1980). Riesenfeld reported:

> For a nominal entrance fee, you were able to see all the outstanding artists of Spain. These were benefit performances for the hospitals; in time of peace you could not have seen so many performers in one evening for any amount of money. They worked indefatigably, giving as many as five different benefits a day. As soon as they finished in one theater, they were hurried in cars to appear at another. Seldom have entertainers been so generous in devoting their services and talents. (97)

The American practiced daily at the Monreal Academy to prepare for a scheduled concert tour, though the studio was an intimate space in which this family of instructors and artists lived, socialized, and welcomed Riesenfeld. She claimed that with her dance partners, they "were kept busy" and "dancing as often as five times a day at the benefits." Significant resistance and defense of Madrid transpired in apartments that doubled as dance studios; groups created performances for the stages and streets of Madrid to support the Loyalist cause in the early months of the war in 1936. At the *Teatro de la Zarzuela*, the largest theater in Madrid and remaining in business through the Civil War, Riesenfeld danced in one of the last significant banquets held in the capital during the war. A massive crowd enjoyed hundreds of performers and paid homage to the recently executed and beloved Spanish poet from Granada, Federico García Lorca (134, 193, 199).

Dance augmented Riesenfeld's romanticized view of Spain, but her support of the II Republic evolved into a genuine one. Anglo-nomadic subject, she learned some of the complexities of the Spanish conflict by forging personal relationships. Through dance, friendships, and intimate conversations with Madrileños the American gained a historical sense of inequality and tensions within a society still largely characterized as "feudal" with wide segments of the population "oppressed" by wealthy landowners. Simultaneously, the dancer recalled Jaime's characterization of Andalusians as in perpetual *siesta* and Madrid only slightly more conducive to industrialism, "We could become a great industrial country with the proper discipline. It would take no time to have the machines and real progress if we had a small and efficient group to run things" (117, 118). Riesenfeld eventually formed her own perspective, "I already had found an apartment, seen Jaime every minute he was not working and encountered a growing circle of friends, ranging from colorful and amusing gypsies to the aristocratic business associates of Jaime. I must say I preferred the gypsies" (75).

Dancer in Madrid offers an overlooked but important counterpoint to foreign, predominately male, representations of the Spanish Civil War. Ernest Hemingway, through his fictional foreign volunteer fighter, Robert Jordan, in *For Whom the Bell Tolls* (1940), provides a political and militarized perspective. Riesenfeld's memoir and Hemingway's novel are examples of foreigners' emotional and documentary accounts of the Spanish Civil War. The novelist went to Spain in 1937 to cover the Civil War for the *North American Newspaper Alliance* and took up arms with the International Brigades—a volunteer military unit organized by the Communist International supporting the Popular Front (Sanders 133, 139). His protagonist joins Spanish *guerrilleros* in the hills and is tasked with bombing a key bridge to disrupt fascist use. Hemingway paints for

220   M. LABBATO

readers the sacrifices of Spanish peasants and International Brigades defending the II Republic. While the novel communicates the suffering of war and the tension of killing, its focus on the soldier and fighting centers attention on violence and death, where, ultimately, Jordan is wounded and faces the decision of suicide to avoid enemy capture.

Alternatively, the US dancer spent little time near the front and, instead, documented ordinary forms of survival and resistance in Madrid, observing economic and consumer life. Riesenfeld's older roommate was named Rosario, who was her constant companion for the next four months. The women frequented the commercial life of Madrid together regularly. From the foreigner's perspective, albeit with some essentialism, "Marketing presented another difficulty. There was seldom a fixed price for anything. Bargaining is an essential, the most exciting part of the Spanish housewife's existence. Hours are spent pleasantly and inexpensively every day haggling over the price and quality of the most humble string of garlic" (Riesenfeld 80–82). She appreciated Madrileños: their grace, passion, camaraderie, and the fierceness of the market women. Despite affectionate empathy, the nomadic subject can fail to see their application of static identity onto the "other." When Riesenfeld left Spain, it was the market women that imprinted most on her memory, as she concluded her memoir: "Looking out of the window I could see Madrid in the early morning rain; sodden piles of mortar, skeleton stone buildings gutted by fire, and before the opening markets endless lines of women in black" (298).

Observing civilians' sufferings, a woman's perspective illuminates how war affects women's access to healthcare and the emotional impacts on female caregivers. Riesenfeld recounted the tragic events of a friend whose wife needed medical assistance for premature birth and could not find any, as doctors hurried to fronts to care for wounded soldiers. She provided emotional descriptions of the suffering of women, children, and wounded soldiers. The International Brigades sent hundreds of auxiliary volunteers; however, Spanish nurses most often attended to injured foreigners.[4] Riesenfeld encountered such volunteers, glimpsing what compelled these young fighters to sacrifice themselves in a far-off country. She received authorization "to pass freely to the ends of all fronts" because of her alias as a newspaper correspondent's translator (66). Taking the opportunity to

---

[4] American women generally assumed more traditionally gendered and supportive roles in the Loyalist cause, such as nursing, with a disproportionate amount of Jewish anarchist women.

visit the front near Madrid, she toured a hospital and upon hearing English, had a brief but meaningful connection with a wounded Anglo fighter and a Spanish nurse:

> Tears were in her eyes. Perhaps she would not have allowed herself this weakness for one of her own to whom she could at least have offered the consolation of understanding his words and answering them; but here she saw herself impotent before the barrier of a language she could not understand. She probably realized that he had not needed words or the knowledge of her language to make him understand the cause for which her people were fighting, and come and offer his life for it, and yet at this moment she was powerless to offer him the little comfort that a few intelligible words might have given him. (169)

Riesenfeld grasped, simultaneously, the barrier and universality of the Civil War for Spaniards and foreigners.

Due to the anti-communist paranoia of the left during the 1930s and early Cold War, US writers in Spain received critiques, yet Riesenfeld avoided such controversies and political partisanship. The Spanish Civil War was viewed by many as "offer[ing] international communism its greatest opportunity since the Soviet revolution" (133). In 1960, American scholar David Sanders confronted the partisan arguments surrounding Hemingway's Spanish novel, "he is concerned with the combatant rather than the political element" (139). Nevertheless, Hemingway's work attracted criticism from both the center-right and devout communist intelligentsia and politicians. It is likely that Hemingway, and other Popular Front writers, wrote with a keen awareness of such political tensions and the need to 'downplay' Soviet intervention in Spain (Takayoshi 104). *Dancer in Madrid*, published before the outcome of the war and the *exposed* authoritarianism of the Soviet Union within the Spanish left, offers a less biased snapshot of the sentiments of the moment. Further, Riesenfeld paid attention to groups that are not located in official archives, and we can better detach her writing from temptations of retrospectively cataloging Civil War witnesses as adhering to political expediencies. In fact, Riesenfeld hoped to stir Americans to defy Non-Intervention with her memoir, while *For Whom the Bell Tolls* is primarily dedicated to the soldier's sacrifice. Hemingway's other reporting made pleas for the II Republic; however, due to the perception of women's lack of political identity, the dancer's publication avoided "red" labeling.

222   M. LABBATO

Like the formal foreign journalists documenting the Spanish Civil War, Riesenfeld's Loyalist sympathies grew as she witnessed the events. Despite serving "both as an information resource and as discourses that convey the acts of feeling that pervaded the journalistic and political fields of that period," professional correspondents often lacked historical and political depth, were partisan, and were not educated in Spanish or conversant in language or culture (Deacon 392, 393). Riesenfeld was proficient in Spanish and immersed herself in the everyday culture of Madrileños. Her command of the Spanish language worked to nuance the conflict in ways unavailable to many other foreign travelers or correspondents. Regarding a lack of Spanish, "The majority of [foreign correspondents]—and I met them later—were equally handicapped." Without understanding Spanish, they had to rely on official handouts about developments that the dancer posits "were biased in favor of the side the writer happened to be reporting." She reckoned that few reporters would go out in the field to corroborate reports, "even those who did could only bring back statistical data or isolated reports of the horrors or unprecedented heroism" (67). Riesenfeld's ability to traverse worlds produced an intimate understanding of the events.

The dancer grew in her own self-awareness. Passionate about a free, democratic Spain, she developed "a deep awareness of others, not only those who were close by but those who had always seemed to be very far away...Now universal problems are also my own" (1, 2). Although Riesenfeld acknowledged herself as an outsider, she believed her ideals connected her to the place and people, feeling at home among the flamenco dancers and gypsies. Interestingly, the only relation in Spain that called her an "outsider" without a legitimate opinion on the conflict was Jaime. As he vigorously disagreed with her Loyalist friends, he repeatedly reminded her that as a foreigner, she could not understand the conflict and the will or needs of the Spanish people. While he highlighted *her* otherness, infantilizing her as a "child" in order to dissuade her support of the II Republic, her friends trained her in Spanish traditions, guided her to the front, invited her into historical and political conversations, and called on her as "one of us" to champion their cause. After discovering Villatora brought her to the front, Jaime initiated a fight, further highlighting his gender expectations and questioning the masculinity of Loyalists: "You're going to be my wife and you spend all your time with other men. And such men!" (Riesenfeld 172, 173).

Dancer in Madrid exposes Jaime's own transformation over the months. He had previously referred to himself as a Catalan; now, as the fighting flared, he proclaimed himself as "Spaniard" and reminded Riesenfeld of her ignorance of Spanish topics. As tensions intensified, the dancer learned more of Jaime's vehemence for the Loyalists' efforts. Riesenfeld's love affair with a Nationalist provided her with a unique experience for a foreign woman exposed to various perspectives. Yet, their ideological differences and estrangement provided a glimpse of the struggles ripping Madrid, and Spain, apart:

> It wasn't an abstraction, but an elemental, concrete question. Living in Spain meant that our whole life would be colored by the outcome of this political issue. In this generation in Spain even love is dominated by devotion to a social belief. If I, as an outsider, found it difficult to compromise, how could Jaime do so? (251)

By the time of the siege on Madrid, a poignant rift pierced their relationship. Riesenfeld realized that her ideological beliefs distanced her from the Catalan's staunchly conservative outlook toward the II Republic's liberalism. She became unwilling to bend her beliefs to appease Jaime when she discovered he had implicated her by boarding an older woman in her home who was later executed on charges of smuggling ammunition to Nationalist snipers in Madrid. Riesenfeld ended her relationship with her fiancé and weeks later in the middle of the siege, she identified his body at the makeshift morgue for government assassinations of rebel spies (160).

With her politics independent from and at odds with her fiancé, Riesenfeld represents a community of women experiencing sexual and political awakenings in Spain. By the 1930s, the USA and most European countries passed women's suffrage. As argued by Gruber and Graves, the expanded political opportunities for women on the left in the interwar period would eventually dim with the entire continent at war (7). Yet, like Graham and other female artists on the left, the Spanish Civil War and dance were a conduit for Riesenfeld's growing anti-fascism. The politics of the Popular Front in the 1930s coincided with a post women's suffrage generation of autonomous women. The young US poet, Muriel Rukeyser (1913–1980), was among London's literary circles when she was sent to cover the People's Olympiad for *Life and Letters Today*. The games were scheduled in Barcelona in July 1936 to protest the official Olympics in Germany but were canceled due to the fascist coup and Rukeyser's

224 M. LABBATO

lover—a German athlete and socialist volunteer in Spain—died at the Saragossa front. She witnessed the outbreak of the war, and before the war's end, she understood that the conflict was beyond a nationally bounded struggle. Although she wished to stay longer and do something "contributory," she was evacuated five days after her arrival. Immediately, the poet began to write *Savage Coast*, an autobiographical novel about the first days of the war and the workers' revolution in Barcelona. She hoped to persuade US readers to aid the II Republic, as the experience grounded her politics firmly on the left and resulted in a sexual awakening. Her life's work repeatedly returned to Spain and demonstrates a commitment to anti-fascism and women's autonomy.

Through their idealization of the anti-fascist struggle, women from the USA identified with and affectionately "othered" Spain. Historians and writers in the nineteenth and early twentieth century, in Edward Said's conception, *orientalized* Spain as Europe's "other" (Morcillo 2010). In her argument that women under Franco were agents of change in contextualizing the dictator's restoration of the "mythic Spanish monolithic Catholic identity," historian of modern Spain, Aurora G. Morcillo summarizes that the persisting myth led "scholars inside and outside of the country to see Spain as a European anomaly or a subaltern appendix at best" (259). While more affectionate than colonial-driven, the US and British foreigners during the Civil War "othered" Spain; *Hispanists*, the term used by Sebastiaan Faber for professional and amateur scholars of Spain, idealized (though distorted) representations of the country (7, 8). Yet, most professionals in the USA, "the field's leading journal in the United States, *Hispania*, all but excluded the war as a subject" (Faber 11). This work fell into the hands of thousands of intellectuals. Still, the major professional journals in the field abstained from passionate political discussions, almost omitting the war altogether. Columbia University founded *Revista Hispánica Moderna* in 1934, and its contributors failed to mention the war until more than a year from its start. When it did, it collected facts and news on literary topics. This section "would include regular, succinct, dispassionate updates on the lives, deaths, and sundry activities of Spanish writers." Instead, women's amateur narratives balance the "self-imposed objectivity" of the masculine academia (Faber 48, 49). As an amateur *Hispanist*, Riesenfeld offered insight and an emotional account that many professionals lacked.

Due to Non-Intervention, the task of aiding the II Republic from the outside fell on the shoulders of volunteers and writers. Over six months,

Riesenfeld gained a more realistic knowledge of the Spanish conflict, which matured from when she arrived in Spain. She concluded that she was a burden on a people already strained and wished as an American to not be an additional responsibility to the government. As the war reached Madrid, Riesenfeld felt the poignancy of her status as a non-Spaniard and noncombatant. Once home, Riesenfeld published her memoir before the end of the war, hoping that having been in Spain she could open Americans' eyes to the struggles of the Spanish people and the extent they were willing to sacrifice themselves to preserve democracy. She felt she "would be doing something contributory" (282). Supporting the Loyalist cause galvanized a generation of socially conscious and anti-fascist volunteers from around the globe. Witnessing war and its ensuing Republican exile, Riesenfeld's experience was a political awakening, as it was for other women who carried the lessons from Spain to battle fascism in Europe or defend democracy at home.

UNA *GRINGUITA* EN MÉXICO

Riesenfeld arrived in Mexico for her second, and permanent, time in 1937 or 1938. Her experiences in Spain helped to launch a prolific film career and marriage in 1945 to Spanish Republican exile, actor, and screenwriter Luis Alcoriza (1918–1992). She used the monikers "Raquel Rojas" and "Janet Alcoriza" during the Golden Age of Mexican cinema, and, as one of the screenplay titles written by Riesenfeld and her husband suggests, *Una Gringuita en México* (1951), the dancer continued to traverse Anglo-Hispanic boundaries. In 1946, *Cinema Reporter* described her as "the intelligent actress and ballerina, Austrian, nationalized Spanish" (14).[5] This is the only known assertion that Riesenfeld was nationalized as a Spaniard. While the reporter may have assumed this through her marriage to Alcoriza or Riesenfeld's own declaration, she is nonetheless firmly situated within the European, even Spanish, exile community in Mexico. Although she had a hand in at least eighty Mexican films, her name is generally forgotten and mentioned briefly in biographies and film critiques of Luis Buñuel (1900–1983), the Spanish surrealist, and Luis Alcoriza. From the Second World War through the 1960s, the decrease in foreign cultural imports fueled Mexican state-funded production. It is during this Golden Age of Mexican cinema that Riesenfeld created a successful niche

[5] "La inteligente actriz y bailarina, austríaca, nacionalizada española."

as a US woman importing Spanish culture into films. At the same time, she disrupted cultural fixities and gender normativity. Her nomadic empathy permitted cultural transgressions in character and plot development between Spanish and Mexican traditions as well as Anglo-Hispanic divides.

Women's life histories, as seen through Riesenfeld, demonstrate more transnational contributions in Mexican cinema during an age of heightened nationalism within the industry, challenging singular and gendered national and cultural narratives, yet exposing paradoxical limitations on women's liberation in the postwar period. In dancing, acting, and screenwriting, Riesenfeld contributed to the "othering" through her recreations of Spanish folk culture inside of Mexico; however, she also recreated herself many times over in her attempts to become the "other" out of the nomad's empathetic affection. Filmmakers discovered Riesenfeld at a cabaret called *El patio*, where she danced flamenco in traditional Andalusian style. Alberto Gout (1907–1966), a famous Mexican screenwriter, producer, and director, solicited the "exotic dancer and femme-fatale" for the female lead to dance flamenco in the film *Café Concordia* (1939) (De la Vega Alfaro 16).[6] She then played a US movie star and an aspiring flamenco dancer in the feature *Cuando viajan las estrellas* (1942).

Riesenfeld's film career demonstrates that she continued to use her nomadic body to trespass various cultures and identities. The dancer once more transitioned from acting to writing with *La hora de la verdad* (*The Hour of Truth*). This may have been Riesenfeld's first screenplay, which US filmmaker Norman Foster adapted to film in 1944. It tells the story of a Mexican bullfighter and his rise to fame and fall due to a traumatic love affair. The work was praised as "a film of the environment of bullfighting that shares all of the conventions and prototypes that follows an example of unusual accuracy, without an itching for demystification or melodramatic transgression, but by embracing it. It is possibly one of the best movies made about the world of bullfighters" (Fernández 11).[7] In 1945, *Cinema Reporter* credited "Raquel Rojas" with the screenplay: she had now moved into writing. By 1947 *La hora de verdad* had a popular showing in New York and *Cinema Reporter* pointed out female audiences'

---

[6] "Bailarina exótica y vampiresa."

[7] "Un film de ambiente taurino que a partir de todas las convenciones y prototipos del caso conseguía una verdad inusitada, sin ningún prurito de desmitificación o transgresión del melodrama, sino asumiéndolo. Es posiblemente una de las mejores películas hechas sobre el mundo de los toros."

affinity for the male lead, Ricardo Montalbán (*Cinema Reporter* 45). Amidst this success, the new screenwriter met Alcoriza in New York and later fell in love once in Mexico as both still acted (Rucar Buñuel 84). They married the same year *La hora de la verdad* was finished, and it was Riesenfeld's collaboration with Norman Foster that resulted in the newly-wed's eventual meeting with Luis Buñuel.[8] Following *La hora de verdad* was *Las rosas del recuerdo*, with Luis Alcoriza only mentioned secondary to Riesenfeld (*Cinema Reporter* 30).

As foreign women had little direct engagement with Mexican political spheres, Riesenfeld's experience exposes the creative challenges, and limitations, to social customs through art and cultural works (Prats 1994). While millions watched their films, in several studies dedicated to Luis Alcoriza, Riesenfeld is relegated to the position of assistant and afterthought. In fact, her name almost always accompanies his as the screenwriters and she introduced her husband to American director Norman Foster—an encounter that launched Alcoriza's screenwriting apprenticeship with the director (Turrent 9).[9] Together, Riesenfeld and Alcoriza produced dozens of films between the years of 1946 and 1960 (Fernández 287). During their most prolific years, the Alcorizas—as the couple was called—created six to seven scripts each year (Turrent 12).[10] Yet, not only was Riesenfeld's cinema career extraordinary at the height of the Golden Age of Mexican cinema, but Riesenfeld and her relationship with Alcoriza challenged dominant gender ideologies among the exile community. Riesenfeld, in her various roles as a wife, professional screenwriter, and political subject, challenged, albeit in a restricted way, traditional gender ideologies.

Culturally ironic, yet with predictable gender dynamics, one of Riesenfeld's first acting roles fictionalizes an American's love for a Mexican

[8] Luis Alcoriza was among the main artistic partners of Luis Buñuel, soon after meeting and writing the screenplay together for *La gran calavera* (1949), directed by Luis Buñuel. This film seemed to cement the career of the Alcorizas.

[9] Turrent describes Riesenfeld as "su bella presencia y su extraño acento (la mujer extranjera, la vampiresa, la actriz gringa que se enamoraba del macho mexicano, la torva espía nazi, la fogosa flamenco)" (11). He describes the two key developments, before meeting Luis Buñuel, in Alcoriza's career as, "el de Janet Riesenfeld, actriz y bailarina de flamenco de origen austriaco que actuaba con el nombre de Raquel Rojas y posteriormente el del guionista y realizador norteamericano Norman Foster."

[10] Alcoriza arrived in Mexico in 1940 as part of the Spanish Civil War exodus. Alcoriza came from a family of performers, but at the outbreak of the Spanish Civil War they took their Compañía Alcoriza into exile.

228   M. LABBATO

ranchero, fueling her ability to recreate a presumed natural and Spanish art. Playing "Olivia Onil" in *Cuando viajan las estrellas* (1942), a Spanish dance instructor living in Mexico City is contracted to teach the American celebrity. As a woman from the USA trained in flamenco in Spain, Riesenfeld successfully characterizes a foreigner who defies the Maestro's disbelief in the ability to "teach" the art. While Riesenfeld demonstrates subtle and somewhat awkward acting skills as the elegant but endearing foreigner, this dissolves during the dance scenes when she enlivens with strength, passion, and sexuality. Notions about national culture are complicated in the Maestro's insistence that Olivia studies the Sevillian style in Mexico. Further, the Maestro proposes that Olivia attend a "typical Spanish" festival with bullfighting, a charming *torero*, and a fiesta in a Spanish home to fix her lack of "natural passion." However, it is only after she falls in love with a Mexican *ranchero* at his hacienda that Olivia can perform a passionately skilled flamenco dance. The nomadic subject desires and has the ability of continual motion highlighted by Riesenfeld, as Olivia, trespassing into typical, yet unstable, Hispanic cultural traditions.

Riesenfeld and Mexican film producers collaborated to develop these multiple identities that straddled Anglo-Hispanic lines and empathetically submerges the "self" in the "other." She plays the foreigner who overcomes the requirement of having "sangre gitana" to pass for a flamenco performer. The American's ability to cross genres of dancing, writing, and acting, as well as represent Spanish folk dance styles to Mexican audiences, exemplifies her nomadic subjectivity. Simaltaneously, such roles expose the pervasive nature of romanticized gender narratives. As Olivia, Riesenfeld finally nails the flamenco routine when the Maestro insists that she use dance to express her feelings for the *ranchero*. Gender and culture combine in her enchantment by this "authentically" macho side of Mexico. Through acting and dance, Riesenfeld uses her nomadic body to trespass various Hispanic cultures; however, her character succumbs to the traditional narrative of love's rescue and its superiority to other ambitions for women.

Professionally, Riesenfeld's rejection of roles in the USA in favor of working in Mexico is a representation of the reality of cross-cultural and natural collaborations in North American cinema (De la Vega Alfaro 16, 17). An article in New York's *Morning Herald* in 1943 praises Riesenfeld as the "first North American actress to make a film career in Latin America" (Adelson 7). Included with the article are photographs of Riesenfeld dancing in flamenco attire and a description of her as a "brilliant" flamenco dancer, a graceful actor, and a fluent Spanish speaker.

> Raquel makes her debut before her fellow New Yorkers in a picture which symbolizes the friendship between her native and her adopted countries, for the picture is the first Mexican, pro-Ally, anti-Fascist film production...the growing Mexican film industry considers Raquel one of its most valuable assets. (7)

The *Morning Herald* quoted a Mexican movie picture's annual report (1942–1943), bolstering their praise of Riesenfeld as embodying "the ideal of our directors who needs a fine and highly sensitive interpreter. Raquel Rojas, a North American but with a strong feeling for the things of Spanish-speaking peoples, has traveled throughout the world, is a newspaperwoman, author, and a marvelous dancer. In short: she is one of the first ladies of our motion pictures" (7). We, therefore, see US influence, and Riesenfeld specifically, play a critical role in US-Mexican cultural relations at the start of the so-called Golden Age of Mexican cinema.

Tropes that played on foreigner-Mexican relationships and corroborations become more significant in Mexican film history considering the growth of the subgenre of Andalusian and Mexican musical folk fusions during the 1940s–1960s. Emilio José Gallardo Saborido analyzes this phenomenon of co-productions and construction of *hispanismo* between Spain and Latin America through romantic love stories and folk music. These stemmed from images produced during the II Republic and began with films like *Jalisco canta en Sevilla* (1948) and continued with Gout's *Cuando viajan las estrellas* (Gallardo Saborido). Of the estimated 25,000 to 40,000 Spanish Civil War exiles in Mexico, more than half were intellectuals, teachers, or professionals (Lida 226). This group of Spaniards worked industriously in Mexico within various intellectual and cultural fields that viewed their renewed relationship with Spain's former colony in a romanticized way, producing cultural and intellectual negotiations of *hispanismo*. It is, therefore, important to consider these processes within Mexican national cinema in which Riesenfeld participated.

Other screenplays by the couple combine romantic or gendered stories with questions about national identity. The film adaptation of their screenplay, *Gitana tenías que ser* (*You Had to Be a Gypsy*) (1953), opens with Carmen Sevilla playing the part of Pastora de los Reyes, dancing flamenco in Spain, singing "España mía." She is drenched in the traditional

230   M. LABBATO

trappings of Sevillano flamenco: the *bata de cola*, the tall *peineta*, a large cross on her neck, with vibrant colors of red and sounds of the Andalusian guitar whirling. The film then cuts to the Mexican producers, who are in fact watching Pastora on screen. The Alcorizas contributed the screenplay, directed by the renowned Rafael Baledón, which starred two of the most quintessential film and music icons of Spanish and Mexican folk traditions at mid-century: Carmen Sevilla and Pedro Infante. The Alcorizas combined the popular charro-gitana and *ranchera comedia* sub-genres while ironically exposing their holes by blending the more classical *ranchera* with "cosmopolitanism." It does this through *demythification*, combining popular iconography of the urban cowboy and the foreigner in romantic melodramas to mock common stereotypes that served to establish a hegemonic homogeneity (Gallardo Saborido 52, 72).[11] Thus, to expose the limits of these folk images they practiced the technique of repeatedly cutting to see the behind-the-scenes production of popular folk images and songs played to the parodic theme. In a similar vein, Infante, as "Pablo," is first shown as the Mexican charro, singing Mariachi, and dressed in the performance cowboy garb. Pablo then ditches the charro look in 'real life," instead he chooses an urban, modern suit.

The Spanish exiles parodied the genre of the gitano(a)/flamenco identity in Mexico to problematize the singular narratives used by Francoists and official usages of Andalusian cultural iconography during the dictatorship (Labanyi 2002). Further, the Alcorizas challenged notions of cultural authenticity. Within Spain, there was growing popularity among elites, Madrid residents, and many intellectuals on the left in the late nineteenth century and early twentieth century of flamenco and "gitano" culture (Mitchell 155).[12] In the 1940s, Fernando Ortiz asserted that Latin America, its people, and culture were a product of "transculturation" and hybrid identities, recognizing the *mezcla* (mixture) of European, indigenous, and African elements present since colonization and to combat the Anglo-centric term, "acculturation" (Davies 141–142). Riesenfeld's life

---

[11] Debates included a nationalistic inclination while also existing an economic imperative for foreign markets; the integration of folklore with romantic and uplifting melodramas would provide such outlets and became a popular genre by the 1940s. Mexicans' Spanish-speaking cousins could offer the image of the Andalusian bandit and flamenco performer, fitting well with such a project.

[12] Many intellectuals on the Spanish left sought to elevate such aspects of Andalusian society to a broader national identity, a process supported by figures like Federico García Lorca and the Concurso de Cante Jondo in his birthplace of Granada in 1922.

and screenplays attest to her ability to thrive in and further produce a new notion of hybridity in Mexican cinematic life. As Braidotti's nomad has no authentic singular self, instead she adapts to her changing context, Riesenfeld remade herself in Spain and in Mexico (Braidotti 5). Her transgressive identity in creative works pokes fun at static cultural symbols defining "foreigner" and "native" and challenges broader, national ideas of authenticity and belonging.

The 1930s theme of gender and sexual liberation reappears in Riesenfeld's films and experiences in the 1940s and 1950s. Remarried without children, she maintained a professional partnership with Alcoriza. Yet, like Riesenfeld's acting roles that centered on romantic relationships, postwar gendered negotiations are a central theme in their screenplays. The Alcorizas wrote *La liga de las muchachas* (*The League of Girls*) (1949), a provocative comedy about a group of women who become fed up with demanding and controlling boyfriends and husbands and are lured to live together free of men. Their mascot is a Greek goddess with their "league of liberty" song asserting "libertad." The men discover and infiltrate the women's compound, with Alcoriza playing a hyper-macho partner who continues a behavior of violence. Ultimately, the house mother, Doña Remedios, financially profits from these young women's relationship frustrations and the love-starved heroines greet the less violent men with open arms, though it is not without negotiation. The men agree to be more mutually loving partners. Alcoriza's girlfriend, however, rejects his machismo and instead opts to adopt a mysteriously abandoned baby as a single mother. While not overturning social customs, the film flirts with an unconventional path for women, an imaginary enabled by the interwar and war periods.

Experimenting with women's complete independence, the film negotiates, as many women did in the postwar era, a revision to traditional gender roles based on mutual respect and the possibility of multiple versions of womanhood and motherhood. At the conclusion of *La liga de las muchachas*, even the goddess—enlivened by the events—leaves the mansion concluding that living with women alone is no way to live. The earlier entrance of many creative and leftist women into politics and anti-fascism may not have been reflective of a far-reaching revolution in gender and women's roles. Yet, the interwar movements, including the Spanish Civil War, left an impact on women's political awakening and sense of autonomy. In an interview, Riesenfeld asserted that her husband planned the scripts but that she added considerable work: "I limit myself as 'critic'

232   M. LABBATO

of what Luis does. I'm more of a collaborator, critical of him" (*Novelas,* 6).[13] Despite the hegemonic narrative that minimized her role, theirs was a mutually generative process. While the leftist "new woman" "remained symbolic of the equality ideal and did not represent a shift towards gender power sharing," the imbalance of power was shaken, exemplified by the Alcorizas' screenplays and lives (Gruber and Graves 13).

The early Cold War years opened, in limited ways, space for foreign women in professional artistic careers and in nontraditional life paths in Mexico. Since Europe halted exports during World War II, including cultural productions, the period favored the expansion of Mexican cinema and provided opportunities for exiles to participate when the industry searched for collaborators.[14] While Luis Buñuel and Luis Alcoriza obtained Mexican citizenship, there was a general sentiment that the European expatriates did not socially assimilate during the first decade or two into Mexican circles. However, within cinema, these foreigners worked extensively with Mexican filmmakers. The industry "continued to focus squarely on issues of cultural nationalism and representational authenticity in a way that resonated with yet departed from earlier criticisms leveled at Hollywood" (Gunckle 124). Riesenfeld's participation, as the insider-outsider, exhibits the Anglo fantasy as she is transformed into the flamenco femme-fatal and critique of absolute "othering" and assumptions of authenticity. The films that she acted in and the screenplays that she and her husband wrote closely represented autobiographies, as they included much of Riesenfeld's life experience into their parodies on cultural essentialism. As an American, Riesenfeld's nomadism adds further insight into the feminine, and foreign, potential to creatively subvert nationalistic narratives.

* * *

As the world witnessed the transformations of war and the rise of European Nazi Fascism, Janet Riesenfeld's symbolic and literal nomadism mirrored the modern mobility of artistic and intellectual women. Under the II Republic, women's public roles and equality expanded in the 1930s, and

[13] "Yo me limito a 'criticar' lo que hace Luis. Soy más que colaboradora, crítica de él."
[14] The 1920s and 1930s saw a decline in Spanish-speaking Hollywood productions; by the late 1930s efforts were underway to bolster the national industry in Mexico. Kirsten Strayer and Marcia Landy argue that the film industry was different from other cultural institutions in that it was more open to foreigners.

modernist women writers and artists across Europe, the USA, and Latin America pursued careers, asserting new levels of political and sexual independence. Dance was Riesenfeld's first spatial metaphor, her way of mapping her path, identity, and navigation of Anglo-Hispanic borders. It was the ordinary people of Madrid, not Riesenfeld's Catalan fiancé, who most influenced her politics and outlook. Flamenco provided a personal awakening, leading her to be politically active for the Loyalist cause and to view Spain as the battlefront to halt fascism. Her voluntary nomadism illuminates the possible bridges and risks of the privileged Anglo "nomadic subject": the affectional exoticization of the "other." However, for Riesenfeld and other foreign women in Spain, this empathy also initiated or intensified broader commitments to democracy, gender liberation, and challenges to traditional, nationalist narratives. Riesenfeld's Spanish Civil War memoir exemplifies how women's narratives reveal emotional and everyday aspects of war often lacking in professional *Hispanist* writings or masculinist political and military explanations in the archive. Transformed by the Spanish conflict, Riesenfeld then remade herself and her career in a second foreign country.

In Mexico, the dancer collaborated on screenplays that defied common sexual tropes and gender norms, though women's exiled lives and works expose limitations on the challenges to traditional values during the earliest stages of the Cold War. Further, reviving Riesenfeld's voice through film provides an examination of exiles' cultural productions and belonging abroad. She was formally recognized in 1998 with Mexico's Ariel Award, which celebrates the best contributions to Mexican cinema. It was awarded posthumously because she passed away weeks before the ceremony (Hernandez 7). The Alcorizas' films subverted gender norms and countered assumptions about natural binaries. While Riesenfeld initially held a romanticized, essentialist view of Spanish culture, the Alcorizas and other exiles parodied and inverted notions of cultural and national authenticity in Mexico. Rather than an insignificant helper to the male-dominated Spanish exile community and Mexican national cinema, Riesenfeld's collaboration with her husband appeared mutually generative. Continually re-fashioning her identity—personally and professionally—she transcended divisions between herself and others, aiding her success across three countries. From the interwar to early Cold War period, *la americanita's* empathetic, nomadic subjectivity trespassed genres and national borders, illuminating women's Anglo-Hispanic spaces of creative, cultural exchange.

234   M. LABBATO

WORKS CITED

Adelson, Dorothy. "Yankee-Born Actress Mexican Screen Star: Manhattan Miss In Film Triumphs South of Border." *Morning Herald*, New York, 29 June 1943, p. 7.

"Argumento de Raquel Rosas." *Cinema Reporter*, vol. 346, no. 303, 1945, pp. 30–31. Centro Documentación, UNAM.

Braidotti, Rosi. *Nomadic Subjects: Embodiment and Sexual Difference in Contemporary Feminist Theory*. Columbia UP, 1994.

Cuando viajan las estrellas. Directed by Alberto Gout, Films Mundiales, 1942.

Davies, Catherine. "Fernando Ortiz's Transculturation: The Postcolonial Intellectual and the Politics of Cultural Representation." *Postcolonial Perspectives on Latin American and Lusophone Cultures*, edited by Fiddian Robin, Liverpool UP, 2000, pp. 141–68.

De la Vega Alfaro, Eduardo. *Alberto Gout (1907–1966). Serie Monografia 3.* Cineteca Nacional, 1988.

Deacon, David. "Elective and Experiential Affinities: British and American foreign correspondents and the Spanish Civil War." *Journalism Studies*, vol. 9, no. 3, Apr. 2008, pp. 392–408.

Domínguez Prats, Pilar. *Voces de exilio: Mujeres españoles en México, 1939–1950.* Madrid, 1994.

Faber, Sebastiaan. *Anglo-American Hispanists and the Spanish Civil War: Hispanophilia, Commitment, and Discipline*. Palgrave Macmillan, 2008.

Fein, Seth. "Myths of Cultural Imperialism and Nationalism in Golden Age Mexican Cinema." *Fragments of a Golden Age: The Politics of Culture in Mexico Since 1940*, edited by Gilbert M. Joseph, Anne Rubenstein, and Eric Zolov, Duke UP, 2001.

Fernández, Jorge. "Luis Alcoriza o la mexicanización del exiliado cinematográfico republicano/Luis Alcoriza or the Mexican Nationalization of the Republican Cinematography Exile." *Espacio, Tiempo y Forma* 28, vol. 2016, pp. 283–305.

Franko, Mark. *Martha Graham in Love and War: The Life in the Work*. Oxford UP, 2012.

Gallardo Saborido, Emilio José. *Gitana tenías que ser: las Andalucías imaginadas por las coproducciones fílmicas España-Latinoamérica*, Centro de Estudios Andaluces, Consejería de la Presidencia, Junta de Andalucía, 2010.

Gitana tenías que ser. Directed by Rafael Baledón, Cesáreo González Producciones / Suevia Films - Cesáreo González, 1953 / Azteca Films, 1954.

Goldberg, Meira K., and Michelle Heffner Hayes, editors. *Flamenco on the Global Stage: Historical, Critical, and Theoretical Perspectives*. McFarland & Company, 2015.

Gómez, Javier Tusell. *La Guerra Civil Española. Exposición organizada por la Dirección del Patrimonio Artístico, Archivos y Museos*. Ministerio de Cultura, 1980.

9 *LA AMERICANITA*: JANET RIESENFELD'S NOMADIC CROSSINGS... 235

Graham, Helen. *The Spanish Civil War: A Very Short Introduction.* Oxford UP, 2005.

Gruber, Helmut, and Pamela Graves. Introduction. *Women and Socialism - Socialism and Women: Europe Between the World Wars,* edited by Pamela Graves and Helmut Gruber, 1st ed., Berghahn Books, 1998, pp. 3–24. JSTOR, http://www.jstor.org/stable/j.ctt1c0gm4g. Accessed 21 Feb. 2024.

Gunckel, Colin. "Now We Have Mexican Cinema?: Navigating Transnational Mexicanidad in a Moment of Crisis." *Mexico on Main Street: Transnational Film Culture in Los Angeles before World War II,* Rutgers UP, 2015.

Hemingway, Ernest. *For Whom the Bell Tolls.* Simon & Schuster, 1940.

Hernandez, Rocío Ramírez. "Murió Janet Alcoriza." *Novedades,* 26 Nov. 1998, p. 7. Expedientes Personalidades (E-05821), Centro de Documentación, Cineteca Nacional, Mexico City, D. F.

"'La hora de verdad' en Nueva York." *Cinema Reporter,* no. 472, 1947, p. 45. Centro Documentación, UNAM.

La liga de las muchachas. Directed by Fernando Cortés, Ultramar Films, 1949.

Labanyi, Jo. *Constructing Identity in Contemporary Spain: Theoretical Debates and Cultural Practice.* Oxford UP, 2002.

Lida, Clara E. *Una inmigración privilegiada: Comerciantes, empresarios y profesionales españoles en México en los siglos XIX y XX.* Alianza América, 1994.

Lines, Lisa Margaret. *Milicianas: Women in Combat in the Spanish Civil War.* Lexington Books, 2012.

Mitchell, Timothy. "Flamenco Deep Song." *Flamenco's Golden Age,* Yale UP, 1994.

Morcillo, Aurora G. "The Orient Within: Women 'in-between' under Francoism." *Women in the Middle East and North Africa: Agents of Change,* edited by Fatima Sadiqi and Moha Ennaji, Routledge, 2010.

Moorhead, Joanna, and Stefan van Raaij, editors. *Surreal Friends: Leonora Carrington, Remedios Varo and Kati Horna.* Ashgate, 2010.

Nash, Mary. *Defying Male Civilization: Women in the Spanish Civil War.* Arden Press, 1995.

Novelas de la pantalla. Año V, no. 249, 5 de enero de 1946, p. 6. Escritores.cinemexicano.unam.mx/biografias/A/Alcoriza_janet/biografia.html.

Novick, Peter. *The Noble Dream: The "Objectivity Question" and the American Historical Profession.* Cambridge UP, 1988.

Ortiz, Fernando. *Cuban Counterpoint: Tobacco and Sugar.* Translated by Harriet de Onís. Duke UP, 1995.

Paquet, Sandra Pouchet. "The Caribbean Writer as Nomadic Subject or Spatial Mobility and the Dynamics of Critical Thought." *Journal of West Indian Literature,* vol. 18, no. 2, 2010, pp. 65–94.

Preston, Paul. *The Spanish Holocaust: Inquisition and Extermination in Twentieth-Century Spain.* W.W. Norton & Company, 2012.

"Raquel Rojas." *Cinema Reporter,* no. 416, 1946, pp. 14–15. Centro de Documentación, UNAM.

236 M. LABBATO

Rucar Buñuel, Jeanne. *Memorias de una mujer sin piano.* Alianza Editorial Mexicana, 1990.

Rukeyser, Muriel. *Savage Coast: A Novel.* Edited by Rowena Kennedy-Epstein, The Feminist Press at the City University of New York, 2013.

Sanders, David. "Ernest Hemingway's Spanish Civil War Experience." *American Quarterly,* vol. 12, no. 2, 1960, pp. 133–43.

Strayer, Kirsten Amy. *Ruins and Riots: Transnational Currents in Mexican Cinema.* 2009. Pittsburgh U, PhD Dissertation. ProQuest Dissertations Publishing.

Takayoshi, Ichiro. "The Wages of War: Liberal Gullibility, Soviet Intervention, and the End of the Popular Front." *Representations,* vol. 115, no. 1, 2011, pp. 102–29.

Torres, August M. *Buñuel y sus discípulos.* Huerga & Fierro Editores, 2005.

Turrent, Tomás Pérez. *Luis Alcoriza.* Semana de Cine Iberoamericano, 1977.

Zimmer, Kenyon. "The Other Volunteers: American Anarchists and the Spanish Civil War, 1936–1939." *Journal for the Study of Radicalism,* vol. 10, no. 2, Fall 2016, pp. 19–52.

CHAPTER 10

From British Sorcery to *El Mundo Mágico De Los Mayas*: Leonora Carrington's Cultural Hybridity

Javier Martín Párraga

Introduction

Leonora Carrington (1917–2011) is not only one of the most important members of surrealism but superior to most of the authors from this movement in several respects. First of all, Carrington is one of the few artists from this disruptive crew who excelled both as a painter and as a writer. Second, due to the fact that she experimented with madness itself, as Hertz explains, "[her] experiences are more genuinely Surreal than any of the psychic experiments—from the hypnotic sleeps to the simulations of mental illness by Breton and Éluard—conducted by the male Surrealists" (91). Finally, "surrealism offered many women their first glimpse of a world in which creative activity and liberation from family-imposed social expectations might coexist, one in which rebellion was viewed as a virtue,

---

J. M. Párraga (✉)
Department of English and German Studies, University of Córdoba, Córdoba, Spain
e-mail: javier.martin@uco.es

© The Author(s), under exclusive license to Springer Nature Switzerland AG 2024
R. M. Silverman, E. Sánchez-Pardo (eds.), *Nomadic New Women*, https://doi.org/10.1007/978-3-031-62482-7_10

237

imagination a passport to a more liberated life" (Chadwick 67). Nonetheless, it was only a minute glimpse of freedom, since surrealism was at the end of the day as patriarchal and male chauvinist as the bourgeois society it pretended to demolish. Thus, surrealist women artists were considered as secondary or, even worse, reduced to the subaltern categories of *femme-enfant*, *femme-fatal*, or *femme-folle*. In spite of these limitations imposed by Breton and his acolytes, Carrington was able to become one of the most important surrealist artists first, and then she went a step beyond surrealism and started producing an exciting artistic corpus which did not renounce those surrealistic aspects which empowered her but ceased to be constrained by the barriers that a full-fledged adhesion to this movement would imply. In this sense, Carrington's art is liminal not only because she navigated the complex threshold between the conscious and the unconscious but also because she permanently placed herself in an in-between territory between surrealism and a new surrealism entirely of her own. Thus, I agree with an article published in *The Economist* which declared that "Carrington became one of the most accomplished Surrealist artists of the 20th century. But not in the way many people of that time understood the genre" (2019).

One of the critics who best knew Carrington, Orenstein, stated in the foreword she wrote to *The Oval Lady* that "Leonora Carrington's art and writings express the mystery of being through occult parables whose true meaning becomes accessible to those who acquire initiation into the specific form of symbolism that her work display" (7). I am convinced that it is impossible to acquire the initiation Orenstein referred to without paying attention to the author's biography, since, as Guiral explains, it is precisely Carrington's biography which contains "the ingredients which will allow us to understand the life and work of this artist" (119).[1]

In this paper, I examine one particular aspect of Carrington's biography which, from my point of view, becomes central to understanding her complex literary corpus: her Mexican experiences and how they help shape her vision of herself, surrealism, feminism, and the world.

---

[1] My translation: "Los ingredientes que nos llevarán a entender el trabajo y la vida de esta artista." All subsequent translations are also mine.

Foreseeing Mexico

In *From Puritanism to Postmodernism* (1991), Ruland and Bradbury expressed the shocking but accurate idea that "America existed in Europe long before it was discovered, in the speculative writings of the classical, the medieval and then the Renaissance mind. American literature began, and the American dream existed, before the actual continent was known" (4). In the case of Carrington, it is safe to affirm that Mexico and what its culture meant to the author played a paramount role in her imagination and artistic corpus years before she arrived in the American country. In fact, this idea is not surprising, since, as Gaensbaeur points out, "Surrealism has always been associated with the act of discovery and the surrealist have frequently been compared to explorers who came to the 'New World' in the 15th and 16th centuries" (271). The connections between surrealism and Mexico as a physical place and Mexican culture (characterized by an ancient and extremely rich folklore populated by magical landscapes and creatures) are indisputable. As Andrade reminds, "There are two levels of exoticism which are appealing to surrealists: the geographical, that of non-Western cultures—among them the Amerindians—and the inner one, the unconsciousness, the dream, and the nonsense" (102).[2]

Consequently, Carpentier defends the thesis that surrealism is innate to Latin America (due to the baroque style in which realism and magic are so often interwoven in this continent's founding myths and daily routines) (Oropesa). Carpentier's idea was fully shared by André Breton, one of the fathers of surrealism, since as Cline points out, when Breton met Leon Trotsky in Mexico, the French artist declared that surrealism had no purpose in a country which was itself surrealistic (2012). Consequently, Guiral affirms, "Mexico is part of the dreamlike territory explored by these adventurers in the nonsense. If Columbus 'needed to get surrounded by mad people to discover America', other 'mad people also came and explored Mexico as they explored their own madness" (60).[3]

It is true that Leonora Carrington's life prior to her Mexican residence did not lack magical inspiration and influence, since, as Davis points out,

---

[2] "Hay dos niveles de exotismo que resultan atractivos para los surrealistas: el geográfico, el de las culturas no occidentales- entre ellas las amerindias- y el interior, el del inconsciente, el sueño y la sinrazón."

[3] "México forma parte del territorio onírico explorado por estos aventureros del sinsentido. Si Colón 'tuvo que rodearse de locos para descubrir América', otros 'locos' también vinieron, y transitaron por México como por su propia locura."

even during her childhood, the artist was exposed to fantastic stories: "From the outset Leonora gravitated toward her Irish mother and her Irish nanny, both of whom satisfied her appetite for tales driven by the marvelous" (iii). However, at the same time, even when nurtured by Celtic fantastic narrations, the young woman, who was utterly unhappy in her British residence, projected herself not into a fairy from the Irish folklore but into wild, exotic animals which were equally alien to the real England and to the rich Irish folklore she enjoyed so much. As a paramount example, it becomes indispensable to remember one of Carrington's best-known short stories, "The debutante." In this story, a young girl, who cannot but be considered as an obvious alter ego of the author, is full of anxiety and dread, caused by an imminent presentation into society that her mother arranges—a situation which mirrors Carrington's own feelings when her respectable and wealthy family made all the preparations in order for her to be introduced to King George V. Leonora resorted to her inner world to find solace, while her alter ego explains, "indeed, it was in order to get away from people that I found myself at the zoo everyday" (3). Out of the many wild animals she gets familiar with, she soon befriends a particular one, a hyena. As it always happens with Carrington, the apparent lack of coherence which permeates her literature and paintings hides a careful process of selection. Chadwick argues that the hyena which helps the protagonist escape her social constraints and obligations represents "the fertile world of the night" (79), and Plunkett considers that "Carrington is using the hyena to represent the bestial, wild side of her own sexuality. The animal's human eyes, swollen breasts and shared gaze unite it with her, suggesting that they are one and the same. Furthermore, Carrington's lack of breasts in the portrait is supplemented and replaced by the swollen breasts of the hyena" (501). By the end of the story, the hyena, which has replaced the protagonist at the feared gala (by using the protagonist's own clothes and the face of a servant she had previously killed as part of the sophisticated disguise process she and the girl had devised), gets finally free from the mask (which she consumes) and shockingly declares to the polite crowd: "So I smell a bit strong, what? Well, I don't eat cakes" (7). I agree with Conley who writes, "Thus Carrington sardonically dramatizes the fantasy of destroying her own beautiful 'mask' in the interest of revealing her true, wilder, freer, but socially unacceptable hidden self beneath. Through the character of the hyena, she expresses her rage against society's expectations of young women" (51).

It is crucial to highlight the fact that in this story, which is key to understanding her necessity to break not only with her bourgeoise family but also with the United Kingdom's orderly and repressive society, Carrington uses as a symbol a hyena rather than any of the several animals or hybrid creatures central to Celtic folklore, which were mostly horses, boars, and dragons (Noodén).

THE ROAD TO MEXICO

In her introduction to *The Hearing Trumpet*, Ali Smith complains that "people who write about Leonora Carrington (and far too little has been written about her extraordinary art and writing) tend to dwell on her life. They revel in her sheer unexpectedness" (v). This expert is certainly right when pointing out that a great deal of the attention given to Carrington tends to focus on her biography. This is not surprising if we take into account two significantly different facts. First of all, and from a literary perspective, her own adventures became central to her artistic corpus (both literary and pictorial) since, as Moorhead (who was the artist's cousin and spent numberless days with her in Mexico) sums up, "One of the ironies of her story was that she had gone so far to get away from us, and then spent most of her time in Mexico exploring and explaining her childhood and adolescence in her art" (15) and "Like all of Leonora's fiction, most of the narrative is true" (93). The second element which makes Carrington's biography so appealing to critics is not exclusively literary, and it involves the short but meaningful sentimental relationship she had with Max Ernst, one of the most prominent surrealist artists of all time. Thus, even when I agree with Smith (and, to a certain extent, adhere to Barthes's concept of the "death of the author") and refuse to focus exclusively on the author's extraordinary biography, I consider it indispensable to explore the road which led Carrington to become one of the most exciting and complex women writers of the twentieth century.

Leonora Carrington was born on April 6, 1917, in the British county of Lancashire. She was the daughter of Harold Wilde Carrington, a prominent businessman, and Mauren Moorhead. Three years later, the family moved to a neogothic castle, Crookney Hall, which was surrounded by magnificent gardens. Being raised in this scenario was influential to Carrington's art, as it becomes evident in paintings such as "Green Tea," many short stories, and the novel *The Hearing Trumpet*. As Guiral explains, the author's education was marked by her parents' bourgeois style, their

242   J. M. PÁRRAGA

Catholicism, and a British society in which the concept of a "new woman" was slowly emerging and starting to challenge heteropatriarchy but which still considered that high-class women should essentially be trained to be good wives and mothers (22–26). The author's refusal to obey rules and learn by the means of repetition caused her numberless problems at every religious institution she was sent to (in England, Italy, and France):

> Leonora preferred to write and paint using her two hands, producing an inverse, mirrored, writing. In fact, she was ambidextrous as well as dyslexic. As a result of this, she was punished and tagged as impossible to educate by the nuns, who considered this condition as a genuine disease which, sometimes, caused unpleasant effects. Probably only for this reason, Leonora started to consider the environment in which she was living as unbearable and to reject the principles of the Catholic Church in which she had been educated. At the same time, she also understood the conventions and behavior of her own social class as equally unbearable." (Scappini 22)[4]

In fact, Janice Helland considers that Carrington's exploration of the Jungian feminine archetype started long before the author started avidly reading the works of Jung (55–56). In 1935, the author traveled to London to start her education as a painter, and in 1936, she enrolled in the Chelsea School of Art, which was directed by Amédée Ozenfant, one of the authors of the 1918 *Aprés le cubisme* manifesto. As Eduardo de la Fuente sums up,

> By separating from her parents, Carrington obtained a new freedom which enabled her to discover the bohemian scene of England and to freely explore her new interests: alchemy and occultism, which opened a path to discover in depth a whole reality which had been shadowed by the rigid social rules which had surrounded her previously.[5]

---

[4] "Leonora, prefería escribir, así como pintar, con dos manos, produciendo una escritura inversa, en espejo. De hecho, era ambidestra y también disléxica; como consecuencia de esto fue castigada y tachada de ineducable por las monjas, que consideraban este trastorno del aprendizaje una genuina enfermedad, a veces causando efectos desagradables. Probablemente solo por esto Leonora comienza a sentir insoportable el ambiente en el que vive y a rechazar los principios de la Iglesia Católica que le habían sido inculcados, resultándole también insoportables las convenciones y los comportamientos de la clase social a la que pertenecía."

[5] "Al distanciarse de sus padres, Carrington obtuvo una nueva libertad que le permitió conocer el ambiente bohemio en Inglaterra y darle rienda suelta a sus nuevos intereses: la alquimia y el ocultismo, lo que resultaba un camino para descubrir el fondo de una realidad plena, que había sido obscurecida por las formas rígidas sociales que le habían circundado."

10 FROM BRITISH SORCERY TO *EL MUNDO MÁGICO DE LOS MAYAS...* 243

In this context, she became familiar with the emerging surrealism and got to know some of this movement's most seminal authors, such as Éluard, Ray, Lee Miller, Roland Penrose, and, obviously, Max Ernst.

When Leonora and Max met, they fell in love almost immediately and started a three-year relationship, which had lasting effects on both artists' lives and careers. As Marina Warner points out, "Ernst was an inspiring companion, she later acknowledged, with whom she discovered a new way of living; he could turn everything into play—cooking, keeping house, gardening" (ix). As a result, "Working side by side with Ernst produced a febrile activity in Carrington. She couldn't have found a better companion" (Caballero 41).[6] After enjoying the summer together in Cornwall, the couple moved to France, where, as Solomon Grimberg explains:

> [D]espite her young age when she arrived in Paris with Ernst—was admired by the older surrealists for her intuitive intelligence and her ability to articulate it. Carrington's appearance in the group was sudden, and her acceptance immediate. Enthralled by her wraithlike persona, the surrealists soon came to admire her kindred spirit as one who lived and created under the belief that invisible forces influenced the world of appearances. Breton made Carrington one of his chosen few; only from her did he accept what he would have interpreted from others as insubordination. She held the key to the door that opened to the other side. (5)

The three years Carrington shared with Ernst had a deep influence on her art, as Ernest Schonfield affirms, "Leonora Carrington's work clearly owes a great debt to her years with Ernst" (249). Nonetheless, Ernst's influence on Carrington had some negative effects as well: "Ernst's overwhelming ego (according to Peggy Guggenheim, he got cross when someone suggested Napoleon was the greatest genius), combined with the coercive, cruel fantasies of surrealist sexuality, infuse many scenes that Leonora wrote and painted at the time with a degree of terror that rises above the usual range of the macabre tale" (Warner xii). Gaensbauer considers that Carrington felt like "one of the caged creatures [she painted and described at the time]" (272) and, according to this scholar, "Carrington's early short stories most of them written in France during her years with Ernst, startling excursions into phantasmagoric night world, generally undertaken by impulsive young mirror images of the offer with long wild dark

---

[6] "El trabajar codo con codo con Ernst supuso para Leonora una actividad febril. El mundo imaginario de Carrington no pudo encontrar mejor compañero."

244   J. M. PÁRRAGA

hair and rebellious itineraries" (273). As we can see, even during the time the author was attached to Ernst and enjoyed the company of the most prominent members of the surrealistic crew, she kept dreaming about escaping to what Gaensbauer defines as "rebellious itineraries" and I would call (after examining the short stories she published during that period) "exotic territories." In several interviews and letters, Carrington has affirmed that she was frankly upset by the critics' obsession with the time she and Ernst were together:

> In later years, Leonora would become angry when fans—like myself— showed intense curiosity about that early phase of her life. She once wrote me a furious letter- and letters from her were rare- because something that I had written about her appeared with a photograph of Ernst leaning, blissed out, eyes closed, on her shoulder. Those old days were long ago for her, and she was not pleased when the intervening decades of work were not given their due. "A lot of people want to make me into gossip," she said, "and it's missing the point of anybody to make them into gossip." (Warner xiv–xv)

In fact, as an elderly woman, Carrington refused to be defined not only according to her relation to Ernst but also according to surrealism as a literary or cultural movement:

> Even the surrealists's ideas were appealing to me, I don't like to be pigeon-holed as a surrealist. I prefer to be a feminist. André Breton and the rest of the men from the group were very male chauvinist. They only wanted us as sensual and crazy muses to entertain them, to take care of them. And my clock didn't stop at that time. I only lived with Ernest for three years and I don't like to be reduced like I was a silly person. I haven't lived under Ernst's charm: I was born with a vocation and my works are only mine. (Haro 3)[7]

As explained in the quotation above, one of the main reasons why Carrington broke with Ernst and surrealism was the male chauvinism that most surrealist authors exhibited, both in their private life and as a basis for

---

[7] "Aunque me atraían las ideas de los surrealistas, no me gusta que hoy me encajonen como surrealista. Prefiero ser feminista. André Breton y los hombres del grupo eran muy machistas, sólo nos querían a nosotras como musas alocadas y sensuales para divertirlos, para atenderlos. Además mi reloj no se detuvo en ese momento, sólo viví tres años con Ernst y no me gusta que me constriñan como si fuera tonta. No he vivido bajo el embrujo de Ernst: nací con mi vocación y mis obras son sólo mías."

their artistic movement. Moorhead explains how shocked Carrington was when she discovered (while living in France with Ernst) the role surrealism gave to women: "Among the friends he had in Paris was the French poet Paul Éluard, whose wife Gala was the central and, in many ways, the essential Surrealist muse, an exponent of free love with a voracious appetite for sex" (44–45), and this same author further expresses how bad Carrington felt when Dalí defined her not as an important artist but as "a most important woman artist" (78). In other words, Carrington discovered that she had abandoned her bourgeois, heteropatriarchal, and constraining family in order to enjoy her own personal and creative freedom but also embrace a movement, surrealism, which was equally (if not more) heteropatriarchal and which imposed similar boundaries for her, both as a woman and as an artist. Carrington's judgment of surrealism as hypocritical and male chauvinist is not exaggerated at all, since, as Chadwick explains, the whole movement was based on such foundations:

> A vision of woman as muse, the image of man's inspiration and his salvation, is inseparable from the pain and anger that gave birth to surrealism. As the stimulus for the convulsive, sensuous disorientation that was to resolve polarized states of experience and awareness into a new, revolutionary surreality, she existed in many guises: as virgin, child, celestial creature, on the one hand; as sorceress, erotic object, and *femme-fatale*, on the other. In each of these roles she exists to complement and complete the male creative cycle. (13)

Together with the fundamental role the *femme-fatale* played in surrealism (while at the same time reducing women to a subaltern role), the concept of *femme-enfant* developed by Breton in *Nadja* and *Arcane 17* was equally important; concurrently, it imprisoned surrealistic women even more. In fact, Breton found Carrington extremely influential. According to Hertz, "The inclusion of Carrington as an exemplar of the future Surrealism reveals both how Breton continued to navigate the fraught and sometimes nefarious gender politics of the movement and how he began to think through Surrealist aesthetics after the war" (90). Breton had been obsessed with the idea of the *femme-folle* (the madwoman) since 1928, when he published *Nadja*. Nonetheless, Breton's incursions into madness are but fictional and literary. Breton, Max, Dalí, and several other surrealist male artists enjoyed madness as a vicarious pleasure, by pushing women to their

246   J. M. PÁRRAGA

very limits. Nin, who met Carrington in New York in 1944, explains in her diary how cruelly Ernst fostered her lover's mental instability:

> I remembered the story I was told about the time he [Max Ernst] was married to Eleanora Carrington [...] The surrealists, as a group, encouraged her neurosis to the point of madness. She was a painter. She would paint a canvas and lay it against a wall. A few days later she would look for it and would not find it [...] he would say to the girl: "Are you sure that you painted anything? I never saw such a painting." (qtd. in Bueno 158)

On the other hand, Leonora Carrington showed Breton a more authentic version of *Nadja* when she succumbed to madness in Madrid and was treated with *Cardiazol*, a drug which produced both epilepsy and altered states of perception. The author's madness was so authentic that her memories about that period have been studied from the perspective of clinical psychiatry (Hoff). Thus, as Hertz points out,

> According to Carrington's own account, *Down Below* was written with Breton's prompting. Carrington had clearly experienced the "deregulation of the senses" which, following Rimbaud, Breton sought to convey through *Nadja* and such collaborative works as *L'Immaculée Conception*. In a sense, as Suleiman has suggested, Carrington had become Nadja, that femme-folle who teaches Breton much about the experience of life through a surfeit of authenticity. Now that one of Surrealism's "own" had experienced that same madness for real, it had to be recounted in some fashion. (98)

Interestingly enough, the "descent into madness [which] consecrated her as a surrealist heroine" (Warner 20) happened because of Max Ernst, since Carrington had traveled to Spain in the hope of securing a passport for her lover, a Jew who was kept captive by the Nazis in France. In Franco's Madrid, Carrington was lost and disoriented in the middle of a big city which was experiencing the turmoil and repression of the post-civil war period, surrounded by strangers who spoke a language she could hardly understand. In *Down Below*, Carrington explains how the linguistic barriers contributed to her own inability to deal with reality at the time: "The fact that I had to speak a language I was not acquainted with was crucial: I was not hindered by a preconceived idea of the words, and I but half understood their modern meaning. This made it possible for me to invest the most ordinary phrases with a hermetic significance" (12). Investing the most ordinary phrases with a hermetic significance and the chaos surrounding her in Madrid certainly affected her mental stability. However, at the same time, as Conley affirms, it also led her to a "liminal psychological state" in which she was hyperconscious:

> All of the distortion of reality to which she testifies seem almost understandable, given the pressure she was under. What she describes coincides with of "liminal psychological state" that leads to the familiar surrealist notion of the marvelous, described by Dr. Pierre Mabille in his *Miroir du merveilleux*, and which is situated "beyond consciousness, in dreams, or even beyond, in a state of superrational, hyperconscious lucidity, if one may indeed describe our interior geography in such a fashion." (62)

The hyperconscious lucidity this expert refers to allowed Carrington to understand the fact that she did not need to help Ernst escape but rather help herself escape Ernst and the surrealist group, as the following passage from *Down Below* clearly shows: "When he refused to take Max's passport, I remember that I replied: 'Ah! I understand, I must kill him myself,' i.e., disconnect myself from Max" (13). Escaping Max Ernst was feasible. On the contrary, escaping Spain was much harder, since soon after trying to get her lover's passport, she was abducted by a group of *requetés*, who "rose and pushed me into a car [...] They showed me into a room decorated in Chinese style, threw me onto bed, and after tearing off my clothes raped me one after the other" (13–14). Even when the author's description of the rape refuses to delve into painful and humiliating details and is presented in a distant, almost clinical manner, this terrible incident moved Carrington from a liminal state of mind into the sheer madness Breton had only been able to know in a speculative, fictional manner. As a result, immediately after being raped, Carrington perceived World War II to be the result of a global conspiracy induced by collective hypnosis and started devising a plan to prevent the conspirators from succeeding:

> That day my freedom came to an end. I was locked up in a hotel room, in the Ritz. I felt perfectly content; I washed my clothes and manufactured various ceremonial garments out of bath towels in preparation to my visit to Franco, the first person to be liberated from his hypnotic somnambulism. As soon as he was liberated, Franco would come to an understanding with England, then England with Germany, etc. (16)

As a result of Carrington's inability to distinguish between the hallucinations her mind presented her with and the reality, the author was first

248   J. M. PÁRRAGA

moved to a convent; however, the nuns were absolutely unable not only to help her recover her sanity but even to keep her within the premises. Consequently, she was taken to a mental asylum in Santander, where she was exposed to some inhuman treatments ("Was it a hospital or a concentration camp?" [22]): "they tore my clothes off brutally and strapped me naked to the bed" (28) and three injections of *Cardiazol*, a drug which produced epilepsy and hallucinations. The effects of this drug were so painful (both physically and emotionally) that Carrington finally surrendered to prevent a new dose from being administered. I have compared the description of her rape (in which she is abused and humiliated but not deprived of her integrity and strength to fight the aggressors) I quoted above to how she reacts to this drug:

> Then, I went back to bed, and tasted despair. I confessed to myself that a being sufficiently powerful to inflict such a torture was stronger than I was; I admitted defeat, the defeat of myself and of the world around me, with no hope of liberation. I was dominated, ready to become the slave of the first comer, ready to die, it all mattered little to me. When Don Luis [the psychiatrist] came to see me later, I told him that I was the feeblest creature in the whole world, that I could meet his desires, whatever they were, and that I licked his shoes. (41)

During her fiendish period at the institution at Covadonga, Carrington was helpless and even more disoriented ("I probably was still in Spain [...] ended believing I was in another world, another epoch, another civilization, perhaps on another planet containing the past and future and, simultaneously, the present" [25]) and constantly afraid of *Cardiazol*. Nonetheless, she also had time to reflect about her own life and future and came to the conclusion that she needed not only to escape the asylum but also "in a moment of lucidity, I realized how necessary it was to extract myself all the personages who were inhabiting me" (56). I am convinced these "personages" refer to the role the character was supposed to impersonate as a female member of the surrealist group (*femme-fatale, femme-enfant*, and *femme-folle*). Lander also points out that in *Down Below*, Carrington identifies the evil psychiatrist who tortured her at Covadonga with the surrealist's fascination with feminine madness and their utter inability to properly understand it:

Once incarcerated, Carrington encounters Don Luis, who is essential in Carrington's critique of the masculine fascination with female visionaries. What is intriguing about the way he is presented is that, speaking from within a position of the mad female subject, Carrington offers a fragmentary view of him that nonetheless manages to illustrate his fundamental incapacity to understand her. (63)

Consequently, when she was finally released from Covadonga and on her way to a (supposedly) gentler mental asylum in South Africa where her parents were sending her, she escaped in Lisbon and did not hesitate to ask the taxi driver to take her to the "Mexican Embassy" (66). There, she hoped to find Renato Leduc, a Mexican artist and ambassador she had met in France and then again in Madrid, with whom she desired to move to Mexico. As Mercedes Jiménez de la Fuente affirms, escaping to Mexico meant not only getting free from her family's controlling shadow and from a future of reclusion at a South African mental asylum but also liberating herself from Max Ernst and surrealism: "Carrington finally splits with the groups and, above all, with Marx Ernst, by moving to Mexico city. After experiencing madness she is no longer the same person, since she knows the consequences and suffering until she reaches a moment in which she is no longer afraid of anything, not even of losing her mind, something which Breton, knowing her rebel and brave nature, has previously encouraged" (14).[8]

Regarding her destination, it is true that Mexico became a feasible option by mere accident since Carrington knew Leduc would be in Lisbon when she was there, on her way to South Africa, and that the poet enjoyed a privileged political position in Mexico (he had fought with Pancho Villa and was considered both as a national hero and a sort of poet laureate of the country), a country which was far enough from her family and the evil Spanish experiences: "Mexico City: conveniently, thousands of miles from Lancashire, and Berlin, and Paris, and Madrid, and Santander. She couldn't say yes quickly enough" (Moorhead 14). However, it is also true that before arriving in Mexico, the author lived for 18 months in New York, where Peggy Guggenheim offered her not only friendship but patronage as well. As a matter of fact, her stay in New York was quite productive, and

---

[8] "Carrington finalmente rompe con el grupo y, sobre todo, con Max Ernst, al irse a vivir a México D.F. Tras el paso por la locura ya no es la misma persona, pues conoce las consecuencias y el sufrimiento de llegar hasta el final, el no tenerle miedo a nada, ni a perder la razón, algo a lo que le había alentado Breton al conocer su naturaleza rebelde y atrevida."

250 J. M. PÁRRAGA

several exhibitions were commenced and received with enthusiasm by the Big Apple's art critics. Nonetheless, as Mar Rey Bueno concludes, "New York was definitively not as she had imagined it. It looked like the houses, of a reddish black color, had mysteriously been raised from London's fire" (167).[9]

As a result, as Moorehead explains, the artist decided to abandon the commodities she started to enjoy in the USA to move to Mexico, a country whose language she had not mastered and whose culture could not be more different from her British upbringing: "In war-time New York she was welcomed as one of the Europeans artists in exile [...] And there she would stay in a Mexico City that seemed sparse and empty when she arrived" (20). However, it was precisely the promise of a *terra ignota* where she could re-imagine, re-consider, and re-write herself that attracted Carrington to Mexico in such a powerful and magnetic manner:

> It was a place of contradictions, of frictions; layers of history, of indigenous people, with their ancient traditions up-ended by the sixteenth century Spanish invaders, had left a trail of fault-lines that were never far below the surface of Mexican life [...] Death, whether an as idea or in reality, was never far away in Mexico. Leonora was fascinated, entranced, excited and amazed by this extraordinary new country, the country André Breton had, when he visited a few years earlier, called the most surreal nation on earth [...] In Mexico Leonora had a new canvas, an empty canvas, and she felt something in her heart that she had not felt for a long time: hope. (Moorehead 174–8)

MEXICAN YEARS

As Carrington confessed to Grimberg, "Crossing into Mexico, she saw people riding horses on unpaved streets, and she felt a comfortable familiarity. But when they drove into Mexico City, and she noticed a trolley with a sign that read 'Misterios,' she knew she had arrived at the right place" (14). Once in Mexico D.C., the artist started to discover the mysteries of the country in Colonia Roma, a neighborhood where Carrington could enjoy the company of several other intellectuals and artists who did not constrain her the way surrealists had: "Inevitably, the Europeans clung together and created their own world in Colonia Roma in Mexico City" (Raay 14). Of all the people Carrington interacted with at Colonia Roma, the most important one would be without any doubt Remedios Varo, an

---

[9] "Definitivamente, Nueva York no era como lo había imaginado. Parecía como si las casas, de color negro rojizo, hubiesen surgido misteriosamente del incendio de Londres."

old friend of hers: "Even though Leonora Carrington and Remedios Varo had been acquainted with each other in Europe, it was in Mexico that their shared sensibility came to the fore. Here they found themselves at a distance from the pressures of the male-dominated Surrealist group" (Kunny 167). At this point, it is important to note that this new country also enabled them to enjoy more freedom as women than in Europe. It is true that during the 1930s, the country was certainly contaminated by toxic masculinity. However, it is also true that it was the most advanced country for women in the Latin American context (Moorhead 178). Further, at the same time, "as Europeans, meant they were not bound by the usual rules ascribed to women in macho Mexican society" (Moorhead 208). Consequently,

> Mexico will become a creative space, a refuge, but, above all, it will be the setting where the relation the two women will maintain would be placed [...] The two artists were to free, magical, spirits. They never saw each other as adversaries, but as two women who complemented each other. Mexico linked their lifes in a very tight manner. (Caballero 55–61)[10]

As Domenella reminds us, Varo, called by Breton as "the sorcerer," and Carrington (referred to by Breton as "the sphynx") did practice sorority long before this term became popular (1997).

As Davis points out, "Even though Leonora described Mexico as 'a familiar swimming pool with sharks in it,' she lived there for the rest of her long and remarkable life. I think it's safe to say her Irish soul (as well as her British tea and her French lingerie) were brought along to keep her company" (vi). That is not to say the author's situation was not often complex in the country. Emerich summarizes Carrington's pleasure and suffering as follows: "She was absent from what she defined as 'the paradigm of reason' which establishes the code for normality [...] Like Lewis's Carrol's Alice in wonderland, Carrington lives the Mexican country like a desired torrent of absurdity, fantasy and, even, horrors" (qtd. in Ingarao 274).[11]

---

[10] "México se convertirá en un espacio creativo, en un refugio pero, sobre todo, será el decorado donde situar la relación que ambas mantendrán. [...] Dos espíritus libres, mágicos, eso eran, en realidad ambas artistas. Nunca se vieron como competidoras, sino como dos mujeres que se complementaban. México unió sus vidas muy estrechamente."

[11] "Ajena a lo que ella llama 'el paradigma de la cordura' que establece el código de normalidad [...] Como Alicia, la de Lewis Carrol, en el país de las maravillas, Carrington vive el país mexicano como una deseable precipitación entre absurdos, rarezas, fantasías e incluso horrores."

252   J. M. PÁRRAGA

Carrington once confessed to Joanna Moorhead that "life in Mexico was hard: it was very tempting to think about how much easier things would be in Lancashire" (202). However, Carrington knew too well that life in Lancashire would be as safe, comfortable, and stable as it would be boring and lethal to her art, since, as Poniatowska explains,

> In Mexico, almost all of us hallucinate [...] Maybe in England Leonora wouldn't have painted as much as she did in Mexico. [...] Maybe she would have gone back to the control of Harold Carrington, the father she never loved. Maybe the conventions that she initially were able to break with would have asphyxiated her in the long term. Maybe her father, Harold Carrington, would have won the battle. (62)[12]

In a recent article published in *The Economist*, it was declared that "Few give Mexico, her adopted home, credit for influencing this fantastical, half-feral dreamscape." Nonetheless, Carrington's first years in Mexico were certainly fascinating, and the author enjoyed the new and shocking world she inhabited by exploring its rich culture, sometimes accompanied by Varo, sometimes alone. This is the case of the many expeditions she took to get to the heart of the mythical and ancient roots of the country:

> Carrington filled sketchbooks with drawings and notes. In addition to her observations of the Indians, Carrington studied all the creatures native to southern Mexico at the state zoo Tuxtla Gutierrez. Once she had informed herself in this way, she began to focus on understanding the otherworld of the Maya that operates behind the world of experience. To discover the Maya vision, Carrington turned to literature, especially colonial manuscripts, which supply philosophical and sacred information gleaned from Maya informants by Spanish missionaries. Two texts served Carrington as primary sources for mythic material: The Popol Vuh, a sixteenth-century record of the ancient creation myth of the Quiche Maya of northern Guatemala; and the eighteenth-century council book of the Yucatec Maya, Chilam Balam. (179)

During the first decades in the country, Carrington wrote several short stories which were characterized by liminality and hybridity, since they all

---

[12] "En México casi todos alucinamos [...] Quizás en Inglaterra Leonora no habría pintado tanto como en México. [...] Quizás hubiera vuelto al redil de Harold Carrington, el padre que no amó. Quizá las convenciones que primero logró vencer a la larga la hubieran asfixiado. Quizá su padre, Harold Carrington, habría ganado la batalla."

10 FROM BRITISH SORCERY TO *EL MUNDO MÁGICO DE LOS MAYAS...* 253

were full of monsters, grotesque landscapes, cannibalistic meals, and a highly complex symbolism which combined her Catholic upbringing, her fascination with the Cabalah, and the Mexican mythos she was discovering. Plunkett, a scholar who has studied the role of hybridity in Carrington in depth, sums up the importance of hybridity in her corpus and how Mexico affects her hybrid creations as follows:

> Carrington painted and wrote of many hybrids throughout her lengthy career. While many of them were deliberately grotesque, such as the aforementioned examples and the painted figures that populate *The Meal of Lord Candlestick* (1938) and *Down Below* (1941), often their monstrosity was intended to make a political statement on bourgeois excess, female desire, women's bodies or the futile nature of binary constructs. Conversely, her Mexican paintings are replete with harmonious hybrids that hint at transcendence and unity. (494)

Orenstein, one of the first scholars to pay critical attention to Carrington and who became one of her closer friends, explains that she did not fully understand the author's complex corpus until she visited her in Mexico:

> This visit was the most extraordinary and generous gift I have ever received. Leonora took me everywhere, and I spent every day with her. We visited the Witches' Market in Mexico City. We went to faith healers in the country, who passed an egg over me to heal me. We traveled to her other house in Cuernavaca where she had dreams of founding a retreat center for women and having the group lead a spiritual, visionary lifestyle [...] I began to understand the mythos that was unfolding in her vision- how the ancestors, like her own Celtic forebears, both the real ones and the mythical ones who had worshipped the Goddess, had vanished into the underworld, with their ancient knowledge. Their knowledge of the beyond, the hereafter, and the origins of all that exists, was most likely buried in the underworld beneath the pyramids, waiting for us to learn to expand our psychic and clairvoyant vision, so that we might begin to perceive these other worlds from which they had come and to which they had gone. (195–97)

One of the things Carrington discovered when exploring rural Mexico and the ancient traditions of the country was related to some of the artist's own obsessions which had accompanied her since her childhood: the abject, cooking as a magical activity, and vomiting as purging. As Caballero

254   J. M. PÁRRAGA

Guiral explains, "Leonora identifies every pitiful thing happening around her with her stomach" (122).[13]

Asia's essay "Gardens of Delight, or What's Cookin'? Leonora Carrington in the Kitchen" deals with this topic:

> Few of her stories fail to include an allusion to eating, and more often to devouring, while the food in question is seldom "innocent." The experience of the body or "corps propre" as represented in her narratives, is that of a body eating/being eaten, a place of culinary alchemies which is also manipulated, or manipulates itself, in order to exercise control over the outside world. In this fictional realm dominated by magic, perversion and anarchic excess, food elaboration and food consumption are posited as the central act of the narrative. A fascination with the abject and a willingness to provoke her readers' disgust in a language that is marked by the extreme nimbleness of phobic speech, seem to me to offer the clue to Carrington's fiction. (212)

As Carrington discovered through contact with native Mexicans in Chiapas (where she traveled with the Swiss anthropologist Gertrude Bloom [Ries]) and other places, ritual feasting and purging as cleansing were also a central part of their culture. Recent archaeological research has proven that these practices date from the Mayan period:

> For the ancient Maya, it would seem that acts of deliberate purging were also important (Henderson 2008), and archaeologically, evidence exists to suggest that these practices were carried out. For example, Henderson (65) refers to a ceramic vessel that depicts a figure inducing self-vomiting by forcing his hand in his mouth, and the use of enemas is iconographically documented (Houston), with vomiting depicted following enema use or heavy drinking (Henderson). Numerous other instances can be found on ceramic vases (see for example the MayaVase Database). (Cagnato 248)

I consider that Carrington's book *The Milk of Dreams* deserves special attention. It includes nine short stories, which were illustrated by Carrington herself. She composed them during her first years in Mexico to entertain her children and gave the notebook as a present to her friend Alejandro Jodorowsky, "to whom she read and taught from the kitchen of her Mexican house" (Ramírez).[14] As Eduardo de la Fuente explains, dur-

---

[13] "Leonora identifica todo lo penoso que ocurre a su alrededor con su estómago."
[14] "al que hacía lecturas y lecciones desde la cocina de su casa en México."

10 FROM BRITISH SORCERY TO *EL MUNDO MÁGICO DE LOS MAYAS...* 255

ing this period, Carrington focused on educating her children and, to do so, became obsessed with the Jungian archetype of "the Great Mother" (2017b); at the same time, she explored the ancient Mayan myths regarding femineity. When Carrington died, Jodorowsky handed the book back to one of her sons, who published it in 2013 in Spanish. The stories and drawings define Carrington's Mexican hybridity in a perfect manner since the stories can be read as re-interpretations or re-writings of ancient European fairytales but which very often take place in Mexico ("the monster of Chihuahua") and are populated by the rich pathos, mythos, and imaginary which characterize the American country (García-Manso).

When Varo died in 1963, Carrington's connections in Mexico basically ceased, since most of the other artists from Colonia Roma had either died or abandoned the country. Consequently, the author could not but feel a certain loneliness, which was echoed in her daily activities and artistic production. As Caballero Guiral explains, "From this moment [Varo's death], the British artist would start her Mexican journey alone. Her work also changes. These last decades will be characterized by Carrington's vital, political and social involvement" (55).[15] The way in which Carrington got involved to improve the sociocultural situation of Mexico was, unsurprisingly, related to feminism, since she contributed in a decisive manner to the creation of the feminist movement in Mexico City in 1972 (Caballero 83). In this way, according to Emre, Carrington, who had renounced surrealism when she arrived in Mexico, became at this time "committed to dissolving the boundaries between the daily work of art and the daily work of care—a feminist project more enduring and surreal than any single romance or school of painting."

From a literary point of view, after Varo's death, Carrington started to focus more on active feminism than on the Jungian spiritual quests, explorations of the Mexican mythos, and the playful spirit of the still surrealistic games and extravagant magical-culinary preparations that she and Varo had produced. In 1974, the author published her best work, *The Hearing Trumpet*.[16] The importance of Mexico to the genesis of this text was fundamental. However, unlike previous literary works written in the

---

[15] "A partir de aquí, la artista inglesa comenzará su andadura en México en solitario. Su trabajo también cambia. Estas últimas décadas se van a caracterizar por el compromiso vital, político y social de Leonora Carrington."

[16] In several interviews, the author explains that the text had been written in the 1950s, when she was about 40 years old, but didn't remember the exact date.

256   J. M. PÁRRAGA

country and which were inspired from the jungle and ancient pyramids, in this case it was the metropolis which had an impact on the creation of the text, since, as Carrington told Ali Smith, "she wrote the entire book while seated in the Café Garibaldi in the Plaza de los Mariachis in the midst of cacophonous noise" (x). At the same time, Carrington's sorrow for the loss of her dear friend and the way she felt Mexico was no longer a real house to her once Varo had gone is also clearly reflected in a text which was written years before but revised and edited at that time (Cabañas 60).

As Kent explains, "described as a novel, or a novella, the format of *The Hearing Trumpet* is difficult to pin down. It has no chapters or sections, contains letters, poetry, incantations, typographical variations, and almost thirty of the 158 pages are given over to a story within a story, the text of a nun's tractate *mise-en-abîme*" (297).

Difficult as it is to define *The Hearing Trumpet*, it is obvious that this literary work is above all a parody on surrealism and the rigid categories in which the movement pigeonholed women. As Bachet points out, the novella constitutes in many ways not only Carrington's revenge on Breton's chauvinism but also the author's final movement to break the ties that still connected her to surrealism and the founders of the movement:

> In a comical reversal of Breton's *Nadja*, the madwoman of Carrington's novel is a fraud. Indeed, Nadja's enchanting madness is transformed into an old woman's poorly staged performance. Natacha does not possess clairvoyant powers. She does not receive visions but rather constructs visions of her own, for she has understood that it is what the doctor desires. She uses madness as a strategy to manipulate the doctor into giving her what she wants. Later on, when the doctor fails to expel Georgina, Natacha tries to kill her, but mistakenly ends up poisoning another resident. The archetypal madwoman turns into a mediocre murderess. In that instance, Carrington's parody seems to be primarily playful. The author plays with the madwoman of Breton and denies the male character the possibility of deriving any creative inspiration or transformation from her (simulated) madness. (9)

Once liberated from surrealism (even when the text is full of dreamlike elements, Jungian archetypes, hybridity, and a constant deconstruction of the binary conscious/unconscious), Carrington uses *The Hearing Trumpet* to carry on a feminist revision:

10 FROM BRITISH SORCERY TO *EL MUNDO MÁGICO DE LOS MAYAS...* 257

And all this underpinned, of course, by the primary structure of the feminist revision [...] The story that emerges as Dona Rosalinda's life, told by what turns out to be an unsympathetic narrator, is a story of antipatriarchal and anti-Christian subversion: the good abbess and her homosexual friend, the bishop of Treves les Freles, are devotees of 'the Goddess', working to destroy the Christian edifice from the inside- which means, to rewrite its story. (Suleiman 174)

By the means of this feminist revision, and no longer tied by the invisible but rigid straps imposed by surrealism, the novella declares the end of patriarchy (González 123); concurrently, it becomes appealing to a wider audience who could not (or did not want to) deal with the excessive complexities of surrealism. And, simultaneously, she creates a literary work which becomes Horatian, by resulting as useful from a social point of view: "*The Hearing Trumpet* is a post-war post-nuclear vision, and one with ramifications in the global-warming era. Its reprint could not be more timely" (Smith x).

Salmerón considers that "*The Hearing Trumpet* is the culmination of a long journey "[...] What started being a powerful but dark and 'gothic' voice becomes, in later texts, into a playful, witty and, over all, very ironic one" (113).[17] Levitt explains, "In her early, Mexican years, Carrington's landscape (both written and painted) became more complex, utilizing new scenes and mythologies, and then the writing stopped entirely" (74). "Then" refers precisely to the moment in which Carrington published *The Hearing Trumpet* and, in fact, stopped producing literature in order to focus on painting and her role as a Mexican feminist. If we consider the fact that "Since her childhood, Leonora Carrington had been a questor, looking for a scripture to match her belief in the metaphysical dimensions of existence" (Warner xxviii) and that her literary corpus can be read as a shamanic crisis journey (Cline), it is not surprising that Carrington arrived at her final destination as a prose writer with a novel in which she rewrote the myth of the grail quest from a feminist perspective while simultaneously freeing herself from surrealism finally and acknowledging the tremendous role Varo and Mexico played in order to enable her successful

---

[17] "*La Corneta Acústica* es la culminación de un largo viaje. [...] Lo que empezó siendo una voz poderosa pero sombría y 'gótica' se convierte, en textos posteriores, en una voz lúdica, ingeniosa y, sobre todo, muy irónica."

258   J. M. PÁRRAGA

arrival. From that moment on, our author did not stop traveling, exploring, investigating, and invoking new routes until the moment she left this world. However, those explorations were no longer literary.

Conclusion

Leonora Carrington's extraordinary biography is key to fully enjoying and understanding (at least as far as her surrealistic-influenced creations can be rationally understood) her outstanding literary production. Nonetheless, so far, most critics have focused on the artist's upbringing as a high-class British girl who refused to conform to the rigid constraints imposed on her by her Catholic, bourgeois family; her short but intense relationship with Max Ernst; or with the mental breakdown she suffered in Franco's Spain and the subsequent reclusion into a mental asylum in Santander, where she was tortured, both physically and psychologically, with a cruel drug. Unquestionably, all these aspects of her biography are fascinating and have a deep impact on Carrington's work. Nonetheless, the attention paid to the author's Mexican phase of life and how this country and its culture influenced her literary corpus has not received similar critical attention so far.

Carrington once told her friend Gloria Orenstein "that I would have to come to Mexico if I wanted to understand her work" (193) and another good friend of the author, Marina Warner, also considers that this country played a fundamental role in Carrington's personal and artistic development, since,

> In Mexico she encountered a culture in which the beliefs of the Indians merged with the imported Catholicism of the missionaries and the conquistadores; in the vigorous spirit of this Mexican syncretism, the artist wanted to communicate her inner visions, and a luxuriant variety of religious symbols bloom in her paintings of this period. "All religions are real." Leonora once commented. "But you have to go through your own channels—you might meet the Egyptians, you might meet the Voodoos, but in order to keep some kind of equilibrium it has to feel authentic to you. (xxxi–xxxii)

Moorhead, cousin and friend of the late Carrington, did not hesitate to refer to the kitchen from the author's Mexican house as "The inner sanctum, Leonora's kitchen, tabernacle-like at the centre of the fortified island" (11). We should not forget that it was at that same kitchen that our author transmitted some of her magic to Jodorowsky, who had traveled to the country to learn from Carrington herself and Erich Fromm (who was, at that time, living in Cuernavaca).

As I have shown in this paper, Mexico was utterly important to Carrington not only because of the surreal and magical nature of the country itself (her visit to Chiapas and the pyramids were two of the most magical moments in her whole life), but also because the artist had projected her own dreams, her own will, and her own necessity to be free in that country even before stepping a foot in it. Mexico had allowed her to escape the horrors of going to a South African mental asylum and Mexico had enabled her to escape the toxic masculinity of Breton's surrealistic sect. At this point, it is important to remember that immediately before leaving New York to finally move to Mexico, she gave a last present to Breton: "On the coat worn by the androgyn, Carrington partly inscribed in mirror writing, 'TIME WAS TIME IS TIME IS PAST.' Carrington gifted the drawing to André Breton before leaving for Mexico" (Grimberg 13).

Carrington could not summarize it in a better way: Europe and the USA were the past, and Mexico was her future: a future that brought her enlightenment, serenity, motherhood, freedom, sorority, and artistic recognition.

WORKS CITED

Andrade, Lourdes. "De la monstruosidad carringtoniana." *Artes de México*, vol. 16, 1992, pp. 102–03.

Assa, Sonia. "Gardens of Delight, or What's Cookin'? Leonora Carrington in the Kitchen." *Studies in 20th Century Literature*, vol. 15, no. 2, 1991, pp. 213–27.

Bachet, Tifaine. "Parody and Femininity in British Surrealism (Ithell Colquhoun and Leonora Carrington)." *Polysèmes*, vol. 23, 2020, pp. 1–15.

Bonnie, Lander. "The Modern Mediatrix: Medieval Rhetoric in André Breton's Nadja and Leonora Carrington's Down Below." *Colloquy: Text, Theory, Practice*, vol. 13, 2007, pp. 51–72.

Breton, André. *Nadja*. Gallimard, 1928.

———. *Arcane 17*. Al Borak, 1972.

Caballero Guiral, Juncal. "Leonora Carrington y sus memorias: una experiencia de violencia y locura." *Arte y Políticas de Identidad*, vol. 6, 2012, pp. 117–32.

———. "El embrujo de las recetas surrealistas." *Dossiers Feministes*, vol. 17, 2013, pp. 51–61.

——. *Hechiceras: un viaje a la vida y obra de Remedios Varo y Leonora Carrington.* Ediciones Trea, 2018.

Cabañas, Salmerón. *Leonora Carrington.* Ediciones del Orto, 2002.

Cagnato, Clarissa. "Sweet, Weedy and Wild: Macrobotanical Remains from a Late Classic (8th Century Ad) Feasting Deposit Discovered at La Corona, an Ancient Maya Settlement." *Vegetation History and Archaeobotany,* vol. 27, 2017, pp. 241–52.

Carrington, Leonora. *The Oval Lady.* Capra Press, 1975.

——. *The Hearing Trumpet.* Penguin, 2005.

——. *The Milk of Dreams.* New York Review Children's Collection, 2013.

——. *Down Below.* New York Review Books, 2017.

Chadwick, Whitney. *Women Artists and the Surrealist Movement.* Little, Brown, 1985.

Cline, Kurt. "Shamanic Praxis and Hermetic Speculation: Leonora Carrington, Giordano Bruno and the Secret of the Flying Horse." *NTU Studies in Language and Literature,* vol. 27, 2012, pp. 71–104.

Conley, Katharine. *Automatic Woman: The Representation of Woman in Surrealism.* U Nebraska P, 1996.

Davis, Kathryn. "Introduction." *The Complete Stories of Leonora Carrington.* Dorothy Project, 2017, pp. i-vii.

De la Fuente Rocha, Eduardo. "Leonora Carrington. Frente a la desestructuración." *Revista Iberoamericana de las Ciencias Sociales y Humanísticas,* vol. 6, no. 12, 2017a, pp. 1–25.

——. "Leonora Carrington. Metamorfosis hacia la autenticidad." *Revista Iberoamericana de las Ciencias Sociales y Humanísticas,* vol. 6, no. 12, 2017b, pp. 1–27.

Domenella, Ana Rosa. "Leonora Carrington en sus ochenta. La creación compartida." *Debate Feminista,* vol. 15, 1997, pp. 359–63.

Economist, The. "The Sorceress in the Jungle; Leonora Carrington," 2019, p. 104.

Emre, Merve. "How Leonora Carrington Feminized Surrealism." *The New Yorker,* 2020. Web.

Gaensbauer, Deborah B. "Voyages of Discovery: Leonora Carrington's Magical Prose." *Women's Studies,* vol. 23, 1994, pp. 271–84.

García-Manso, Angélica. "Sentido didáctico de *Leche del sueño, Cuaderno de Leonora Carrington.*" *Ogigia-Revista Electrónica de Estudios Hispánicos,* vol. 26, 2019, pp. 93–107.

Gómez Haro, Germaine. "Leonora Carrington, la inasible." *La Jornada Semanal,* vol. 857, 2011. Web.

González Madrid, María José. "Leonora Carrington y Remedios Varo: Alquimia, pintura y amistad creativa." *Studia Hermetica Journal,* vol. 1, 2017, pp. 116–44.

Grimberg, Salomon "Traveling toward the Unknown." *Woman's Art Journal,* vol. 38, 2017, pp. 3–15.

10 FROM BRITISH SORCERY TO *EL MUNDO MÁGICO DE LOS MAYAS...* 261

Helland, Janice. "Surrealism and Esoteric Feminism in the Paintings of Leonora Carrington." *Racar, Société pour Promouvoir la Publication en Histoire de l'Art au Canada, Départment d'Histoire, Université Laval, Québec*, vol. 16, 1989, pp. 53–61.

Hertz, Erich. "Disruptive Testimonies: The Stakes of Surrealist Experience in Breton and Carrington." *Symposium*, vol. 64, 2010, pp. 89–104.

Hoff, Anne. "'I Was Convulsed, Pitiably Hideous': Convulsive Shock Treatment in Leonora Carrington's *Down Below*." *Journal of Modern Literature*, vol. 32, 2009, pp. 83–98.

Ingarao, Giulia. "México y el surrealismo: Leonora Carrington y *El laberinto fantástico de Xilitla*." *Boletín de Arte*, vol. 29, 2008, pp. 273–83.

Jiménez de la Fuente, Mercedes. "La Joven Leonora Carrington y El Movimiento Surrealista." *1616: Anuario de Literatura Comparada*, vol. 6, 2016, pp. 149–70.

———. "Mitos del surrealismo en *Memorias de abajo*, de Leonora Carrington." *Estudios de Literatura Comparada 1: Las Las Artes De La Vanguardia Literaria*, edited by Ana González-Rivas Fernández and Luis Martínez Falero, Sociedad Española de Literatura General y Comparada, 2018, pp. 7–16.

Kent, Alicia. "'Are We to Be Contented with Dreams?' Getting Older in the Work of Leonora Carrington." *Journal of Romance Studies*, vol. 17, 2017, pp. 293–309.

Kunny, Clare. "Leonora Carrington's Mexican Vision." *Art Institute of Chicago Museum Studies*, vol. 22, 1996, pp. 166–79.

Levitt, Annette Shandler. "The Bestial Fictions of Leonora Carrington." *Journal of Modern Literature*, vol. 20, 1996, pp. 65–74.

Moorhead, Joanna. *The Surreal Life of Leonora Carrington*. Virago, 2017.

———. "Great Embarkation: A Witness to Leonora Carrington's Life in War-Threatened Lisbon." *Times Literary Supplement*, 2019.

Noheden, Kristoffer. "Leonora Carrington, Surrealism, and Initiation Symbolic Death and Rebirth in *Little Francis* and *Down Below*." *Correspondences*, vol. 2, 2014, pp. 35–65.

Noodén, Lars. "Animal Symbolism in Celtic Mythology." U Michigan, 1992. Web.

Orenstein, Gloria. "Foreword." *The Oval Lady*. Capra Press, 1975.

———. "In Memory of the Most Magical Friend I Ever Had, Leonora Carrington." *Femspec*, vol. 17, 2016, pp. 193–225.

Oropesa, Salvador A. "La pintora surrealista y expatriada en la Colonia Roma. *Leonora* (2011), de Elena Poniatowska." *Chasqui: Revista de Literatura Latinoamericana*, vol. 43, 2014, pp. 82–91.

Plunkett, Tara. "'Melusina after the Scream': Surrealism and the Hybrid Bodies of Leonora Carrington and Remedios Varo." *Bulletin of Spanish Studies*, vol. 95, 2018, pp. 493–510.

Poniatowska, Elena. "Un mural en la selva, el de Leonora Carrington." *Revista de la Universidad de México*, vol. 62, 2009, pp. 59–64.

van Raaij, Stefan. *Surreal Friends: Leonora Carrington, Remedios Varo and Kati Horna*. Lund Humphries: In association with Pallant House Gallery, 2010.

Ramírez, Noelia. "El dramático encierro español de la pintora surrealista Leonora Carrington." *El País*, 2020. Web.

Rey Bueno, Mar. "Armada de locura: mi viaje a Leonora Carrington." *Studia Hermetica Journal*, vol. 1, 2017, pp. 150–75.

Ries, Olga. "El exilio y la política nacionalista mexicana: Remedios Varo, Leonora Carrington y el nacionalismo mexicano." *Revista IZQUIERDAS*, vol. 3, 2010, pp. 1–20.

Ruland, Richard, and Malcolm Bradbury. *From Puritanism to Postmodernism: A History of American Literature*. Viking, 1991.

Salmerón, Julia. "El sortilegio de la repetición, o cómo invocar la revolución a través de las palabras." *Studia Hermetica Journal*, vol. 1, 2017, pp. 84–115.

Scappini, Alessandra. *El paisaje totémico entre lo real e imaginario: Leonora Carrington, Leonor Fini, Kay Sage, Dorothea Tanning y Remedios Varo*. Benilde Ediciones, 2018.

Schonfield, Ernest. "Myths of Anglo-German Surrealism: Max Ernst and Leonora Carrington." *The Embrace of the Swan: Anglo-German Mythologies in Literature, the Visual Arts and Cultural Theory*, edited by Rudiger Görner, DeGruyter, 2010, pp. 231–59.

Smith, Ali. "Introduction." *The Hearing Trumpet*. Penguin, 2005, pp. v–xvi.

Suleiman, Susan. *Subversive Intent. Gender, Politics and the Avant-Garde*. Harvard UP, 1990.

Warner, Marina. "Introduction." *Down Below*. New York Review Books, 2017, pp. vii–xxxvi.

PART III

New Women, New Art Forms

CHAPTER 11

How to Narrate a War: Kati Horna's Photography During the Spanish Civil War (1936–1939)—Moving Across the Real and the Symbolic

Aránzazu Díaz-Regañón Labajo

Memories of the Spanish Civil War are constructed through written documents as well as visual artifacts in the propaganda that both sides of the fight promoted with determination and tenacity. Photographs provide an eyewitness account of the social history of that moment, including images not only from the front, the battles, and the main characters but also from the ordinary life of common people and their experiences, beliefs, pleasure, and suffering. Gaining great value as evidence of social history, photography helps historians construct a "history from below" (Burke 12), focusing on the daily life of ordinary people.

Foreign journalists, photographers, and writers traveled to Spain, where they worked as both professionals and activists. Photographers such as Kati Horna saw and used their work as a resolute tool of propaganda at the

---

A. Díaz-Regañón Labajo (✉)
IES María Moliner, Segovia, Spain
e-mail: arandi@usal.es

© The Author(s), under exclusive license to Springer Nature
Switzerland AG 2024
R. M. Silverman, E. Sánchez-Pardo (eds.), *Nomadic New Women*,
https://doi.org/10.1007/978-3-031-62482-7_11

265

266   A. DÍAZ-REGAÑÓN LABAJO

service of the loyalist cause, expecting their war chronicles to impact readers' consciences. Famous artist Josep Renau thought that in the extreme circumstances of the war, artists lost their personal and subjective characters to turn into something collective, solidary, and "objective." They served the common cause—the collective task of defeating the enemy—as a step before social justice and freedom (López Mondejar 162–4). This "activist aspect" of photographic work deeply marked the photography taken in Spain during 1936–1939, by both Spanish and foreign photographers, including Horna's work.

In the pages that follow, I focus on Kati Horna's photography. Many studies and exhibitions of Horna's photographic work address the perspective of Kati Horna during the Spanish Civil War. Her visual style typically focuses on the consequences of war—without showing a drop of blood—and the presumption that viewers ponder those consequences. She utilized different techniques, genres, and topics before, during, and after the war. In fact, the influence of different schools and artistic styles, such as Dada, the New Vision, the Bauhaus, Surrealism, and documentary and social photography, throughout her professional career makes it impossible to frame her in just one of them. It is well known that the most common fieldwork she participated in included the illustrated magazines of the country she was living in; however, the use of her Spanish photographs in the foreign press and in propaganda pamphlets, albums, and posters has only been recently identified. As new documents and artifacts appear concerning herself and her work, as happened in 2016 when new artifacts were discovered in the International Institute of Social History (IISH) in Amsterdam,[1] knowledge about her perspective can be further developed.

Her traveling spirit, deepened by the circumstances that forced her to constantly move from one country to another, made her walk the edges of photography and society, creating her personal style that crosses aesthetic

---

[1] According to Rubio, the artifacts include 522 negatives of 6 × 6 mm, preserved in numbered paper envelopes (22). The new material does not have online open access, and individuals must request to examine it in a reading room, or it is temporarily not available due to digitization (see International Institute of Social History, https://search.iisg.amsterdam/Record/COLL00138. Regarding this discovery, a recent exhibition took place, titled *The Amsterdam Boxes: Kati Horna and Margaret Michaelis in the Spanish Civil War*. 03 Jun 2022–24 Jul 2022, Royal Academy of Fine Arts of San Fernando, Madrid, https://www.phe.es/en/exposiciones/las-cajas-de-amsterdam-kati-horna-margaret-michaelis-en-la-guerra-civil/.

frames as she crossed the physical borders of Hungary, Germany, France, Spain, and Mexico.

The sources that form the basis of this study belong to the "Photographic File of Kati Horna," deposited in the Centro Documental de la Memoria Historia (CDMH) in Salamanca, under the Ministry of Culture of Spain. In 1983, Horna donated to the Spanish Ministry the negatives she shot in service of the social revolution launched by the Confederación Nacional del Trabajo-Federación Anarquista Ibérica (CNT-FAI) during the Spanish Civil War. Until 2020, these negatives were thought to be the only surviving artifacts of her original work. They include 270 black-and-white cellulose nitrates of 6 × 6 mm, numbered from 1 to 272 (Nos. 175 and 176 do not exist). Horna herself arranged the order pattern when she donated the artifacts, and Desantes and Hernández compiled and inventoried any existing dates and titles that Horna provided.

In creating a compilation of the most remarkable viewpoints and uses, I explain in the following text how the war was narrated through Horna's visual representation of it, establishing connections between her education in Europe and her practice before and after the Civil War. As Otayek states, "a powerful storytelling impulse runs through much of Kati Horna's work" ("Loss" 21).

Horna's Professional and Activist Origins in Europe

Many references exist about Kati Horna's life and work. The different surnames she adopted throughout her life make it difficult to follow her path: she had at least five names, as she adopted the name closest to her reality and most intimate relationship of the moment (Horna Fernández 9). For clarity, I consistently refer to her in this text as Horna.

She was born Katalin Deutsch Blau in Hungary on May 19, 1912, in Szilasbalhás, a city near Budapest, to a wealthy Jewish family. As I explain in the following pages, she lived in five different countries throughout her life, most of them in Europe. Everything she learned in both her profession and her activism she practiced in her career before and during her Spanish stay and later in her lifetime in Mexico—except for ideology, as will be shown.

Her first training occurred in Hungary, where she met the Hungarian activist Lajos Kassák, a member of the second generation of the avant-garde (Everett 9–10). As a young woman, she gravitated toward Kassák's network of left-wing artists and intellectuals. From him she learned to use

268   A. DÍAZ-REGAÑÓN LABAJO

photography as a tool of condemnation and political commitment. There she also met her future husband, the activist Pal Partos. Eventually, as their views became more radicalized, particularly regarding the Stalinist party rule in the Soviet Union, Horna and Partos split from Kassák's circle (Otayek, "Loss" 22).

Partos's activism against the military government of Miklós Horhy pushed the young couple to move to Berlin in 1928. There they met the poet and playwright Bertolt Brecht, the anarcho-syndicalist writer Erich Mühsam, and the journalist Augustin Souchy, head of the CNT-FAI in Barcelona.

Berlin was important in Horna's life for two other reasons. At the beginning of the 1930s, the couple became involved with an antifascist community of intellectuals, at whose center was the Marxist theorist Karl Korsch, a leading intellectual in dissident circles from the German Communist Party. Horna's later move to Spain and her involvement with the anarchist cause during the Civil War were related to her membership in this political community.

Equally significant to the future direction of her photography practice was the rapid rise of new conventions of visual representation. A variety of innovative narrative genres, from the photo essay to the photobook, pushed the boundaries of how the printed page could engage images, text, and design to tell stories and convey complex ideas. While Horna lived in Berlin, a second remarkable event occurred: she came into contact with groups from the Bauhaus and the New Vision, and specifically with the Hungarian Láslo Moholy-Nagy, from whom she learned the photomontage technique.

Just before Hitler seized power, Berlin was the meeting point for Hungarians, Czechs, and other politically exiled individuals, along with German intellectuals. It was also where the first great photojournalists worked for the first successful photographic agencies and illustrated press (Pelizzon 22–4). When Horna abandoned Berlin, she had created for herself a cosmopolitan outlook and a background in radical politics.

In 1933, the couple returned to Budapest and married. During this time, she studied with József Pèczi and made her first portraits. Pèczi's concentration on the interplay of photography, design, and typography in advertising work provided Horna with the technical skills to build a career in the illustrated press. Pèczi's teachings, crucial to the development of Horna's vision, provided her with a distinctive sense of photography as a tool for image construction and persuasion rather than just a means for detached documentation (Otayek, "Loss" 22).

Her first famous portrait was shot in Pèczi's studio: one of Endre Freidmann (Robert Capa) as he took one of her. She also shot her first photographs of a social documentary nature, such as vagabonds lying on benches, children playing on the banks of the Danube, toys she herself created, and anchors left on the street.[2]

Only six weeks after their marriage, they moved to Paris, just as the French capital was gathering the artistic avant-garde and cultural movements. Photographers from all of Europe, including many exiled from Germany and Hungary, were forming what Emmanuel Sougez called the "Parisian School of Photography" (302). In Paris, Horna created her first photographic series influenced by surrealism: in a *flâneur* style, her photos portrayed flea markets, cafés, street life, and "wandering poetics." There she practiced her ethnographic viewpoint which she would later use in Valencia and Barcelona.

Around 1936, she worked with Wolfgang Bürger, a young German illustrator in exile, on several series of satirical photo stories featuring eggs, vegetables, and household objects. These stories bring inert items to human life, parodying domesticity, romance, and other aspects of everyday life. However, some reflect antifascist militancy: "Hitler-Ei"[3] ridicules the seditious oratory of the Nazi leader using a boisterous egg featuring the dictator's familiar hairstyle and mustache (Otayek, "Loss" 25). In 1937, the story's comical tyrant was dubbed "Das Franco-Ei," a direct reference to Francisco Franco. These satirical pieces were enthusiastically disseminated across Europe through the thriving antifascist press of the late 1930s.

Although she returned to Paris in less than two years, the following section discusses Horna's arrival at Barcelona, for which official documentation is yet to be determined.

---

[2] The photographs studied here belong to the Museo Amparo (2013) and Americas Society (2016) exhibition catalogs.

[3] Horna, Kati. "Serie Hitlerei". 1937, Museo Amparo, Puebla, Mexico https://museoamparo.com/exposiciones/pieza/2555/serie-hitlerei.

270 A. DÍAZ-REGAÑÓN LABAJO

KATI HORNA'S ARRIVAL TO SPAIN

Kati Horna went to Spain to work as a photojournalist for the anarchist institutions supporting the Spanish Second Republic, as she explained in 1983 in a letter to the General Director of Fine Arts and Archives of Spain (Vicent Monzó 16–17).

This institution was the Foreign Propaganda Office, formed by a group of foreigners cooperating with the Regional Committee of CNT and led by Augustin Souchy since 1922. It was in charge of radio broadcasts and news bulletins edited in several languages, as it promoted the complicated anarchist position by producing and internationally distributing a wide range of propaganda materials. In its graphics section, photography was used with an exclusively propagandistic aim (Rubio 25). Its first photographer was the Polish anarchist, Margaret Michaelis. In 1937, the Spanish Photo Agency (Photo SPA) was created.

Starting in the autumn of 1936, Pal Partos worked in Paris as the journal editor of *L'Espagne Antifasciste*, funded by the Comité Anarcho-Syndicaliste pour la Défense et la Libération du Prolétariat Espagnol (Rubio 26). However, the journal was interrupted in early 1937, and Horna and Partos decided to move to Spain after being officially invited by the CNT-FAI. She took her husband's new nom de plume "Polgare," and according to the CNT archives in the IISH, on January 9, 1937, the entrance of "Kathe Polgare" to Barcelona was authorized.[4] This evidence is why Rubio (27) rejects the idea that she entered Spain with the help of the Ministry of Foreign Propaganda of the Spanish Government, even though Pelizzon believes otherwise (35).

González Quintana denies that the Republican government intervened (10). In his opinion, Horna's work was almost unknown until the 1990s because official Republican propaganda kept her work outside international press circuit distribution. However, this was not the case for Robert Capa, Deschamps, or Serrano, who worked for *Life*, *L'Illustration*, and *The Illustrated London News*, respectively (Miravitlles 9–16). Although it is clear today that Horna worked for the CNT-FAI and Photo SPA, the scope of these institutions was probably smaller than that of the other cases. Moreover, it is also evident that some of her pictures were used by the Republican government and distributed throughout the international circuit.

---

[4] According to Otayek, the entry is under the name of Catalina Partos ("Loss" 39).

11 HOW TO NARRATE A WAR: KATI HORNA'S PHOTOGRAPHY... 271

The truth is that no document exists in the "Authorized Photographers" files or in the Department of Press and Propaganda in Madrid, preserved in the CDMH,[5] concerning Kathe Polgare or Partos (or her maiden name). However, the identification cards of Gerta Pohorylle (better known as Gerda Taro), Antoine Saint Exupéry, and David Szymin "Chim" have been maintained. The names of neither Kati Polgare nor Paul Polgare appear in the CNT-FAI Foreign Propaganda Office, located in the Arxiu Nacional de Catalunya (ANC).[6] In fact, "Pablo Polgare" appears just once in a report on the Ebro front, "Bericht von der Frontreise 20–23.2.37," in relation to a "Brigada Internacional Especial" with no other reference to it.[7]

The only mention of Polgare in the Spanish archives is in the "File of Repression," in which at least six cards refer to "P.," "Paul," or "Pablo Polgare," as the nickname of Pal Partos.[8] They refer to a letter Pablo Polgare signed about material the Cultural Council of Madrid of CNT-FAI bought in September 1938.[9]

Whatever the case may be, Kati Horna—then Polgare—started her journey through Spain armed with her Rolleiflex: her first job—to clean the name of anarchism for what the international right-wing press was saying of it. For that, she accepted one of Souchy's assignments, as is shown next.

"HORROR TALES AND FASCIST CALUMNIES": A PHOTOGRAPHIC ALBUM

Posters, photomurals, magazines, and pamphlets are the main propaganda materials used in wars and studied by historians. However, photographic albums are less known and even considered a "relic of the Spanish Civil War" (Otayek, "Loss" 27).

---

[5] Fichero de fotógrafos autorizados, Subsecretaría de Propaganda del Ministerio de Estado. PS-Madrid, C. 1870, Leg. 633. and Político-Social. Madrid. Prensa y Propaganda (Subsecretaría). Administración. PS-Madrid, C. 2361, Leg. 2984, No. 1–2. CDMH, Salamanca, Spain.

[6] Fitxes d'estrangers del Departament de Propaganda Exterior. Arxiu Nacional de Catalunya (ANC), Barcelona, Spain, ANC1-886-T-3159.

[7] Correspondència de Souchy, Agustín. ANC, Barcelona, ANC1-886-T-3157. Image 15/101.

[8] Card of Pablo Polgare. CDMH, Salamanca, DNSD-Secretaría, Fichero No. 52, P0138549 to P013555.

[9] Letter by Pablo Polgare. 1938, CDMH, Salamanca, PS-MADRID, 1188, 43.

272   A. DÍAZ-REGAÑÓN LABAJO

In early 1936, the CNT-FAI Foreign Propaganda Office promoted *Impressions of the Spanish Revolution: July 19, 1936*, which included exclusive illustrations by José Luis Rey Vila under the name "Sim," some of which were reproduced in *Life* on February 22, 1937 (34–36). It was printed by the collectivized Grafos in Barcelona. The reception was enthusiastic, and it continued to be advertised in various periodicals, such as *Spanish Revolution*, long after the events of May 1937, during which factions on the Republican side engaged one another in street battles in Catalonia, ending with government control over the anarchists in the region.

The success of *Impressions* led Emma Goldman to suggest that Souchy should target the English-speaking anarchist networks and engage the mainstream press in the United States and Canada. Souchy and his team did not follow the suggestion (Otayek, "Keepsakes" 312), but the CNT's next project was more ambitious and used several languages. It was commissioned to Kati Horna, after being entrusted with the bureau's photographic agency from January to June 1937 (González et al. 10).

Entitled *España? A Picture Book of Horror Tales and Fascist Calumnies*, the 20 × 25 cm illustrated book was written in Spanish, French, English, and Swedish. It challenged the characterizations of anarchist control in large portions of Catalonia and Aragón as a reign of terror, by then a recurring subject in much of the international mainstream press. Drawing from her expertise as a photographer and *photomonteur* and her acquaintance with the narrative in the illustrated press, Horna produced a noteworthy account of what Spanish anarchists viewed as a revolutionary order. With nearly forty pages, the album follows an imaginative outline in which sensationalist headlines from the European right-wing press, caricatures, and numerous photographs taken by Horna in Barcelona, Aragón, and Valencia demonstrate the reality of everyday life in anarchist-controlled territories. The images are treated as an unequivocal testimony of truth, but they are also used to demystify the goodness of the rebels:

> The stupid and coarse lies spread by the fascists are innumerable. Fascist planes bombarded schools. Children at tender age were torn to pieces by shrapnel.—And the photographs of this little corpses were published in the fascist press with the title: "Bolshevik hordes assassinate the sons of national[10] parents." This also is horrible. (CNT-FAI Foreign Propaganda Office)

---

[10] Consider that the word "national" here refers to the Francoist rebels or *nacionales*.

Text, drawings, and photographs shape a continuous collage to create a story of a triumphant social revolution. Except for the front and back covers, which use the anarchist red and black, the entire interior is in black and white. The topics to consider are multiple: the evolution of the war and the imminent capture of Madrid, carelessness for children, food shortage and hunger, destruction and desecration of churches, sacking of artistic heritage, treatment of enemy prisoners, and so on.

It is never mentioned that the pictures belong to Kati Horna, in neither the album itself nor the bibliographic description of the preserved artifacts in the CDMH library. The literature on photography or illustrated magazines did not mention it either, until 2016 in an article by Otayek ("Keepsakes" 302–27) from the United States and in 2017 in my work (Díaz-R. Labajo, 466). However, the discovery is quite clear once you view the album: you come across Horna's work.[11]

The cover itself is one of Horna's iconic images: a young, smiling militiaman of the Ascaso Division (photo No. 30), likely from March 1937, during Horna's first trip to Aragón. The militiaman's silhouette is cut out, with an arm on his hip and a sweater with the FAI and CNT flags. He is precisely placed over the anarchist flag colors, facing his alter ego, the drawing of an ugly, ferocious anarchist carrying a bomb and a severed head. Without a doubt, the image the rebel's propaganda spread was what the album aspires to eradicate (Fig. 11.1).

A controversial theme addressed in the album is the Catalan authorities' appropriation of religious buildings through a policy on artistic heritage safeguarding. Contrary to the bad press about burning churches, they protected many religious buildings (CNT-FAI 19). This was the case for the Cathedral of Barcelona: originally the Assault Guards protected the building and saved it from burning. Soon after, on July 21, 1936, the Catalan government confiscated the buildings and protected them from sackings, burnings, and desecrations (Gudiol i Ricart 90). Several photographs report this event as "Church in Barcelona" (photo No. 159), in which a poster showing protection by the authorities hangs next to the blessing *Salvator Mundi* Christ.

Also in Barcelona, the Church of Our Lady of Bethlehem is shown covered by posters against fascism (photo No. 158). It was burned on July 19, 1936, and only the façade and lateral walls remained. Other churches

[11] Full document accessible in Biblioteca Digital (AHCB), Arxiu Històric de la Ciutat de Barcelona, Spain, https://ahcbdigital.bcn.cat/ca/biblioteca/visualitzador/ahcb-d021436.

Fig. 11.1 CNT-FAI Foreign Propaganda Office of CNT. *España?* 1938. CDMH, Salamanca, CDMH BIB FA00431 001

were used as warehouses for sacks and barrels of vinegar and wine, such as one in the province of Teruel (photo No. 49). Although unidentified, it is surely the Church of the Piarist School in Alcañiz, where several disputes between the religious and the anarchists occurred in which the priests were eventually killed. Later, as the image shows, the building was confiscated and reused (CNT-FAI 21). Churches were not closed down: they remained open for religious purposes or to serve as hospitals or food distribution centers.

Another remarkable issue covered in *España?* is refuge and assisting displaced people, particularly the elderly and children. The centers in Vélez-Rubio and Alcázar de Cervantes were not the only ones Horna knew: she also visited several in Barcelona and one in Gandía, Valencia.

Although a headline had reported that fifty thousand children were roaming around Spain, *España?* defends the work of the Consejo de la Escuela Nueva Unificada (CENU), a project promoted by the Catalan government to create a free, secular, coeducational school. It was first established as a committee in Barcelona on June 27, 1936, soon after the military coup d'état as part of the revolutionary process of forming the Antifascist Militias, and it had great prominence until May 1937 (Cortavitarte Carral 147–53).

During the time the public school system depended on CENU, approximately 128,000 school posts were created, covering more than 80% of the existing deficit. The lack of resources during the conflict led new schools to be created in private mansions and factories that had been confiscated and prepared for educational needs. The CENU involved the CNT in children's camps or *colonias* in places such as Figueres, Olot, and Banyoles (Navarro 174–5).

In these camps and schools, children lived healthy lives, enjoying fresh air and sunlight far away from the horrors of war. The open-air schooling process is exhibited in several pictures from the series "Children's Center in Barcelona's Surroundings," likely referring to a location in Puente Rodrigo. In the series, young teachers are surrounded by boys and girls attending to their lessons (photos Nos. 161 and 160). The children appear to be clean, adequately clothed, and in good health. Some of them are listening carefully, some are distracted, and some are looking toward the photographer, beyond the field of vision (CNT-FAI 15).

The educational scenes continue with children reading, drawing, and practicing gymnastic exercises. All the shots of this report (photos Nos. 164, 165, and unknown) have in common the same group of students (CNT-FAI 17). Although the photographs all suggest that the children's gestures and movements were spontaneous, it can be assumed that the scenes were prepared for the visitors and photographer. As this series tries to show, children during this time were not wandering the streets, forming bad habits, or being chased by anarchists and communists.

Prisons and the treatment of prisoners is another aspect that the album aims to clarify. It shows the interior of the Penitentiary Center in Barcelona, known as *Cárcel Modelo* because it served as a model for other Spanish prisons. The images include cells, common corridors and aisles, the library, bundles for the prisoners, guards, and so on (CNT-FAI 33). Photograph No. 119 shows the vaults and superior galleries with prisoners leaning out into the central corridor, undoubtedly attracted by the visit. Moreover, this image is representative of Horna's photographic technique: the shot is directed from the bottom left corner toward the background on the top

276   A. DÍAZ-REGAÑÓN LABAJO

right corner (a low-angle shot), a straight but inclined outline with a clear use of perspective, and representative of the New Vision.

Additional topics were also depicted in the album. Settled in Barcelona, Horna traveled to Aragón and Valencia to produce the reports she was commissioned for, and the CNT granted her access to restricted areas. Horna's interest in showing ordinary life in the rear-guard, working men and women, the means of transport, and the market's supply can be seen in the album's pages. Reports and poses are complemented with the spontaneity of her flâneur spirit, shooting buildings, objects, and people while they continue living as life—and war—goes on in the Ramblas and the red-light district in Barcelona.[12]

The scope of the album is difficult to measure. It was thought to be published in early 1937, given that the introduction is dated April of that year. However, it was not actually published until March 1938. Otayek suggests that Souchy and his team lacked coordination in the timely flow of information and materials through transnational networks ("Keepsakes" 312). At the same time, the rapid deterioration of the situation in Spain impaired the CNT-FAI's efforts to gather support abroad. By the time the Foreign Propaganda Office started dispatching copies of *España?* the embattled Republican government, pressured by the Soviet Union, had stripped anarchists of their effective power. For all practical purposes, the revolution was finished. It also seems that the company in charge of reproducing the album was more than six months delayed in the delivery and increased the print prices at a time when the anarchist bureau could not afford it.[13]

CNT considered the album to be hard to sell inside Spain. At least 7000 copies were dispatched to individuals and groups in numerous countries, but *España?* went largely unnoticed in the United States (Otayek, "Keepsakes" 319). This result contrasts with the remarkable success of *Impressions* in engaging audiences beyond the anarchist movement.

Nevertheless, *España?* was not the only attempt at promoting the loyalist story through Horna's photographs among international agencies. These cases are examined in the following section.

---

[12] Horna, Kati. "In the streets of the red-light district in Barcelona". CDMH, Salamanca, photo No. 129, http://pares.mcu.es/ParesBusquedas20/catalogo/show/118115.

[13] Foreign Propaganda Office of CNT-FAI to Industrias Gráficas Seix Barral. 12 March 1938, *The Amsterdam Boxes.*

The International Scope of Horna's Photographs

Regarding the international stage, Spanish studies have usually considered Horna's work not to have been spread outside Spain during the war, as explained above. However, since 2016, this idea has started to change under the new approaches to her photos.

In 2016, a series of three flyers or pamphlets were identified in Salamanca under the general title *Aid for Spain*, promoted by the Ministry of Labor and Social Assistance. They were printed by a collectivized photolithography business, Fotolitografía Barguño E.C., in Barcelona. Written in English, they are thought to be part of the foreign propaganda in favor of the Republican government.

These materials focus on the civilians whose lives were most affected by the war: refugees and those evacuated from the bombed cities of the South. Each flyer is dedicated to a specific issue, including the elderly, women in their roles as mothers, and the displaced in general. The text is anonymous, as are the drawings and pictures. Once "Amsterdam Boxes" becomes digitized and available to the public, additional images should be able to be identified, but for now it is sure that only one brochure reproduced photographs taken by Kati Horna.

This brochure is *Aid for Woman*,[14] which was dated August 1937. At that time, Horna had already abandoned Photo SPA and started working for *Umbral*. However, the pamphlets were edited and funded by the Oficina General de Evacuación y Refugiados, which adopted that name in January 1938.

Similar to her photographic album, *Aid for Women* includes text, photographs, and drawings that intermingle to create collages. The central drawing represents a mother nursing her baby, a hand separating them from the battlefield. The outline followed is the same in the interior of all the pamphlets: a drawing on the top left corner presents the problem, then a text explains the action directed at the institutions in charge of assisting the victims, and another drawing on the bottom right corner represents the emotional and physical recovery of the victims thanks to the assistance program.

According to the pamphlet, women and children were the main targets of the rebels, so they needed a preferential place in the Republic. The Oficina General de Evacuación y Refugiados was in charge of three million

---

[14] Hojas de propaganda. CDMH, Salamanca, Panfletos, P0086-1, 2, 3.

278   A. DÍAZ-REGAÑÓN LABAJO

people, all refugees and evacuees, and funded two maternity homes, one in Fuente Podrida, Valencia, and the other in Vélez-Rubio, Almería (Clavijo 161), the latter of which Horna visited. In these wards, they handled birth and postpartum care and taught mothers hygienic and medical care for newborns—that is, the "scientific care" of children, assisted by specialist doctors and nurses. By receiving this care, women would become "perfect mothers" raising "men of the future," of the Republican future, indeed.[15]

The back page includes four photographs and a brief text near the exposition. The photograph on the top right corner belongs to the series "Committee for Refugees in Alcázar de Cervantes," a village now known as Alcázar de San Juan, in the province of Ciudad Real. It shows a woman with her two children eating in the dining room the Committee for Refugees created in that municipality. The photograph's negative has not been preserved, and neither this picture nor any from the series are dated, although some were published in different magazines in October 1937.

The other pictures are cuttings from shots No. 99 and No. 100, from the series "Scenes in a Refugee Center in Vélez-Rubio," dated August 1937.[16] As can be seen, these pictures attest to the effort and care for children, newborn babies, and mothers in this maternity home. This center was created to care for refugees from Madrid, although many of them came from the massacre of the Malaga-Almería highway, popularly known as *La Desbandá*, and it was promoted by the Ministry of Health under Federica Montseny.

In addition to appearing in pamphlets, Horna's photos were published in the foreign illustrated press when Photo SPA was born in April 1937. The illustrated press had already achieved a critical role during the interwar period. Although starting earlier, the idea of a purely photographic magazine was revived in 1936 by Henry Luce, publisher of *Time* and *Fortune*. The previously haphazard taking and publishing of pictures had been replaced by the "mind-guided camera" (Newhall 229–30). During the Spanish Civil War, press photography and magazines played a fundamental role in narrating the events. The technological changes in photography throughout the first decades of the twentieth century allowed the

---

[15] Hojas de propaganda. CDMH, Salamanca, Panfletos, P0086-2.

[16] Horna, Kati. "Scenes in a Refugee Center in Vélez-Rubio". Aug. 1937, CDMH, Salamanca, photos No. 100, http://pares.mcu.es/ParesBusquedas20/catalogo/show/118351 and No. 99, http://pares.mcu.es/ParesBusquedas20/catalogo/show/118084.

"visual communication of facts" to be born during the Spanish Civil War (Colombo 17). In the period of mass communication, a new and powerful domain of participation, emotion, outrage, and exaltation was built, identical to life but framed and "staged."

Paul Polgare became the Photo SPA agency manager in April 1937, and Horna was its official photographer[17] until the agency moved to Valencia in July. As stated earlier, Photo SPA was a self-managed, independent agency. It supplied photos to the proletariat press and bourgeois journals through the distributor Imago Photo Service. According to Rubio, during this time Horna shot 300 photographs, 296 of which were sent to Paris.

From what is known, a few of Horna's pictures were published in April in a Swedish journal and the British *Weekly Illustrated*. León and Otayek collected this work in 2016 (Goldman). The report in *Weekly Illustrated* had an anonymous author and was published as a full page on December 3, 1938 (I–II).[18] It includes seven pictures with a brief text that discusses the "heroic Spanish people" in their fight and resistance against the rebels. The text commented on the ferocity and resilience of the civilians, who had a "fierce, proud and unconquerable" spirit after two years of conflicts. The final sentence is absolutely solemn: "They may be killed, but they will never be defeated."

The first group of photographs, Nos. 148 "Marina Street. Bombings in March" and 179 "Bombed Houses," belongs to a series taken in Barcelona during the bombings on March 17 and 18, 1938. Curiously, the original low-angle shot that Horna used to take was corrected in picture No. 148 for publishing, making the building straighter and higher. Photo No. 179 shows multiple belongings piled up and saved after the bombings—it is reminiscent of her work featuring the accumulation of typical flea market objects in Paris, now with a quite different background.

A second theme refers again to the evacuation center in Vélez-Rubio, Almería, and the Committee for Refugees in Alcázar de Cervantes, in Ciudad Real (Nos. 99 and 105), except in these images, the foregrounds have been cropped to focus on the babies and the mother eating with her baby.

---

[17] It appears now to be under the name "Catalina Partos" (Rubio 31).

[18] *Whitehot Magazine of Contemporary Art*, https://whitehotmagazine.com//UserFiles/image/b/1b/ddeca0145e66b2894cdc8ae7e96db85f.jpg.

280   A. DÍAZ-REGAÑÓN LABAJO

A different story is told about leisure time at the front, represented with two images depicting scenes of the Ascaso Division in the areas of Banastás and Monte Carrascal in Huesca. These pictures (Nos. 24 "Scenes in Monte Carrascal" and 53 "Meal. Ascaso Division") belong to a series taken in March 1937, almost a year before the final battle, when Horna took a second series in Aragón. Here the militiamen pose for the photographer or are portrayed in their daily lives while waiting for battle.

While few records have been recovered about Horna's published works in international magazines, the circulation of her photographs in the Spanish circuits was larger, as discussed in the next section.

HORNA'S PHOTOS IN SPANISH ILLUSTRATED MAGAZINES

Kati Horna cooperated with several Spanish magazines during the Civil War, all of which were exclusively allocated for libertarian ideals. Publishing periodicals was central to the grassroots organizing and fundraising strategies of anarchists everywhere.

After working for Photo SPA, she put her camera into service in July 1937 as graphics editor for *Umbral*, although she also collaborated with *Tierra y Libertad*, *Tiempos Nuevos*, *Libre Studio*, and *Mujeres Libres*, aligned with the CNT propaganda agenda. Despite readjustments after the events of May 1937, Horna's vantage point as a foreign woman and press collaborator with close ties to those running the anarchists' propaganda machine gave her privileged insight into the shortcomings of their revolutionary agenda. In the following text, I refer to the most significant contents.

Umbral, subtitled *Semanario de la Nueva Era*, was published between July 1937 and January 1939, with some interruptions. Sixty-two editions were published, two of which were special editions. The first twenty were published in Valencia, and starting in January 1938, publishing occurred in Barcelona. It was a weekly journal, but funding problems and the progression of the war made it difficult. Horna continued collaborating with *Umbral* through 1939, even though she had abandoned Spain in mid-1938.

Horna's understanding of the media potential of the printed page made *Umbral* an illustrated magazine that combined text, drawings, and photographs, following the avant-garde style already mentioned. Its print technique was the rotogravure, and it was composed of different types of articles: national and international news, theater, cinema, health, and, of course, war propaganda. Overall, it discussed the anarchist contribution to war and revolution.

Photographs authored by Horna appeared early, in the second edition, on July 17, 1937. Although it is uncommon to see Horna's pictures in every issue, she was one of the regular photographers, along with Pérez de Rozas, Mauro Bajatierra, M. Santos Yubero, Vidal Corella, and "Finezas." Her final work published there, although taken long before, appears in No. 60, January 7, 1939. Her most active period was from September 1937 to April 1938. In fact, during this time, she started to sign her photographs with "Fotos Kati."

Horna's first cover in *Umbral* is photo No. 27, again from the series of the Ascaso Division (March 1937).[19] The militiaman portrayed was known as "Pacho Villa." A symbol of the struggle, the photo narrates the story of a man "done in" by the hazards of war and a hard life, demonstrating his warrior look and rifle.

One of Horna's most sensitive and representative series is that of the final battle of Teruel and the evacuation of the population, produced during her second visit to the front in Aragón. This series is dated December 24, 1937, Christmas Eve, and includes eighteen shots (photos Nos. 1 to 18).

The photo "Civilians Evacuated from Teruel and Militiamen Arriving" (No. 1) was the cover of *Umbral*, No. 21, January 8, 1938,[20] and it represents the evacuation as an escape toward freedom. Consider that when this edition went public, definite defeat had not happened yet. Here two groups of people meet on a road: in one direction, those arriving (the militiamen), and in the opposite, those leaving (women and children resting and letting the others pass). The scene shows a moment of greetings and conversation, of spontaneity, as the militiamen continue walking and turn their heads to look at the women (in close-up), just as one has stopped to talk to them (middle ground). The shot's point of interest is the women's white headscarves, using light in the photographer's interest. Rhythm flows through the photograph's narrative.

---

[19] *Umbral.* No. 3, 24 July 1937, Hemeroteca Digital, Biblioteca Nacional de España (BNE), Madrid, Spain, https://hemerotecadigital.bne.es/hd/es/viewer?id=e889f791-e72d-4584-bd0f-edcbe5b840ea.

[20] *Umbral.* No. 21, 8 Jan. 1938, BNE, https://hemerotecadigital.bne.es/hd/es/viewer?id=8acfef99-903d-465b-909d-4180c325f6e3.

Mujeres Libres (Free Women), an anarchist movement that promoted women's emancipation in 1936, was founded by physician Amparo Poch y Gascón, journalist Mercedes Comaposada Guillén, and Lucía Sánchez Saornil, distinguished member of Solidaridad Antifascista Internacional (SIA). They thought that the problems of the female proletariat in bourgeois society were specific and different from those of males. Their main aim was to free women from triple slavery: of ignorance, gender, and work (Sánchez Blanco 229–38). According to Nash, about 20,000 activists were in this organization, with 170 local groups throughout Spain (127).

Before 1935, an open debate in *Solidaridad Obrera* had started about women's marginalization in the libertarian movement being a male problem. Sexist attitudes, traditional roles, feminine sexualization, male hegemony, and so on all contributed to diminishing women's participation in anarchist organizations. Sánchez Saornil suggested that specific propaganda should be delivered to male and female activists and proposed the creation of an expressive tool particularly for and by women. Mujeres Libres became the first organization to join both ideals: feminism and revolution. It was the first large organization that attempted to put anarcho-feminism into practice, and its efforts gained momentum during the war (Nash 129).

The initial principles of Free Women were essentially cultural and educational, and its magazine *Mujeres Libres* was an efficient tool to spread the organization's ideals. The first edition appeared in May 1936, an attempt at a monthly journal; but the publishing dates were uneven, probably because it received scarce support from most libertarian sectors. The last editions were published in 1938, and a final edition went public when the front reached Barcelona (Nash 102). However, no copy has remained. For *Umbral*, it was printed by Fotolitografía Barguño.

When considering Kati Horna's work, it is clear that she gave prominence to women as a portrayed subject. This aspect leads to the assumption that she frequently cooperated with *Mujeres Libres*. However, a detailed analysis of the magazine shows that this happened on just a few occasions in 1938, and only one photo is authored "Foto Katti." Again, "Amsterdam Boxes" will confirm or correct this.

Nevertheless, the topics she featured were intimately anarchist: motherhood and female peasants. As an example of the first case, a woman in close-up nursing her baby (photo No. 97) was published in No. 11 of

Mujeres Libres, a photo taken in Vélez-Rubio, this time to illustrate the article "Motherhood."[21]

Additionally, the female agrarian proletariat was a theme with little representation in Horna's published work until No. 13 of *Mujeres Libres.*[22] The series (photos Nos. 88 to 96) was taken in September 1937, when Horna photographed female peasants in a vineyard on the road between Madrid and Alcalá de Henares. The subjects include a mother and her daughter in their work clothes, mainly depicted in American shots. Their faces show the anguish of those working in full sunshine, a praise to women who fight every day to get ahead.

POSTERS AND PHOTOMONTAGES: WHERE ARTISTIC TECHNIQUES COME TOGETHER

The format of propaganda posters underwent major development based on the use of the photomontage technique, a process Dadaists and Constructivists had already implemented. The Republicans used posters prolifically—although others did as well—and the most renowned artists were Renau, Monleón, Bardassano, and Amster. Spanish anarchism had some of the greatest graphic designers of the period, including Arturo Ballester, Vicente Ballester, and Muro. In posters, several techniques came together, such as drawing, lithography, rotogravure, and spraying paint with compressed air. This combination shaped the expressive force of the message, the rhythm of the typographic composition, and the vibrant colors (Brihuega 36–45; Satué 46–54).

However, no evidence exists of Kati Horna's personal dedication to creating posters. In fact, neither her photography nor her authorship is mentioned in the large collection of Civil War posters. In the file "José Mario Armero" of the CDMH in Salamanca, more than three thousand posters exist, and only three of them contain images by Horna,[23] although her name is not identified in the inventory's description. They were all created for the circulation and propaganda of *Umbral.* The preserved negatives allowed me to locate at least two more posters edited by FAI and

---

[21] *Mujeres Libres.* No. 11, 1938, Confederación General del Trabajo (CGT), https://cgt.org.es/wp-content/uploads/2017/10/Mujeres-Libres-11_0.pdf, pp. 9–10.

[22] *Mujeres Libres.* No. 13, 1938, CGT, https://cgt.org.es/wp-content/uploads/2017/10/Mujeres-Libres-13.pdf, p. 7.

[23] Fondo Armero, José Mario. CDMH, ARMERO, Carteles, 82, 70 and 83.

284   A. DÍAZ-REGAÑÓN LABAJO

other prints that indicate there were further attempts. Although it is not certain that all the images belong to Horna, at least the negatives and themes can be attributed to her.

Phototypography and photomontage, critical tools in avant-garde proposals (Sougez 303), are combined here to welcome an anarchist icon, the prototype of the Ascaso Division militiaman featured in *España?* The poster is dated June 20, 1937, from Barcelona, according to the handwriting on the back.[24] The same photo is used in a photomontage in honor of anarchist Buenaventura Durruti in *Umbral*, No. 19, November 20, 1937.[25]

The other two posters promote *Umbral* in an attempt to reach a wider audience beyond the anarchists. Both use the division of society in professions as a reference: the first one dated July 9, 1938, with the triad proletariat–peasantry–soldiers, and the second broadening the range. In both cases, women are included.

In the first poster, at least one photograph (topmost) belongs to Horna (No. 81), depicting a peasant from a rice collectivity in Silla, Valencia, in July 1937. On the second, the photomontage reproduces the shape of a soldier's head, a silhouette composed of eight images, two of them Horna's: a female (photo No. 93, "Peasants in a Vineyard on the Way from Madrid to...," September 1937, also published in *Tierra y Libertad*, No. 22, June 18, 1938) and a male (No. 79, "Rice Collectivity in Silla").[26]

Reflecting a clear anarchist theme, these agrarian workers are represented in the typical clothes of Spanish Mediterranean rice and vinegar farmers. In the original picture, other typical elements can be seen: whitewashed walls, canes for pushing the boats, clay vessels, rice sacks, and so on. Several of Kati Horna's series allow examining how her ethnographic work was influenced by the anarchist perspective—not only the series about rice farmers in Silla, female peasants in vineyards in Madrid, and sheep shepherds in Aragón but also the series about women and children in Valencia and Barcelona, the markets and red-light districts, and the

---

[24] "Forthcoming: Magazine of the People, Umbral, 16 Large Photogravure Pages For a better view, visit SPAIN". 1937, Museo Nacional Centro de Arte Reina Sofia (MNCA Reina Sofia), Madrid, Spain, https://www.museoreinasofia.es/en/collection/artwork/proximamente-umbral-revista-pueblo-soon-umbral-revista-pueblo.

[25] *Umbral*. No. 19, 20 Nov. 1937, BNE, https://hemerotecadigital.bne.es/hd/es/viewer?id=09c676b1-b579-405d-9d6f-8a0494717c18.

[26] "Umbral, Weekly Graphic Publication in Photogravure". 1938, MNCA Reina Sofia, https://www.museoreinasofia.es/en/collection/artwork/umbral-semanario-grafico-huecograbado-umbral-weekly-graphic-publication.

11 HOW TO NARRATE A WAR: KATI HORNA'S PHOTOGRAPHY... 285

churches and traditional architecture. She portrayed loneliness, the situation of the outcast, and traditional workers in the war context—a narrative and visual field in which speech on cultural marginalization and resistance is built and shaped. Those viewing the photographs can consider what is and is not seen in them, as Horna moves in what Buxó calls "ambiguous borders" (13).

Horna creates her own visual narrative, and as Ruby explains, "photographs are seen as socially constructed artifacts that tell us something about the culture depicted as well as the culture of the picture taker" (1346). An aesthetic component also exists, as the author's taste prompts her to choose specific compositions that explain her personal concept of beauty. The ways that artists choose the elements and frame them reveal their preferences for the sphere of expression (Brisset).

Additional negatives and experiments of other sharp, intense, and emotional posters and photomontages exist. They are quite interesting because they show her creative process, and they also mark the beginning of her collaboration with José Horna. Having met in 1938 in the context of their involvement with *Umbral*, they soon became lifelong collaborators.

This collaboration can be observed in photo No. 272[27] that belongs to a photographic glass plate used to create the photomontage. It is a rare exception in a mass of cellulose nitrate of 6 × 6 mm. Published as the cover of *Tierra y Libertad*, No. 10, March 10, 1938, it also became a poster promoting FAI (photo No. 186) to define the suffering that fascism caused. The tension of the scene is described by a bombed house framing the profile in a waist shot of an elderly woman and a child's face looking down.

Although the CDMH inventory attributes its complete authorship to Kati Horna, this project is surely one of those the couple created together, having two signatures assembled on the bottom right: the surname "Horna"—clearly José Horna's signature in his own works[28]—over the name "Kati," as she usually signed as "Fotos Kati."

Another montage used the image of this elderly woman placed over the penitentiary center of Barcelona. Published in *Umbral*, No. 24, January

---

[27] Horna, Kati. "Glass Palte for Film Projection...". CDMH, Salamanca, photo No. 272, http://pares.mcu.es/ParesBusquedas20/catalogo/show/118272.
[28] To consider José Horna's signature as an author, visit *Umbral*. No. 15, 23 Oct. 1937, BNE, https://hemerotecadigital.bne.es/hd/es/viewer?id=534d99d2-c48c-4190-940c-c877b64a0291, p. 3.

29, 1939,[29] when Horna no longer resided in Spain, it belongs to the short series "Model Prison in Barcelona" (Nos. 119, 120, and 121).
Other negatives show evidence of different designs and montages. Clearly influenced by surrealism, photo No. 184 depicts a woman's eye meeting a wall's window, providing clear identification of eyesight and a

[29] *Umbral.* No. 24, 29 Jan. 1938, BNE, https://hemerotecadigital.bne.es/hd/es/viewer?id=feaa77ba-3335-4220-ac1a-1fc971b9b92e, p. 6.

Fig. 11.2 Kati Horna. "The Spanish Woman Before the Revolution." March 1938. CDMH, Salamanca, photo No. 184

window as vehicles of connection with the outer world. The woman has ringleted, dark hair typical of Spanish folklore (no negative preserved), and the stairs head toward the cathedral in the Gothic District in Barcelona (photo No. 169) (Fig. 11.2).

According to the CDMH inventory, various posters with this photomontage were published, including one in *Libre Studio*, March 1938, titled "The Spanish Woman Before the Revolution" and on the back cover of *Umbral*, No. 29, March 31, 1938, as part of the collage "We Fight Until Death or Victory."[30]

As the war progressed and the Republican government was forced to control the left-wing factions in a desperate struggle to contain Franco's advance, the anarchists' revolutionary order fell apart. Anarchist groups engaged in vicious internal polemics, and Horna began drifting away from those clinging to a dogmatic commitment to the revolution, including Partos, who remained involved with the CNT's Foreign Propaganda Office (Horna Fernández 9, Otayek, "Loss" 22).

Rather than expressing revolutionary enthusiasm, many of Horna's works during her last months in Spain reveal awareness of the likely defeat. Among her most traumatic experiences during this period were the fall of Teruel and the air raids in Barcelona in 1938, which left a powerful imprint on some of her work.

THE LAST FRONTIER: A PHOTOGRAPHER IN MEXICO

In 1938, once again in Barcelona, her relationship with Spain and her former husband passed the point of no return. According to Rubio, in the beginning of that year, Kati and José Horna would have started a relationship beyond professional interest, and in June 1938, she and Paul Polgare made their last journey together to Paris to buy photographic material (38).[31] This fact is the last connection between Horna and the CNT in Spain, as she did not return to Barcelona. She finally abandoned the libertarian utopia to which she had committed herself.

In Paris, she waited for José Horna to cross the Pyrenees. Once in France, they decided to go into exile in Mexico. While waiting to arrange credentials, she continued producing work, using the 270 negatives she

[30] *Umbral*. No. 29, 31 March 1938, BNE, https://hemerotecadigital.bne.es/hd/es/view er?id=310b6207-856c-4de7-9989-b6ab8de1f194, p. 16.

[31] Although Polgare appears in the document, she does not. Receipt. 1938, CDMH, Salamanca PS-MADRID,1188,43.

288   A. DÍAZ-REGAÑÓN LABAJO

managed to take with her, which today rest in Salamanca. The other 522 negatives were hidden in the CNT in Barcelona, and they were moved from there to Oxford and finally to Amsterdam in 1947, where they were discovered almost sixty years later.

Most of her published work from this time includes several series of photomontages, created in cooperation with José Horna, that recall defeat and the war's miseries, the fear and solitude of inert objects, and buildings in low-angle shots.[32] Here, the most famous series were "What Goes to Garbage" and "Fearing Dolls," published in Paris in 1939.

With the help of the Mexican ambassador Narciso Bassols, Horna received new documents, as her Hungarian passport had been annulled (Otayek, "Loss" 29, 39). She then moved to Mexico under a new identity: a Spanish woman born in Jaén called Catalina Fernández Blau.[33] According to this documentation, she and José Horna were already married. The couple arrived in Veracruz in October 1939.

In Mexico, she took her second husband's surname, although she chose "Catalina Fernández" as her nom de plume (Rubio 39). Nevertheless, she continued being known as Kati Horna. She lived in Mexico City for the remainder of her life, and she died on October 19, 2000.

In December 1939, she published her first series in Mexico, starting a long engagement with the country's illustrated press. Her technical skills and aesthetic sensibility helped her be easily incorporated into the expanding Mexican publishing industry, although adapting to the country's culture was probably not as easy. In time, the Hornas became part of a tight-knit community of exiled artists and intellectuals in Mexico City, and their home and workshop in Colonia Roma developed into a place for gathering and creation. Moreover, working as a field photographer for numerous periodicals gave her access to a variety of social, political, and cultural networks, creating an eclectic group of friends. Names such as Remedios Varo, Leonora Carrington, Chiki Weisz, Gunther Gerzso,

---

[32] Horna, Kati and José Horna. "Childhood". 1939, https://www.museoreinasofia.es/en/collection/artwork/lenfance-childhood; "Mussolini: Sporting Dictator". 1938, https://www.museoreinasofia.es/en/collection/artwork/mussolini-dictador-deportivo-mussolini-sporting-dictator, and [Untitled], 1938, https://www.museoreinasofia.es/en/collection/artwork/sin-titulo-untitled-468, MNCA Reina Sofia.

[33] Identification Card. Registro Nacional de Extranjeros, Archivo General de la Nación (AGN), Mexico. Digital copy in Archivo General de la Administración (AGA), Madrid, REIM, 083, 099.

Edward James, Beatriz Sheridan, and Victor Flores Olea were part of this group (Otayek, "Loss" 30–1).

She alternated between commissioned works and series, experiments, and private works, some in collaboration with her husband. The bitter experience of the Civil War left a deep mark on her, despite occupying less than two years of her lifetime. Thenceforth, Horna maintained a deeply critical posture toward all types of dogmatism. Through her works she reflected on the failure of political illusion and the suffering caused by uprooting; however, she understood how to leverage the new opportunities that Mexico offered (Horna Fernández 9). She did not support any political movement as she had done in Spain, yet she remained faithful to the socially disadvantaged.

During her long career in Mexico, three main fields stand out among her vast body of photographic work. First, the series in La Castañeda mental asylum in the outskirts of Mexico City is an example of her social photography that underscores a sense of criticality toward Mexican urban modernity. The series, published in *Nosotros* on July 22, 1944, was commissioned to praise the government's commitment to patients' well-being. Nevertheless, some of the pictures seem to highlight the lack of care and almost negligence toward the patients (Otayek, "Loss" 32). The most remarkable and famous photograph of this series was "The Enlightened One,"[34] a portrait of a patient. Through Spanish eyes, the image is reminiscent of the Baroque imagery of a crucified Christ asking his father to be released from torment. The series also recalls her work in refugee centers and the red-light districts in Barcelona.

Second, a variety of personal series date back to the beginning of the 1960s, considered to be the creative peak of her career. The subject matter of her photographic commissions for magazines such as *Arquitectura México* and *Mujeres* extended to her life experiences and questions of gender, belonging, and transcendence. She moved from large-scale architecture to the architecture of the uncanny, from articles on the work of creative women to magical stories. When discussing architecture and design, Horna's practice was definitely urban, registering the effects of the industrialization and the fast-growing developmentalist urbanism from the 1940s to the 1970s. Her photos become a testimony of the rapid

---

[34] Horna, Kati. "El iluminado". 1944, *Arts Summary, A Visual Journal*, https://i0.wp.com/artssummary.com/wp-content/uploads/2016/09/1-el-iluminado-the-iluminated-19447.jpg?ssl=1.

290   A. DÍAZ-REGAÑÓN LABAJO

expansion of the Mexican metropolis, connecting shots and perspectives to those she learned during her stay in Germany.

Third, in 1962, for the journal *S.nob*, she conceived of a series including "Ode to Necrophilia," "Artificial Paradises," and "History of a Vampire: It Happened in Coyoacán,"[35] set in an atmosphere of ludic complicity between her and some of her closest friends, who she photographed (Degano 67–77). Probably the nearest series to surrealism, they are marked by symbolism and a meditation on love, loss, and mourning. *S.nob*'s provocative agenda offered her a place to develop irreverent content and a daring design. It is also her greatest period of artistic experimentation: in *S.nob* she approaches a specifically Mexican anthropology of the death, where life and death merge, walking away from her European production.

CONCLUSION

Throughout this chapter, I have demonstrated the strong influence that the cultural movements of the interwar period had on Kati Horna's photography. Specifically, this essay has focused on the techniques, genres, and themes she learned and later practiced during her Spanish experience, which was a small part of her career. It is difficult to categorize her into one artistic movement, as she practiced many of them. She even tried to distance herself from any label that could imprison her personal vision.

Some elements endure in her photography career: the survivor's condition, melancholy, and the feeling of loss and uprooting. Having reached her creative maturity in Mexico in the early 1960s, she continued creating photo stories that explored the themes of love, death, concealment, delights, and displacement, representing what she not only saw but also lived. Her collaborative spirit, techniques, and themes remained.

Some interruptions occurred once she arrived in Mexico. Her trajectory as a politicized woman in interwar Europe was later kept private in exile. She experienced a process of political education, then political practice, and finally a political withdrawal caused by the hard experience of the war. Portraying the marginalized was no longer one of her main subjects, becoming only occasional.

---

[35] Horna, Kati. "Serie 'Oda a la necrofilia' and 'Paraísos artificiales'". 1962, Museo Amparo, Puebla, https://museoamparo.com/colecciones/pieza/3983/serie-oda-a-la-necrofilia-y-paraisos-artificiales-los-fetiches-de-s-nob-de-kati-horna.

Moreover, considering that she lived in a country with a robust tradition of folklorist photography such as Mexico, it is worth mentioning that she hardly photographed the country's indigenous traditions or the rural countryside as she had in Spain. However, she incorporated into her work the daily inevitable experience of death, following the Mexican codes for living and sharing the mourning; a theme she indirectly represented in Spain through destruction, loneliness, and desolation.

In Mexico, she remained an urban photographer. In her photographs from that time, piled objects, isolated statues out of context, ruined buildings, and furniture still appear, but there are no people in the cafés, drunkards in the streets, shoppers at the flea markets, peasants working, or children playing. Instead, she continued narrating stories with portraits and photomontages.

The permanent themes in Horna's work are her personal sense of humor, the consistent use of irony, the intersection between fine art and popular media, the conscious inclusion of psychology and memory, and the transgression of the boundaries proposed by the dominant discourse of the period. Whatever boundaries she met in life—physical, metaphorical, stylistic, and technical—she never doubted to cross them.

Works Cited

Americas Society, editor. *Told and Untold: The Photo Stories of Kati Horna in the Illustrated Press.* Americas Society, 2016.

Brihuega, Jaime. "Formas de urgencia. Las artes plásticas y la Guerra Civil española." *Carteles de la Guerra, 1936–1939. Colección Fundación Pablo Iglesias,* edited by Fundación Pablo Iglesias, Lunwerg Ediciones, 2004, pp. 36–45.

Brisset Martín, Demetrio E. "Acerca de la fotografía etnográfica." *Gazeta de Antropología,* no. 15, 1999, http://hdl.handle.net/10481/7534.

Burke, Peter. *Eyewitnessing: The Uses of History as Historical Evidence* Reaktion Books, 2001.

Buxó, María Jesús, and Jesús M. de Miguel, editors. *De la investigación audiovisual. Fotografía, cine, vídeo, televisión.* Proyecto A. Ediciones, 1999.

Clavijo, Julio. *La política sobre la població refugiada durant la guerra civil, 1936–1939.* U Girona, 2003.

CNT-FAI Foreign Propaganda Office. *¿España?* CNT-FAI, 1938, Biblioteca Digital, Arxiu Històric de la Ciutat de Barcelona, (AHCB), https://ahcbdigital.bcn.cat/ca/biblioteca/visualitzador/ahcb-d021436.

292 A. DÍAZ-REGAÑÓN LABAJO

Colombo, Furio. "Para la muestra fotográfica sobre la guerra de España." *Bienal de Venecia, Fotografía e información de guerra. España 1936–1939*. Gustavo Gili, 1977, pp. 17–34.

Cortavitarte Carral, Emil. "El CENU, un sistema educativo público revolucionario en la Catalunya del 36." *Viento Sur*, no. 147, 2016, pp. 56–62.

Degano, Giulia. "Poder a la imaginación: la colaboración de Kati Horna con la revista *S.Nob.*" *Quiroga*, no. 8, 2015, pp. 66–76.

Desantes, Blanca, and Margarita Hernández. *Fotografías de Kati Horna en el Archivo General de la Guerra Civil Española*. Ministerio de Educación y Cultura, 1999.

Díaz-R. Labajo, Aránzazu. "Miradas para la guerra de España. Los usos de las fotografías de Kati Horna en la propaganda del Gobierno republicano, de la CNT-FAI y en las revistas ilustradas *Weekly Illustrated*, *Umbral* y *Mujeres Libres* (1937–1939)." *Liberales, cultivadas y activas. Redes culturales, lazos de amistad*, edited by Adelaida Sagarra Gamazo, U Salamanca, 2017, pp. 449–528.

Everett, Martyn. *War and Revolution: The Hungarian Anarchist Movement in World War I and the Budapest Commune (1919)*. Kate Sharply Library, 2006.

Goldman, Alexandra. "Women Photographers in Exile: A Conversation with Curators Christina De León and Michel Otayek." *Whitehot Magazine of Contemporary Art*, December 2016, https://whitehotmagazine.com/articles/de-le-n-michel-otayek/3575.

González Quintana, Antonio, *et al.* "Presentación." *Kati Horna. Fotografías de la guerra civil española (1937–1938)*, edited by Ministerio de Cultura, 1992.

Gudiol i Ricart, Josep Maria. *Tres escritos*. Opera Minora, 1987.

Horna Fernández, Ana María Nora. "Memory and the Recovery of Lived Experiences: Kati Horna, 'Invisibilist.'" *Told and Untold: The Photo Stories of Kati Horna in the Illustrated Press*, edited by Americas Society, 2016, pp. 6–13.

López Mondejar, Publio. *150 años de fotografía en España*. Lunwerg, 1999.

Miravitlles, Jaume. "Introducción a la edición castellana." *Fotografía e información de guerra. España 1936–1939*, edited by Bienal de Venecia, Gustavo Gili, 1977, pp. 7–16.

Museo, Amparo. *Kati Horna*. Fundación Amparo Museo Amparo–Jue de Paume, 2013.

Nash, Mary. *Mujeres Libres: España 1936–1939*. Tusquets, 1976.

Navarro, Ramón. *L'Educació a Catalunya durant la Generalitat 1931–1936*. Edicions 62, 1979.

Newhall, Beaumont. *The History of Photography from 1839 to the Present Day*. MOMA, 1949.

Otayek, Michel. "Loss and Renewal: The Politics and the Poetics of Kati Horna's Photo Stories." *Told and Untold: The Photo Stories of Kati Horna in the Illustrated Press*, edited by Americas Society, 2016, pp. 20–39.

———. "Keepsakes of the Revolution: Transnational Networks and the U.S. Circulation of Anarchist Propaganda during the Spanish Civil War." *Writing Revolution: Hispanic Anarchism in the United States*, edited by Christopher J. Castañeda and Montse Feu, U Illinois P, 2019, pp. 302–24.

Pelizzon, Lisa. *Kati Horna. Constelaciones de sentido*. Sans Soleil Ediciones, 2014.

Rubio, Almudena. "Las cajas de Ámsterdam." *Historia Social*, no. 96, 2020, pp. 21–40.

Ruby, Jay. "Visual Anthropology." *Encyclopedia of Cultural Anthropology*, edited by David Levinson and Melvin Ember, Henry Holt and Company, vol. 4, 1996, pp. 1345–51.

Sánchez Blanco, Laura. "El anarcofeminismo en España: las propuestas anarquistas de Mujeres Libres para conseguir la igualdad de géneros." *Foro de Educación*, no. 9, 2007, pp. 229–38.

Satué, Enric. "El diseño del cartel de guerra en España." *Carteles de la Guerra, 1936–1939. Colección Fundación Pablo Iglesias*, edited by Fundación Pablo Iglesias, Lunwerg, 2004, pp. 46–54.

Sougez, Marie-Loup. *Historia general de la fotografía*. Cátedra, 2007.

Vicent Monzó, Josep. "La mirada de Kati Horna en la España de 1937." *Kati Horna. Fotografías de la Guerra Civil Española (1937–1938)*, edited by Ministerio de Cultura, 1992, pp. 13–19.

CHAPTER 12

"It's where she belongs, isn't it?" Lupe Vélez and Dolores del Río in Hollywood

R. Hernández-Rodríguez

HOLLYWOOD IN THE 1920S—"AND THE MEXES WERE THE HOTTEST"

The decade of the 1920s represents a period of change for the American film industry. This is the moment when the studio system is instituted in Hollywood, and thus when its golden age begins. It is also a period of cinematic technical, artistic, and social transformations. Toward the end of the decade, movies transitioned from silent into talkies, experimented with new techniques and color, and established a set of self-regulating rules to control the content of the films, avoiding controversial, irreverent, or offensive topics for mainstream America. Topics such as profanity, nudity, sexuality, drug trafficking, lustful kissing, childbirth, detailed surgical procedures, men and women sharing a bed, antireligious sentiment, sedition, and miscegenation were considered taboo and discouraged in films under religious and political pressure but also as an attempt to reach an ever-larger audience, particularly of women who were the barometer of the emerging middle class. These regulations were left up to the directors and

R. Hernández-Rodríguez (✉)
Southern Connecticut State University, New Haven, CT, USA

© The Author(s), under exclusive license to Springer Nature Switzerland AG 2024
R. M. Silverman, E. Sánchez-Pardo (eds.), *Nomadic New Women*,
https://doi.org/10.1007/978-3-031-62482-7_12

295

producers, although not always enforced. Eventually, however, the industry came up with strict rules presented in the Motion Picture Production Code.

Making money and expanding their influence around the world was the main goal of the studios, based on two principles: developing a star system and controlling distribution as well as production. The strategy ended up being very successful, and by the 1930s, the film industry was a monopoly controlled by eight major studios, out of the sixty or so that were active in the previous decades. It also resulted in the preeminence of American films around the world, since "By the 1920s, most large European companies had given up film production altogether" (Gomery 9), unable to compete with Hollywood. As the American film industry rose, so did the demand for talent. Hollywood had already gone global, hiring European, Latin American, and Asian actors, but with the arrival of sound, many of them needed to be groomed to Americanize their accents and looks to appeal to US audiences. Not all of them made it in the end. With little or no competition, Hollywood was free to promote the image that America wanted to project of itself, as a white, Christian, modern nation, where other ethnicities and races were used primarily to frame dramas in exotic locations or as background to provide a sense of realism or "authenticity" in period stories, all of them with white protagonists.

Such a view was immediately challenged by the Black press, which not only criticized the lack of African Americans on screen but the distasteful practice of hiring white actors to play Black characters with painted faces. As a result, there was an increased visibility of African Americans in movies, however, mostly as extras. And in many cases, as extras of indistinctive race, like in the case of *Where East is East* (1929), "Where Negroes are being used with a few Chinese and Filipinoes as natives of Siam," according to Floyd Covington (qtd. in Regester 102). Similarly, other non-European ethnicities played different roles in movies, but for the most part as extras or secondary characters. Mexicans were an interesting case, since they came to Hollywood early on and many of them, like Ramón Novarro, Lupe Vélez, and Dolores del Río, played starring roles of different ethnicities (Russian, Roman, Latin, European, Asian, or even American like in the case of *Where East is East*, in which Lupe Vélez plays the daughter of Estelle Taylor and Lon Cheney) (Fig. 12.1).

The early twentieth century also saw the role of women in society change. Women were very active during the 1910s, fighting for the right

Fig. 12.1 Promotional photo of Novarro and Vélez in *Laughing Boy*. 1934

to vote and more freedom. However, after the ratification of the 19th Amendment in August of 1920, giving women the right to vote, they disappeared from public view prompting critics to ask, "What happened to feminism during the decade after the political goal of suffrage had been achieved?" (Freedman 372). And to wonder where was the New Woman, as these activists were generally known. Increasingly, "women in the 1920s began to be presented as flappers, more concerned with clothing and sex than with politics" (Freedman 379), and for some, this was the result of their activism, which had caused them to want nothing more than "sexual freedom [...] the automobile, and Hollywood" (Freedman 379). And if movies were perceived as pernicious and dangerous for society, Hollywood was determined to change that view by crafting a new image for women that would preserve the status quo, while maintaining its dominance over American audiences. It was clear that "women were a crucial element of the industry's efforts to establish respectability with middle-class audiences and thus to retain industry power" (Wasson 15). So, women were increasingly portrayed as idealized girlfriends, mothers, and housewives, preferably American-born, instead of racially ambiguous foreign beauties, whose accents and sex appeal were intimidating to women and seductive to men, and thus disruptive of the American way of life.

298   R. HERNÁNDEZ-RODRÍGUEZ

Previously adored foreign movie stars began to decline in popularity and their foreignness exposed, in part due to the introduction of sound. That was the case with Dolores del Río and Lupe Vélez who, as we will see, maintained an ambivalent relationship with Hollywood. Both actresses were part of the avalanche of Mexican talent working in movies in the 1920s. But the presence of Mexico at the time went beyond Hollywood and included many other artists and intellectuals who visited the country or lived and worked temporarily in the United States. It was particularly the *Tres Grandes* of Muralism, Diego Rivera, José Clemente Orozco, and David Alfaro Siqueiros, who left an indelible mark in American society. Not only did they bring their innovative art to this country but were also seduced by American culture, allowing it to permeate them, establishing a dialogue with their American counterparts.[1] An example of this is the case of Orozco and Thomas Hart Benton, who were commissioned a mural at the New School in New York City at the same time and together "fueled the nation's growing excitement about public art depicting contemporary issues in modern vocabulary" (Haskell 20).

Jazz, modern architecture, urban landscapes, industrialization, a cosmopolitan environment, and new artistic sensibilities influenced these Mexican artists. Of all cultural manifestations, the most influential was film, that quintessential American art form. Film was particularly important for Siqueiros, who in Los Angeles painted some of his most revolutionary murals, and who developed his idea of *plástica fílmica* through his contact with Hollywood.[2] Muralism, certainly, has many affinities with film—both communicate through images, have a popular intention, monumentality, and a narrative structure. Although there is not a lot of documentation about it, it is possible that these Mexican artists were encouraged and perhaps even influenced by the large number of Mexicans appearing on the silver screen at the time. Names such as Ramón Novarro, Donald

---

[1] Orozco, for example, joined the Delphic Circle, a gathering of expatriated artists organized by the Greek poet Angelos Sikelianos, and engaged in "esoteric discussions on topics spanning Greek mythology, William Blake, Eastern religion, Friedrich Nietzsche, and Dynamic Symmetry, the compositional system formulated by Jay Hambidge based on the diagonals of squares" (Haskell 18).

[2] According to Ana Indych-López, "Siqueiros's direct contact in Los Angeles with industry artists, the technical and material innovations of U.S. film culture, and its social context" (188), deeply affected him. Siqueiros, in fact, not only had direct contact with Hollywood actors and directors but also taught at the Chourinard Art Institute, where he entered in contact with some of the most innovative and artistic movie workers.

Reed, Gilbert Roland, Lupita Tovar, José Mojica, Delia Magaña, Tito Guízar, and, of course, del Río and Vélez were everywhere in the 1920s and 1930s and must have been familiar to the muralists. At the same time, the prestige of these painters must have reaffirmed the acceptance of Mexican actors.

Ideologically and artistically, Mexican culture was present and appreciated in American society from the 1920s to the 1940s. The revolution had a lot to do with it, in part because of the romantic idea it offered to adventurous young Americans flirting with socialism, and in part because of the groundbreaking artistic manifestations it made possible, particularly Muralism, which was seen as a revitalization of public art, and which later was adopted as part of the social programs of the New Deal.[3] This interest in the southern neighbor was also driven by Mexicans living in the United States, like poet José Juan Tablada, who opened the first bookstore in Spanish in the country on 23rd Street in New York City in 1924, and who regularly gave lectures on Mexican art. Anita Brenner was another Mexican promoter of art and culture living in New York City, who published an influential book, *Idols Behind Altars*, in which she claimed that Mexico was experiencing a renaissance in art, which was summed up in the works of the muralists and other artists of post-revolutionary Mexico. Such artistic and intellectual presence, unfortunately, was not able to change completely the popular notion of Mexico as either a primitive country or as a nation with an artistically sophisticated elite. And in a symbolic way, Lupe Vélez and Dolores del Río could be seen as embodiments of these perceptions.

Lupe Vélez is often remembered as a temperamental, capricious, sexy beauty that somehow mirrors the wild and primitive idea some Americans had of Mexico. And yet, she was also recognized as a versatile artist, a sort of rarity that triumphed in Hollywood and succeeded in Broadway. In the words of Rosa Linda Fregoso, she "was one of a handful of actresses who

---

[3] The emergence of Mexican Muralism coincided with the Great Depression. In an attempt to minimize the devastation and to stimulate the economy, President Franklin Delano Roosevelt created his famous New Deal, a series of social programs and economic incentives, as well as the promotion of federal jobs, which included a cultural project inspired by Mexican Muralism. The government offered federal aid to artists to paint public spaces, convinced that it was important to stimulate the economy, but also to boost the nation's morale, and murals in public buildings depicting the national spirit and local scenes, were ideal for that purpose.

excelled both on the screen and in Broadway musicals. By the time she died, at age thirty-five, Lupe Vélez had starred in forty-five feature films, working in Hollywood, London, and Mexico" (112). She was neither the first nor by any means the only Latina making a name for herself at the dawn of the American film industry. Before her, Myrtle González and Beatriz Michelena, for example, had worked in silent motion pictures often portraying all sorts of heroines; and actresses like Raquel Torres, Lupita Tovar, Mona Rico, and Delia Magaña arrived in Hollywood from Mexico around the same time as Lupe Vélez. It was, however, Dolores del Río who surpassed them all in success, fame, and grace, and who came to represent that sophisticated and artistic aspect of Mexico. Del Río had already made a few pictures by the time her *The Loves of Carmen* (1927) made her a star and prompted *Photoplay*, the most influential film magazine of the time, to compare her to Greta Garbo and consider her one of the most beautiful women on the silver screen.

Like del Río, Vélez was a real movie star. Directed by Cecil B. DeMille, D. W. Griffith, and Victor Fleming, she costarred in movies with Douglas Fairbanks, Gary Cooper, Laurel and Hardy, and Ramón Novarro. She was a familiar face in Hollywood, in part because she was able to transition from silent films into talkies, something even American actors were not always able to do, but also because of her charismatic presence on and off screen. Although she was very famous during the 1920s and 1930s, soon after her death, she was forgotten. Some critics claim that she was forced to perform the most stereotypical aspects of her nationality and to exaggerate her sexuality for American amusement, and offer the image projected by Dolores del Río as a contrast. But this provides only a partial picture of the complex person that Lupe Vélez was. I would argue rather that Vélez and del Río were aware of the dilemma they were presented with as women and as Mexican in a changing Hollywood, and made the decision of continuing working and succeeding even if the price they had to pay was to overplay or underemphasize their ethnicity and accept their prescribed roles.

This essay will center on Lupe Vélez and Dolores del Río and their artistic accomplishments, looking also into the challenges they had to overcome as artists: the literal border crossing between Mexico and the United States, and the figurative cultural divide they faced as women and foreigners in a changing world and at a time when silent films were transitioning to sound.

Lupe Vélez—*Sailors, Beware!*

The image most people have of Lupe Vélez is the one provided in the titles of many of her latest films, a Mexican spitfire. Anyone who writes about her reminds us that she was also referred to as Whoopee Lupee, Hot Tamale, and Tropical Hurricane; she was often described as volatile, uninhibited, unrefined, childish, and capricious. However, these adjectives are the ones that describe many of the characters she played in movies, thus pointing toward the possibility that they are the result of a publicity strategy in which she was forced to create—or at the very least allowed to be created—a persona that would help studios promote her movies and herself as a *spicy* Mexican woman in hopes of enticing male audiences to movie theaters. Her much-publicized romance with Gary Cooper also contributed to portray her as the complete opposite of that dignified, quintessential American man. Against Cooper's tranquil Midwestern demeanor, Lupe was an exotic, exciting other that would sprinkle their monotonous lives with shouts in Spanish and suggestive gazes and gestures, promising mysterious adventures.

Born in San Luis Potosí in 1908 to a military family, Lupe was always independent and determined, even when, at age thirteen, she was sent to study at a convent in San Antonio, Texas, where she entertained her friends by mocking the strict nuns in charge of her education. While in San Antonio, her father disappeared during the Revolution and she was forced to return to Mexico. Fascinated by acting, singing, and dancing, she dreamed of a future in the theater. Eventually, she started working as a performer, founding a niche for herself and becoming famous in Mexico by performing songs in English and dancing the shimmy and other jazz-age dances. Her modern act contrasted sharply with that of veteran performers, dominating the stage at the time, like legendary vaudeville singer María Conesa, called the "White Kitten." According to Michelle Vogel, Lupe wanted to help her family and that motivated her to look for work in the theater; in fact, "Lupe's determination to succeed and her decision to share her financial rewards when she did succeed ensured that her family lived in comfort and without financial burden for the rest of their lives" (Vogel 23).

In Lupe's own words, the time she and her boyfriend went to the Teatro Principal to see María Conesa, when Conesa came out, a disappointed Lupe exclaimed: "She is an old woman. I can do better than her!" (qtd. in Vogel 25), prompting her to see the manager of the theater to ask

302   R. HERNÁNDEZ-RODRÍGUEZ

for a job. In an interview in 1973, Conesa claimed that she was the one who gave Lupe her first opportunity to work in the theater, claiming "I also discovered Lupe Vélez. I gave her the opportunity to appear at Teatro Principal, and I did it against everybody's advice"[4] ("María Conesa" 00:05:44-00-05-51). Against everybody's advice because nobody considered Lupe a real artist. Vélez's own version of her beginning as an artist emphasizes determination, always claiming that she fought hard to become a performer, showing that she had a genuine artistic temperament and that her career was no accident. It also reveals that from early on she tried to create a persona for herself adapting to the circumstances.

Clearly aware of her audiences and of what they wanted or were ready for, both in Mexico and in Hollywood, Lupe performed the roles that would be more effective, playing the modern flapper in Mexico, for example, or the impetuous *señorita* in Hollywood, manipulating to her advantage the stereotypical view these two countries had of each other. Recruited to come to Hollywood by Richard Bennet, she got her first opportunity when she was given a screen test and, as a result, was asked to play the Baroness Behr in the silent short film *Sailors, Beware!* (1927) with Stan Laurel and Oliver Hardy. It was a brief, yet memorable part, in which Lupe already showed a strong personality. In one of her two scenes, she is being photographed before boarding the steamship Mirimar, which is sailing to Monte Carlo "with the greatest collection of millionaires ever known to steamship travel." Charming and beautiful, she poses for the camera, but when she realizes the photographer is on his knees taking pictures of her legs, she strikes him on the head with a bouquet of roses she was holding. The scene is charming and funny.

That role must have made an impression because the same year she appeared as the costar of *The Gaucho* (1927), opposite Douglas Fairbanks. This film was soon followed by *Stand and Deliver* (1928) and by Griffith's *Lady of the Pavements* (1929). According to Molli Caselli, reviewing the film for the San Francisco Silent Film Festival in 2009, *Lady of the Pavements* received excellent reviews, particularly Vélez, who, although was not the star, managed to steal the film. According to *Variety*, she "gets everything in the picture [considering that] nine-tenths of the close-ups are hers" (qtd. in Caselli). This film introduces Vélez as a serious actress, as she portrays a heroine that "defies the typical Griffith female protagonist, steeped in Victorian mores [since] Vélez's potent character does not

---

[4] "Yo también lancé a Lupe Vélez, yo la lancé en el Teatro Principal, en contra de todos."

need any rescuing" (Caselli). Paradoxically, Caselli sees in this film the beginning of that image that would follow Vélez for the rest of her life, the unpredictable and capricious hot-tempered girl. In fact, many of her early films emphasize that persona in roles that are charged with lavish sexuality and a strong character.

Unlike other actresses, including Dolores del Río, "Lupe brought an earthiness to her roles which was new to the movies" (Conner 14). Films like *Hell Harbor* (1930) or *The Cuban Love Song* (1931) reinforced that image. Particularly *Hell Harbor*, where she plays a girl forced to marry a man she does not love. She is actually sold to that man by her drunken father, and when she recriminates him for treating her that way, he tries to hit her. She fights back and threatens to kill him, knife in hand, if he ever touches her. Roles like this one suggest that the impulsive Lupe is an image imposed on her by her career, in part because of her ethnicity, and in part because of her temperament and attitude. But Caselli insinuates that this is also due to Lupe's commitment to her art, since she "embraced her role in promoting the film, attending the premieres and living up to reviews, which focused on her rowdy nature rather than on the story or technical issues." The image created for Lupe in Hollywood, which she herself embraced, has to be seen as a promotional stunt that somehow got out of control, culminating with the mendacious description of her suicide infamously propagated by Kenneth Anger's *Hollywood Babylon* (Fig. 12.2).

The real Lupe was of course more complex. A more balanced view of her as a person and as an artist emerges when we review what was written about her in her lifetime. Not only the copious praise for her acting and presence on screen but also what was said about her personal life. As an example, we can look at an article published in the December 1930 issue of *Photoplay*, "Lupe—No change!" Here Barbara Lawton writes some ambivalent, but in the end tenderly favorable, opinions about Lupe that summarize the way she was seen by Americans. The article begins with fake shock at something the writer claims she heard, that Lupe Vélez had become a lady. If that is the case, she declares, "better to learn that Ronald Colman had turned hey-hey boy or that Buster Keaton was cast in the title role of 'Hamlet' or even that Greta Garbo had become a leading social light and attended all wild parties" (73), since Lupe symbolizes all the excitement and glamour of Hollywood. Fortunately, this turned out not to be the case and Lawton is relieved because if "Lupe has been called temperamental. She is, but she is never arbitrary or hard to handle" (73), and if she is sometimes late to work, "once she is at the studio she works

Fig. 12.2 Lupe Velez and Gibson Gowland in a still photo from *Hell Harbor*. 1930

hard and when she swears, as she does freely, it is usually at herself" (74) and mostly as a way of calling attention to what she needs to improve as an actress.

If people sometimes spread rumors about her, she continues, it is only because of her generosity since she loves making people laugh and see them happy, and is not afraid of being silly if it helps her to accomplish that. "Lupe has a heart as big as the Grand Canyon, except that it isn't empty, and she allowed herself to do whatever popped into her head because [...] nothing so delights Lupe as to be laughed at" (Lawton 74). Being laughed at has a double meaning here. On the one hand, it refers to Lupe's genuinely good intentions of pleasing her public; on the other hand, it makes it clear that she puts herself in a position of ridicule since nothing is so outrageous that she wouldn't do for an audience, as, for example, one occasion "when she pulled her skirts above her head and flung herself into a wild dance" (Lawton 74). After, when Lupe's own secretary pointed out that her free-spirited attitude, even though generous, was the reason "her audience spread fantastic reports of her misbehavior," Lupe seemed truly hurt, and began to change her attitude, causing in her the change that so shocked Lawton (74). From that moment on, she started to be more discreet in the way she talked and acted, assuming a "dignified manner," particularly in front of her fans; she was also vigilant of the way she dressed, opting for "gowns that any Park Avenue lady would be delighted to own" (74).

Although, Lawton adds, nobody would mistake her for a Park Avenue lady "merely because she is too striking a type" (74). Again, being too striking a type can be read in many ways, including an ethnic reference, of course, but not exclusively or primarily. Lupe is a type of free, modern girl who does not care for conventions. When we read the entire article, we realize it is mostly positive and even tender toward Lupe. Lawton reminds us that though she "wears the garments of a lady. Inside she is the same" (74). She is nothing like those stuck-up women on Park Avenue, because she is too much of a free spirit. The real contrasting element here is not ethnicity, but the opposition between the upper classes and the modern working masses. And Lupe is well aware of it, as she declares, according to Lawton, that if they say that she has changed and now she is a lady, they do not understand that "In a church I am a saint. In a public place I am a lady. In my own home I am a devil" (74).

Lawton's article portrays Lupe as determined and independent but also as generous with "abundance of kindliness and real affection"; a woman always willing to help anybody with talent, like two "little girls, twelve or thirteen, who were excellent tap dancers" and whom she sponsored; or a Mexican guitar player she hosted at her house and "schooled [...] in aggressive American ways" (135). In a strange sense, Lupe became the champion of the people. As an immigrant, she was well aware of the restrictive role immigrants were assigned, culturally, socially, economically. Having suffered hardship, she also understood poverty; and having fought for everything she had, she knew what resilience was. Paradoxically, it is her foreignness, her literally having crossed the border, that makes her such a heroine. At the same time, as we will see, her exaggerated Latin femininity can be seen as a way of questioning the role Hollywood was assigning to women, presenting it as authentic American. As Victoria Sturtevant writes, Lupe Vélez

> represents an ambivalent vision of immigrant identity, one that acknowledges the limitations of the American fears about ethnic pollution while simultaneously offering a subversive outsider's vision of Anglo feminine values like restraint, sexual passivity, and the performance of helplessness. (21)

306   R. HERNÁNDEZ-RODRÍGUEZ

Despite all her success, Lupe's career was never secure. The accomplishments of her earlier films were not enough and she went from studio to studio all through the 1930s. Whether it was her foreignness, emphasized by her accent; whether it was the roles she was offered, which began to seem repetitive and less interesting; whether it was her love life, particularly her turbulent marriage to Johnny Weissmuller, along with her reputation as unpredictable and capricious, the truth is that her career seemed to be in decline by the late 1930s. So, in 1938, she decided to cross the southern border to film *La zandunga*, which was very well received by public and critics in Mexico. Nonetheless, after that success, she returned to Hollywood. Lupe had already invested so much time and energy in her Hollywood career that abandoning it now could not have been a real option.

After her return, she starred in the successful *The Girl from Mexico* (1939), the first film in the Mexican spitfire series. These are among the last films she made and in which she truly embraced the exaggerated image of a Mexican woman living in the United States. They were based on the conventional fish-out-of-the-water situation, but even here she demonstrated her talent and intelligence. Rosa Linda Fregoso writes that Vélez's presence on and off screen "was predicated on an identity that she herself cultivated [...] a woman who broke with all social conventions" (116). And that is what we see in these movies disguised as "ethnic" comedy. The acknowledgment that she "cultivated" this image is important because it gives Vélez agency over the way she was portrayed. If Lupe crossed borders, both physical and cultural, she did it in order to take control of her life and to succeed in a business that was the most glamorous and envied at the time, and nothing was off limits, not even her image. But these films, according to Brian O'Neil, were also subversive since they "broke new ground in depicting a Latina not just hopelessly in love with an Anglo male, but actually married to one" (366–67).

The Girl from Mexico is about Carmelita (Vélez), a charming, impulsive Mexican girl who was brought to New York as a singing talent, and because of her impulsiveness, she often gets in trouble, complicating things for her protector Dennis (Donald Woods), who eventually becomes her husband. Carmelita's misfortunes are often caused by the other women in Dennis's life, namely, his aunt and his fiancée, who are tirelessly plotting against her. Aunt Della (Elisabeth Risdon) despises Carmelita because she considers her unworthy of her all-American, successful nephew who seems to be falling in love with her. Instead, she favors Elizabeth (Linda Hayes),

Dennis's fiancée, because she "can track her family back to the pilgrims." Carmelita is often reminded by words and actions that she does not belong in the house of a WASP family. Not everybody, however, feels the same way. Dennis's uncle Matthew (Leon Errol), who himself seems a little out of place in this family, likes Carmelita and helps her to fit in and conquer Dennis's love. Together, they form a charming comic duo (Fig. 12.3).

When Carmelita loses her voice, the main reason for her coming to the United States, Dennis decides to send her back to Mexico, although he does not want her to go back. However, his aunt convinces him that naturally the girl wants to return to her own country. Confused and desperately looking for any signs that Carmelita wants to stay, since by now he has fallen in love with her, he asks his aunt if Carmelita has expressed any sadness at having to return to Mexico. She, who all this time has been

Fig. 12.3 Lupe Velez, publicity portrait for *Mexican Spitfire*

making plans for Dennis's wedding to Elizabeth, simply exclaims, "Of course not. It's where she belongs, isn't it?" In *Mexican Spitfire* (1940), the second movie of the series, Dennis and Carmelita are newlyweds, however, Elizabeth, who for some reason continues to hang around, tries to break up their marriage. The duality of female desire continues to be performed in the figure of the American Elizabeth and the foreign Carmelita, while Aunt Della continues to lament the marriage of her nephew to that "little Mexican wild cat."

The disappointment she feels because Dennis broke his engagement with Elizabeth and married Carmelita will continue to be central to the plot of all the movies in the series. The antagonism between her and Carmelita will only increase with each one. In a revealing scene in *Mexican Spitfire Sees a Ghost* (1942), the screwball comedy turns into physical comedy. Here Carmelita jumps, screams, laughs, hangs from a rope outside of a skyscraper, and swings into a high-rise apartment through the window. A disapproving Dennis (Charles "Buddy" Rogers) tells her that her attitude is a little too "unladylike, is the word," volunteers Aunt Della. "That's right, as we grow older we must become more dignified," he agrees. To which Carmelita replies: "You mean I've got to be old and dignified?" "Well, yes," says Dennis. And Carmelita sarcastically asks: "Like Aunt Della?" When Dennis responds that yes, she declares "if I've got to be old like Aunt Della, and dignified, then I don't want to be dignified because I don't want to be old." Again, Vélez and her character are not dignified enough for mainstream America. But the real problem is that conventional society cannot mold her into what it wants her to be. Dignified is associated with old, which helps to make the point that old, that is, traditional, America can only be revitalized by the new, that is, immigrants.

Watching all the movies of the series, we realize that Lupe Vélez, far from being a passive victim of ridicule, was a more complex figure. The image of the Mexican spitfire was a mask that helped her navigate the intricacies of life in Hollywood as a single, non-American girl. Lupe's persona was built by a mix of authenticity and pantomime, an image created as a publicity stunt that she took and ran with, in part for necessity, in part for fun, and in part as a defiance to convention, be it in the figure of Aunt Della or those supercilious Park Avenue ladies mentioned by Lawton. But these movies are "also an opportunity for the audience to see the mainstream culture from an outsider's position and laugh at the very language, customs, and institutions that are being abused in the narrative. [And thus, they are] a richly ambivalent comic form" (Sturtevant 23).

Dolores del Río—Queen of "the brilliant and cosmopolitan society of Mexico City"

It is almost impossible not to compare Lupe Vélez and Dolores del Río. For one, they both came from Mexico seeking the same dream of becoming movie stars and both were in Hollywood at the same time, competing for similar roles, so much so that they actually starred in different versions of the same film, under the same director, like in the case of *Resurrection*. The first version of Leo Tolstoy's novel about love and deceit, was a silent film directed by Edwin Carewe and released in 1927. The film presented Dolores del Río as the innocent country girl Katyusha who is seduced and then abandoned by Prince Dimitry. In 1931, Carewe directed another version of the novel, this time a talkie starring Lupe Vélez. Vélez also starred in the Spanish version of the same film produced in Hollywood for Spanish-speaking audiences. Vélez and del Río displayed their beauty and talent playing all sorts of characters; at the same time, their sex appeal was displayed by playing "exotic" types, like Asian (*East is West* or *Bird of Paradise*), Native American (*Laughing Boy* or *Ramona*), and Latin American women (*The Gaucho*, *The Cuban Love Song*, *Hell Harbor*, or *Flying Down to Rio*).

Even though they were very successful movie stars, in the end, they were marginalized, relegated to a footnote in the history of Hollywood, or worse yet, the butt of a joke. Critics look at Latin American women—mostly women—working in Hollywood in an oversimplified light, discussing their skin color and features, something we rarely hear about male movie stars. Latina movie actresses' temperament, and idiosyncrasies, on the contrary, are constantly on display and under scrutiny. Thus, "The Mexican actress Dolores Del Río played the warm, sensitive, and sensual Latina in the 1920s and 30s. Lupe Velez, another Mexican actress, played the spitfire Latina between the 1930s and 40s [while the] Brazilian actress Carmen Miranda played the frivolous woman" (Ruiz 31) from the 1930s through the 1950s. Almost as if in order to make sense of them, they needed to be compartmentalized. However, these comparisons require some context.

With her mysterious beauty, charming personality, and aristocratic presence, many critics argue, Dolores del Río represented a type of Mexican that was welcomed in Hollywood; an aristocratic woman not associated

310   R. HERNÁNDEZ-RODRÍGUEZ

with the lower classes that had to migrate out of need.[5] However, the arguments for this assessment are not always clear, except they serve the purpose of contrasting her against her rival, Lupe Vélez. If Vélez was passionate, loud, impulsive, outspoken, in other words, not a lady, del Río was calm, sensitive, aristocratic, a lady. Such contrasting views of character are followed with some persistency by sometimes contradictory assertions about the color of their skin, hair, or eyes to match their personalities, or most often to "match" their nationality. Despite the impossibility to really talk about their true skin color based on the images we have of them, which are either publicity photographs or movies—that is highly composed images manipulated and altered by lighting and make-up—they are described either as dark-skinned or light-skinned to prove the rejection of Mexicans or the acceptance of certain type of Mexicans in Hollywood.

Linda Hall mentions skin color as a distinguishing characteristic of del Río, but her opinion only confirms that skin color in the case of these Mexican actresses is a construct, rather than a fact. She writes that del Río's "very beauty and social class diminished the significance of her Mexican background and her somewhat darker rather than lighter skin" (6), making it possible therefore for her to succeed in Hollywood. It is hard to know how she came to the conclusion that del Río's skin was darker rather than lighter or what spectrum of skin color she was measuring it against. Without arguing against or in favor of this sort of analysis, a quick look at pictures of del Río next to say, Marlene Dietrich or Orson Wells, does not seem to corroborate without a doubt that her main distinguishing characteristic is "her darker rather than lighter skin." Likewise, Fregoso writes that "the dark-skinned Vélez had been explicitly singled out in the media's anti-immigrant campaigns" (116) in favor of American actresses; she bases her comment on an article originally published in *Continental* in December of 1931, arguing that "It is time for [Lupe Vélez] and her foreign accent to disappear so that our own American actresses can occupy the space that corresponds to them" (qtd. in Fregoso 117).

Here again is hard to know how Fregoso reaches a conclusion about Vélez's dark skin color, except that it *must be* since she is Mexican. However, what the *Continental* article points out, which is something that

---

[5] The tagline for the article of St. Johns, "A Daughter of the Dons," reads, "Dolores del Río came to Hollywood seeking neither fame nor romance or money. She went into the movies 'just for fun.' But the movies refuse to let her go" (66).

was mentioned often about both actresses, is her accent. What distinguishes Vélez and del Río as foreign actresses is their accent. Skin color is somehow different from the categorization of race. White is a social construct that encompasses many aspects, including a variety of skin tones, but it is closely tied to geographical origins, as well as class, culture, and even religious practices. Joanne Hershfield makes a more balanced assessment of the American perception of these actresses, although she also mentions "Del Río's 'dusky' beauty" (18). But she does so referring to the Polynesian woman she plays in *Bird of Paradise* (1932); furthermore, she is citing an article from the *New York Herald Tribune* mentioning how del Río's "alien beauty" is perfect for the role. She continues to explain how even when del Río "performed on one level like white, female movie stars as an object of the white hero's desire, she could not occupy exactly the *same* narrative and visual space as foreign 'white' actresses" (18) such as Dietrich and Garbo (Fig. 12.4).

Fig. 12.4 Still from the movie *Bird of Paradise*. 1932

312   R. HERNÁNDEZ-RODRÍGUEZ

However, before discussing the dusky aspect of del Río's skin, Hershfield acknowledges the importance of her accent as an impediment for her film career. Del Río herself seemed to be aware of the fact that her biggest obstacle was her diction: "Despite her accent and her insistence that she would 'nevair make a talkie,' del Río weathered the industry's shift to sound" (Hershfield 18) only to play "a variety of roles as an exotic, foreign woman" (18). Nonetheless, it is important to remember that del Río became a real movie star early on, playing all sorts of roles, and that neither her name nor her nationality were ever an obstacle for her fame. In fact, she was one of the first legendary movie stars, with a career acclaimed by critics and public alike and considered one of the most beautiful women in the world. Her presence on screen was equal to that of her male counterparts and to that of other female movie stars of the time, like Garbo or Dietrich who also played all sort of roles, including some in which they were the object of the desire of Latin leading men like Ramón Novarro or Antonio Moreno. Dolores del Río was, in the words of Linda Hall, "the first major Latina cross-over star in Hollywood" (3).

Like Lupe Vélez, she worked hard on creating an image for herself based on her nationality; in her case, she cultivated the image of the aristocratic Mexican beauty who was educated in Europe and ended up in the movie business almost by accident and became a star without intending to do so. In an article about del Río in *Photoplay*, "A Daughter of The Dons," the fascination with the actress is evident for her talent but also because of her class. After all, not only was she schooled in France but was "born in a magnificent old Spanish ranch home which had belonged to her forefathers over three hundred years" (St. Johns 102), and lived her life as "one of the reigning belles and beauties" (St. Johns 67) of "the brilliant and cosmopolitan society of Mexico City" (St. Johns 67). And yet, even here, what distinguishes her as a foreigner is "her quaint and delicious English, all of which she has acquired in the time since she came to Hollywood" (St. Johns 102).

This perception of del Río contrasts with that of Lupe Vélez, who, according to Hershfield, was "black-haired, black-eyed, slender, small, and untamed" (4), and therefore "most definitely Mexican" (4). It is true that in the case of Vélez, manners have been read as an extension of nationality or even ethnicity. Thus, being untamed *has to match* eye and hair color. However, this assumption is brought to the argument from the outside. If we look at *Photoplay*, we find many references to the national origin of del Río and Vélez, in terms of attitude, temperament, accent, education,

12 "IT'S WHERE SHE BELONGS, ISN'T IT?" LUPE VÉLEZ AND DOLORES DEL...   313

values, even food,[6] but rarely, if at all, in terms of skin color, even when given the opportunity. In an advertisement for Max Factor in the September 1931 issue of *Photoplay*, for example, we read: "Leading stars...Evelyn Brent, Lupe Velez, Joan Crawford, Renee Adoree, and scores of others have given you a glimpse of the faultless beauty to be gained with make-up in correct color harmony" (17). Color harmony here refers to Society Make-up Hollywood, a product that enhances the natural skin color, since "Cosmetics must be in color harmony, if beauty is to be emphasized" (17). The ad includes a chart that women can cut from the magazine, fill up, and send with their order to indicate their personal complexion going from light to olive. One imagines that the names of the actresses mentioned attempt to offer the *standard* varieties of skin tones. Likewise, a previous ad in March of 1926, also in *Photoplay*, described del Río as the perfect Hispanic woman of "creamy skin" (104).

Nationality in the case of these Mexican actresses was determined mostly by accent and by opposing personality traits: artistic, well-bred, old-fashioned traditions of aristocratic Mexico embodied by del Río, and the impulsive, hot-blooded, reckless post-revolutionary temperament of Lupe Vélez. The characterization of these actresses is, above all, a matter of a clash between a traditional attitude, idealized as proper, and a more modern and free-spirited one. We already saw how in 1930 Barbara Lawton lamented the possibility of Lupe turning into a proper lady. A year later, there is another mention of Vélez not being a lady in the same magazine, to which she responds "To act like everyone else—is that what they call a lady? Then I am not a lady!" (November 1931, 106). In an article about her relationship with Gary Cooper, "Love on the Rocks," Leonard Hall writes that it is not secret that Cooper's parents never approved of their relationship because "The Judge and his wife are quiet, dignified Montana folks, accustomed to a placid life and a sane one—for themselves and for the long-legged lad" (51).

While Vélez is inappropriate, del Río is a lady. Both represent different versions of being Mexican, one more in keeping with traditional, albeit fading, American values than the other. According to Clara E. Rodríguez,

---

[6] There is a curious anecdote about food that illustrates the playing with national stereotypes. It appeared in *Photoplay* in July of 1929: "Hoping to give Dolores del Río a treat, while the star was filming 'Evangeline' in Louisiana, a Spanish girl brought her some piping hot tamales and some homemade chili-con-carne. 'I thought that being Mexican, you would enjoy some real Mexican food,' the donor of the tamales and chili said. 'I do appreciate your thoughtfulness, my dear,' replied Dolores, 'but I never ate a tamale or chili in my life!'" (84).

314   R. HERNÁNDEZ-RODRÍGUEZ

despite the different personae they presented to the public, they were more alike, not only in terms of age, height, and weight but also in that both "were fairly light-skin with European facial features" (74). What distinguished them was the opposition of the aristocratic and the ordinary; the old-fashioned and the modern. Each had a preestablished role to play. It is important to remember that Lupe Vélez had made her career in Mexico playing with similar contradictions, representing a new woman, a jazz-age flapper of sorts, modern, uninhibited, singing in English and dancing the modern rhythms coming from America, in direct opposition to the popular matrons of the time, plump women like Maria Conesa, Lupe Rivas Cacho, or Celia Montalván.

In addition, del Río and Vélez had to constantly negotiate an imposed demand of "representing" Hispanic cultures,[7] not just Mexican, as well as keeping their careers afloat, despite popular perceptions of their ethnicity. The roles they had to play, the stories they starred in, and the dialogue and situations they encountered in their films were not their making, and it was not their job to correct them; their job, which they did superbly well, was to embody characters.[8] Not acknowledging this robs them of their talent and their right to be admired and recognized for it, instead of demanding that they represented a race, a culture, a nation. This forces us also to read their comments and pronouncements carefully. If del Río, as Rodríguez mentions quoting other critics, "strongly identified with her Mexican heritage despite her growing fame" (83) and explicitly expressed her desire "to play a Mexican woman and show what life in Mexico really is" (83), she was probably trying to please the audience for whom such declaration was intended.[9]

Without denying the possibility that there was some real interest in representing Mexico in a more positive light, the truth is that del Río was,

[7] In the words of Rodríguez, "There is evidence that both stars viewed their community ties (and connections to Mexico, Mexicans, Spain, or Latinos in general) as sources of sustenance, identity, and pride" (83). Although she does not provide this evidence, this is probably generally true, except the idea of identity and pride sounds suspiciously much more contemporary.

[8] The praises for their acting were constant, even when they starred in talkies. Their movies were often reviewed favorably, particularly their acting. Even Cecil B. De Mille said of Vélez, in a brief note on *Photoplay* from August 1931: "Lupe is the greatest embryonic actress since Swanson; she is a combination of Lenore Ulric and Swanson" (108).

[9] Let's remember that when she had the opportunity to do so, when she moved to Mexico, the roles she played were hardly any better. No one would consider playing an Indian woman in *Maria Candelaria* (1944) an example of "what life in Mexico really is."

and should have been, focused on her own career. There were some major obstacles she and all the other Mexican actors had to overcome if they wanted to continue having a successful career in Hollywood. The biggest obstacle of all was, as we saw, the arrival of sound. "The silence of cinema allowed actors like Del Río, Vélez, Roland, Novarro, and Moreno to play characters of various nationalities" (Ramírez Berg 266), but with the talkies it became less possible. Del Río, being one of the most established of them, had to work harder to maintain her status; she knew she was up against the enormous challenges that the talkies presented to the industry but also to American culture in general. Since she did not have Lupe's ability for histrionics, she had to rely on her "serious" acting and gravitas; and histrionics went better with accents than gravitas. As Ann Douglas observes, the first decades of the twentieth century were also the ones that marked definitely the preeminence of American culture in the world, and the American vernacular was a huge part of it since "People were beginning to listen hard to the way Americans talked" (356). If Hollywood could manipulate the titles in silent films, adapting them to many languages and cultures, even Anglicizing them for British audiences, "When talkies arrived, their gritty American language proved once again a draw to their English fans" (357), and indeed to the world.

When movies went from silent to talkies, they became even more important as a tool for the creation of a modern American identity through language, a language that was carefully crafted yet "authentic" and delivered with ideal enunciation and the perfect pitch. The demand for a specific type of voice and, later, for a specific "neutral" accent, that is "before time and television made Nebraskans of us all" (Kehr), meant that even many American actors and actresses were not able to make the transition from silent movies to talkies due to their own timbre, enunciation, or regional drawl. This was a huge change in the industry and the culture; even *Photoplay* dedicated its December 1929 issue to the "terror of the studios," the microphone. On the cover of that issue, silent movie actress Norma Talmadge is pictured attempting to talk in front of a mike with the tagline on top reading "The microphone—The terror of the studios," and the one on the bottom: "You can't get away with it in Hollywood." The main article in that issue, by Harry Lang, is also called "The microphone—The terror of the studios," and in it, Lang declares that "Mike, the demon [...] sends the vocally unfit screaming or lisping from the lots" (29).

As the article points out, "you can't even begin to write the half of the story of Terrible Mike and what he's done [including] laughs and sobs,

316   R. HERNÁNDEZ-RODRÍGUEZ

heart-leaps and heart-aches, sudden wealth and sudden ruin" (29) that has caused. Since the tragedy of some, like Clara Bow, was the fortune of others, like Bebe Daniels or Joan Bennet. Among some of the unfortunate ones, were many Mexicans ("and the Mexes were the hottest," 124), who despite their sex appeal, couldn't make the transition to talking pictures. The article then centers on the case of Mona Rico, another Mexican movie star of the silent era, who went from an extra to play "lead opposite John Barrymore [and] put all the stuff that went with it—apartments, maids, autos, chauffeurs, clothes" (124). Only to lose it all, since "Terrible Mike has a Nordic superiority complex or something [and] planted himself before her, and said: You!—how do you speak English?" (124). The article ends by stating that Mexicans "aren't the only ones to suffer from Terrible Mike's linguistic demands. It's tough on other outlanders" (124) as well, including Scandinavians like Nils Asther and Greta Garbo.

The cultural divide Lupe Vélez and Dolores del Río had to cross and overcome to succeed in Hollywood manifested itself in the barrier of language—or accent—and the assumed social attitude expected from a Mexican woman in the eyes of the American public. In its more grotesque form, it appeared in accounts of Lupe Vélez's suicide in December of 1944. The reported "reason" for her suicide, as told even today by most biographers and critics, is that "A Catholic, Velez wouldn't have an abortion, but she also couldn't handle the shame of being pregnant and unmarried" (King). Yet, although she does indicate in her suicide note that she preferred to take her life and the baby's "before I bring him with shame," the note also, and more emphatically, recriminates her lover, Harald Ramond, an unemployed actor who seemed to have been taking advantage of her to advance his own career, with these words: "How could you, Harald, fake such great love for me and our baby when all the time you didn't want us" (Conner 229).

To assume that she couldn't have an abortion because of her religion, as if Protestant girls were having abortions left and right, and that instead she would commit an even greater sin, is hard to accept, if in fact she was such a devout Catholic. Against her religion would have also been other things she did, like divorce or sex—according to some critics plenty of it—out of marriage. Yet, the mentioning of her religion in relation only to her death reveals that it is considered basically a cultural trait. Being Mexican, it makes sense to use Catholicism to create a narrative about Lupe's demise while emphasizing her cultural otherness, just like the color of her eyes and hair, her accent, as well as her effervescent personality had done before. To contemplate the convincing possibility proposed by Michelle Vogel, that "bipolar disorder may have played [a role] on her suicide" (King), would make Lupe appear less ethnic. Had it not been for her suicide and the need to create a "Mexican" narrative for it, Catholicism would have never been brought up. Dolores del Río, who had also a history of divorces and well-publicized affairs with producers and actors, was never mentioned in terms of her religion. The reason, is clear, each one of them had a role to play in the representation of the two extremes Americans (and the movies) perceived Mexicans to be.

CONCLUSION

As we saw, Mexican artistic influence at the beginning of the twentieth century was prevalent in America, when "the U.S. opened its doors to a large group of Mexican painters, writers, musicians, actors, and actresses" (Muñoz). This boom of all things Mexican must have had some influence in the way that country was perceived in the United States, even if it still was understood in a broad way as either folkloric or artistically sophisticated. That also influenced the way Lupe Vélez and Dolores del Río, the most successful Mexican actresses in early Hollywood, were appreciated. Vélez and del Río knew that they were up against major obstacles because they were women and foreign. Nonetheless, they were willing to fight for their careers and the lives that they wanted for themselves. They were aware of the cultural divide they faced and knew there was a price to pay in a business where the public decided, or as Samuel Goldwyn, of Metro-Goldwyn-Mayer, put it, "If the audience don't like a picture, they have a good reason. The public is never wrong" (qtd. in Douglas 189). So, if that price was to become antagonists and to overplay earthy Mexicaness, in the case of Vélez, or emphasize an aristocratic, refined image, in the case of del Río, they were ready to pay it, despite reinforcing a distorted view of Mexico.

Vélez and del Río had come to Hollywood, like many others, in search of opportunities and to fulfill their dream of a career in the movies. They wanted to be noticed, to be appreciated for their talents, and to be remembered. And for a time, it seemed that they had done it. At first, they were able to play a variety of roles in silent movies, which allowed them to rise to the top. However, once sound arrived, their accents made obvious their foreignness at a time when American culture was beginning to spread around the world and to establish its preeminence, mostly through

318   R. HERNÁNDEZ-RODRÍGUEZ

movies, music, and the American vernacular.[10] Lupe Vélez and Dolores del Río found themselves in the middle of a battle for cultural supremacy, where there was very little room for them. America, a modern nation in search of its own identity as a world power, relied on an image it wanted to create and promote of itself. One way of doing that was by contrasting an idealized view of America against an archetypical Other. Emphasizing a Mexico that was at once Latin, conservative, Spanish, aristocratic, Catholic, Spanish-speaking, artistic, impulsive, sensuous, and raunchy presented a golden opportunity for America to erect that Other *par excellence*. And these heavily accented actresses and their personae were evidence of that.

WORKS CITED

Anger, Kenneth. *Hollywood Babylon*. Straight Arrow Books, 1975.

Bird of Paradise. Directed by King Vidor, performances by Dolores del Río, Joel McCrea, John Halliday, Bert Roach, and Lon Chaney Jr., RKO Radio Pictures, 1932.

Caselli, Mollie. "Lady of the Pavements." *San Francisco Silent Film Festival*, 2009, https://silentfilm.org/lady-of-the-pavements/, accessed 23 January 2021.

Conner, Floyd. *Lupe Velez and her Lovers*. Barricade Books, 1993.

Dobrzynski, Judith H. "Vida Americana." *Wall Street Journal*, 18 Feb. 2020, www.wsj.com/articles/vida-americana-mexican-muralists-remake-american-art-1925-1945-review-ideas-without-borders-11582065680. Accessed 18 Jan. 2021.

Douglas, Ann. *Terrible Honesty. Mongrel Manhattan in the 1920s*. Farrar, Strauss, and Giroux, 1995.

East is West. Directed by Monta Bell, performances by Lupe Vélez, Lew Aires, Edward G. Robinson, E. Alyn Warren, and Mary Forbes, Universal Pictures, 1930.

Flying Down to Rio. Directed by Thornton Freeland, performances by Dolores del Río, Gene Raymond, Raul Roulien, Ginger Rogers, Fred Astaire, and Blanche Friderici, RKO Radio Pictures, 1933.

Freedman, Estelle B. "The New Woman: Changing Views of Women in the 1920s." *The Journal of American History*, vol. 61, no. 2, Sept. 1974, pp. 372–93.

Fregoso, Rosa Linda. *Mexican Encounters. The Making of Social Identities on the Borderlands*. U of California P, 2003.

---

[10] Ann Douglas mentions that Virginia Woolf "praised Ring Lardner in 1925 for refreshing the language with America's 'expressive ugly vigorous slang'" (357).

Gomery, Douglas. *The Hollywood Studio System: A History.* British Film Institute, 2005.

Hall, Linda B. *Dolores del Río: Beauty in Light and Shade.* Stanford UP, 2020.

Hall, Leonard. "Love on the Rocks." *Photoplay,* vol. 40, no. 4, September 1931, pp. 51, 95.

Haskell, Barbara. "América: Mexican Muralism and Art in the United States." *Vida Americana: Mexican Muralists Remake American Art, 1925–1945,* edited by Barbara Haskell, Whitney/Yale UP, 2020, pp. 14–45.

Hell Harbor. Directed by Henry King, performances by Lupe Vélez, Gibson Gowland, Jean Hersholt, John Holland, and Harry Allen, United Artists, 1930.

Hershfield, Joanne. *The Invention of Dolores del Río.* U of Minnesota P, 2000.

Indych-López, Anna. "Celluloid América: Siqueiros, Hollywood, and Plástica Fílmica." *Vida Americana: Mexican Muralists Remake American Art, 1925–1945,* edited by Barbara Haskell, Whitney/Yale UP, 2020, pp. 188–95.

Kehr, Dave. "When Hollywood Learned to Talk, Sing and Dance." *The New York Times,* 15 Jan. 2010, www.nytimes.com/2010/01/17/movies/homevideo/17kehr.html. Accessed 18 Dec. 2020.

King, Susan. "Lupe Velez: Early Hollywood Path-Paver." *Los Angeles Times,* 13 Aug. 2012, www.latimes.com/entertainment/movies/la-xpm-2012-aug-13-la-et-mn-classic-hollywood-20120813-story.html. Accessed 20 Feb. 2021.

La zandunga. Directed by Fernando de Fuentes, performances by Lupe Vélez, Arturo de Córdova, Rafael Falcón, María Luisa Zea, and Joaquín Pardavé, Clasa Films Mundiales, 1938.

Lady of the Pavements. Directed by D. W. Griffith, performances by Lupe Vélez, William Boyd, Jetta Goudal, Albert Conti, and George Fawcett, United Artists, 1929.

Lang, Harry. "The Microphone—The Terror of the Studios." *Photoplay,* vol. 37, no. 1, Dec. 1929, pp. 29–30, 124.

Laughing Boy. Directed by W. S. Van Dyke, performances by Ramón Novarro, Lupe Vélez, William B. Davidson, Chief Thunderbird, and Catalina Rambula, Metro-Goldwyn-Mayer, 1934.

Lawton, Barbara. "Lupe—No Change!" *Photoplay,* vol. 31, no. 1, Dec. 1930, pp. 74, 135.

"María Conesa La Gatita Blanca. Entrevista" *YouTube,* uploaded by Guillermo Pérez Verduzco, 24 Jan. 2012, www.youtube.com/watch?v=HQIfzMjK1RY.

Mexican Spitfire. Directed by Leslie Goodwins, performances by Lupe Vélez, Donald Woods, Leon Errol, Linda Hayes, Elisabeth Risdon, and Cecil Kellaway, RKO Radio Pictures, 1940.

Mexican Spitfire Sees a Ghost. Directed by Leslie Goodwins, performances by Lupe Vélez, Charles "Buddy" Rogers, Leon Errol, Elisabeth Risdon, Donald MacBride, and Minna Gombell, RKO Radio Pictures, 1942.

320   R. HERNÁNDEZ-RODRÍGUEZ

Muñoz, Sergio. "When Mexico was a Star." *Los Angeles Times*, 25 Feb. 2007, www.latimes.com/archives/la-xpm-2007-feb-25-op-munoz25-story.html. Accessed 15 Feb. 2021.

O'Neil, Brian. "The Demands of Authenticity: Addison Durland and Hollywood's Latin Images During World War II." *Classic Hollywood, Classic Whiteness*, edited by Daniel Bernardi, U of Minnesota P, 2001, pp. 359–85.

Ramírez Berg, Charles. *Latino Images in Film: Stereotypes, Subversion, and Resistance*. U of Texas P, 2002.

Ramona. Directed by Edwin Carewe, performances by Dolores del Río, Warner Baxter, Roland Drew, Vera Lewis, and John T. Prince, United Artists, 1928.

Regester, Charles. "African American Extras in Hollywood During the 1920s and 1930s." *Film History*, vol. 9, no. 1, 1997, pp. 95–115.

Resurrection. Directed by Edwin Carewe, performances by Rod La Rocque, Dolores del Río, Marc McDermott, Lucy Beaumont, Vera Lewis, Eve Southern, and Ilya Tolstoy, United Artists, 1927.

Rodríguez, Clara E. "Dolores del Río and Lupe Vélez: Working in Hollywood, 1924–1944." *Norteamérica*, vol. 6, no. 1, 2011, pp. 69–91.

Ruiz, Marisol. "The Taxonomy of the Latina Body: Adrian Lee in the Secret Life of the American Teenager." *Humboldt Journal of Social Relations*, vol. 37, 2015, pp. 30–45.

Sailors, Beware! Directed by Fred Guiol and Hal Roach, performances by Stan Laure, Oliver Hardy, Anita Garvin, Frank Brownlee, Dorothy Coburn, and Lupe Vélez, Hal Roach Studios, 1927.

St. Johns, Ivan. "A Daughter of the Dons." *Photoplay* vol. 33, no. 1, June 1927, pp. 67, 102.

Stand and Deliver. Directed by Donald Crisp, performances by Rod LaRocque, Lupe Vélez, Warner Oland, Louis Natheaux, and Jimmy Dime, DeMille Pictures Corporation, 1928.

Sturtevant, Victoria. "Spitfire: Lupe Vélez and the Ambivalent Pleasure of Ethnic Masquerade." *The Velvet Light Trap*, no. 55, 2005, pp. 19–32.

The Cuban Love Song. Directed by W. S. Van Dyke, performances by Lawrence Tibbett, Lupe Vélez, Ernest Torrence, Jimmy Durante, Karen Morley, and Louise Fazenda, Metro-Goldwyn-Mayer, 1931.

The Gaucho. Directed by F. Richard Jones, performances by Douglas Fairbanks, Lupe Vélez, Joan Barclay, Eve Southern, Gustav von Seyffertitz, and Michael Vavitch, Elton Corporation, 1927.

The Girl from Mexico. Directed by Leslie Goodwins, performances by Lupe Vélez, Donald Woods, Leon Errol, Linda Hayes, Elisabeth Risdon, and Donald MacBride, RKO Radio Pictures, 1939.

The Loves of Carmen. Directed by Raoul Walsh, performances by Dolores del Río, Don Alvarado, Victor McLaglen, Nancy Nash, Mathilde Comont, and Fred Kohler, Fox Film Corporation, 1927.

Vogel, Michelle. *Lupe Vélez: The Life and Career of Hollywood's Mexican Spitfire.* McFarland, 2012.

Wasson, Haidee. "Electric Homes! Automatic Movies! Efficient Entertainment!: 16 mm and Cinema's Domestication in the 1920s." *Cinema Journal*, vol. 48, no. 4, 2009, pp. 1–21.

Weinberger, Adam D. "Foreword." *Vida Americana: Mexican Muralists Remake American Art, 1925–1945*, edited by Barbara Haskell, Whitney/Yale UP, 2020, pp. 8–11.

Where East is East. Directed by Tod Browning, performances by Lon Chaney, Lupe Vélez, Estelle Taylor, and Lloyd Hughes, Metro-Goldwyn-Mayer, 1929.

CHAPTER 13

A Double Exile: Crossing the Female Figure in Maruja Mallo's Art—From Spain to America

Renée M. Silverman

Spanish painter Maruja Mallo's (1902–95) career as an artist took off in 1928, borne on the wings of a solo exhibition sponsored by the *Revista de Occidente*, the highly influential beacon of modernity and avant-garde aesthetics directed by the philosopher José Ortega y Gasset. Not only was the exhibition of Mallo's work the first ever to be mounted under the journal's auspices but also the homage to a woman artist that it paid remained remarkably rare for the *Revista de Occidente* and Ortega y Gasset.[1]

---

[1] Maruja Mallo (Ana María Gómez González) was born on January 5, 1902 in Viveiro, a town in the province of Lugo, in Spain's northwestern region of Galicia (Ferris 33; Mangini, *Maruja Mallo* 35). For biographical information on Mallo, see: José Luis Ferris, *Maruja Mallo: la gran transgresora del 27*; Shirley Mangini, *Maruja Mallo y la vanguardia española*; and Carme Vidal, *Maruxa Mallo*. José Ortega y Gasset (1883–1955) was the founder (in

---

R. M. Silverman (✉)
Department of Modern Languages, Florida International University, Miami, FL, USA
e-mail: silvermr@fiu.edu

© The Author(s), under exclusive license to Springer Nature Switzerland AG 2024
R. M. Silverman, E. Sánchez-Pardo (eds.), *Nomadic New Women*, https://doi.org/10.1007/978-3-031-62482-7_13

323

324   R. M. SILVERMAN

Notwithstanding Ortega y Gasset's appreciation for Mallo, as well as a small cluster of other similarly inclined women artists, writers, and intellectuals, as "a positive contribution to the new era," his aesthetic philosophy relies on an idea of abstraction into which masculine "objectivity" has been encoded. In his watershed *La deshumanización del arte* [The Dehumanization of Art; 1925], Ortega y Gasset detaches what he calls "pure art," "new art," and the "new style" from the body, and the emotion and sentimentality that he associates with nineteenth-century bourgeois art forms (19–20).[2] In the treatise's well-known narrative about a dying man attended by his wife and doctor, a journalist, and an artist, the artist's "objective" perspective, paradigmatic of the new modern aesthetic, constitutes the polar opposite of the subjective and sentimental, embodied in the scene's lone female figure—the dying man's wife (21–25).

Mallo's art transcended the "feminine" and its sundry negative connotations, fitting with the concepts of the "new art" and "new style" established and promoted by Ortega y Gasset.[3] Certainly, the Mallo of the 1928 *Revista de Occidente* exhibition was "A conscientious and expert painter, who studies mathematical proportion, who draws with a sure hand, who is neat and correct, endowed with great imagination and provided with much joy, humor, and irony" (De la Gándara 24).[4] In Francisco Ayala's estimation, expressed in a 1929 review of her work in the preeminent journal *Alfar*, "the assured hand of M. Mallo has found the *new*, the super-real, solely by transforming the elements that the modern world offered her."[5] Yet, Ayala, aware of the limitations of Ortega y Gasset's aesthetic philosophy, lauds Mallo for exceeding them, noting, "[...] for this she has not needed to dispense with the values of the spirit, as other pure painters want to do. Rather she has generously incorporated them."[6]

1923) and Editor of the *Revista de Occidente*. All translations are mine unless otherwise noted. I use the Spanish-language version of Mangini's *Maruja Mallo y la vanguardia española* except where indicated.

[2] "arte puro"; "arte nuevo"; "el nuevo estilo."

[3] See also Susan Kirkpatrick, *Mujer, modernismo y vanguardia en España (1898–1931)* (242–43) and Francisco Rivas, "Maruja Mallo, pintora del más allá" (16–17).

[4] "Unha pintora aplicada e experta, que estudia a proporción matemática, que dibuxa con man segura, que é pulcra e correcta, dotada de gran imaxinación e provista de moita ledicia, humor e ironía."

[5] "la mano segura de M. Mallo ha encontrado lo *nuevo*, lo suprareal, sólo con transformar los elementos que el mundo moderno le ofrecía." Emphasis in the original.

[6] "...no ha necesitado para ello prescindir de los valores del espíritu, como quieren otros pintores puros. Sino que los ha incorporado generosamente."

13 A DOUBLE EXILE: CROSSING THE FEMALE FIGURE IN MARUJA MALLO'S... 325

Mallo's consciousness of the potential shortcomings of abstraction became acute, especially after her experience of the Spanish Civil War's outbreak (July 18, 1936) and her subsequent exile (in the winter of 1937):

> Cubism had an abstract concept of the external world. It is a subjective, conceptual reality, comprehensible to a minority of people.
> [...]
> But art cannot sustain itself only through formal conquests. To a new humanity corresponds a new art. Because an artistic revolution does not content itself solely with technical discoveries [...].[7]
> The function of abstract art is to seize the new reality.
> ("Proceso histórico" 32)

Standing out amidst the display of thirty engravings and ten paintings at Mallo's 1928 *Revista de Occidente* exhibition were the *Verbenas* [Fairs], representations of popular street culture, painted in a post-Expressionist style, whose searing social criticism must have struck a chord in the politically charged atmosphere of the 1920s and 30s, prior to the Spanish Civil War of 1936–39. In Mallo's posterior 1937 lecture, *Lo popular en la plástica española a través de mi obra 1928–1936* [The Popular in the Spanish Plastic Arts through my Work, 1928–1936],[8] given not long after she began her life in exile in Buenos Aires, her affinity for the popular ties in to her solidarity with Spain's Second Republic (1931–39) and opposition to the 1936 *coup d'état*. In the lecture, Mallo describes the way in which she came to take inspiration from Madrid's street culture, making reference to her 1928 *Revista de Occidente* exhibition: "What surprises me most in these moments is present in my production: it was the street. What most attracted me was the popular. The multiplicity of beings, things, and objects" (7–8).[9]

It is in great part through her portrayal of the female figure and female body that Mallo dissociates her brand of "new art" from the

---

[7] "El cubismo tuvo un concepto abstracto del mundo exterior. Es una realidad subjetiva, conceptual, comprensible para las minorías [...]. Pero un arte no puede sostenerse solamente por conquistas formales. A una humanidad nueva corresponde un arte nuevo. Porque una revolución artística no se contenta solamente de hallazgos técnicos [...]. La función del arte abstracto es apoderarse de la nueva realidad."

[8] Losada published the lecture as a book in 1939.

[9] "Lo que más me sorprende en estos momentos está presente en mi producción: era la calle. Lo que más me atraía era lo popular. La multiplicidad de seres, cosas y objetos."

326   R. M. SILVERMAN

masculine-as-objective perspective with which modern art is inextricably linked in Ortega y Gasset's *The Dehumanization of Art*. This uncoupling occurs on three main levels: one, Mallo's taking of a socially engaged stand, mirrored in her (often overlapping) depiction of both women and popular culture, distinguishing her work from so-called "pure art"; two, her foregrounding of the female figure and the material experience of the female body; and three, her troubling of the masculine, objectivizing and objectifying perspective, as related to the desiring male gaze and classificatory ontology. In her work of the 1920s and 30s, Mallo circumvents gendered expectations with respect to her representation of the female figure and female body, implicitly critiquing the foundations of Ortega y Gasset's masculinist objectivity. Later on, in the 1940s, Mallo's contact with South America's natural beauty while living there in exile brings a sensuality and consciousness of female bodily experience, including the sexual, to her art, especially the *Naturalezas vivas* [Live Nature] series.[10] With the *Live Nature* series, Mallo also reclaims for herself as a female artist the taxonomic function which, similar to Ortega y Gasset's objectivizing perspective, has ordinarily been male territory. This *taxinomia*, as Foucault has argued in *Les mots et les choses: Une archéologie des sciences humaines* [The Order of Things: An Archaeology of the Human Sciences], is bound up with the ontology—the categorization in keeping with principles of sameness and difference—encoding the language of representation. Mallo's art then comes to challenge the power and authority of the male gaze with the *Retratos bidimensionales* [Two-dimensional Portraits] of the 1940s and early 50s. As an exile, her concern for social justice and the harmony of humankind, after the conflagrations of the Spanish Civil War and World War II, leads her, in the series, to depict the variety of (frequently mixed) ethnic and racial archetypes encountered during her time in South America. As problematic as Mallo's portrayal of the Other might be from a twenty-first-century viewpoint, into which a thorough criticism of the process of viewing and cataloguing the Other has been assimilated, a number of the *Two-dimensional Portraits* should be understood as actually questioning the classificatory operation that Foucault deems the defining

---

[10] Mangini translates the *Naturalezas vivas* paintings as "Live Nature"—a translation that I have adopted ("Atlantic" 95). Yet, the title of the series can also be considered as a pun on the term "*naturaleza muerta*" ("*bodegón*"), or "still life." Mallo's *Naturalezas vivas* are, in this sense, "not-so-still lifes."

characteristic of the classical episteme—particularly regarding this classifying operation's gendered underpinnings.[11]

Since Laura Mulvey's seminal essay, "Visual Pleasure and Narrative Cinema" (1975), feminist psychoanalytic film theory has connected the structure of vision and the associated economy of pleasure to masculine needs and unconscious obsessions. Male desire, according to this line of thought, has generated the prevailing fascination with the female object of vision—the "woman as representation/image" (Mulvey 26). Parallel to narrative cinema, there can be identified a comparable controlling fascination with the female object in other genres and media, such as portrait painting. Mallo's *Two-dimensional Portraits* by turns invite, evade, and defy the gaze of the viewer, circumventing the visual economy as regulated by masculine desire. Through the expression, or lack thereof, on their faces, the meeting or avoidance of the viewer's gaze, the female subjects (or objects) of the *Two-dimensional Portraits* vex their classification and pleasurable consumption.

Turning back to Mallo's works of 1927–28, her revolt against traditional Spanish social and gender norms turns on her depiction of the female figure and the female body, which throws into question both the valorization of her art in consonance with a masculinist conception of the "new style" and the "new art" itself.[12] For instance, across the center of *La verbena* [The Fair (1927)], two figures, marked as female by the curvaceous shapes of their breasts and buttocks, and dressed in the modern fashion, stride forcefully, opening their legs and moving their bodies in a manner that at the time would doubtless have been judged indecorous. Just as in *The Fair*, in *Ciclista* [Cyclist (1927)], *Mujer tenista* [Woman Tennis Player (1927)], and *Dos mujeres en la playa* [Two Women on the Beach (1928)], Mallo portrays the female body as at once athletic, powerful, and feminine. The contradictory mixture of these qualities, in *Two Women on the Beach*, includes a knowing play on the nude; one of the two figures in the painting stays shrouded in the folds of fabric covering her

---

[11] Foucault's skepticism of *taxinomia*—the ordering system in the biological sciences that provides for the "arrangement of identities and differences into ordered tables"—is fundamental to his critique of the classical episteme (71–72).

[12] See Kirkpatrick's *Mujer, modernismo y vanguardia en España (1898–1931)* ironic commentary on the contradiction between the espousal of modernity and progress by Ortega y Gasset and the Spanish avant-garde, and (with a few exceptions, such as Mallo and María Zambrano) the tendency of each to treat the female as either a mere object to be represented or the source of "feminine" sentiment.

328   R. M. SILVERMAN

body, while the other's exposed form flirts with nakedness, one of her strong legs kicking backward at the same time as her softly rounded breasts and demure countenance, eyes downcast, suggest femininity. Such a contrast between modern and conventional views of the female body serves to simultaneously contest gender roles and subvert the power of the male gaze—whether its perspective be shaped by traditional or modern aesthetic values.

Mallo put her own body on the line in rising against the behavioral codes then in force. Her conduct as a young woman living in Madrid in the 1920s and 30s flew in the face of convention: she and her friend, the writer Concha Méndez, on whom many of the female figures in her works of the 1920s are modeled, became as *flâneuses*, enjoying the city's popular cultural expressions and street life, like the fairs depicted in the *Verbenas* ([Fairs]; Kirkpatrick 226–29). Mallo cross-dressed on an excursion to the historic Silos monastery with her friends, the poet and playwright Federico García Lorca and the artist Salvador Dalí, entered the Madrid Church of San Miguel on a bicycle, and, notoriously, engaged in the *sinsombrerismo* that would have her, along with Lorca, Dalí, and painter Margarita Manso Robledo, dodge stones thrown for the sartorial violation of going hatless in public (Pérez de Ayala, "Álbum" 78; Balló 120).[13] Mallo's boundary-breaking "performances" sabotaged male authority in a way analogous to the masquerade as social subversion in Mikhail Bakhtin's carnivalesque.[14] Moreover, by adopting an object position parallel to that of the female figures protagonizing her paintings, she created both the frame and ground for resisting masculinist visual and representational economies.

In the 1930s, Mallo's commitment to societal issues steadily increased, propelled considerably by her relationships with other women artists and

[13] "*Sinsombrerismo*" means, literally, "without-a-hat-ism." See also Tània Balló, *Las sinsombrero. Las pensadoras y artistas olvidadas de la generación del 27*; Kirkpatrick, *Mujer, modernismo y vanguardia en España (1898–1931)*; Ferris, *Maruja Mallo. La gran transgresora del 27* (81–85, 89–90); and Paloma Ulacia Altolaguirre, *Concha Méndez. Memorias habladas, memorias armadas*. With respect to Mallo's 1932 Galerie Pierre exhibition, see *Maruja Mallo*, edited by Pérez de Ayala and Rivas in 1992 (125), and Balló (118). Mallo and Salvador Dalí met and became friends while both were students at the *Escuela de San Fernando de Bellas Artes* (Ferris 56, 67). With respect to Mallo's friendships with such members of the Generation of 1927 as Dalí and Federico García Lorca, see Rosa Ruiz Gisbert, "Maruja Mallo y la Generación del '27."

[14] Regarding Mallo's transgressions as "performances," see Mangini, "The Gendered Body Politic of Maruja Mallo" (161, 166–67). See also María Alejandra Zanetta, *La subversión enmascarada: análisis de la obra de Maruja Mallo* (16–17). Mikhail Bakhtin explains the concept of the carnivalesque in his 1965 book, *Rabelais and His World*.

13 A DOUBLE EXILE: CROSSING THE FEMALE FIGURE IN MARUJA MALLO'S... 329

intellectuals. Following a crucial year abroad in Paris (1931–32) from an artistic standpoint, during which the prestigious Galerie Pierre (Pierre Loeb) recognized her work with an exhibition (May, 1932), Mallo reconnected with the writers Méndez, Rosa Chacel, and Ernestina de Champourcín, and participated in the *tertulias* hosted by the philosopher and essayist María Zambrano (another of the tiny cluster of women anointed by Ortega y Gasset), further strengthening her sense of identity as an artist and intellectual (Balló 119–21).[15] Mallo soon coupled this identity with a dedication to causes such as labor, aligning herself with Zambrano, the poet Miguel Hernández, and the union organizer and political militant Alberto Fernández Mezquita. In 1936, shortly before the July outbreak of the Civil War, Mallo left Madrid for her native region of Galicia to join the *Misiones Pedagógicas* [Pedagogical Missions], educational programs sponsored by the II Spanish Republic that were designed to uplift rural populations through a focus on literacy and the arts (Balló 125–26).

One special series of paintings to emerge from this time of civic engagement, *La religión del trabajo* [The Religion of Work (1936)], constitutes a transitional phase in Mallo's art.[16] For *The Religion of Work* bridges home and exile with respect to her representation of the female form, as well as to subjects related to popular culture as entwined with the social ideals of the Second Republic. The large female figure dominating the first canvas in the series, *La sorpresa del trigo* [The Surprise of the Wheat], is the embodiment of the Greek goddess Demeter in the course of her transformation into wheat. Since ancient Greek mythology regarded Demeter as the goddess of the harvest and Earth's fertility who presided over natural life cycles, it can be inferred that Mallo's depiction of the goddess reflects a nature-based spirituality and belief in women's centrality to the Republic (Zanetta 159–60).

In the 1937 *Arquitectura humana* [Human Architecture], the earliest canvas in *The Religion of Work* series to be painted in Mallo's refuge of Buenos Aires, a large female figure wearing clothing fashioned from fishing nets stands at center foreground holding a fish in her hands, while the background features two boat-like geometric forms (Zanetta 188–89).

---

[15] "*Tertulias*" are informal gatherings in which artists, writers, and intellectuals converse.

[16] Mallo painted *La sorpresa del trigo* [*The Surprise of the Wheat*] in Spain, in May of 1936, just a few short months before the Civil War's opening salvo. She brought it with her when she went into exile in Argentina (Rivas 23; Mangini, *Maruja Mallo* 205).

330   R. M. SILVERMAN

The boat motif suggests "'la barca de San Pedro'" [the Barque of Saint Peter], symbolic of the Church, and the maternal womb or cradle (Zanetta 189). *Human Architecture* brings to mind the pagan and Christian identification of bodies of water with the feminine, and the traditional association of female mythological figures and Virgins with the sea; the painting can also be understood as referring to the zodiac-figure of Virgo (tied, in Greek and Roman mythology, to Demeter), a maiden who is customarily portrayed as bearing an ear of wheat. In *The Surprise of the Wheat* and *El canto de las espigas* [The Song of the Ears of Wheat; 1939], another canvas in the *The Religion of Work* series, the representation of fish and wheat together alludes to Christ's miracle of the loaves and fishes.[17]

Mallo emphasizes, in *The Popular in the Spanish Plastic Arts through my Work*, the links between the imagery and social themes of *The Religion of Work*, her earlier creations centering on the popular, and her vision for the future of her native land and humanity:

> This is the evolution of my painting, a production that stems from the popular art of men, the form of which goes underground through the transformation of my work and flowers in conjunction with other realities. *Sorpresa del trigo* [Surprise of the Wheat] (May of 1936), which I announce as a prologue to my work on the laborers of sea and land, the compenetration of material elements. The wheat, universal plant, symbol of struggle, earthly myth. The manifestation of a belief that surges out of the severity and grace of the two Castiles, from my materialist faith in the triumph of the fishes, in the kingdom of the ear of wheat. (40)[18]

In *The Surprise of the Wheat*, Demeter and the wheat stalks, her homologue in Nature, stand for the humanistic and egalitarian society as envisioned by the architects of the Second Republic, but the female figure's

---

[17] The miracle of "Jesus Feeds More Than Five Thousand" is described in the Bible, in Matt. 14.13–21, Mark 6.30–44, Luke 9.10–17, and John 6.1–15; and the miracle of "Jesus Feeds More Than Four Thousand," in Matt. 15.32–39 and Mark 8.1–9.

[18] "Así es la evolución de mi pintura, producción que arranca del arte popular (1928) del hombre, cuya forma va subterráneamente por debajo de la transformación de mi obra y brota en conjunción con otras realidades. *Sorpresa del trigo* (mayo de 1936) que anuncio como prólogo a mi labor sobre los trabajadores de mar y tierra, compenetración de elementos materiales. El trigo, vegetal universal, símbolo de la lucha, mito terrenal. Manifestación de creencia que surge de la severidad y la gracia de las dos Castillas, de mi fe materialista en el triunfo de los peces, en el reinado de la espiga."

13 A DOUBLE EXILE: CROSSING THE FEMALE FIGURE IN MARUJA MALLO'S... 331

taking of center stage bespeaks a gynocentrism that far exceeds the Republican model (Zanetta 164).

The geometric stylization of the figures in *The Religion of Work* series liberates them from the confines of feminine stereotypes, rendering them as universal archetypes of mythology, spirituality, and social justice.[19] Such stylization fits with Mallo's conceptualization of the "integration of background and form, Unity," inspired by the "constructive universalism" of the Uruguayan painter Joaquín Torres-García—a constructivism that she adapted to suit her idiosyncratic aesthetic (36):[20]

---

[19] See Zanetta (166–67).

[20] "integración del fondo y la forma, la Unidad"; "universalismo constructivo." As Mallo writes, in *Lo popular en la plástica española a través de mi obra* [The Popular in the Spanish Plastic Arts through my Work]:

> La Naturaleza es lo que comienza a atraerme: hallar un nuevo orden. El orden es la arquitectura íntima de la naturaleza y del hombre, la matemática viviente del esqueleto. En la naturaleza clarividente y misteriosa, espontánea y construída [sic], desprovista de fantasmas anacrónicos, analizo la estructura de los minerales y vegetales, la diversidad de formas cristalinas y biológicas, sintetizadas en un orden numérico y geométrico, en un orden viviente y universal.

> Nature is what started to attract me: to find a new order. Order is the intimate architecture of Nature and Man, the living mathematics of the skeleton. In Nature, intuitive and mysterious, spontaneous and constructed, devoid of anachronous phantasms, I analyze the structure of minerals and vegetables, the diversity of crystalline and biological forms, synthesized in a numeric and geometric order, in a living and universal order. (36)

Regarding Mallo in connection with Joaquín Torres-García and "el arte constructivo," see Mangini, *Maruja Mallo y la vanguardia española* (213), Mangini, "The Gendered Body Politic of Maruja Mallo" (174), and Guillermo de Osma, "Maruja Mallo: Catálogo Razonado y Archivo" (6). As Rivas notes, "Progresivamente interesada por las matemáticas y la geometría, en 1933 frecuenta el menguado círculo madrileño de Torres-García." ["Progressively interested in math and geometry, in 1933 she frequented the reduced Madrid circle of Torres-García." (22)] The Uruguayan artist, theorist, and pedagogue Torres-García founded the Grupo de Arte Constructivo in Madrid in 1933, of which Mallo was a member; he later explained his vision of constructivism in the visual arts in his 1944 treatise *Universalismo constructivo* (Bonet 599; Osma, "Argentina" 388). See also Éric Darragon, "Torres-García, una visión utópica." As Osma explains, in "Maruja Mallo en Argentina: más luces que sombras," Torres-García introduced Mallo to the books of the mathematician Matila Ghyka (388).

332   R. M. SILVERMAN

Triangular, rectangular and pentagonal nets over circles are the living organisms mentioned, live ordered structures, recreated reality where law and content mutually need each other.

This human presence and absence, a constant in my work, which appears in the *Popular Subjects, Machines and Mannequins, Cinematic Subjects, Sewers and Church Towers, Humanized Nature,* and *Living Architecture,* are magical presences that engender a plastic conception of Man. They are precursor signs that determine original human forms in accordance with a new conception of the universe, a universe that demands a new order, human forms that respond to a new reality and can be translated into language. [...]

Parallel to content, the plastic evolves from objective realism, 1928, to objective destruction, 1932. These visual realities turn into a subjective reality, 1936. In ordering reason, a reason that fulfills a function of reintegrating into unity the plastic properties of a painting. (*Lo popular* 39–40)[21]

It is not coincidental that Mallo attaches the date of 1936—the year in which the Spanish Civil War began—to the transformation of her "objective realism, 1928" and "objective destruction, 1932" into a "subjective reality" founded on an "ordering reason."[22] Indeed, this evolution, as explained in *The Popular in the Spanish Plastic Arts through my Work,* forms the basis of Mallo's second lecture in exile, pronounced on June 22, 1937 at the Buenos Aires branch of the *Sociedad Amigos del Arte,* the organization that sponsored her travel to South America, which became an escape from the existential threat posed by the Civil War and, later, Francisco Franco's 1939–75 dictatorship (Pérez de Ayala, "Vida vibrante"

---

[21] "Redes triangulares, rectangulares y pentagonales sobre círculos son los organismos vivientes mencionados, estructuras vivas ordenadas, realidad recreada donde la ley y el contenido se requieren mutuamente.

Esta presencia y ausencia humana, constante en mi labor, que aparece en los *Temas populares, Máquinas y maniquíes, Temas cinemáticos, Cloacas y Campanarios, Naturalezas humanizadas* y *Arquitecturas vivientes,* son presencias mágicas que engendran una concepción plástica del hombre. Son signos precursores que determinan formas humanas inéditas de acuerdo con una nueva concepción del universo, universo que reclama un nuevo orden, formas humanas que respondan a la nueva realidad y puedan traducirse en lenguaje. [...]

Paralelamente al contenido la plástica evoluciona del realismo objetivo, 1928, a la destrucción objetiva, 1932. Estas realidades visuales se transforman en realidad subjetiva, 1936. En razón ordenadora, razón que cumple una función de reintegrar a unidad las propiedades plásticas de un cuadro."

[22] "realismo objetivo, 1928"; "destrucción objetiva, 1932"; "realidad subjetiva"; "razón ordenadora."

13 A DOUBLE EXILE: CROSSING THE FEMALE FIGURE IN MARUJA MALLO'S... 333

22). Mallo's first South-American lecture, "Proceso histórico de la forma en las artes plásticas" [Historical Development of Form in the Plastic Arts], given in Montevideo on the prior date of April 28, a few weeks after her arrival on the continent, connects aesthetics with her political and social stance, and condition as a Spanish-Civil-War exile:

> The new art should discover laws, consider Nature as a whole. Art should be a compendium of knowledge, it must make exact realization of the place that it occupies in the entirety of natural and historical facts.
>
> Art is a universal compendium, it has its history in time like Nature and it represents contemporary thought.
>
> Nature, historical facts, and art go together unceasingly. Consciously or unconsciously art is propaganda. Revolutionary art is a weapon that a conscious society employs against a broken down society. The new art is not a weapon, but rather a result; it is the incarnation, the symbol of a new society.
>
> The new order, comprehensive art, is that which emerges after the last battles. That which becomes established after heroic combat. (32)[23]

To these social themes, and concern with form and structure, during the first part of Mallo's exile, would soon be added a renewed focus on the female figure and body. According to Shirley Mangini, "As her [Mallo's] exile in Latin America continued, she gradually replaced her socialist subject matter with a language that exalted the female body; feminine oceanic motifs and mythological female figures. She rarely painted male figures at

---

[23] "El arte nuevo debe descubrir leyes, considerar la naturaleza como un todo. El arte debe ser un compendio de conocimientos, tiene que darse cuenta exacta del lugar que ocupa en el conjunto de los hechos naturales e históricos.

El arte es un compendio universal, tiene su historia en el tiempo como la naturaleza y representa el pensamiento contemporáneo.

La naturaleza, los hechos históricos y el arte van unidos incesantemente. El arte consciente o inconscientemente es propaganda. El arte revolucionario es un arma que emplea una sociedad consciente en contra de una sociedad descompuesta. El arte nuevo no es un arma, sino que es un resultado; es la encarnación, es el símbolo de una sociedad nueva.

El nuevo orden, el arte integral, es el que surge después de las últimas batallas. El que se establece después de los heroicos combates."

Mallo was able to escape from Spain to Portugal thanks to an invitation from the Amigos del Arte de Buenos Aires. Once in Lisbon, she was protected by the poet Gabriela Mistral, future Nobel laureate, who was then Chile's ambassador to Portugal (Pérez de Ayala, "Álbum" 83). See also Mangini, "From the Atlantic to the Pacific: Maruja Mallo in Exile" (89). Mallo arrived at the port of Buenos Aires on February 9, 1937, aboard the English steamship *Alcántara* (Pérez de Ayala, "Álbum" 83; "Vida vibrante" 21).

334   R. M. SILVERMAN

all in the 1940s" ("From the Atlantic" 94). Mallo takes on the patriarchal aspect of European art and aesthetics in *Esquema* [Diagram (n.d.)], a drawing that reworks Leonardo da Vinci's *The Vitruvian Man* (1487/1490). Da Vinci's drawing places the male body at its perspectival nexus—comparable to the way in which the masculine occupies the center of Renaissance art and Humanism. In Mallo's ironic reworking, the female, instead of the male, body stands inside a pentagon—reversing Da Vinci's paradigm of "universal man" to make it "universal woman" (Zanetta 163–66). She leaves the sex organs to the imagination (in contradistinction to Da Vinci's *The Vitruvian Man*) and draws two circles at the chest area, using geometric forms to suggest the presence of breasts. In *Diagram*, Mallo's foregrounding of the female figure destabilizes the androcentric concept of art and ontology that undergirds *The Vitruvian Man*, reclaiming the female body and, by extension, women's role in shaping a future utopia (Zanetta 163–66).[24]

In the first complete series created by Mallo while in exile, the *Live Nature* series, the female retains its central place. At the same time, there is a shift in attitude and aesthetic: the natural beauty of South America and Mallo's exhilaration at having found a new life infuses the works in this series with a palpable *joie de vivre*. Created between 1941 and 1944, the sixteen works in the *Live Nature* series marry a sensual materiality with what Guillermo de Osma describes as "a geometric structure, the 'harmonic design,' authentic skeleton of the painting which all the lines and brushstrokes obey" (Preface).[25] According to Osma, Mallo initiated her artistic process by making highly structured "trazados armónicos," which followed the Golden Rule of Geometry and the proportions found in Nature ("Argentina" 406). As Juan Pérez de Ayala explains, America transformed Mallo, engendering in her work "a vibrant explosion of creativity"—a vibrancy indicated by the title of Mallo's 1943 *Naturaleza viva. Vida Vibrante* ([Live Nature. Vibrant Life]; "Vida vibrante" 23;

---

[24] Leonardo da Vinci based his drawing, *The Vitruvian Man*, on the work of the Roman architect Vitruvius, who, in his work, established a canon of proportions for architecture and the human body.

[25] "una estructura geométrica, el 'trazado armónico', auténtico esqueleto del cuadro al que obedecen todas las líneas y pinceladas." Osma believes it quite possible that Mallo also found inspiration in the Darwinian naturalist Ernst Haeckel's book *Kunstformen der Natur* (1904), with its vibrantly colored prints and display of the most elaborate shapes of marine plants and animals, noting that the book enjoyed wide popularity among artists of the early twentieth century ("Argentina" 401–402).

13 A DOUBLE EXILE: CROSSING THE FEMALE FIGURE IN MARUJA MALLO'S...   335

Naturalezas vivas 65).[26] The explosion of bright colors in the painting—blues, purples, and magentas, striking against muted pastels evocative of sandy beaches—is held in equilibrium by clearly traced lines and demarcated shapes.

At this point, social themes and imagery recede from Mallo's art as she conceives a new artistic language that exalts the female body, integrating "feminine" sea motifs and female mythological figures (Mangini, *Maruja Mallo* 224). Mallo's physical proximity to the sea during her frequent travels in South America provides inspiration for her maritime motifs, which evoke the experiences of the female body, incorporating the sensual and sexual. Illustrative of this tendency is a 1939 photographic portrait (retouched in ink by the artist) taken on a Chilean beach during a visit there with the poet Pablo Neruda. Covered in long curling tendrils of seaweed, Mallo poses as if she were a divinity, uniting her woman's body with Nature and turning herself into a feminine mythological figure of the sea; she is at once mermaid, siren, and Aphrodite, the Greek goddess of love and beauty born of sea foam whose attributes include a scallop shell.[27]

The new vitalism in Mallo's art can be traced to her initial discovery of Valparaíso, Viña del Mar, and the Chilean Pacific coast in 1939 (Pérez de Ayala, "Vida vibrante" 24–25):[28]

> That extraordinary coast of Chile is full of surprises. That violent Pacific sea bathes beaches whose sands are colored stones, where the palm trees rise

[26] "una vibrante explosión creativa." See also Mangini, *Maruja Mallo* (224).

[27] Venus is the Roman version of the Greek Aphrodite (Bulfinch 23, 69, 82). Demeter (Ceres) is the goddess of grain and agriculture, and the mother of Proserpine, who is associated with both the growth of crops in Spring and the underworld, to which she was abducted, prompting her mother's search for her there (Bulfinch 18, 51–56). In *Maruja Mallo, Naturalezas vivas 1941–1944*, Pérez de Ayala identifies the photograph as *Maruja Mallo en las playas de Chile* (55). Mallo's photograph serves as an illustration in the exhibition catalog, *Mujeres en vanguardia: La Residencia de Señoritas en su centenario [1915–1936]*, edited by Almudena de la Cueva and Margarita Márquez Padorno (376). See also the cover illustration of Pérez de Ayala, ed. *Maruja Mallo: Naturalezas vivas (1941–1944)*.

[28] Mallo had been invited by the Alianza de Intelectuales de Chile to speak at the University of Santiago on January 25, 1939. Her lecture, however, was suspended in the wake of the great 1939 earthquake. In solidarity with the Chilean people following the tragedy, Mallo changed the topic of her talk (rescheduled to February 3) to the deleterious effects of the 1936 military uprising on her native Galicia (Pérez de Ayala, "Vida vibrante" 23–24). Mallo published a reportage on the tragic events in Galicia in the Barcelona newspaper *La Vanguardia* in 1938; "Relato veraz de la realidad en Galicia" ["True Story of the Reality in Galicia"] was published in three installments (August 14, 21, and 26).

336   R. M. SILVERMAN

and over which the sea hurls stones charred by the volcanoes and polished by the waters. There are enormous geraniums and spherical hydrangeas there that flower on the beaches among enormous seaweed and starfish. A surprising panorama, a marvelous garden that is completed, in color, with the fire of the volcanoes and the intense blue of the ocean's waters. (qtd. in Pérez de Ayala, "Vida vibrante" 24)[29]

Mallo turns the different sensations experienced on Atlantic shores, such as the sight of the abundant orchids at Punta Ballena, into fresh ideas and motifs for the *Live Nature* paintings.[30]

Yet, the *Live Nature* canvases cannot be understood as a simple reflection of Mallo's evident joy in South America's natural environs. In contrast with her previous work, the *Live Nature* series of the 1940s alludes to female sexuality; what Tilly Craig has described as a "profound connection with the natural world" leads to a "mythic and definitively female eroticism" (45). For example, the shape of the conch shell and orchid in *Naturaleza viva con orquídea* [Live Nature with an Orchid; (1942)], and the piercing of the starfish by two roses in *Naturaleza viva con estrella de mar* [Live Nature with a Starfish (1943)], evoke the female body, sex organs, and sexual pleasure achieved through penetration (Zanetta n. pag.; Mangini, *Maruja Mallo* 225).[31]

At the same time, the *Live Nature* paintings are typified by the same attention to abstract form and the geometric as in Mallo's previous work. Significantly, the series evinces an ontological inclination—a predilection that stretches back to the "multiplicity of beings, things, and objects" in the *Fairs* (Mallo, *Lo popular* 8).[32] Mallo's encounter with the Chilean

---

[29] "Esa extraordinaria costa de Chile está llena de sorpresas. Ese violento mar Pacífico, baña unas playas cuyas arenas son piedras de colores, donde brotan las palmeras y sobre las cuales el mar arroja piedras calcinadas por los volcanes y pulidas por las aguas. Allí hay enormes geraneos [sic] y esféricas hortensias que florecen en las playas entre las enormes algas y las estrellas de mar. Un panorama sorprendente, un jardín maravilloso que se completa, en color, con el fuego de los volcanes y el azul intenso de las aguas del océano." Pérez de Ayala quotes Rafael B. Esteban, "Maruja entre rosas y orquídeas," *Estampa*, Buenos Aires, 25 de enero de 1943.

[30] See Pérez de Ayala, "Vida vibrante" (24–25).

[31] The treatment of sexuality in Mallo's work may be compared with Surrealism (a topic that is beyond the scope of this article). In her review article, "Surrealist Women," Ara H. Merjian considers Mallo as a Surrealist artist and discusses her involvement with the movement.

[32] "multiplicidad de seres, cosas y objetos."

Pacific Coast only trains her focus more intensely on the architectonic order of Nature:

> I was amazed at your beaches. There were blue, golden, and white ones. I gazed at them and didn't believe it. I rubbed my eyes fearing that the illusion would disappear from sight; but they remained and were real. And then, the large shells
> [...] what a profusion of beauty, what harmony of forms, what a dazzling architecture of finished geometry! (qtd. in Lombay 40–41)[33]

The delineation of natural objects in the *Live Nature* series can be compared in this sense with the meticulous detailing of the shapes and colors of various sorts of algae in a number of Mallo's studies, a good many of which date from 1943.[34]

Parallel to the *Live Nature* canvases, Mallo's orientation toward detail is in evidence in the *Two-dimensional Portraits*. However, in the *Two-dimensional Portraits*, contrastingly, Mallo turns back to the female figure—the heads and busts of women from different South-American ethnic and racial groups—rather than indirectly evoking the material experience of the female body. In the *Two-dimensional Portraits* (also known as the *Cabezas de mujer* [Heads of Women]), created between 1941 and 1951, Mallo explores the polyethnic character of South America through the lens of her exile's desire for the harmonious and just co-existence of humankind, as well as the renewed ontological thrust of her work.[35]

Francisco Rivas has argued in his catalog essay for the 1992 Mallo exhibition at the Madrid Galería Guillermo de Osma that the artist's representation of ethnic and racial archetypes in the *Two-dimensional Portraits* is part of an optimistic vision for a future renascence in response to the oppression and violence of the 1930s and 40s: "The successive American cycles of Maruja Mallo arise like iconographic proposals, mythic models,

---

[33] "Maravillábame de vuestras playas. Las había azules, doradas, blancas. Las miraba y no lo creía. Me frotaba los ojos temiendo ver desaparecer la ilusión; pero permanecían y eran realidad. Y luego, las caracolas [...] ¡qué profusión de belleza, qué armonía de formas, qué deslumbradora arquitectura de acabada geometría!" Reinaldo Lombay quotes Mallo. See also Pérez de Ayala, "Vida Vibrante" (24).

[34] See Pérez de Ayala, *Maruja Mallo: Naturalezas vivas*, figs. 13, 14, 16, 17, 18, 19, and 20 (42, 44, 46). Figs. 13–18 are dated 1943; 19 and 20 are undated. All are oil and pencil on cardboard (54).

[35] The women portrayed in the series range from Black, multi-racial and multi-ethnic, to blond and fair. See Mangini, *Maruja Mallo* (223).

338   R. M. SILVERMAN

for that new reality that emerges from the ashes of the World War. The beyond that will soon be close at hand" (24–25).[36] Rosa M[a]. Ballesteros García, writing in 2004, has similarly focused on the depiction of "futuristic racial archetypes" in the portraits (18).[37] The views of Rivas and Ballesteros are consonant with the opinion expressed by Zoila Villadeamigo decades earlier, in 1948, the year of Mallo's successful show at the Carroll Carstairs Gallery in New York, which encompassed five *Cabezas de mujer* [Heads of Women]:

> Maruja Mallo's master work is represented in her paintings of heads with the five races, with a tonality faithful in color and form, which characterizes the races. In this work, considered an incomparable novelty in modern pictorial art, the artist has magisterially captured racial archetypes plastically, in the humanized order that corresponds to each race. (qtd. in Pérez de Ayala and Rivas 90)[38]

Estrella de Diego emphasizes the influence of post-World War II anthropological theories, and related contemporary discourses of race and ethnicity, on Mallo. She underscores the year 1941 as common to the first canvas of the *Two-dimensional Portraits* series (which would illustrate the cover of Ramón Gómez de la Serna's 1942 monograph on the artist) and

---

[36] "Los sucesivos ciclos americanos de Maruja Mallo surgen como propuestas iconográficas, modelos míticos, para esa nueva realidad que surgirá sobre las cenizas de la Guerra Mundial. Un más allá que pronto será un más acá."

[37] "arquetipos raciales futuristas."

[38] "La obra maestra de Maruja Mallo está representada en sus cuadros de cabezas con las cinco razas, con una tonalidad muy fiel en color y la forma, que caracteriza a las razas. En este trabajo, considerado una novedad incomparable en el arte pictórico moderno, la artista ha captado magistralmente los arquetipos raciales plásticamente, en el orden humanizado que corresponde a cada raza." Pérez de Ayala and Rivas quote from the original text: Zoila N. Villadeamigo, "Visitó nuestra redacción la eximia pintora española Maruja Mallo," *Nueva York al día,* Nueva York, 16 de octubre de 1948. In Gisbert's account, "On October 11, 1948, she presented in the Carroll Carstairs Gallery a retrospective with 24 oils, the *Fairs,* the series *The Religion of Work,* 9 *Live Nature* [paintings], 2 *Bunches of Grapes,* and 5 *Heads of Women.* The reviews were extraordinary, irrefutable proof of her establishment." ["El 11 de octubre de 1948 presenta en la Caroll Castairs (sic) Gallery una retrospectiva con 24 óleos, las *Verbenas,* la serie *La religión del trabajo,* 9 *Naturalezas vivas,* 2 *Racimos de uvas* y 5 *Cabezas de mujer.* La crítica fue extraordinaria, prueba irrefutable de su consagración."] (235) She notes that a few months before the Carroll Carstairs exhibition, Mallo won the prize in painting at the XII New York Exposition for her *Cabeza de negra* [Head of a Black Woman] of 1942 (235). See also Enrique de Ezcurra, "Maruja Mallo triunfa en Nueva York."

the Spanish-language translation of Ruth Benedict's book-length study, *Raza: ciencia y política* [Race: Science and Politics; 1940], published by the Mexican *Fondo de Cultura Económica*. Benedict, a disciple of the anthropologist Franz Boas, takes inspiration from Boas's idea of cultural relativism, in which cultures are conceptualized according to their own, as opposed to external, criteria (Diego, "Retratos" 79).[39] In her essay "Retratos" (2009), Diego surmises that Mallo would likely have been familiar with Benedict's *Race: Science and Politics*, given the particular interests of her contacts in Spanish-American intellectual and artistic circles, and the 1941 date of the Mexican translation (79). For Diego, in the 2009 essay, part of the motivation for the *Two-dimensional Portraits* comes from the new anthropology as conceived by Boas and Benedict, documentation for which she finds in a preparatory sketch for the series with the phrase, "the five races" in the artist's handwriting ("Retratos" 79–80).[40] Yet, in "Maruja Mallo en América" (2021), Diego instead ventures that inspiration for Mallo's representation of an idealized world of ethnic and racial harmony, in which hybridity is regarded positively, may have come from paleoanthropologist José Imbelloni's study, *Poblamiento primitivo de América* [*Primitive Settlement of America*] (431). Whichever Mallo's sources might have been, in the *Two-dimensional Portraits*, the artist becomes as an ethnographer, examining and cataloguing the adornments and embellishments, jewelry, and hairstyles of her portraits' female subjects (Diego, "Retratos" 79).

Mallo's firsthand experience of the autochthonous American, gained during travels through Argentina, Uruguay, Chile, Easter Island, Bolivia, and Brazil makes a significant mark on the *Two-dimensional Portraits*.[41] Gómez de la Serna singles out *La cierva humana* [The Human Deer; 1948], honored by inclusion in the 1951 First Hispano-American Biennial of Art in Madrid, as typical of Brazil's impact on the series ("Nueva actualidad" 100).[42] Pérez de Ayala observes that *The Human Deer* comes out of Mallo's experiences in Rio de Janeiro and that the painting portrays "a Black-Asian model that she had" in that city, who, "according to Mallo's recollection, danced the *macumba* for her, a rite that she also managed to

[39] See Franz Boas, *Race, Language, and Culture*.
[40] "las cinco razas."
[41] Mangini describes Mallo's extensive travels in her article, "From the Atlantic to the Pacific: Maruja Mallo in Exile."
[42] See also Mangini, "From the Atlantic to the Pacific: Maruja Mallo in Exile" (99).

340   R. M. SILVERMAN

attend in the company of the director of the newspaper *O Journal* [Jornal], possibly in the year 1946, the first confirmed reference of her visit to Brazilian lands, or in her more than likely second visit" ("Cotas de ascensión" 105).[43]

In his 1942 monograph on Maruja Mallo, published in Buenos Aires by Losada, Gómez de la Serna interprets the *Two-dimensional Portraits* at once in terms of their modernity and proximity to Renaissance aesthetics. He remarks on the modern quality of the *Two-dimensional Portraits*: "The new paintings represent portraiture stylized with a renewed freshness, the oil tranquil and luminous in effect, the possibility of assembling a series of heads of our times with the new coquetry of very drawn eyebrows and immense lashes and lips painted with surprising reds" (14).[44] He also relates them to Renaissance portraiture: "[...] Maruja Mallo before the immensity of the portrait—eyes as windows on galleries of souls—that correspond in a maze and in this moment like El Greco, like the great Italian portrait artists, she meditates on the solitude of the human figure, the only formula proper to life, whose resolution deserves to be studied" (14).[45]

Gómez de la Serna's observations about the *Two-dimensional Portraits* may be used as a springboard to a comparative analysis of Renaissance aesthetics and representational modes, and Mallo's work in the series. Such a comparison brings into focus how, in the portraits, Mallo makes a similar kind of wry commentary on the underpinnings of Renaissance perspective as in her *Diagram*. Just as in Mallo's ironic transformation of Da Vinci's *Vetruvian Man* in *Diagram*, a number of the *Two-dimensional Portraits* subvert the hierarchies of gender, ontology, and representation

---

[43] "una modelo negro-asiática que tuvo"; "[...] según recordaba Maruja Mallo, le bailaba la macumba, rito al que también llegó a asistir en compañía del director del periódico *O Journal* [Jornal], posiblemente en el año de 1946, primera referencia contrastada de su visita a tierras brasileñas o en un más que probable segundo viaje." Pérez de Ayala refers to anecdotes taken from a transcription of conversations with Mallo recorded by Rivas in 1978 ("Cotas de Ascensión" 105).

[44] "Los cuadros nuevos representan el retrato estilizado con una frescura renovada, el óleo tranquilo y luminotécnico, la posibilidad de armar una serie cabezas de nuestro tiempo con la coquetería nueva de las cejas muy dibujadas, y las pestañas inmensas y los labios pintados con rojos de sorpresa."

[45] "[...] Maruja Mallo ante la inmensidad del retrato—ventanas de ojos hacia galerías de almas—que se corresponden en laberinto y en este momento como el Greco, como los grandes retratistas italianos medita en la soledad de la figura humana, la única fórmula condigna de la vida, la que merece estudiar su resolución."

13 A DOUBLE EXILE: CROSSING THE FEMALE FIGURE IN MARUJA MALLO'S... 341

inherent in the Renaissance art of which Da Vinci has become emblematic. In particular, some of the paintings in the series, including *Cabeza de mujer* (*Cabeza de negra*) [Head of a Woman (Head of a Black Woman); 1946]) and *The Human Deer*, question the structure and economy of the gaze which, from Da Vinci to Ortega y Gasset, has emanated from the male subconscious and a perspective that is implicitly masculine.

Shirley Mangini's characterization of the *Two-dimensional Portraits* as enigmatic, elusive, and evasive points toward the way in which the female subjects of the portraits spurn participation in androcentric perspectival and visual economies:

> This was the first time Mallo displayed an interest in the multicultural nature of America. Some of the women appear to be interracial, others are golden colored, some are black. Some are androgynous like *The Religion of Work* figures. Others are classical, geometrically-conceived heads which evoke 'exotic' people. Although the paintings are small, the heads appear to be massive. The women have thick lips and strange, geometric eyes with prominent tear ducts; most are profiles with voluptuous mouths and deep, dark, coloring and, generally, expressionless faces. Her American painting, like her personality in this phase of her life, is elusive and enigmatic. (*Maruja Mallo* 168)[46]

Mallo's representation of the ethnic and racial diversity, in the portraits comprising the series, constitutes a continuation of the centrality of the female figure in her work and its corresponding destabilizing of masculinist viewpoints and aesthetic ideologies. Diego interprets the systematizing drive—the "classificatory desire"—of the *Two-dimensional Portraits* and *Live Nature* series as a subversion of the spatial and architectonic order controlled by, and reserved for, men ("Retratos" 78).[47] She similarly characterizes Mallo's extensive papers as an "archive of knowledge," underlining the artist's desire to create an order for all that she learns ("América" 419).[48]

---

[46] Here I am quoting Mangini's English-language *Maruja Mallo and the Spanish Avant-Garde.*

[47] "deseo clasificatorio."

[48] "archivo de conocimiento." Estrella de Diego points to Mallo's encyclopedic work on shells, and ethnicity and race, including an unpublished manuscript entitled, *América aborigen* [Aboriginal America] ("América" 419, 432–33).

Mallo's reclaiming of *taxinomia* in several of the *Two-dimensional Portraits* disturbs the classificatory ordering of her female subjects in line with a logical system of sameness and difference.[49] This taxonomic process, which Foucault associates with the classical episteme, and which links to the structuring of perspective and knowledge in Da Vinci's Renaissance *Vitruvian Man*, is destabilized by the female subjects' return or refusal of the gaze, or blank indifference. *Head of a Black Woman* pictures the bust of a Black woman, in which her neck, shoulders, and face are partially in shadow. The woman in the portrait gazes directly out at the viewer or the artist, perhaps warily or maybe defiantly, but her otherwise impassive aspect frustrates any attempt to fix such interpretations. Apart from the ethnic inflection of her elaborate hairstyle, in combination with the rich dark tones of her skin, the woman remains as a cipher: the classificatory process involved in her representation cannot reach completion, and the would-be male gaze and masculine perspective lose their control over emotional responses and potential identification, on the one hand, and objectivization (perspectival and emotional distancing) and objectification, on the other hand (Fig. 13.1).

A comparable tension between the classificatory and the vacancy of the female subject's expression—which implies a lack of engagement and cooperation with the prevailing ordering and representational systems—is

Fig. 13.1 Maruja Mallo. *Cabeza de mujer (Cabeza de negra)*. 1946. Museo de Pontevedra. © 2024 Artists Rights Society (ARS), New York / VEGAP, Madrid

---

[49] Foucault refers to the Classical episteme's "great tables of knowledge developed according to the forms of identity, of difference, and of order." As he argues, "What makes the totality of the Classical *episteme* possible is primarily the relation to a knowledge of order.... When dealing with the ordering of complex natures (representations in general, as they are given in experience), one has to constitute a *taxinomia*, and to do that one has to establish a system of signs." (71, 72)

likewise present in the oil-on-canvas portraits *Oro* [Gold, n.d.] and *Joven rubia* [Young Blond, n.d.]. Both portraits depict busts of blond women and catalogue the various ethnic features and skin tones that, in South America, may become mixed with fair hair.[50] Each female subject is portrayed in profile, her bright blue eyes staring intently toward the side, absorbed by thoughts or perceptions inaccessible to artist and viewer alike. Particularly in *Young Blond*, Mallo distances the subject further by giving her an androgynous air—at once attracting and thwarting the gaze.

In *The Human Deer*, Mallo takes this detachment to an extreme: the female subject's glazed-over eyes stare straight ahead as if she were hypnotized, catatonic, or dead—the victim of the hunt to which the painting's title possibly alludes. Her likeness could be envisioned as a severed head akin to that of a deer mounted as a hunter's trophy, and in fact, the ethnically inflected and intricate arrangement of her hair recalls the antlers of a deer, or *cierva* in Spanish. Given the polyvalence of the image, it remains difficult to explain *The Human Deer* solely through the lens of ethnology, with its implications of ordering and classifying. Mallo, a woman artist who has mastered several visual languages of representation, portrays the female subjects of the *Two-dimensional Portraits* in a double-edged fashion: She recuperates the predominant taxonomic, ontological, and perspectival systems while simultaneously challenging their very bases (Fig. 13.2).

Fig. 13.2 Maruja Mallo. *La cierva humana*. 1948. Patrimonio Museo de Bellas Artes de La Boca de Artistas Argentinos "Benito Quinquela Martín." © 2024 Artists Rights Society (ARS), New York / VEGAP, Madrid

---

[50] *Oro* [Gold] and *Joven rubia* [Young Blond] have been reproduced as illustrations (Figs. 10 and 11) in the 1992 catalog, *Maruja Mallo*, edited by Pérez de Ayala (58–59).

Young Blond, *Gold*, and *The Human Deer* are all, in a way, ciphers. At the same time, the blankness, and even deadness, of their eyes and facial expressions contrast markedly with the specificity of their skin, hair, and decorative accessories. Here, then, lies the irony of Mallo's work. Her depiction of ethnic and racial archetypes in the *Two-dimensional Portraits* as a feature of her exile's vision for the future of humanity, conditioned by the intellectual currents generated by Boas and Benedict, depends on a *taxinomia* that is part and parcel of an ontological and visual economy that privileges a masculine gaze and distanced perspective. Rather than becoming coin in this economy, however, the female subjects of Mallo's portraits interrupt their circulation and consumption precisely by their unnerving emptiness and unknowability. Mallo further undermines such an economy by repossessing for herself, as a female artist, the objectivizing perspective and classifying (objectifying) gaze normally accorded to the male, and reintroducing at the same time the material experience of the female body, as in the *Live Nature* series. Mallo's *Live Nature* paintings embody this seeming contradiction, so essential to her art, in that they are at once architectonic catalogues of Nature's geometric forms—*taxinomia*—and sensual and allusive of the female body. Yet, from even another angle, *Young Blond*, *Gold*, and *The Human Deer*, among other *Two-dimensional Portraits*, destabilize the taxonomic operation that Mallo by turns re-appropriates and re-circuits by means of the overdetermined and variable significance of their subjects' alternating "femininity," androgyny, and ethnic inflection. These paradoxes in Mallo's work ultimately throw into question the certainties of the new art, as well as this new art's neutralization of the female, sentiment, and the body, through framings that remain only apparently objective.

Works Cited

Ayala, Francisco. "Maruja Mallo," *Alfar*, Año VII, no. 63, mayo–junio 1929, n. pag.

Bakhtin, Mikhail. *Rabelais and His World*. 1965. Translated by Hélène Iswolsky, prologue by Michael Holquist, Indiana UP, 1984.

Ballesteros García, Rosa Mª. "Maruja Mallo (1902–1994). De las cloacas al espacio sideral." *Aposta: Revista de Ciencias Sociales*, no. 13, diciembre 2004, pp. 1–34.

Balló, Tània. *Las sinsombrero. Las pensadoras y artistas olvidadas de la Generación del 27*. 2nd printing, Espasa Libros, 2020.

13 A DOUBLE EXILE: CROSSING THE FEMALE FIGURE IN MARUJA MALLO'S...   345

Benedict, Ruth. *Raza: ciencia y política.* Fondo de Cultura Económica, 1941.

The Bible. King James Version, Christian Art Publishers, 2016.

Boas, Franz. *Race, Language, and Culture.* 1910. U of Chicago P, 1982.

Bonet, Juan Manuel. "Torres García." Revised ed., *Diccionario de las vanguardias en España (1907–1936)*, Alianza Editorial, 1999, pp. 598–600.

Bulfinch, Thomas. *Mythology.* A modern abridgment by Edmund Fuller with a new index, Doubleday, 1959.

Craig, Tilly, and Maruja Mallo. *Sea Monster*, words by Tilly Craig and art by Maruja Mallo. Ortuzar Projects, https://www.ortuzarprojects.com/attachment/en/5f3d7f3dc8aa2c0d0a8b4567/News/5e8cd93272d8505509d2deb9. Accessed 2 Mar. 2021.

De la Cueva, Almudena, and Margarita Márquez Padorno, editors. *Mujeres en vanguardia: La Residencia de Señoritas en su centenario [1915–1936].* Publicaciones de la Residencia de Estudiantes, 2015.

Darragon, Éric. "Torres-García, una visión utópica." *Joaquín Torres-García: un mundo construido*, Museo Colecciones ICO, Madrid, 22 de octubre de 2002–6 de enero de 2003, Fundación ICO, 2002, pp. 47–86.

Diego, Estrella de. "Maruja Mallo en América." *Maruja Mallo: catálogo razonado de óleos*, by Antonio Gómez Conde, Guillermo de Osma, and Juan Pérez de Ayala, Fundación Azcona, 2021, pp. 415–33.

———. "Retratos." *Maruja Mallo*, edited by Juan Pérez de Ayala and Fernando Huici, vol. 1, Casa de Artes, Vigo, 10 de septiembre de 2009–10 de enero de 2010 / Real Academia de Bellas Artes de San Fernando, Madrid, Ministerio de Cultura / Fundación Caixa Galicia / Real Academia de Bellas Artes de San Fernando / Sociedad Estatal de Conmemoraciones Culturales, 2009, pp. 71–87. 3 vols.

Esteban, Rafael B. "Maruja entre rosas y orquídeas." *Estampa*, Buenos Aires, 25 de enero de 1943.

Ezcurra, Enrique de. "Maruja Mallo triunfa en Nueva York." *El Hogar*, Mexico, 31 de diciembre de 1948, p. 17.

Ferris, José Luis. *Maruja Mallo: la gran transgresora del 27.* Ediciones Temas de Hoy, 2004.

Foucault, Michel. *The Order of Things: An Archaeology of the Human Sciences [Les mots et les choses: Une archéologie des sciences humaines].* 1966. Vintage Books, Random House, 1994.

De la Gándara, Consuelo. "Maruja Mallo." "Homenaje a Maruxa Mallo," *II Bienal de artistas galegas*, Antigo Edificio Banco de España, Vigo, 29 de marzo–30 de abril, Concello de Vigo, 1990, pp. 24–28. Originally published in De la Gándara, Consuelo. *Maruja Mallo*, Ministerio de Educación y Ciencia, 1978.

Gisbert, Rosa Ruiz. "Maruja Mallo y la Generación del '27." *Isla de Arriarán*, vol. XXVIII, diciembre 2006, pp. 223–40.

346 R. M. SILVERMAN

Gómez de la Serna, Ramón. *Maruja Mallo*. Losada, 1942.

———. "Nueva actualidad de Maruja Mallo." *Guadalimar: Revista bimestral de las artes*, no. 117, octubre–noviembre, 1992, p. 43. Originally published in *Atlántida*, mayo, 1956.

Imbelloni, José. *El poblamiento primitivo de América*. Talleres Gráficos Radio Revista, 1938.

Kirkpatrick, Susan. *Mujer, modernismo y vanguardia en España (1898–1931)*. Translated by Jacqueline Cruz, Ediciones Cátedra / Universitat de Valencia / Instituto de la Mujer, 2003.

Lombay, Reinaldo. "El pincel de Maruja Mallo descubre el mar de Chile." *Zig-Zag*, Santiago de Chile, Año XL, Edición 2081, 9 de febrero de 1945, pp. 40–41.

Mallo, Maruja. *América aborigen*. Fondo Maruja Mallo, Archivo Lafuente, Cantabria, Spain. 1909–1995.

———. *Arquitectura humana*. 1937. *La subversión enmascarada: análisis de la obra de Maruja Mallo*, by María Alejandra Zanetta, Biblioteca Nueva, 2014, n. pag.

———. *Cabeza de mujer (Cabeza de negra)*. 1946, Museo de Pontevedra, Pontevedra, Spain.

———. *Cabeza de mujer (Cabeza de negra)*. 1946, Museo de Pontevedra, http:// catalogo.museo.depo.es/inweb/ficha.aspx?t=o&id=3665. Oil on canvas, 56.5 × 46.5 cm. *Maruja Mallo*, edited by Juan Pérez de Ayala and Fernando Huici, Casa de Artes, Vigo, 10 de septiembre de 2009–10 de enero de 2010 / Real Academia de Bellas Artes de San Fernando, Madrid, Ministerio de Cultura / Fundación Caixa Galicia / Real Academia de Bellas Artes de San Fernando / Sociedad Estatal de Conmemoraciones Culturales, 2009, detail on cover.

———. *El canto de las espigas*. 1939. *La subversión enmascarada: análisis de la obra de Maruja Mallo*, by María Alejandra Zanetta, Biblioteca Nueva, 2014, n. pag.

———. *Ciclista*. 1927. *La subversión enmascarada: análisis de la obra de Maruja Mallo*, by María Alejandra Zanetta, Biblioteca Nueva, 2014, n. pag.

———. *La cierva humana*. 1948, Museo de Bellas Artes de La Boca de Artistas Argentinos "Benito Quinquela Martín," Buenos Aires, Argentina.

———. *La cierva humana*. 1948, Private Collection. Oil on canvas. *Maruja Mallo*, by Estrella de Diego, Fundación MAPFRE, Instituto de Cultura, 2008, p. 89.

———. *Dos mujeres en la playa*. 1928. *La subversión enmascarada: análisis de la obra de Maruja Mallo*, by María Alejandra Zanetta, Biblioteca Nueva, 2014, n. pag.

———. *Esquema*. n.d.-a *La subversión enmascarada: análisis de la obra de Maruja Mallo*, by María Alejandra Zanetta, Biblioteca Nueva, 2014, n. pag.

———. *Joven rubia*. n.d.-b, Private Collection, Madrid. Oil on canvas, 49 × 40 cm. *Maruja Mallo*, edited by Juan Pérez de Ayala and Francisco Rivas, Guillermo

13 A DOUBLE EXILE: CROSSING THE FEMALE FIGURE IN MARUJA MALLO'S... 347

de Osma Galería, Madrid, 21 octubre-20 diciembre, 1992, Guillermo de Osma Galería, 1992, p. 59.

———. *Maruja Mallo en las playas de Chile*. c. 1939, Guillermo de Osma Galería, Madrid. Photograph, vintage copy retouched in ink by the artist, 23'8 × 19-6 cm. *Mujeres en vanguardia: La Residencia de Señoritas en su centenario [1915–1936]*, edited by Almudena De la Cueva and Margarita Márquez Padorno, Publicaciones de la Residencia de Estudiantes, 2015, p. 376. *Maruja Mallo, Naturalezas vivas 1941–1944*, edited by Juan Pérez de Ayala, Guillermo de Osma Galería, Madrid, junio–julio, 2002 / Fundación Caixa Galicia, Vigo, septiembre–octubre, 2002, Guillermo de Osma Galería, 2002, cover.

———. *Mujer tenista*. 1927. *La subversión enmascarada: análisis de la obra de Maruja Mallo*, by María Alejandra Zanetta, Biblioteca Nueva, 2014, n. pag.

———. *Naturaleza viva con estrella de mar*. 1943. *La subversión enmascarada: análisis de la obra de Maruja Mallo*, by María Alejandra Zanetta, Biblioteca Nueva, 2014, n. pag.

———. *Naturaleza viva con orquídea*. 1942. *La subversión enmascarada: análisis de la obra de Maruja Mallo*, by María Alejandra Zanetta, Biblioteca Nueva, 2014, n. pag.

———. *Naturaleza viva. Vida vibrante*. 1943, Guillermo de Osma Galería, Madrid. Oil on drawing board, 42 × 30 cm. *Maruja Mallo, Naturalezas vivas 1941–1944*, edited by Juan Pérez de Ayala, Guillermo de Osma Galería, Madrid, junio-julio, 2002 / Fundación Caixa Galicia, Vigo, septiembre-octubre, 2002, Guillermo de Osma Galería, 2002, p. 45.

———. *Oro*. n.d.-c, Colección Arte Contemporáneo, Madrid, Spain. Oil on canvas, 49 × 40 cm. *Maruja Mallo, Naturalezas vivas 1941–1944*, edited by Juan Pérez de Ayala, Guillermo de Osma Galería, Madrid, junio-julio, 2002 / Fundación Caixa Galicia, Vigo, septiembre-octubre, 2002, Guillermo de Osma Galería, 2002, p. 59.

———. *Lo popular en la plástica española a través de mi obra 1928–1936*. Editorial Losada, 1939.

———. "Proceso histórico de la forma en las artes plásticas." *Maruja Mallo*, by Ramón Gómez de la Serna, Losada, 1942, pp. 27–32.

———. "Relato veraz de la realidad en Galicia." *La Vanguardia*, Barcelona, 14, 21, 26 agosto 1938: 7, 11, 5.

———. *La sorpresa del trigo*. 1936, Private Collection. Oil on canvas, 66 × 100 cm. *Maruja Mallo*, by Estrella de Diego, Fundación MAPFRE, Instituto de Cultura, 2008, p. 91.

———. *La verbena*. 1927, Museo Nacional Centro de Arte Reina Sofía, Madrid. Oil on canvas, 119 × 166 cm. *Maruja Mallo*, by Estrella de Diego, Fundación MAPFRE, Instituto de Cultura, 2008, pp. 66–67.

Mangini, Shirley. "From the Atlantic to the Pacific: Maruja Mallo in Exile." *Studies in 20th and 21st Century Literature*, vol. 30, no. 1, Winter 2006, pp. 85–106.

348 R. M. SILVERMAN

———. "The Gendered Body Politic of Maruja Mallo." *Modernism and the Avant-Garde Body in Spain and Italy*, edited by Nicolás Fernández-Medina and Maria Truglio, Taylor and Francis, 2016, pp. 160–81.

———. *Maruja Mallo and the Spanish Avant-Garde*. Ashgate, 2010.

———. *Maruja Mallo y la vanguardia española* [*Maruja Mallo and the Spanish Avant-Garde*]. Translated by Roser Berdagué, Circe, 2012.

Merjian, Ara H. "Surrealist Women." Rev. of "Maruja Mallo: Paintings 1926–1952," Ortuzar Projects, New York, Sept. 26–Dec. 1, 2018, and "Leonor Fini: Theatre of Desire, 1930–1990," Museum of Sex, New York, Sept. 28, 2018–Mar. 4, 2019, *Art in America*, vol. 106, issue 11, December 2018, pp. 94–96.

Mulvey, Laura. "Visual Pleasure and Narrative Cinema." *The Sexual Subject: A Screen Reader in Sexuality*, Routledge, 1992, pp. 22–34.

Ortega y Gasset, José. *La deshumanización del arte y otros ensayos de estética*. 1925. *Revista de Occidente en Alianza Editorial*, 2002.

Osma, Guillermo de. "Maruja Mallo: Catálogo Razonado y Archivo." *Maruja Mallo: orden y creación. Óleos, dibujos, bocetos y su Archivo*, edited by Juan Pérez de Ayala and Guillermo de Osma, Guillermo de Osma Galería, Madrid, 14 septiembre–10 noviembre, 2017, Guillermo de Osma Galería, 2017, 5–7.

———. "Maruja Mallo en Argentina: más luces que sombras." *Maruja Mallo: catálogo razonado de óleos*, by Antonio Gómez Conde, Guillermo de Osma, and Juan Pérez de Ayala, Fundación Azcona, 2021, pp. 383–413.

———. Preface. *Maruja Mallo, Naturalezas vivas 1941–1944*, edited by Juan Pérez de Ayala, Guillermo de Osma Galería, Madrid, junio–julio, 2002 / Fundación Caixa Galicia, Vigo, septiembre–octubre, 2002, Guillermo de Osma Galería, 2002, n. pag.

Pérez de Ayala, Juan. "Álbum biográfico." *Maruja Mallo*, edited by Juan Pérez de Ayala and Francisco Rivas, Guillermo de Osma Galería, Madrid, 21 octubre-20 diciembre, 1992, Guillermo de Osma Galería / Fundación Banesto, 1992, pp. 77–91.

———. "Cotas de ascensión/puntos de contemplación." *Maruja Mallo*, edited by Juan Pérez de Ayala and Fernando Huici, vol. 1, Casa de Artes, Vigo, 10 de septiembre de 2009–10 de enero de 2010 / Real Academia de Bellas Artes de San Fernando, Madrid, Ministerio de Cultura / Fundación Caixa Galicia / Real Academia de Bellas Artes de San Fernando / Sociedad Estatal de Conmemoraciones Culturales, 2009, pp. 89–105. 3 vols.

———. "Vida vibrante." *Maruja Mallo, Naturalezas vivas 1941–1944*, edited by Juan Pérez de Ayala, Guillermo de Osma Galería, Madrid, junio–julio, 2002 / Fundación Caixa Galicia, Vigo, septiembre–octubre, 2002, Guillermo de Osma Galería, 2002, pp. 21–31.

———, ed. *Maruja Mallo, Naturalezas vivas 1941–1944.* Guillermo de Osma Galería, Madrid, junio–julio, 2002 / Fundación Caixa Galicia, Vigo, septiembre–octubre, 2002, Guillermo de Osma Galería, 2002.

Pérez de Ayala, Juan, and Francisco Rivas, editors. *Maruja Mallo.* Guillermo de Osma Galería, Madrid, 21 octubre–20 diciembre, 1992, Guillermo de Osma Galería / Fundación Banesto, 1992.

Rivas, Francisco. "Maruja Mallo, pintora del más allá." *Maruja Mallo,* edited by Juan Pérez de Ayala and Francisco Rivas, Guillermo de Osma Galería, Madrid, 21 octubre–20 diciembre, 1992, Guillermo de Osma Galería / Fundación Cultural Banesto, 1992, pp. 15–29.

Torres-García, Joaquín. *Universalismo constructivo.* Poseidón, 1944.

Vidal, Carme. *Maruxa Mallo.* Edicións A Nosa Terra, 1999.

Da Vinci, Leonardo. *The Vitruvian Man.* 1487/1490, Gallerie dell'Accademia, Venice, http://www.gallerieaccademia.it/en/node/1582. Metalpoint, pen and ink, touches of watercolor on white paper, 34.6 × 25.5 cm.

Ulacia Altolaguirre, Paloma. *Concha Méndez. Memorias habladas, memorias armadas.* Editorial Renacimiento, 2018.

Zanetta, María Alejandra. *La subversión enmascarada: análisis de la obra de Maruja Mallo.* Biblioteca Nueva, 2014.

INDEX[1]

A

Abstraction, 324, 325
Acculturation, 213, 230
Activism, 267, 268
Adorno, Theodor, 8, 20, 44, 47, 207
African American actors, 296
Agrupación Femenina de Acción Republicana, 103
Agustini, Delmina, 53
Alaimo, Stacy, 78, 92
Alberti, Rafael, 123
Alcalá de Henares, 283
Alcázar de Cervantes, 274, 278, 279
Alcoriza, Luis, 225, 227, 227n8, 227n9, 227n10, 230–233
Alfar, 324
Alfaro Siqueiros, David, 298
Altolaguirre, Manuel, 123, 126n9
America Hispana, 132, 135
American film industry, 295, 296, 300
American identity, 315
Americas, 2, 15

Amsterdam, 266, 287
Anarchism, 271, 283
Anderson, Sherwood, 205
Angel in the house, 8
Anglo-Hispanic, 212–214, 225, 226, 228, 233
Anti-fascism, 223, 224, 231
Antifascist, 268, 269
Anti-Semitism, 216
Anzaldúa, Gloria, 18, 19
Aragón, 272, 273, 275, 280, 281, 284
Arendt, Hannah, 44, 123
Ariel Award, 233
Arquitectura México, 289
Art, 76, 77, 85, 89, 95, 96
Arte nuevo (new art), 324n2
Arte puro (pure art), 324n2
Artistic influence, 317
Ascaso Division, 273, 279, 284
Asociación Femenina de Educación Cívica, 103

---

[1] Note: Page numbers followed by 'n' refer to notes.

© The Author(s), under exclusive license to Springer Nature Switzerland AG 2024
R. M. Silverman, E. Sanchez-Pardo (eds.), *Nomadic New Women*, https://doi.org/10.1007/978-3-031-62482-7

352 INDEX

Asociación Nacional de Mujeres de
España, 102
Astrana Marín, Luis, 54
Ateneo de Madrid, 102
Atlantic, 2, 3, 5–8
Aub, Max, 123
Augustine, *Confessions*, 137
Autobiography, 77, 80–81, 87
Ayala, Francisco, 324, 328
Azaña, Manuel, 123, 154

B
Bakhtin, Mikhail, 185, 190, 191,
197–200, 207, 328, 328n14
Baledón, Rafael, 230
Banastás, 279
Barad, Karen, 78, 92, 98
Barcelona, 223, 224, 268–277, 279,
280, 282, 284–287, 289
Barnes, Djuna, 185
Battle of Teruel, 111, 111n15
Baudelaire, Charles, 10n1
"The Painter of Modern Life," 10n1
Beauvoir, Simone de, 123
Benedict, Ruth, 339, 344
Race: Science and Politics (*Raza:
ciencia y política*), 339
Bennett, Jane, 78, 92
Berenguer, Dámaso, 104
Berlin, 268
Berry, Ellen, 199
Besant, Annie, 6
Bilingualism, 80
Bird of Paradise, 309, 311
Birth, being born, 140
Boas, Franz, 339, 344
Bombardment/bombing/bombs,
111, 112, 114, 115
Border-crossing, 1–20
Border-crossing creative women, 8

Borders, 122, 122n1, 136,
138, 139n52
Border Theory, 18
Borges, Jorge Luis, 4
Borges, Norah, 4
Boundaries, 2, 4, 5, 8, 10, 16, 17, 20
Braidotti, Rosi, 8–12, 212, 217,
218, 231
Nomadic Subjects, 8–10
Brenan, Gerald, 4
Breton, André, 237–239, 243–247,
244n7, 249–251, 249n8,
256, 259
Bridgman, Richard, 191
British Parliament, 108
Budapest, 267, 268
Buñuel, Luis, 201, 225, 227, 227n8,
227n9, 232
Bürger, Wolfgang, 269
Burgos, Carmen de, 7, 102
La mujer moderna y sus derechos, 7

C
Cabrera, Lydia, 18, 18n3
El monte, 18, 18n3
Campoamor, Clara, 3, 6, 14, 102
El voto femenino y yo, 14
Camprubí Aymar, Zenobia, 75
Camprubí, Zenobia, 2–5
Cárdenas, Lázaro, 108, 116
Carewe, Edwin, 309
Caribbean, 2, 4, 11, 13, 15, 121–143
Carrington, Leonora, 3, 5, 19,
237–259, 288
Cartographic method, 9
Cartography, 3, 4, 18, 20
Casa del Pueblo (Madrid), 103
Castro, Rosalía de, 13
Centro de Hijos de Madrid, 103
Cernuda, Luis, 123, 134

INDEX 353

Cervantes, Miguel de, 183n1, 186, 190, 191, 201
Don Quixote, 183n1, 186, 202
Chacel, Rosa, 7, 77, 123, 148, 161, 173, 329
Champourcín, Ernestina de, 7, 123, 329
Charro, 230
Chopin, Kate, 185
Cigar Workers' Union, 155
Cinema Reporter, 225–227
Cold War, 221, 232, 233
Committee for Refugees, 278, 279
Communist International, 219
Concentration camp, 108, 115, 117, 118
Conesa, María, 301, 302, 314
Confederación Nacional del Trabajo (CNT), 267, 270, 272, 273, 275, 276, 280, 287
Conferencia Internacional del Trabajo de la Sociedad de Naciones, 103
Conferencia sobre el Desarme (Geneva)., 103
Cooper, Gary, 300, 301, 313
Corral, Rose, 151
Cronos, 140
Cuba, 5, 13, 76, 76n2, 79, 82, 83, 86, 90, 93, 95, 97
The Cuban Love Song, 303, 309
Cultural essentialism, 232

D
Da Vinci, Leonardo, 334, 334n24, 340–342
The Vitruvian Man, 334, 334n24, 342
Dalí, Salvador, 7, 183, 328, 328n13
Dance, 214, 216–219, 217n3, 223, 226, 228, 233

Dancer in Madrid, 211, 219, 221, 223
Dante, 189
Daydreaming, 130
de Ibarbourou, Juana, 53
de Prada, Juan Manuel, 52, 53, 60, 73
DeKoven, Marianne, 191
del Río, Dolores, 295–318
Delaunay, Robert, 4
Delaunay-Terk, Sonia, 4
Deleuze, Gilles, 9
Deleuzian, 9, 12
DeMille, Cecil B., 300
Democracy, 124n5, 128, 133, 136, 139, 140, 142
Demythification, 230
Deraismes, Maria, 6
Destierro, see Exile
Deterritorialization, 9, 12
Deutsch Blau, Katalin, 267
Diaghilev, Sergei, 4
Diary, 75–99
Diaspora, 2, 15, 57n25, 58, 67, 72
Diaspora of modernist women philosophers, 123
Dictatorship, 51, 58, 72
Dietrich, Marlene, 310–312
Diplomacy/diplomatic, 105–109, 110n14, 113, 114, 118
Discontinuity, 27, 31, 35
Dislocated, 67
Displacement, 2, 10, 11, 13, 15, 16, 59, 66, 68, 70, 72
Dispossession, 26, 31, 36, 40
Domesticity, 1, 6, 7
Dos Passos, John, 181, 182
Down Below, 246–248, 253
Drottingholm, 117
Durruti, Buenaventura, 57
Dwelling, 28, 36, 40–42, 44, 45, 47
Dydo, Ulla, 204

354 INDEX

E

East is West, 309
Ekphrasis, 175
Ellis, Havelock, 186
Éluard, Paul, 237, 243, 245
Empathy, 212–214, 220, 226, 233
Enciso, María, 123
Epiphany, 95
Ernst, Max, 241, 243–247, 243n6,
  244n7, 249, 249n8, 258
Errol, Leon, 307
Estampas, 52, 61, 64, 67,
  68, 72
Ethnicity, 296, 300, 303, 305,
  312, 314
Ethnic representation, 317
Ethnographic, 269, 284
Euro–American divide, 122
Exile, 1, 2, 4, 5, 8, 10–13, 15–20,
  26–37, 39, 40, 42–45, 47–49,
  51–73, 75–99, 104, 104n3,
  105, 106n5, 107, 107n10,
  108, 113, 114n20, 117–119,
  122–126, 126n9, 129n13,
  130n19, 134–136, 134n42,
  138–142, 138n51, 147, 148,
  158, 160, 161, 164n70, 166,
  169n85, 174n103, 211–233,
  269, 287, 290, 323–344
Exile, double, 135
Exilic, 52, 59, 60, 66–68,
  70, 72
Expatriation/expatriate, 106, 113

F

Falange, 215
Falcón, Irene, 14
Fascism, 5, 14, 15, 161n58, 211, 212,
  218, 225, 233
Federación Anarquista Ibérica (FAI),
  273, 283, 285

Federación Universitaria Escolar
  (FUE, University Student
  Federation), 151, 153
Female figure, 323–344
Feminism, 55n15, 56, 56n19, 238,
  255, 282
Feminism, first wave, 7
Feminist, 55, 55n15, 56, 56n19
Feminist ideals, 102, 109
Femme-enfant, 238, 248
Femme-fatale, 245, 248
Femme-folle, 238, 245, 248
Fernández Blau, Catalina, 288
Film, 3, 5, 19, 213, 225–233, 226n7,
  227n8, 232n14, 295, 296, 298,
  298n2, 300–303, 306, 309,
  312, 314
  transition to sound, 300
Firing squad, 168–175
Flamenco, 211, 211n1, 214–218,
  222, 226, 227n9, 228–230,
  230n11, 232, 233
Flâneur, 10, 10n1
Flâneuse, 10, 328
Fleming, Victor, 300
Flying Down to Rio, 309
Foreign accent, 310
Foreign correspondents, 222
Foreign Propaganda Office of
  CNT, 270–272, 274, 276,
  276n13, 287
Foster, Norman, 226, 227, 227n9
"Fotos Kati"/"Foto Katti," 281,
  282, 285
Foucault, Michel, 326, 327n11,
  342, 342n49
*Les mots et les choses: Une archéologie
  des sciences humaines* (The
  Order of Things: An
  Archaeology of the Human
  Sciences), 326
France, 122, 122n1, 126, 139n52

INDEX   355

Franco, Francisco, 51, 52, 57, 58, 61, 71, 72, 108, 110, 111n15, 112, 116–118, 200
Franco's dictatorship, 16
Frank, Waldo, 134, 135, 135n43, 181–183
Freeman, Elizabeth, 201, 204
Freidmann, Endre (Robert Capa), 269
Fuente Podrida, 277

G
Galán Rodríguez, Fermín, 171
García Hernández, Angel, 171
García Lorca, Federico, 7, 123, 219, 230n12, 328, 328n13
García Marruz, Fina, 134, 136, 142n67
The Gaucho, 302, 309
Gender normativity, 226
Generación del 98 [Generation of 1898], 200
Generation of 1898, 13
Generation of 1927, 13
Generation of 1936, 13
Generation of 27, 123, 126n9
Gentic, Tania, 156
Gil Roësset, Marga, 7
Gilman, Charlotte Perkins, 6
Giménez de Asúa, Luis, 154
The Girl from Mexico, 306
Gitana tenías que ser, 229
Gitanos, 211
Golden Age of Mexican cinema, 211, 213, 225, 227, 229
Goldman, Emma, 272, 279
Gómez de la Serna, Ramón, 338–340
González-Ruano, César, 53, 53n6, 54n8, 55
Gossy, Mary, 184
Gout, Alberto, 226, 229
Goya, Francisco de, 11

Goya, Francisco de (Goya y Lucientes, Francisco José de), 168–175
El tres de mayo (*The Third of May*), 168–175
Graham, Martha, 217, 217n3, 223
Granada, Spain, 184, 189, 201
Graves, Robert, 4
Greece, 126
Griffith, D. W., 300, 302
Guattari, Félix, 9
Guzmán, María De, 183
Gynocentrism, 331

H
Hardy, Oliver, 300, 302
Harmon, William, 185, 186n2, 197, 205
Hart Benton, Thomas, 298
The Hearing Trumpet, 241, 255–257
Hegemony, 230, 232
Heidegger, Martin, 28, 28n7, 30, 32, 41, 44
Hell Harbor, 303, 304, 309
Hemingway, Ernest, 4, 181, 182, 219, 221
Hernández, Miguel, 329
Hesiod's Theogony, 140, 140n58
Heteroglossia, 190, 198
Heterotopia, 139, 143
Hispanism/Hispanismo, 213, 229
Hispanists, 224, 233
Hollywood, 214, 232, 232n14, 295–318
cinema, 5
1920s, 295–300
studio system, 295
Homecoming, 25–49
Homeland, 103, 105–107, 113–116, 114n19, 118
Homelessness, 25–49, 67
Homogeneity, 230

356 INDEX

Horna, José, 285, 287, 288
Horna, Kati, 3, 5, 17, 265–291
Howells, William Dean, 183,
  197, 198n6
Hungary, 266, 267, 269
Hybrid, 5, 11, 18–20, 122, 124,
  134n42, 136
  hybrid genre, 125
  hybridization, 121
  hybrid philosophical essay, 142
Hybridity, 9–11, 13, 18, 19, 217,
  231, 237–259

I

Ibárruri, Dolores, 14, 123
Identity, 305, 306, 314n7, 318
Ignatius of Loyola, 206
II Spanish Republic [Second
  Republic], 215, 218–224,
  229, 232
Ilie, Paul, 16
  Literature and Inner Exile, 16
Illustrated magazine, 273, 280–283
Illustrated press, 268, 272,
  278, 288
Imago Photo Service, 279
Imbelloni, José, 339
  Poblamiento primitivo de América
  (*Primitive Settlement of
  America*), 339
Immigrant, 305, 308
Immigration laws, 116
In-between, 18, 19
Infante, Pedro, 230
Insular, 125, 126, 127n10, 128n12,
  142, 143
Intellectual pilgrimage, 128
International Brigades, 219, 220
Introspection, 78, 98
Irigaray, Luce, 10, 16, 19
  "Women's Exile," 16, 17

Island of Puerto Rico, 121, 133, 136
Italy, 122
Itinerancy, 130

J

Jaca uprising, 171
Jackson, Laura Riding, 4
Jiménez, Juan Ramón, 75–77, 79, 80,
  82, 83, 85, 86, 89–91, 94–96, 98
Jodorowsky, Alejandro, 254, 255, 259
Johnson, Roberta, 151, 153n25

K

Kagan, Richard, 184, 200
Kassák, Lajos, 267, 268
Keats, John, 204
Kent, Victoria, 14, 77, 102, 106
Kollontay, Alexandra, 110n14
Krieger, Murray, 175

L

La americanita, 211–233
La Castañeda, 289
Lady of the Pavements, 302
Latin America, 122–123, 122n1, 139
Laughing Boy, 297, 309
Laurel, Stan, 300, 302
La zandunga, 306
Lejárraga, María, 102
León, María Teresa, 7, 106,
  106n5, 123
Levinas, Emmanuel, 41, 44
Lezama Lima, José, 126, 126n7,
  127, 134
Libertarian, 280, 282, 287
Libre Studio, 280, 287
Life writing, 77, 79
Liga de Educación Social (League for
  Social Education), 155

INDEX 357

Liminality, 252
Lines of flight, 9, 12
Lorris, Guillaume de, 197
The Loves of Carmen, 300
Loy, Mina, 201
Loyalist, 215, 218, 219, 220n4, 222, 223, 225, 233
Lukács, Georg, 201
Luxemburg, Rosa, 123

M

Machado, Antonio, 13, 122n2, 123, 134, 141
Macho, 227n9, 228
Madariaga, Salvador de, 123
Madness, 237, 239, 245–249, 256
Madrid, 81, 82, 86, 89, 211, 214–216, 218–221, 223, 225, 230, 233, 270, 272, 278, 283, 284, 288n33
Madrileños, 215–217, 219, 220, 222
Maeztu, María de, 123
Mallo, Maruja, 3, 4, 7, 11, 13, 323–344
  América aborigen (Aboriginal America), 341n48
  Ciclista (Cyclist), 327
  Dos mujeres en la playa (Two Women on the Beach), 327
  Esquema (Diagram), 334
  La religión del trabajo (The Religion of Work); *Arquitectura humana* (Human Architecture), 329; *El canto de las espigas* (The Song of the Ears of Wheat), 330; *La sorpresa del trigo* (The Surprise of the Wheat), 329, 329n16
  Maruja Mallo en las playas de Chile (Maruja Mallo on the Beaches of Chile), 335n27

Mujer tenista (*Woman Tennis Player*), 327
Naturalezas vivas (Live Nature); *Lo popular en la plástica española a través de mi obra 1928-1936* (The Popular in the Spanish Plastic Arts through my Work, 1928-1936), 325; *Naturaleza viva con estrella de mar* (Live Nature with a Starfish), 336; *Naturaleza viva con orquídea* (Live Nature with an Orchid), 336; *Naturaleza viva. Vida Vibrante* (Live Nature. Vibrant Life), 334
Retratos bidimensionales (Two-dimensional Portraits) *or Cabezas de mujer* (Heads of Women); *Joven rubia* (Young Blond), 343, 343n50; *La cierva humana* (The Human Deer), 339, 343; *Oro* (Gold), 343, 343n50
Verbenas (Fairs), 325, 328; *La verbena* (The Fair), 327
Mallorca, 183, 189, 200, 201
Manso Robledo, Margarita, 328
Manso, Margarita, 7
Marañón, Gregorio (Marañón y Posadillo, Gregorio), 154, 155n31
Marginality, 53–59, 72
Marginalization, 211n1, 213, 217
Mariátegui, José Carlos, 124n5, 128
Martínez Sagi, Ana María, 3, 4, 18, 51–73
Materiality, 76, 78, 91, 94, 95, 98
Maternity home, 277, 278
Maternity/motherhood, 111, 112, 112n18
Matter, 78, 88, 92, 96, 98, 99
Maya, 252, 254

358 INDEX

Méndez, Concha, 7, 106, 123,
    328, 329
Mental asylum, 248, 249, 258, 259
Mestiza consciousness, 19
Mestizaje, 213
Meun, Jean de, 197
Mexican actors, 299, 315
Mexican culture, 299
Mexican Muralism, 299n3
Mexican spitfire, 301, 306, 308
Mexican Spitfire (movie), 308
Mexican Spitfire Sees a Ghost, 308
Mexico, 4, 5, 17, 19, 122, 122n1,
    126, 126n8, 126n9, 211, 213,
    225–233, 239, 239n3, 241,
    249–259, 251n10, 266,
    267, 287–290
Mexico City, 211, 214, 228, 288, 289
Miami, 83, 86, 90, 95–97
Michaelis, Margaret, 270
Migration, 101–119
Migration systems theory, 105
Migration theory, 108
Migrations, 2, 3, 15, 20
Militiaman/militiamen, 273, 280,
    281, 284
The Milk of Dreams, 254
Mind, 76, 78, 81, 88, 93, 96, 97
Ministry of Labor and Social
    Assistance, Government of
    Spain, 277
Minority population, 107, 108
Mistral, Gabriela, 54, 54n8
Mistral, Silvia, 77
Mobility, 212, 232
Modernist literature, 7, 10, 12, 13
Moholy-Nagy, Láslo, 268
Monte Carrascal, 279
Montseny, Federica, 14, 77, 106
More-than-human (world), 76, 78,
    88, 92, 93, 95, 98
Mother tongue, 122

Mujeres, 289
Mujeres Libres, 280, 282, 283
Mulder, Elisabeth, 52, 56, 57, 57n21
Mulvey, Laura, 327
Munich Agreement, 113
Murad, David, 183

N
National, 2, 4, 5, 8, 15, 16, 20
Nationalism, 213, 226, 232
Nationalists, 211, 212n2, 223,
    232, 233
Nelken, Margarita, 14, 102
New woman, 187, 232
New York, 80–82, 84, 89, 126
Nomadic, 52, 67
Nomadic existence, 122
Nomadic New Women, 1–20
Nomadic subject, 212, 213, 216, 218,
    220, 228, 233
Nomadic subjectivity, 9–11
Nomadic women, 2, 3, 17
Nomadism, 75, 212–214, 217,
    232, 233
Non-American actors, 300, 315
Non-intervention, 212n2, 213, 218,
    221, 224
Non-Intervention Pact, 108
Nostalgia, 52, 59–61, 67–69, 71, 72,
    128, 130, 130n18, 131, 137, 138
Novarro, Ramón, 296–298, 300,
    312, 315
Novella, 256, 257

O
Oficina General de Evacuación y
    Refugiados, 277
Ontology, 326, 334, 340
Orígenes, 125, 126, 134
Orozco, José Clemente, 298, 298n1

INDEX   359

Ortega y Gasset, José, 54, 134, 150,
  323, 323n1, 324, 326, 327n12,
  329, 341
  La deshumanización del arte (The
    Dehumanization of Art), 324
Ortiz, Fernando, 18, 18n3
Ostranenie [defamiliarization], 205
Other, 124
Othering, 226, 232
The Oval Lady, 238
Owens, David, 183

P

Painter, 237, 242, 246
Painting, 92, 95–97
Palau de Nemes, Graciela, 78–84,
  78n3, 83n4, 84n5, 93
Palencia, Ceferino, 103, 110
Palencia, Isabel de, 2, 4, 17
Palma, Mallorca, 201
Pamphlet, 266, 271, 277, 278
Pan–Americanism, 128
Pankhurst, Christabel, 6
Pankhurst, Emmeline, 6
Panza, Sancho, 186, 195
Paradiso, 128n12
Paris, 269, 270, 279, 287, 288
Partido Socialista, 102
Partos, Kathe/Kati, 270
Partos, Pal, 267, 268, 270, 271, 287
Patriarchal, 8, 16, 20
Patriarchal order, 11
Paul, Alice, 6
Pèczi, József, 268, 269
Pedagogical Missions (Misiones
  Pedagógicas), 161
Pedreira, Antonio, 127
  Insularismo (*1934*), 127
People's Olympiad, 223
Perception, 92, 97, 99
Pérez de Ayala, Ramón, 154

Persona, 301–303, 308, 314, 318
Personal is political, 3
Photographer, 265, 266, 269, 270,
  272, 275, 279–281, 287–291
Photographic album, 271–276
Photography, 3, 265–291
Photojournalist, 268, 269
Photomontage, 268, 283–287, 291
Pícara, 185, 186, 186n3, 190, 196,
  200, 207
Picaresque, 183–200, 202, 204, 207
Picasso, Pablo, 183, 184, 200, 201
  Guernica, 112
Plástica fílmica, 298
Plenipotentiary Minister, 106, 109
Poetic reason, 128, 135, 139, 141
Polgare, Kathe/Kati, 270, 271
Polgare, Paul/Pablo, 271, 279, 287
Popular Front, 161, 212, 213, 215,
  216, 219, 221, 223
Porosity, 92
Poster, 266, 271, 273, 283–287
Postwar, 108, 114n20
Prados, Emilio, 123
Presence, 30, 32, 35, 36, 47
Primo de Rivera, Miguel, 104, 151,
  156, 164n70, 165
Propaganda, 265, 266, 270, 271, 273,
  277, 280, 282, 283
Puente Rodrigo, 275
Puerto Rico, 5, 13, 76, 76n2, 79, 80,
  82, 83, 85, 86, 93, 97, 121, 122,
  124, 124n5, 125n6, 126–132,
  126n8, 127n11, 129n13,
  130n19, 134, 136, 139, 142

R

Ramona, 309
Ramond, Harald, 316
Ramon Llull of Mallorca, 206
Ranchera comedia, 230

360 INDEX

Rape, 247, 248
Refugee, 107, 116, 117
Reid, John, 181–184, 200
Republic, 51, 55–57, 56n19, 59, 65, 71, 72
Republic(an), 54, 55, 57, 58n26, 60, 65, 66, 122, 122n1, 123, 126n9, 136, 139
Responsabilidades políticas, 116
Resurrection, 309
Return, 32, 37, 42–44, 42n56, 46–49
Revista de Occidente, 323–325, 324n1
Riding, Laura, 182
Riego, Rafael del (Riego y Flórez, Rafael del), 171
Riesenfeld, Hugo, 214–232, 227n9
Riesenfeld, Janet, 3, 5, 17, 211–233
Río, Dolores del, 3, 5, 19
Rivera, Diego, 298
Rivoli Theater, 214
Roche, Hannah, 202
Rogers, Gayle, 184
Rojas, Raquel, 214, 225, 226, 227n9, 229
Romani, 216, 217
Rome, 126
Romero, Marina, 3, 4, 17, 25–49
Rukeyser, Muriel, 4, 182, 223

S
Sade, Marquis de, 197
Said, Edward, 15, 36, 40, 44, 59, 60, 66, 67, 224
Sailors, Beware!, 301–308
St. John of the Cross, 206
St. Teresa of Ávila, 206
Salamanca, 267, 274, 277, 283, 286, 287, 287n31
Salinas, Pedro, 123
Sánchez Albornoz, Claudio, 123
Sanger, Margaret, 3, 6

Santos, Ángeles, 7
Schirmacher, Käthe, 6
Scopophilic, 206
Screenwriting, 213, 226, 227
Second Republic (II Spanish Republic), 151, 171
Second Spanish Republic, 4, 13
Seidel, Michael, 60, 61n33, 66
Sevilla, Carmen, 229, 230
Shimmy, 301
Shklovsky, Viktor, 205
Short stories, 240, 241, 243, 244, 252, 254
Sicalíptico [erotic, suggestive], 201, 203
Silence, 52, 57, 60, 63, 68–73
Silent film, 300, 309, 315
Silla, 284
Silver Age, 102
Sinsombrerismo, 328, 328n13
Skin color, 309–311, 313
Slavery Commission of the League of Nations, 103
S.nob, 289, 290
Social photography, 266, 289
Sociedad abolicionista, 103
Sociedad General de Autores, 116
Solitude, 95, 97, 128, 129, 135
Souchy, Augustin, 268, 270–272, 276
Sound in movies, 300, 315, 317
Soundscape, 92, 96
Spahr, Juliana, 204
Spain, 2, 4, 5, 7, 13–15, 17, 18, 25, 26, 33, 35, 42–45, 42n56, 47, 211–225, 211n1, 228–231, 233, 265–271, 274, 276, 280, 282, 285, 287, 289–291
Franco, Francisco, 332
Misiones Pedagógicas (Pedagogical Missions), 329
Second Republic (II Spanish Republic), 325, 329, 330
Spanish Civil War, 325, 326, 332

INDEX   361

Spanish-American War, 13
Spanish American War of 1898, 200
Spanish Civil War, 4, 11, 13, 14, 17,
  18, 25, 75, 79, 82, 90, 95, 98,
  103–105, 107, 122, 138n51,
  148, 161, 164n70, 167, 168n84,
  169n85, 170, 173, 211–233,
  252, 265–291
Spanish diaspora in México, 116
Spanish Legation (embassy),
  Sweden, 104
Spanish Photo Agency (Photo
  SPA), 270
Spanish Republican exiles, 213, 225
Spanish Second Republic, 269
Stein, Edith, 123
Stein, Gertrude, 2, 4, 181–207
  Autobiography of Alice B. Toklas,
    184, 201, 206n9
  "Lifting Belly," 183, 184, 201,
    206, 207
  Q.E.D., 183–187, 190–192, 194,
    197, 199, 201, 202, 207
  Tender Buttons, 184, 200,
    201, 203–207
  Three Lives, 183–185, 191, 196,
    197, 199
Stereotypes, 313n6
Stopes, Marie, 6
Style, 129, 131
Subjectivity, 27, 30, 47, 60
Surrealism, 237–239, 243–246,
  249, 255–257, 266, 269,
  286, 290
Switzerland, 122, 126
Syncretic consciousness, 19, 20
Syncretic forms of writing, 11

T
Tabori, Paul, 59
Tagore, Rabindranath, 76

Talkies, 295, 300, 309, 312,
  314n8, 315
Taxinomia, 326, 327n11, 342,
  342n49, 344
Teruel, 273, 281, 287
Thing-power, 92, 96, 98
Thomas, M. Carey, 6
Thomson, Virgil, 204, 206n9
Tiempos Nuevos, 280
Tierra y Libertad, 280, 284, 285
Toklas, Alice B., 184, 200, 201, 204
Torre, Josefina de la, 7
Torres-García, Joaquín, 331, 331n20
  constructive universalism, 331
Tovar, Lupita, 299, 300
Trans-corporeality, 78, 92, 95
Transculturación, 18, 18n3
Transculturation, 213, 230
Transit, 75, 78–86, 91, 98
Transnationalism, 212
Transportation, 7
Trauma (of exile), 124, 139
Travel, 75, 80, 86, 96
Travel journal, 124, 125
Truth, 122, 132, 138n51, 139–143

U
Ugarte, Michael, 57n25, 59, 60, 64
Umbral, 277, 280–285, 287
Unamuno, Miguel de, 13
Unión General de Trabajadores, 103
United States, 25–27, 31, 35, 42–44,
  46, 76, 76n2, 79–84, 86,
  93, 95, 96
Uprooted, 52, 64, 72
Utopia, 137, 138

V
Valencia, 269, 272, 274, 275, 277,
  279, 280, 284

362 INDEX

Valle Inclán, Ramón del (Valle Inclán,
  Ramón María del), 154
Vanguard, 3, 20
Varo, Remedios, 250–252,
  255–257, 288
Veblen, Thorstein, 188
Vélez, Lupe, 3, 5, 19, 295–318
Vélez-Rubio, 274, 277–279, 282
Veracruz, 288
Veracruz, Mexico, 117
Victorian "True Woman," 6
Vitality, 78, 87, 88, 92, 93, 96, 98

W
Wald, Priscilla, 199
Wandering, 66, 67, 69
War of Independence, 148, 167
Washington, 76, 83–86, 90, 95
Weekly Illustrated, 279
Weil, Simone, 123
Weissmuller, Johnny, 306
Wells, Orson, 310
West, Rebecca, 6
Wharton, Edith, 182
Women's exile, as double, 16
Women's rights, 296, 297
Women's suffrage, 6, 14
Woods, Donald, 306

Woolf, Virginia, 3, 6–8, 10, 12, 15,
  16, 20, 185, 207
  A Room of One's Own, 6, 12
  "Street Haunting," 10
  Three Guineas, 8, 15, 16, 20
World War I, 4, 15
World War II, 4, 5, 127, 247, 326, 338

Z
Zambrano, María, 3, 4, 7, 11, 13, 17,
  106, 106n5, 121–143, 168–175,
  327n12, 329
  The Agony of Europe, 121, 136, 138
  Clearings in the Woods,
    142–143, 143n68
  *Delirio y destino: Los veinte años de
    una española* (*Delirium and
    Destiny: A Spaniard in Her
    Twenties*), 11, 147
  Horizontes del Liberalismo, 124n5
  "La Confesión, género
    literario," 141
  Las palabras del regreso, 17
  Persona y Democracia, 139
  "Time and Truth," 121, 139, 140,
    142, 143
Zubiaurre, Maite, 185, 200,
  201, 202n8

Printed in the United States
by Baker & Taylor Publisher Services